CONGRESS
AND THE
PUBLIC TRUST

CONGRESS AND THE PUBLIC TRUST

Report of
The Association of the Bar
of the City of New York
Special Committee on Congressional
Ethics

James C. Kirby, Jr., Executive Director

Armin Rosencranz, Associate Director

Ellen W. Ober, Administrative Assistant

ATHENEUM 1970 *NEW YORK*

The members of the Special Committee wish to express thanks for permission to quote from the following copyright works:

Congressional Ethics by Robert S. Getz, copyright © 1966 by Litton Educational Publishing, Inc.; reprinted by permission of Van Nostrand Reinhold Company.

Lawyers and Politics: A Study in Professional Convergence by Heinz Eulau and John D. Sprague, copyright © 1964 by The Bobbs-Merrill Company, Inc.; reprinted by permission of the publishers.

Legislative Assemblies by Robert Luce, copyright © 1924, 1952 by the President and Fellows of Harvard College; reprinted by permission of the copyright proprietors.

Power, Corruption, and Rectitude by Arnold A. Rogow and Harold D. Lasswell, copyright © 1963; reprinted by permission of Prentice-Hall, Inc., Englewood Cliffs, New Jersey.

THE COMMITTEE

On this and the succeeding page are listed the members of the Committee and its staff, together with public and professional positions held by them.

LOUIS M. LOEB, CHAIRMAN · *Partner: Lord, Day & Lord, New York City; former President of The Association of the Bar of the City of New York, former Vice-Chairman of the New York State Temporary Commission on the Courts; Chairman, New York Mayor's Committee on the Judiciary; Member, New York City Board of Health.*

H. BRIAN HOLLAND · *Partner: Ropes & Gray, Boston, Massachusetts; former Assistant Attorney General in charge of Tax Division, Department of Justice.*

EVERETT L. HOLLIS · *Partner: Mayer, Friedlich, Spiess, Tierney, Brown & Platt, Chicago, Illinois; former General Counsel, Atomic Energy Commission.*

CHARLES A. HORSKY · *Partner: Covington & Burling, Washington, D.C.; former Assistant Prosecutor at Nürnberg with the Chief of Counsel for War Crimes; former Advisor to Presidents Kennedy and Johnson for National Capital Affairs.*

WILLIAM JOSEPHSON · *Partner: Strasser, Spiegelberg, Fried & Frank, New York City and Washington, D.C.; former General Counsel, Peace Corps.*

ROBERT M. KAUFMAN · *Partner: Proskauer Rose Goetz & Mendelsohn, New York City; former Legislative Assistant to Senator Jacob K. Javits.*

THE STAFF

EXECUTIVE DIRECTOR

JAMES C. KIRBY, JR. · *Professor of Law, New York University; Dean-elect, the Ohio State University College of Law; former Chief Counsel, U.S. Senate Judiciary Subcommittee on Constitutional Amendments.*

ASSOCIATE DIRECTOR

ARMIN ROSENCRANZ · *former Consultant to the Executive Office of the President; former assistant to Senator Joseph D. Tydings; former Congressional Fellow, American Political Science Association.*

ADMINISTRATIVE ASSISTANT

ELLEN W. OBER

RESEARCH ASSISTANTS

ROBERT N. CHESTER and G. WILLIAM SISLEY

STAFF ASSISTANT

SUSAN CHRISTIE

PREFACE BY THE CHAIRMAN

On October 4, 1967, the Executive Committee of The Association of the Bar of the City of New York adopted resolutions creating this Special Committee on Congressional Ethics "to conduct research and related studies on conflicts of interest and ethical standards in Congress."

The then President of The Association, Russell D. Niles, had already asked me to serve as Chairman of such a committee, had selected the distinguished lawyers from Boston, Chicago, Detroit, New York, and Washington to comprise the Committee, had arranged for the financing by The Ford Foundation, had provided office space at the house of The Association, and had obtained Professor James C. Kirby, Jr., then of the faculty of Northwestern University School of Law and now of New York University School of Law, as Executive Director, and Armin Rosencranz, a lawyer and social scientist, as Associate Director. A brief description of the credentials of the members of the Committee, all of whom had much more exposure to the Congressional scene than I had, is set forth following the title page.

At the beginning, the task to which the Committee was assigned seemed almost hopeless. But as the work progressed we became increasingly optimistic that we could and would provide answers and recommendations which would be realistically constructive and helpful to enable the Members of Congress to render better service and earn a substantially greater degree of public confidence.

The staff provided enormous quantities of background material. The interview program was pursued carefully and intensively and provided invaluable practical assistance in helping to formulate our views.

From the beginning the Committee determined not to conduct any kind of a witchhunt, but to concentrate on an objective, constructive analysis of both houses, what the problems were and how they might best be solved. We recognized early the diversity in the tasks of Senators and Representatives caused by the difference in size of the two houses and variations in the populations of their constituencies. There were also differences due to geography and due to urban and rural constituencies. We have endeavored throughout not to lose sight of the problems which these differences emphasized.

From the background material and interviews we hammered out in intensive discussions at numerous meetings ideas of how best to overcome or minimize the problems. The staff then prepared and circulated position papers which were subjected to Committee dissection, and then followed by drafts of chapters for the Committee's Report. These in turn were circulated and considered page by page at Committee meetings. Revisions were then prepared, circulated, and considered until the Committee was satisfied. Thus *Congress and the Public Trust* was created.

This has been a most interesting and stimulating experience. The members of the Committee without exception have been scrupulous in doing their homework, in attendance at meetings, many of which were of two days' duration, and were single-minded in devotion to the task entrusted to them. I take tremendous pride in producing a unanimous Report coming from the give-and-take of study and discussion without any member seeking to grind any personal axes.

It should be clear from the above summary that we would in all probability have floundered hopelessly if we had not enjoyed the matchless inspiration and spade work of Professor Kirby. I find myself incapable of adequately expressing the Committee's indebtedness to him. His thinking and writing have been superb. Mr. Rosencranz, too, made valuable contributions, particularly in the interview program which he primarily conceived and executed, and which we believe was a unique achievement in Congressional research. He also drafted portions of the Report. In addition, the Committee and the staff enjoyed the able, dedicated, ever gracious help of our Administrative Assistant, Miss Ellen Ober, without whom we would all have been helpless. We are similarly grateful to Research Assistants G. William Sisley and Robert N. Chester, students at the New York University School of Law, for their painstaking and substantial contributions.

I would be remiss if I failed to pay tribute to the cooperation we have received from so many Members of Congress, and the officers and staff of The Association, and to the advice and help of individuals too numerous to mention here but who are listed in the research note in the Appendix.

The Ford Foundation grant was generously adequate, and no attempt whatsoever was made to influence or effect in the slightest degree our work or the end product. For this, we are indeed appreciative.

Time alone will tell if our recommendations will be adequately implemented. Public reaction to the recommendations must spark the implementation. The subject is worthy, the effort has been great, and I know I speak for all the Committee and staff when I express the confidence that we can anticipate substantial realization of our objectives.

LOUIS M. LOEB
Chairman

CONTENTS

Contents

Contents

xvi

TABLES

Tables

INTRODUCTION

Origins of the Committee

The idea that "public office is a public trust" is an ancient one, traceable to the Romans and even to Plato. It is an underlying assumption of representative government that its officers will view themselves as trustees for the public. In referring to the "solemn trust" committed to the Congress under our Constitution, it was stated in THE FEDERALIST:

> As there is a degree of depravity in mankind which requires a certain degree of circumspection and distrust: So there are other qualities in human nature, which justify a certain portion of esteem and confidence. Republican government presupposes the existence of these qualities in a higher degree than any other form.[1]

Although conceded by all as a general principle of government, the public-trust concept has only recently begun to emerge as a basis for workable rules of conduct for public officials. The efforts of this Committee are a development in a movement which began less than two decades ago.

The public's power to "throw the rascals out" may have been an adequate remedy when the government had relatively little effect upon daily lives of the citizenry, but the New Deal and developments following World War II brought realization that ballot-box remedies are insufficient. Expansions of governmental activity, increased public awareness of the conduct of public officials, and escalating public expectations of those entrusted with power have combined to produce unprecedented demands for higher standards of governmental ethics.

Post-war scandals in the Federal government produced one of the first recognitions of the need for codes of governmental ethics. In 1951 a Senate subcommittee headed by Senator Paul Douglas of Illinois conducted hearings on ethical standards in the Federal government and issued a provocative report developing the need for ethics codes for all Federal officials and recommending a permanent Federal commission on ethics.[2]

In 1953 a Senate committee forced a Presidential Cabinet appointee to dispose of automobile-stock holdings as a condition of serving as Secretary of Defense, and during the next few years several highly placed Federal appointees had similar conflict-of-interest problems with the Congress. Partly as a result, the staff of a subcommittee of the House Judiciary Committee made a special study of Federal conflicts of interest in 1958,[3] and inconclusive hearings on the subject were held in the House in 1960[4] and 1961.[5]

In the meantime a citizens' study much like the present one was under way. In 1958 a special committee of The Association of the Bar of the City of New York, financed by a grant from The Ford Foundation, began a full-scale review of conflict-of-interest problems in the Federal government. After surveying its full jurisdiction, this Committee wisely decided to exclude Congress from the scope of its research and recommendations. It noted in its report:

> The analysis and research required for a study of the congressional conflict of interest problem would differ materially from that of the present study, and any effort to apply conclusions drawn from the one to the other would be certain to be dangerous and at least in part unworkable.

However, the Committee strongly recommended that conflicts of interest of Members of Congress be examined in a separate project.[6]

The work of the earlier Committee (which will be referred to as "our predecessor committee" throughout this Report) was published in book form in 1960 under the title CONFLICT OF INTEREST AND FEDERAL SERVICE. Comprehensive recommendations were made for recodification and revision of existing statutes on the subject, and these proposals, along with the report of an Advisory Panel on Ethics and Conflict of Interest in Government appointed by President Kennedy, were the basis of 1962 legislation which completely overhauled the Federal conflict-of-interest laws governing the Executive Branch.[7] These reforms were joined and supplemented in the Kennedy and Johnson Administrations by a series of executive orders, the final one of which required separate codes of conduct for each department and agency of the Executive Branch.[8]

While ethical regulation of the Executive Branch was being strengthened, the case was being reinforced for similar reforms in the Legislative Branch. In 1962 two Representatives were indicted upon conspiracy and conflict-of-interest charges growing out of a Maryland savings-and-loan scandal. In 1963 Senate Majority Secretary Robert G. (Bobby) Baker resigned after revelations of extensive financial manipulations which exploited his official position. Subsequent investigations by the Senate Rules Committee produced widespread demands for formal regulations, particularly for public disclosure of financial interests. At the same time a series of public and private events began which culminated in 1967 with the exclusion of Representative-elect Adam Clayton Powell from the House of Representatives. In 1966 and 1967 Senator Thomas E. Dodd was investigated and censured by the Senate for misuse of political funds.

This appeared to be a timely point for The Association of the Bar of the City of New York to complete the work begun by our predecessor committee. On May 2, 1967, then-President Russell D. Niles requested another Ford Foundation grant for a study of ethical standards and conflict of interest in Congress, citing among other things the great need for measures to increase public confidence in the legislative process, particularly in view of the critical issues with which Congress and the nation are faced today. On July 7, 1967, the Foundation granted the request. By October this Committee had been organized and began its work.

SCOPE

Under the title Special Committee on Congressional Ethics, we commenced with a broader jurisdiction than we chose to exercise. The term "ethics" in its broadest sense would have authorized inquiry into the private morality and personal lives of Members. This would have been unmanageable and involved matters largely unrelated to the public's business.

In the other direction, we could have narrowed our study to the single subject dealt with by our predecessor committee—conflict of interest. This would have excluded consideration of salaries, allowances, and campaign financing—matters which are undoubtedly of public concern and which give rise to ethical issues akin to those created by conflicts of interest. Such a narrowing of the study would also have had the disadvantage of excluding any consideration of Congress' use of its disciplinary powers to police Members' ethics on other grounds, a topic greatly needing analysis. The outline of the book shows the middle course which the Committee adopted.

Several important subjects which might have been regarded as within our purview were examined briefly and put aside. The most important of these was lobbying. The methods used by lobbyists to influence Congress obviously raise ethical issues within the total legislative process, but involve the ethics of constituents and pressure groups more than the ethics of Members of Congress. Also, the Joint Committee on the Organization of Congress in 1967 reviewed lobbying regulations and issued thorough proposals for needed reforms in this area.[9] Lobbyists who are campaign contributors are considered in that broader context in our report.

The second major topic to be excluded was intervention by Members of Congress in matters pending before Executive and administrative agencies. The essential concern in this area is protection of administrative decision-making from improper influence from all sources. The subject is best considered by focusing on the administrative process and studying off-the-record communications of all types. The Administrative Conference of the United States has a continuing concern with the over-all subject. The Conference has recognized that the problem varies among agencies and has called upon each to promulgate its own code on *ex parte* contacts with outside persons.[10] If a Member of Congress uses his office to intervene with an agency for his personal gain, the issue then is an ethical one as well as one of administrative procedure. In this event, the evil is similar to that of advancing legislation for personal gain and is within the conflict-of-interest problems discussed in Chapter 2.

Much criticism of Congress goes to matters of governmental efficiency rather than ethics. The seniority system, for instance, is regarded by many as detrimental, but it raises no issues which can be resolved under any generally accepted ethical norms. Accordingly, we have not presumed to deal with it.

After this Committee began its work, some of the issues with which it was concerned were narrowed or simplified by the actions of both houses of Congress. In 1964 the Senate had established a permanent Committee on Standards of Official Conduct, and the House established such a committee in 1968. Also in 1968, both houses adopted formal codes of ethics and a measure of public financial disclosure. Although these steps may have rendered less controversial the questions of the need for such codes and committees, the subject is nonetheless treated in Chapter 7. The House Committee on Standards of Official Conduct and the Senate Select Committee on Standards and Conduct are referred to in this report as the "Ethics Committees" of the respective houses.

METHOD

The Committee recognized early that its task was unique. The Congress is both the subject of our inquiry and the object of our recommendations. The Committee then decided to rely almost exclusively on information voluntarily furnished us by Members of Congress and on matters of public record.

The keystone of our factual research was the individual-interview program which is described in detail in Appendix C. In preparation for the individual interviews, exploratory conversations were first held with members of the leadership of both parties in both houses of Congress. We found these leaders cooperative and generally appreciative that the study had been undertaken. Some felt that the subject was one on which it was difficult for Congress itself to be fully objective, and that a comprehensive outside study such as we proposed could help in arriving at needed solutions. Every Member of Congress was then invited to assist us by a letter substantially as follows:

Dear —— :

I am writing on behalf of this Committee to acquaint you with its objectives and to seek your assistance in their accomplishment. As you probably know, in 1958–60 a committee of this Association conducted a study, financed by the Ford Foundation, of conflicts of interest and related ethical problems in the Executive Branch and produced an extended report which contributed to executive orders and new legislation on this subject (Pub. Law 87-849). At that time, the Association noted the need for a separate and independent analysis of such problems in the Legislative Branch. The Association and the Ford Foundation have now returned to this endeavor by establishing this Committee.

We undertake this task with great respect for the Congress and a sympathetic understanding of the unique difficulties faced by Senators and Representatives. A majority of the members of the Committee and its staff have either served on Congressional staffs or have worked in the Executive Branch where they had considerable dealings with Congress. We hope to focus upon your problems from several perspectives and will be aided in this by a diversity of personal and geographic backgrounds within the Committee.

We are determined that our findings and recommendations shall be based upon the real world in which Members of Congress must work and seek election. We are well aware of the high costs of seeking and retaining public office. Accordingly, we are also considering campaign financing and the adequacy of Congressional salaries and office allowances. We believe the public should be educated to a better understanding of the financial demands upon Members.

Needless to say, the Members of Congress are the real experts on these matters and must be our prime source of information and ideas. We earnestly solicit your views and any legislative solutions which you support. We will seek personal discussions with a broad cross-section of both Houses. Time and resources will not permit individual discussions with every Member, but we expect to see a sufficient number to guarantee a reliable factual basis for our ultimate recommendations. Individual data furnished in these discussions will be held in confidence, and no personal information furnished us will be published so as to be attributable to a particular Member. The objective of our research is to obtain general data upon which to base prospective recommendations.

Other Committee members and I have conferred recently with representatives of the leadership of both political parties in both Houses of Congress. We acquainted them with our purposes and received valuable and cooperative suggestions.

We will be most grateful for your cooperation and ask that you favor us with any views and comments which you think will be helpful.

Yours faithfully,
/s/ Louis M. Loeb
CHAIRMAN

We then interviewed 120 Senators and Representatives. They were selected by a process described in detail in Appendix C. We greatly appreciate the candor which was shown by the Members interviewed. This Report draws heavily upon their statements. We have fully protected their confidentiality, even to the point of omitting any list of their names. In several instances we have obtained consent of a Member to attribute to him a quotation from his interview. In some instances consent to attribution was withheld. No statement made to us has been attributed to a Member without his express approval.

This procedure enabled us to learn much that has not been generally known or understood about Congressional attitudes and patterns of behavior. We believe we succeeded in our efforts to learn the realities of Congressional problems. As a result, the Committee achieved a much greater appreciation of the practical problems faced by those who seek and hold Congressional office. We completed this study convinced that the ethical standards followed by most Members are generally high.

GENERAL OBSERVATIONS

Cynics who assume that many Senators and Representatives seek personal monetary gain from office fail to understand the drives of men who devote their lives to elective office. Most of them want political power and the chance to render public service. Men who will undergo the rigors of political campaigning and Congressional service are not apt to risk loss of respect of colleagues and constituents for the sake of money. Political power involves something else and goes to the fundamentals of the incentives which move men to seek public office. Men derive personal satisfaction from being in a position to influence the course of events, particularly on a national scale. Washington observer George S. Allen has written of Federal officeholders:

> They will sometimes go along with policies they don't believe in personally for votes but almost never for any other kind of gain. Some consider this corruption; others call it response to the will of the people and therefore democracy in action.[11]

Despite our general conclusions that ethical standards of Members of Congress are generally much higher than the public realizes, the contents of this Report show that we nonetheless find significant room for improvement. If all Members came up to the standards of the great majority, there would be little problem. Most of our recommendations simply urge that a minority of Members emulate the self-imposed standards of the majority. Above all, our recommendations are also designed to enhance public confidence in the Congress and to show the people that their representatives are actually adhering to the highest standards.

It is unlikely that Congressional imperfections exceed those of other institutions. One of the most critical observers, Professor H. H. Wilson, has attributed Congressional ethical deficiencies to corresponding deficiencies in society as a whole. He said:

> Most important of all . . . is the fact that we cannot expect a legislative body to demand of its members very much higher standards of personal integrity than those prevailing in the society it represents. . . . What . . . businessman or leading citizen, it

may be asked, can, in honesty, volunteer to throw the first stone . . . ? Is there any man in business, no matter at what level, who has not found it "necessary" to resort to illegal or extra-legal practices . . . to "get along"?[12]

A sharply contrasting view has been stated by Dean Bayless Manning. He concluded that the behavior of elected officials generally rises above that of society as a whole because people demand more of public officials than of themselves, saying:

> In our Democracy we look to the political process to identify, produce, and articulate many of our ideals, our goals, our standards, our heroes, our examples for our society, for ourselves, and for our young. . . .
>
> The vocabulary of our politics conforms to its role as a national Morality drama. That vocabulary is formal, dogmatic, simplified, symbolic, repetitive, and goal-setting; it is not descriptive and must not be thought of as being descriptive. And the actors in the political drama must, as in epic drama, appear as more than life-size, establishing, declaring, and appearing to live in accordance with, standards that are not of this world.[13]

While we cannot presume to settle the question of how Congressional ethics compare with those of society in general, we are greatly encouraged by the rise in ethical values in the Congress and throughout government.

As leaders, lawmakers, and examples to others, the ethical standards of Members of Congress should be the highest attainable. The pages which follow contain our judgments of some deficiencies in this regard and develop twenty-nine specific recommendations for improvement. These recommendations are summarized at pages 233–38. Continual re-examination by the Congress and constructive criticism by concerned citizens can move our national legislature to those levels of ethical practice and appearance which are imperative for public confidence in the conduct of public affairs. This Report is submitted as a tool for the assistance of all those engaged in this ongoing process.

CONGRESS
AND THE
PUBLIC TRUST

CHAPTER ONE

THE PRESSURES OF CONGRESSIONAL SERVICE

It is the bane of public life that unspectacular but dedicated and meritorious service, which is the standard of service of the overwhelming majority of today's Members of Congress, is too seldom recognized. From its labors of the past two years, this Committee is convinced that standards of Congressional conduct have probably never been so high as they are today. Public awareness of this fact is lower than it might be, and to the extent that this Committee can do so, it hopes to educate the public to a greater appreciation of the demands and pressures of Congressional service.

Service in Congress is unique. No other public office is beset by quite the same mixture of conflicting demands and pressures. As outsiders presuming to discuss the ethical problems of those who devote their lives to this difficult business, this Committee determined early that it needed to comprehend the real world in which they operate.

Members of Congress share the common human desire to be well regarded. As politicians and elective officials, they must necessarily cultivate public approval. Nonetheless, students of American history

3

find it replete with widespread public dissatisfaction with Congress.

In 1925 Speaker Longworth acknowledged the historic public irreverence for the House of Representatives in these resigned words:

> I have been a member of the House of Representatives . . . twenty years. . . . During the whole of that time we have been attacked, denounced, despised, hunted, harried, blamed, looked down upon, excoriated, and flayed.
>
> I refuse to take it personally. I have looked into history. I find that we did not start being unpopular when I became a Congressman. We were unpopular before that time. We were unpopular even when Lincoln was a Congressman. We were unpopular even when John Quincy Adams was a Congressman. We were unpopular even when Henry Clay was a Congressman. We have always been unpopular.
>
> From the beginning of the Republic it has been the duty of every free-born voter to look down upon us, and the duty of every free-born humorist to make jokes at us.[1]

How can such unpopular men gain re-election? Obviously, there is much difference between particular constituencies' opinions of their individual Representatives and the view of the nation as a whole toward the House as a group and as an institution. To each Member there are two publics—the one which elects him, and the entire public of the nation. Individually, he may care for either less than for the other, but only his local public controls his political livelihood.

Much of the general dissatisfaction described by Speaker Longworth has been due to Members who took courses popular at home but unpopular with organs of national opinion. Much of it has been due to misunderstanding of the tasks of Congress. A leading historian of Congress, George Galloway, attributes the public's traditional dissatisfaction with Congress to its failures to do all that it could to meet national needs.[2] This suggests that ethical standards are not the entire problem, but Congressional responsiveness to public needs and Congressional conflicts of interest are very closely related. Both involve assessments of Congressional motives and ethics.

Ethical standards for Congress can only be evaluated against the background of the pressures that weigh upon Members from constituents, colleagues, and personal circumstances. To be fair, an observer

4

must attempt to appreciate the demands upon the Member of Congress, the adequacy of the resources provided him, and the forces which guide and influence his personal conduct. This chapter's aim is to place in perspective the many pressures which affect Congressional behavior.

THE INCREASINGLY HEAVY WORKLOAD OF CONGRESS

Historical Changes

The Congress of 1789 was composed of 26 Senators and 65 Representatives. The largest state, Virginia, had a population of 950,000. Congressional constituencies averaged about 33,000 persons, enabling a Congressman to know a large portion of his constituency personally. A constituent would have had no reason to visit his Congressman in Washington; he could have seen him at home. There was no question of a Member's commuting back and forth since sessions were relatively short and distances were great. Congress had comparatively few matters on which to legislate. Public issues were relatively few, and most were state and local in scope.

The heavy representation of busy, successful lawyers in early Congresses was due partly to the fact that they could so easily absent themselves from their practices and take on representative duties for short periods.[3] Modest sums, if any, were spent campaigning for election. There was no Federal bureaucracy as such, and Federal employees numbered in the hundreds rather than millions.

During the first third of the twentieth century, legislative service still was part-time and relatively uncomplicated. Congressman Martin Dies wrote in 1954 that during his father's first term in Congress, from 1909 to 1911:

> Congress sat for six months the first session and three months the second session. A representative got about 15 letters a week. Only at rare intervals would a constituent come to see him. He had no pressure groups to contend with. Because Congress enacted only a few bills each session, legislation got the deliberative attention it deserved. Every member had plenty of time to study bills in

5

committee before they came on the floor. Debate was important in the consideration of every bill. A member did not take the floor until he had carefully got together as many facts as were available. When he spoke, he knew his subject. A good debater had no trouble getting a large audience in the chamber. Most of a member's time was spent on legislation. There was little else for him to do.[4]

Writing about his early years in Congress, the late Representative and former Speaker Joseph Martin, who began his service in the House in 1925, observed that

> From one end of a session to another Congress would scarcely have three or four issues of consequence besides appropriation bills. And the issues themselves were fundamentally simpler than those that surge in upon us today in such a torrent that the individual member cannot analyze all of them adequately before he is compelled to vote. In my early years in Congress the main issues were few enough so that almost any conscientious member could with application make himself a quasi-expert at least. In the complexity and volume of today's legislation, however, most members have to trust somebody else's word or the recommendation of a committee. Nowadays bills which thirty years ago would have been thrashed out for hours or days go through in ten minutes. . . .
>
> [M]embers of Congress . . . had a single clerk and a one-room office. Mail was light. I doubt that I received in the beginning twenty-five letters a day until veterans' pension cases started piling up.[5]

Thus, Members still had ample time to spend at home practicing law or attending to private businesses.

The enormous expansion in the workload of Congress dates from the First World War, the Depression, and the recovery efforts following it. The Second World War then imposed vast new responsibilities on both Congress and the Executive in conduct of national and international affairs. "Still functioning for the most part with the machinery inherited from the simpler days of the nineteenth century, [Congress'] calendars and committee schedules became increasingly

6

congested . . . and its members . . . harrassed by multiplying complex problems and local pressures." [6]

Since the New Deal, letters have rolled in at an ever increasing rate. More and more constituents demand service from their Congressmen and visit and telephone them in the hopes of accelerating such service; the mushrooming Federal bureaucracy requires ever increasing legislative appropriations and oversight; Federal taxes and spending multiply; and Federal programs burgeon geometrically. Federal grants-in-aid to states and localities increased very sharply during the Kennedy and Johnson Administrations. Today's Congressman responds to time, work, and financial pressures in a way that the eighteenth-century citizen-legislator could not have dreamed of.

The Congress has now grown to 100 Senators and 435 Representatives, and the average Member represents more than 400,000 constituents. Congress and its committees are in session for most of the year. Virtually all Congressmen today, except those living within commuting distance, maintain homes in Washington in addition to their district homes.

Just as Congressional service has become a full-time job, it is more likely to be a long-term career. The average Member of Congress now serves at least five terms. In contrast, the average service before 1901 never exceeded two terms. In 1903 only 2.3 percent of the Members served ten terms or more; by 1963, however, 17.0 percent had served this long.[7] A professionalism has emerged which better equips the busy Member to cope with his difficult tasks.

Contemporary Dimensions of the Job

During the session many Members honestly claim to work six-day weeks of 60 to 80 hours. A number have described typical days which are long, hectic, and strenuous.[8] As Professors Roche and Levy wrote recently, after analyzing then Representative, later Senator, Estes Kefauver's account of such a day:

> . . . the conscientious American legislator puts in a prodigious work week. And Kefauver does not mention in this selection the obligations that he has back in his district: the speeches he must give, the high-school ceremonies and college commencements he must attend, and the endless political banquets (fund-raising

7

affairs or, often, ego-assuagement for local leaders) he must somehow survive. American politics is no place for the dilettante! Perhaps Kefauver's premature death was in part the penalty for responding so fully to the demands of his office.[9]

Table 1.1 shows the growth in the Congressional workload from 1791 to 1969.

TABLE 1.1

First and Ninetieth Congresses Compared

Points of Comparison	1st	90th
Number of bills introduced	268	24,786
House of Representatives	142	20,587
Senate	126	4,199
Number of laws enacted	118	1,002
Public	108	640
Private	10	362
Number of Members	91	535
Representatives	65	435
Senators	26	100
Number of committees*	2	46
House of Representatives	1	21
Senate	0	16
Joint	1	9
Committee reports	155	3,645
House of Representatives	85	1,975
Senate	70	1,670
Nominations confirmed	211	118,231†

Source: 114 CONG. REC. D943–44 (daily ed. Nov. 1, 1968) and G. Galloway, HISTORY OF THE HOUSE OF REPRESENTATIVES 120 (1961).
* In the 90th Congress there were also four special or select committees in the Senate and one in the House. All Senate committees were such in the 1st.
† The majority of these are routine military promotions.

It should not be assumed that Members are uniformly burdened by long sessions and long workdays. It is no secret that floor debates are very sparsely attended. A Member will generally respond to quorum and roll calls and is almost always in the vicinity of the Capitol when such votes are scheduled, but he is so beset by other duties, centered on his constituents or his committee responsibilities, that he assigns low priority to the obligation to participate in debates.[10] Admittedly, not all are hard-working. One senior Congressman whom we interviewed said, "All we need do is be present for votes, introduce bills without necessarily pressing them forward, and issue frequent press releases." A small but indeterminable number undoubtedly do this and no more.

Even the most conscientious Member cannot meet all legitimate demands upon him. Try as he may, he is unlikely to be able to devote a preponderance of his time to legislation, including committee hearings, floor debate, and simple "homework" on legislative issues. Most Members are unable to fix any routine whatever. Their activities change from day to day and from hour to hour, although there are recurrent patterns.

Each Member normally has to supervise a staff of at least 10 for a Representative, 16 for a Senator.[11] If he heads or is ranking minority member of a committee or subcommittee, the figure may be much larger. By remote control and frequent telephone contact, he must also operate a district office or offices. He must greet countless social visitors who come through his office[12] and hear the legislative demands of constituents, lobbyists, and Executive Branch representatives. He may have to entertain his more important visitors at lunch or dinner. He may be asked to arrange for tours or other Washington meetings for a large number of these visitors. He must carry on a steady stream of telephone conversations with constituents, Executive Branch officials, fellow legislators, and representatives of interest groups. He is constantly receiving information upon which he is expected to act. His staff frequently has a continuing struggle to catch scraps of his time to brief him or get his approval of something.

The mail that comes to a Member's office may be staggering. In 1964 the Capitol's Post Offices handled 100,000 letters a day.[13] Former Senator Joseph Clark (D-Pa.) never received fewer than 1,000 letters a week and averaged 110,000 a year.[14] Former Senator Thomas Kuchel (D-Cal.) received between 1,000 and 2,000 letters a day.[15] Most busy Senators have at least one employee who does nothing but open and sort incoming mail.

The average Representative receives 100 letters a day, although those who have active and articulate constituents are likely to receive more.[16] Most Representatives handle at least some of their mail personally and in many cases draft or dictate personal responses.[17] Even

9

in the cases of Senators and Congressmen who have streamlined their mail operation with form-letter replies, robo-typewriters, and automatic signature machines, virtually every letter receives some sort of reply and requires staff time and resources; and a good portion of the mail requires further attention and case work.

One House Member has said that a typical week brings him "at least 300 letters, visits or phone calls from [his] constituents asking [him] to mediate for them with the Federal bureaucracy." [18] In one 12-month period the Department of Agriculture recorded 13,477 letters and 43,201 telephone calls from Congressional sources exclusive of requests for publications. The Treasury reported 21,500 "information requests" from Congress during the same period.[19]

This casework or service function has become a major responsibility of Members of Congress today. In the performance of this function, a Senator or Representative negotiates in his constituents' behalf a whole range of problems and difficulties that arise out of their relations with the Federal government. This can involve the Member in helping to obtain a Federal contract for his district, interceding on behalf of a Selective Service registrant, inquiring why a constituent's Social Security check has not been delivered, setting up a meeting with a Federal official, and arranging for a tour of the White House for an important constituent.

One close observer of Congress, Kenneth Olson, has stated unequivocally that the service function is central to all the work of Congress.[20] When a Member does favors for his constituents, the fact spreads by word of mouth and has a multiplier effect. Moreover, it seems to ensure a "voluntary reciprocity" which produces loyalty to the Member at campaign time.[21] Many Members find that their ombudsman function builds up a cushion of support among their constituents which is totally unrelated to their legislative record. One experienced legislator was quoted as justifying this function on more principled grounds:

When I first came here I was dumbfounded by the number of requests. I was inclined to think I didn't have time to take care of them, and that I would have no time for legislation. My first reaction was, "Why don't they contact the executive agencies or the proper department with which these problems are associated?

Why should they expect me to take care of this for them?" Gradually I came to realize that each of these problems is very important to the person writing me, and that it is important for me to treat them as significant. Many people are baffled by our bureaucracy and don't know where to turn for help. Eventually somebody says, "Why don't you write your Congressman?" and they do. I now realize that one of my most important functions is to help these people. If they are entitled to go through a door they cannot find, it is my job to locate that door so they can go through.[22]

Many Members derogate their service function and regret any time they must spend fulfilling it. But, surprising as it is, one study found seasoned Members who still devote 90 percent of their time to case work.[23]

Although there is little patronage within the gift of a Member of Congress, many Members, or their staffs, spend considerable time in screening candidates for service-academy appointments and for postmasterships.

A Member will normally spend a substantial portion of his time conferring with party and interest-group representatives on matters of mutual interest. Also, as a matter of political necessity, he must speak to civic and philanthropic meetings.

When Congress is out of session, Members who are not campaigning can profitably supervise staff research, consult more adequately with constituents, or take much-needed vacations and catch up on reading. Some find that their duties require traveling abroad on committee business. Most of these trips have an undisputed legislative purpose, and many Members follow exhausting itineraries. They are understandably peeved when the press and people back home look upon such trips as "junkets." Some critics of Congress applaud the trips, expressing hope that narrow perspectives may be broadened.

Communication with constituents goes beyond merely answering mail. Although motivated in large part by political considerations, newsletters and local TV and radio reports unquestionably serve informational purposes and have become part of the Congressional way of life.

Frequent trips home are also a necessity for some Members. Some constituencies insist upon frequent local exposure of their Congress-men. One New York City Congressman reported that he was ex-pected to appear at local political and civic occasions on virtually the same basis as if his job were in the city.

Each Member has a unique style and problems all his own. The nature of Senators' work has been said to vary "partly because of their different conceptions of the role and partly as a result of such other factors as the size of their states, the security of their seats, their positions in the chamber's hierarchy, and the level of their political ambitions." [24] Populous-state Senators bear the greatest burdens of constituent case work, while Senators from nearby states are constantly besieged by visitors; and those from insecure seats, toward the ends of their terms, must constantly return home for fence-mending and publicity-seeking. As they gain seniority and chairmanships, their time is consumed in committee work. One of the few things all Senators were found to have in common was the complaint of insufficient time to do the job as they would like.

There can be no doubt that a conscientious Member of Congress must work long hours each day. The vast majority of the Members whom we interviewed either declared or implied that Congress is a full-time job, meaning, of course, the job of *being a Congressman*, not merely legislating. Asked how much time they spent on outside inter-ests, fewer than 12 percent of the House Members interviewed, and no Senators, indicated that they spent more than one day a month on outside activities. Members frequently observed that they could not see how any Member could find time to practice law. A majority have abandoned all forms of such activity, including corporate director-ships, as they gain seniority and job demands increase.

For Congress as a whole, the demands of their work and conse-quent pressures upon their time must be counted the dominant facts of Congressional life. It has truly become a full-time job.

CONGRESSIONAL DECISION-MAKING

Needless to say, the Congressman should conduct all his hectic ac-tivity and make all his decisions according to some principles and standards of the proper conduct of the public's business. In this respect, his problem is similar to that which faced his early predecessors. The debate on the proper nature of the representative function in a democratic republic will never fully be settled, and legislators must resolve conflicts between pressures on them without fixed guidelines.

The stage was set for this debate in 1774, when one of two members elected to represent Bristol in the English Parliament stated his view of the representative function:

> It has ever been my opinion that the electors have a right to instruct their members. For my part, I shall always think it my duty in Parliament to be guided by your counsels and instructions. I shall consider myself the servant of my constituents, not their master—subservient to their will, not superior to it. And let me add, I hold myself accountable to you for every action of my life which respects the public.[25]

The second member from Bristol was Edmund Burke. He took a very different position:

> [Your member's] unbiased opinion, his mature judgment, his enlightened conscience, he ought not to sacrifice to you, to any man, or to any set of men living. These he does not derive from your pleasure—no, nor from the law and the Constitution. They are a trust from Providence, for the abuse of which he is deeply answerable. Your representative owes you, not his industry only, but his judgment; and he betrays, instead of serving you, if he sacrifices it to your opinion.[26]

A recent analysis of the functions of the legislator identifies three major role types:[27] (1) the trustee, who is a free agent and follows his own convictions and judgment; (2) the delegate, who consults and follows the instructions of his constituents; and (3) the "politico," who expresses both orientations simultaneously.

An interesting example of a Senator's balancing the competing values at stake is Senator Fulbright's (D-Ark.) 1946 comparison of his decisions on poll taxes and isolationism:

> Regardless of how persuasive my colleagues or the national press may be about the evils of the poll tax, I do not see its fundamental importance, and I shall follow the views of the people of my

state. Although it may be symbolic of conditions which many deplore, it is exceedingly doubtful that its abolition will cure any of our major problems. On the other hand, regardless of how strongly opposed my constituents may prove to be to the creation of, and participation in, an ever stronger United Nations Organization, I could not follow such a policy in that field unless it becomes clearly hopeless.[28]

Thus, Senator Fulbright acted the delegate role with regard to the poll tax and the trustee role with regard to the United Nations. Throughout American history, Members of Congress have acted courageously in the national interest, often at great risk to their political careers.*

Modern legislators must coordinate and integrate diverse social, economic, and political interests in ways their constituents cannot possibly appreciate. In theory at least, they must move toward the trustee role if they are to cope with the problems of modern government.

The natural tendency of Members of Congress as politicians is to equate the interests of their districts with the interests of the nation and to be unable to see conflicts between the two. The more diverse a constituency, however, the more difficult it becomes to identify controlling constituent interests. Senators from the big industrial states and Congressmen from the large cities must pay attention to a plethora of political preferences of racial and ethnic groups,[29] while those from rural areas with relatively homogeneous constituencies have much less of a problem. But, as one scholar points out, there is no clear district viewpoint for either type of Member on the overwhelming majority of issues.[30] It is likely that "[i]n the very multiplicity of demands and pressures . . . the legislator finds a significant degree of freedom of maneuver." [31]

The risk of "role strain" is also reduced by the fact that the dis-

---

* Former President John F. Kennedy's classic work, PROFILES IN COURAGE (1955), included references to a number of Members of Congress. Among those who voted against their sectional interests and in favor of the national interest were: John Quincy Adams, who voted for the embargo against England in 1807, against the interests of New England, and thereby forsook his Senatorial career; Daniel Webster, who alienated all of New England by supporting Clay's Great Compromise; Senator Edmund Ross of Kansas, who cast the deciding vote to acquit President Andrew Johnson; Thomas Hart Benton and Sam Houston, who defied secessionist sentiments of their constituents in their efforts to preserve the Union.

14

trict's attitude, if there is one, is likely to coincide with the Member's own policy attitudes. This, of course, could be the rationalization of policy demands. It conveniently enables him to follow his own perception of what the district's attitude is in order to win re-election.[32]

An interesting irony shown by recent political-science research is that the behavior of the electorate is virtually unaffected by its knowledge of the policy positions of the candidates.[33] Party loyalty is a more important factor to many voters, but there is a remarkable tendency to vote on factors such as conscientiousness and diligence more than upon policy. Thus, many states appear to be happy with both a very conservative and a very liberal Senator at the same time. In a single election voters may deliver majorities to both a liberal Representative and a very conservative Senator.

A Member of Congress may not have clearly thought out his role as *representative*, but he quickly takes on a role as *legislator*. He does so by attempting to reconcile a variety of external pressures with internal pressures of Congress itself. Interest groups, constituents, and the Administration work from without; the committee system, debates, and subtle institutional influences work from within.[34] His relations with his constituents are in large part determined by the fact that he will soon be up for re-election; his relations with his colleagues are determined by his reaction to the folkways of the body.

Members of all types complain, though, of the difficulties of decision-making and seek new forms of assistance. In a recent survey of problems of Congressmen, the one most frequently mentioned (cited by 62 percent of all Members interviewed) was the complexity of decision-making, and particularly the lack of information on which to make decisions.[35] All observers of Congress agree that Members need better information and improved analytical tools and methods. It is not uncommon for Executive agencies of many thousand personnel to be watched over by committees or subcommittees with staffs of five. Committees are generally understaffed, and a Member's personal staff generally is too busy with case-work problems to devote any time to legislation. In general, expertise in policy areas is monopolized by the Executive Branch. One Senator said in desperation, "I just don't have time to study bills as I should. . . . I'm just dealing off the top of the deck all the time." [36]

Congressmen undoubtedly make many decisions on the basis of less

15

information and less study than is desirable from many viewpoints. The claim of inadequate resources for Congressional decision-making finds much support among Congressional scholars and some Members who have conducted extensive research. Many outside recommendations, including expansion of personal and committee staffs and modernization of procedures, were placed before the Joint Committee on the Organization of Congress and were incorporated in that Committee's final report to the 90th Congress.[37] The implementing legislation passed the Senate, but never came to a vote in the House.

In sum, one can only say that the Congressional decision-making process is both imperfect and inexact. It involves resolution of conflicts and accommodation of competing interests which should weigh heavily on the conscientious Member. Those who attempt precise determinations of exactly what produces a given decision are doomed to failure. The Member himself may not be sure. Positive judgments that improper considerations produce certain action, or inaction, are usually impossible. Any Member who is closely scrutinized may find himself caught by suspicious circumstances and encounter a claim that his decision was improperly motivated.

INTERNAL INSTITUTIONAL FORCES

"To get along, go along" is a basic admonition to young Representatives commonly attributed to Speaker Sam Rayburn. An example of one freshman Member who was educated to it the hard way is Representative Sam Steiger (D-Ariz.). During his first year in office he appeared on a network radio conversation show and stated some highly questionable judgments about his House colleagues. When asked if some Members show up drunk, Steiger said, "I have never seen them drunk on the floor. I have seen them drunk during the day," and added that he had seen "some Members assisted to their offices during the morning." He went on to question the quality of both the leadership and the rank-and-file and said, "There are Members of Congress that you wouldn't hire to wheel a wheelbarrow."

In a few months Representative Steiger needed a normally routine suspension of the rules so that a piece of surplus government real estate could be transferred to a city in his district for use as a park.

House Members, angered at Steiger, forced a roll-call vote and defeated his move. No one questioned press accounts which described the House action as "punishment" of Steiger for his indiscreet comments.[38]

Sanctions to keep aberrant Members in line are usually more subtle, but the "Establishment" in both houses has powerful means of compelling conformity to its written and unwritten norms of Congressional conduct.[39] Congressional scholars agree that the prevailing norm in each house is to revere Congress as an institution and to avoid conduct which would tend to bring it into disrepute. One noted Congressional scholar, Donald Matthews, lists the major unwritten normative rules or "folkways" of the Senate as follows:[40]

1. "[N]ew Members are expected to serve a proper apprenticeship." They are expected to perform cheerfully such thankless tasks as presiding over floor debate. They should seek advice of senior Senators and make no speeches or remarks on the floor unless specifically instructed.

2. Senators should devote a major share of their time, energy and thought to dull, often politically-unrewarding legislative work.

3. A Senator should specialize and "focus his energy and attention on the relatively few matters that come before his committees or that affect his state."

4. Senators should at all times be courteous to fellow Senators and not allow political disagreements to influence personal feelings.[41]

5. Senators should help one another out and be repaid in kind. Important reciprocity, according to Matthews, is the trading of votes.

6. Senators are expected to believe that they belong to the greatest legislative and deliberative body in the world and are expected to "revere the Senate's personnel, organization, and folkways and to champion them to the outside world."

These folkways perform some important and worthwhile functions, such as providing motivation for diligent performance of legislative duties, discouraging endless debate, encouraging the development of expertise and division of labor, softening the inevitable personal conflicts so that adversaries and competitors can meet in an atmosphere of cooperation and mutual respect. Conformity to these norms unquestionably maximizes Senators' effectiveness and admits them to what journalist William S. White calls the Senate's "Inner Club."

Unfortunately, it also tends to perpetuate old methods and may induce timidity in reform-minded Members. Caution toward procedural reform was undoubtedly a by-product of the 1963 experience in committee assignments of a group led by Senator Joseph S. Clark (D-Pa.) which sought unsuccessfully to amend the Senate cloture rule to make it easier to halt filibusters. Only five of 14 non-freshman Members who favored the rule change were granted requests for new committee assignments, and only one received his first choice. Seven of the eight non-freshmen who opposed the change were granted their requests, and six got their first choice.[42] Reporters Evans and Novak have detailed elsewhere the use of committee assignments by Majority Leader Lyndon B. Johnson as a means of exercising power.[43]

The House of Representatives has similar norms of behavior. Members are expected to treat each other respectfully, and, as Steiger's experience shows, it is cardinal sin to bring the group into disrepute. Political scientist Richard Fenno has identified some norms which he believes are unique to the House, including (1) devotion to the House and avoidance of pursuing internal conflicts to the point where the effectiveness of the House is impaired;[44] (2) the "seniority-protégé-apprentice" system, to ensure harmony both within the leadership and without;[45] and (3) norms for negotiation and bargaining, which ensure harmony among the leaders.[46]

In the House, voting with its leadership—the Congressional party leaders and committee chairmen—is essential to the working of the body. Most decisions are made by these leaders. This causes the rank-and-file to feel they have very little power as individuals. Representative Charles S. Joelson (D-N.J.) made some revealing statements when he announced in 1969 that he was leaving Congress after five terms to become a state trial-court judge. Stating his great concern for social-welfare problems, but a frustrated feeling of powerlessness to effect change in his Congressional job, he said:

> If you're John Q. Citizen and you see the country in deep trouble, you cluck and say, "Isn't that too bad" and go about your business.

18

But when you're one of 435 members of the House and charged with the responsibility of doing something about our problems and you feel you're practically powerless to effect change, a feeling of frustration, of deep uneasiness sets in.

. . . I've enjoyed Congress, but I'd like to be in a position to do more than shout aye and no. I'd like to have a chance to tackle some of this country's real problems.[47]

Both houses are to some extent centralized or decentralized according to the personal style of those in leadership.[48] The general assumption that committee chairmen have undisputed power over matters within their committees' jurisdictions may not be fully accurate.[49] In his massive study of the House Appropriations Committee, Professor Richard Fenno found that the power of the Appropriations Committee in either house depends heavily on support in the parent chamber. Fenno believes that the House Appropriations Committee is one of the most stable units of either house of Congress because of its adherence to the "integrative" norms of negotiation, bargaining, and compromise.[50]

To this point we have discussed bipartisan norms designed to regularize the functioning of each house as an institution. Each political party also has great power to compel conformity to norms of party loyalty.[51] Members who actively support another party's candidate for President or who refuse to support their party's candidate for Speaker of the House may lose seniority or committee assignments as a penalty.

In 1925 Speaker Nicholas Longworth disciplined 13 Republican insurgents who had supported Robert LaFollette for President in 1924 and who refused to support Longworth for Speaker the following year. All the insurgents were demoted on their committees to the bottom of the lists, and two were ousted from their seats on the powerful Rules and Ways and Means Committees. Following his support of the Democratic Presidential candidate in 1952, Senator Wayne Morse of Oregon, then a Republican, lost his committee posts and was assigned to two minor committees.[52] At the start of the 89th Congress in 1965 the House Democratic Caucus stripped John Bell Williams (D-Miss.) and Albert W. Watson (D-S.C.) of seniority rights for publicly supporting the Republican Presidential candidate in the previous election, and for similar reasons deprived John Rarick (D-La.) of his seniority in 1969.[53] The 1967 exclusion of Representative

Adam Clayton Powell (D-N.Y.) from the House was preceded by action of the Democratic Party Caucus, which stripped him of seniority and his chairmanship of the Education and Labor Committee.

This leads to the ultimate weapon of institutional regulation: the Constitutional powers of each house to judge Members' qualifications, punish for misbehavior, and expel Members by a two-thirds vote. These powers are the subject of a later chapter, but their relative disuse through most of our history should be mentioned here. It is fair to say that each house will formally discipline a Member only in reaction to aroused public opinion which threatens the group institutionally. Its main use is to relieve public concern rather than to elevate the general level of official conduct.

Writing admiringly, William S. White was moved to say of the Senate's self-protectiveness:

> [The Senate] is a place . . . where privilege in personal behavior is high and inhibitions on personal behavior are very rare. The easiest and somewhat oversimplified way to express the real situation is simply to say that the great ones do about as they please, short of action so outrageous as not possibly to be overlooked. The rest, except for the unhappy few in any session who somehow are not acceptable at all, can in the vulgar phrase get away with *almost* anything so long as it is not directed against anybody in the Inner Club.[54]

Senator Joseph McCarthy's downfall came largely from his failure to appreciate the principle stated by White. When the Senate finally turned against him, it was not for what generally are regarded as McCarthy's sins against the public interest, but for his sins against the Senators on the subcommittees which were investigating his major offenses. In White's words again, "the Senate never conceded that this was a truly *public* problem; it was a *Senate* problem and the Senate moved in its way to solve it." [55]

On analysis, the recent actions against Representative Powell and Senator Dodd have some of the same quality. Powell was excluded partly because of his arrogance and defiance of a committee which investigated him, and he was seated with punishments when he returned two years later. Close observers of the Dodd proceedings noted that the tide turned against him only after he dissipated much Senatorial sympathy and antagonized the Senate Ethics Committee by accusing it of treating him unfairly and demanding that one Member be disqualified for bias.[56]

In sum, a Member of Congress in the past has had little to fear from formal use of Congressional disciplinary powers. Whether this must continue to be true is a subject of this report. The new Ethics Codes and permanent committees may or may not change this, but a Member still has more to fear from the subtle and intangible forces which cause diminished effectiveness with colleagues for certain types of misconduct. The evidence is that these go mostly to matters of internal etiquette and regularity, seldom to unethical conduct which has no institutional effects.

STATUTORY CONTROLS

Those who say Congress has never regulated itself do it a great disservice. In its report accompanying the new House Code of Conduct, the House Ethics Committee listed 32 Federal statutes which supply rules of conduct for Members.[57] They range from the criminal statute on bribery, with severe maximum punishments,[58] to a hortatory requirement that deductions be made from Members' salaries for each day of absence from the Senate or House unless the reason assigned is family illness.[59]

Much legislation relevant to our subject is directed at non-Members. Since 1852 Congress has regulated Capitol Hill lobbyists by rule and statute.[60] In that year the House of Representatives denied newspapermen access to the floor if they were employed as agents to prosecute claims pending before Congress. In 1867 the House excluded former Members from the floor if they were interested in claims pending before Congress. There followed a great hiatus in regulations affecting lobbyists or investigations into their activities until the 1930's, when a number of laws were passed requiring the registration of lobbyists in particular cases.[61] Purportedly complete regulation of lobbying did not arrive until 1946, when the Federal Regulation of Lobbying Act was incorporated in Title III of the Legislative Reorganization Act of 1946.[62]

Regulation of campaign financing dates from 1907, when it was

21

made unlawful for a corporation to contribute to candidates for Federal office.[63] The general subject is covered by the Corrupt Practices Act,[64] enacted in 1925, which limits individual political contributions and total spending on Federal campaigns, and provides for reporting of campaign receipts and expenditures to the Clerk of the House and Secretary of the Senate. Candidates early found that they could circumvent its limits on individual contributions by establishing numerous committees, to each of which a donor could then contribute the statutory maximum. The statute requires filing of reports only by committees operating with the candidate's knowledge and consent, and the fiction is freely indulged that committees operating in his behalf do so without his consent. Finally, the filing requirements of the Corrupt Practices Act do not apply to a committee operating entirely within the borders of a single state. There have been virtually no prosecutions under the Corrupt Practices Act. Its inadequate and unrealistic limits are partly responsible. Another factor may be the natural reluctance of most Attorneys General to offend Members of Congress, especially those of their own party.

In addition to these direct regulations of Congressional conduct, Members are subject to most civil and criminal laws which govern the lives of ordinary citizens. They share, for instance, the general liabilities for non-payment of taxes, an area where Members are peculiarly vulnerable because of the complexity of their total financial problems, including campaign financing and official and semi-official expenses.

It should not be assumed that Members of Congress may disobey the law with impunity. Criminal prosecution of Members occurs rarely but often enough to give pause to one tempted to think he is "above the law." According to CONGRESSIONAL QUARTERLY, 11 Members of Congress were indicted for various crimes between 1940 and 1963.[65] Seven of these were convicted and received jail sentences of up to two years and fines of up to $40,000. Their crimes included mail fraud, bribery, payroll padding, accepting salary kickbacks, and income-tax evasion. Only one of these seven, Thomas J. Lane, was subsequently returned to office by the voters. Three cases resulted in acquittals, and one case was dismissed.

The most significant recent prosecution of a Member of Congress involved two Representatives, Frank W. Boykin and Thomas F. Johnson, who were indicted in 1962 on charges growing out of a

Maryland savings-and-loan scandal. Both were defeated for re-election in 1962. In June 1963 they were convicted of conspiring to defraud the government and on seven counts of conflict of interest. Boykin did not appeal; he paid a $40,000 fine and received a suspended sentence. Johnson's conviction was upset by the Court of Appeals for the Fourth Circuit on grounds that proof of the conspiracy count violated Congressional immunity. The government's reliance on a speech delivered by Johnson on the House floor was held to be prohibited by the Constitutional guarantee that "for any Speech or Debate in either House [a Member] shall not be questioned in any other Place.[66] This judgment was affirmed by the United States Supreme Court.[67] Johnson has since been retried and convicted on the conflict-of-interest counts, which were based upon his efforts to influence the Justice Department. As of this writing, his sentence to six months' imprisonment is stayed pending further appellate proceedings.

Political considerations have doubtless prevented some possible prosecutions of Members, but instances have occurred when an Attorney General prosecuted a Congressman of his own political party. Republican Attorney General Herbert Brownell authorized the 1954 prosecution of Representative Ernest K. Bramblett, a California Republican, and Democrat Robert F. Kennedy approved that of Johnson, a Maryland Democrat.

The judicial rulings in the *Johnson* case point up the importance of Congress' using its own disciplinary powers. Such matters as a bribe-induced speech or vote are insulated from criminal prosecution as a part of a Constitutional scheme to protect the independence of the Legislative Branch. As a corollary, it was empowered and expected to keep its own houses clean by using its powers to expel and punish for misbehavior. For the most part, it has deferred to the electoral process to purge Congressional ranks of bad actors.

CAMPAIGN COSTS
AND RE-ELECTION PRESSURES

"Though he may not admit it even to himself," writes Professor James MacGregor Burns, "the Congressman's chief aim is re-election." [68] Staying in office means gaining added Congressional power

23

and prerogatives. A Congressman observed that while all Members of Congress have a primary interest in being re-elected, "*Some members have no other interest.*" [69] Campaigning is itself a major pressure on time and energy, but the costs in money are without doubt the greatest single source of ethical problems for Members. They spend much emotional and sometimes physical energy raising funds, and then try to fulfill their official duties without being unduly influenced by contributors.

Their need for campaign funds is a pressure common to all Members. Even those who are wealthy are loath to spend personal funds after their initial election. It is a matter of pride, plus avoidance of the image of "buying" the office.

The candidate is very much on his own. Few get large sums from the party organization. All candidates receive contributions from some friends and supporters who have no axes to grind, but many campaign funds are made up of large contributions from individuals and groups with vital interests in the candidate's behavior in office. The late Senator Neuberger observed, "The twilight zone between huge campaign contributions and outright bribes . . . [is] murky." [70] All agree that, at the very least, the generous contributor gains access to the Member and has greater opportunity to influence him.

Campaigning itself must be viewed as central to a democratic system. Professor Matthews believes that campaigns have an ethos all their own and do something which leaves an everlasting imprint on the candidate:

> Months "on the road,"—traveling from city to city, town to town, hamlet to hamlet, meeting and talking and listening to all kinds of people—leave a permanent imprint upon a man. . . . Political campaigning forces a man out of the comfortable cocoon of self-imposed uniformity within which most of us live. It results in an acute awareness of the vast differences in the conditions, interests, opinions, and styles of life of the American people and a detached tolerance toward this diversity.[71]

In our interviews a number of Congressmen volunteered that they believed campaigning to be an integral part of public life. It keeps them in touch with their constituents and gives them a first-hand understanding of the problems of the people they represent. Also, it is an antidote to the insularity and unreality of Washington life.[72]

The fact that Members must run on records which cannot possibly please everyone is thought by many of them to put incumbents at a disadvantage against aggressive young opponents, many of whom have no public record to be attacked. Many Members concede that incumbency carries advantages which more than offset this.[73]

The Chairman of the Democratic Congressional Campaign Committee, Mike Kirwan (D-Ohio), wrote a few years ago: "No Congressman who gets elected and who minds his business should ever be beaten. Everything is there for him to use if he'll only keep his nose to the grindstone and use what is offered." [74] The incumbent does favors through the "case work" previously mentioned, which should result in the fervent support of the persons helped, and even of their relatives and friends. He has an impressive forum by virtue of being a Congressman, and, by using the frank, he can communicate with his constituents at little or no cost throughout the year. Representatives participating in the 1959 Brookings Institution "Round Table Conference on Congress" declared that elections are won in the off year: *i.e.,* by doing favors for constituents; using the frank extensively to send out newsletters, questionnaires, and reprints of Congressional speeches; informing one's constituents through radio and television tapes (produced in the subsidized House and Senate studios); constantly sending out press releases; and making non-political speeches both in Washington and in the state or district. The story has been told of a Representative whose father preceded him in the House and told his son, "Son, I have three pieces of advice for you if you want to stay in Congress. One, use the frank. Two, use the frank. Three, use the frank." [75]

In 1962 novelist James Michener waged an unsuccessful campaign in Philadelphia. He observed that

> . . . the incumbent . . . mails his letters free. You pay for yours. For him to send a piece of literature to every family in his district costs about $6,000 paid for by the taxpayers. You cough up your own $6,000, in cash.
>
> He has at his command a staff of about five secretaries and helpers with a total yearly salary of around $45,000 paid for by the taxpayers. You find one girl and pay her yourself.[76]

Referring to the incumbent's campaign advantages, a Western Congressman told this Committee, "A challenger needs $25,000 just to get even with me." This figure did not take into account the $100,-000 worth of staff at the incumbent's disposal.

While campaign funds remain a problem for the incumbent, particularly in closely contested two-party districts, they are much more of a problem for the challenger, hard-pressed to make up for the incumbent's advantages. He may feel compelled to obligate himself to his large contributors—obligations which may seriously compromise him once elected.

In one important sense Senators have more job security than Representatives because they are elected for a six-year term. Against this is the empirical fact that a much larger proportion of House seats are so-called "safe seats." One scholar's research shows that the trends toward two-party competition in statewide elections are not operating within the narrower confines of House districts. In six of the seven elections held from 1950 to 1962, less than 100 of the 435 House seats were won by narrow majorities (under 55 percent of the vote).[77] He concludes that more than three fourths of House seats are relatively safe year after year.[78] Table 1.2 shows the consistently high percentage of incumbents re-elected from 1956 through 1968.

In the 1968 election, only 13 of the 409 Representatives (3.2 percent) who sought re-election were defeated; whereas in the Senate, 8 of the 28 (28.6 percent) who sought re-election were defeated. Here, the explanation may lie in the fact that their opponents were better known. A Governor, for instance, is much more likely to seek the Senate than the House.[79] The incumbent Representative, a big man in his district by this fact alone, is not apt to face an opponent whose prestige and popularity approach his own.

Regardless of whether they are actually in danger of defeat, most Congressmen "run scared," which means that they are running for election all the time. The need for campaign funds is a recurring burden and an inevitable source of both financial and ethical pressures.

PERSONAL FINANCES

Most Members of Congress without independent means, except for senior Members from safe districts, spend all they get from their salaries. It appeared from our interviews that the only Members able to

TABLE 1.2

Number and Percentage of Incumbents Who Won Re-election, 1956–68

Year	Incumbents Seeking Re-election	Lost Primary		Lost Gen. Election		Re-elected	
		HOUSE OF REPRESENTATIVES					
1956	411	6	1.5%	16	3.9%	389	94.6%
1958	394	3	0.8	37	9.4	354	89.8
1960	403	5	1.2	26	6.5	372	92.3
1962	393	11	2.8	14	3.6	368	93.6
1964	397	8	2.0	44	11.1	345	86.9
1966	407	5	1.2	40	9.8	362	89.0
1968	409	4	1.0	9	2.2	396	96.8
		SENATE*					
1956	30	0		4	13.3%	26	86.7%
1958	26	0		9	34.6	17	65.4
1960	28	0		1	3.6	27	96.4
1962	30	0		3	10.0	27	90.0
1964	30	0		2	6.7	28	93.3
1966	31	2	6.5%	1	3.2	28	90.3
1968	28	4	14.3	4	14.3	20	71.4

Source: CQ ALMANAC for above years.

* The term "incumbent" excludes those appointed to fill unexpired terms. During this period only four such appointees served longer than one year. All four were Governors who resigned to accept appointment to the Senate, and all were subsequently defeated.

save anything are those without minor children to raise and educate. Most of these now have sufficient seniority to be entitled to generous retirement benefits. For the rest, and particularly for less secure Members who must pay out of pocket to cover "semi-official" extra expenses (those unreimbursable expenses which a man would not have but for his being a Congressman), financial pressures can be a source of worry.

The general adequacy of official allowances will be discussed separately, but a few individual cases merit passing notice here. One fairly affluent Representative plowed his entire salary into office "extras" for his first three terms. Another of relatively modest means said he spent 57 percent of his salary on such expenses. Senator Javits (R-N.Y.) is known to spend his entire salary, including the 1969 raise, on such "extras." Some Members use surplus campaign funds for the same purpose, and some find it necessary to let supporters provide supplemental office funds.

The costs to a Member of supporting his family in an appropriate life style are considerable. Typically, the Member will have two homes, since, with Congress in session virtually the year round, most Members choose to bring their families to Washington. At the same time, as Professor Matthews points out, "they can ill afford to sell the old homestead, for to do so is to run the risk of being labeled a 'hotel room senator.' " [80]

Members, especially Senators, incur heavy expenses of entertaining constituents, representatives of the press and interest groups, and fellow Members,[81] and generally hosting people whose guests they have been at other times during the year. One veteran Senator complained that most people seemed to think the Senate dining room was free to Senators and their guests. Constituents, members of the press, lobbyists, and committee witnesses frequently let the Senator pick up the tab for such hospitality. Matthews estimates that the average cost of such invitations among Senators is $1,500 a year. Many Members, at their own expense, send flowers to constituents' funerals.

Members must contribute substantially to many charities and other civic appeals and keep up their membership in benevolent and fraternal organizations. Most Members say they are besieged by requests of charitable organizations for money and the purchase of ads in their publications. One Congressman we interviewed observed, "These organizations will nickel and dime you to death."

Although few Members live extravagantly, our interviews indicated that many have found it necessary to dip into their savings to make ends meet. Most find it necessary to travel home many more times than are officially reimbursable. This may be politically essential in marginal districts. Since Members' legislative responsibilities necessarily require that they spend a large majority of their time in Washington, many are generally hyperconscious of the need to mix frequently with "their people." [82]

In addition to all the special financial drains of their offices, Members have the customary expenses of family support and, presumably, would prefer to provide some financial cushions for future uncertainties. The 1969 salary increase of $12,500 per year should take off most of the severe financial pressure, according to our information, but Members' situations differ so widely that salary can never be a complete answer. They have financial needs of types which salaries cannot reach. Until answers are found to the vexing problems of campaign financing and office allowances, these items will continue to place severe strain on personal resources of Members, with continuing ethical implications.

PUBLIC OPINION AS A FORCE ON CONGRESS

In any system of self-government by elected representatives, public support and approval must rank highly as a force upon lawmakers. It is an unfortunate fact of political life that zealous journalists and political opponents are always present to criticize a Member's behavior and actions, but no one is there to say what a good job he is doing. As Congressional historian George Galloway has observed, "The case against Congress varies with changing times and circumstances, but there is always more interest in and a wider market for fault-finding than for praise." [83] The electorate generally evaluates Congressional performance in terms of the issues of the moment.

From the earliest days of the nation, there have been Members whose misdeeds were fueling the fires of public suspicion of Congressional motives. In the very first Senate session (1789–91) a Pennsylvania Senator kept a detailed journal of the Senate's proceedings. He observed with dismay that many fellow Senators were deeply involved in the widespread speculation on the theretofore worthless Continental Certificates while proposals to redeem them at full value were being considered.[84] The high number of Members of Congress whose personal debts were carried by the Bank of the United States became an issue in the dispute over its charter in the 1830's.[85]

Congressional law practices played a large part in mid-nineteenth-century scandals. In 1853 Representative Stephens of Georgia, defending a Senator who had been exposed for representing a fraudulent claimant before the Mexican Claims Commission, said it had been common:

29

> . . . from the beginning of this Government, for Senators and members of this House to appear as counsel for fee and reward or compensation before the Supreme Court of the United States, to appear before any of the courts of the Union, and before commissioners appointed to adjudicate claims [against the government].[86]

This matter of prosecuting claims against the United States became a special sore spot.[87] Until the Court of Claims was established in 1855, and in large part after its establishment, private claims against the government were dealt with by private Acts of Congress or by the various government departments. Either way individual Congressmen could play a part:

> Not only were some high-ranking members of the executive and legislative branches willing to hire out to claimants, but some members of Congress went so far during the Civil War period as to advertise their availability for such services in the Washington newspapers.[88]

Outright bribery and vote-buying has seldom been reported, but strategic retention of lawyers, personal loans, and issuance of corporate stock have raised doubts as to Congressional motives. Another device usable with Members who liked to gamble was recorded by one historian of the period:

> In the years just before the Civil War, Pendleton's gambling establishment on Pennsylvania Avenue "became the recognized clearing house for purchasable votes. . . ." The business was handled in two ways. Either the Congressman was permitted to win at poker or faro, in which case Pendleton would put in a good word for a bill while the happy legislator counted his chips, or things were arranged so that he would lose.[89]

The editor of HARPER'S MAGAZINE wrote in its October 1856 issue:

> Corruption culminates at Washington. It is a propensity elsewhere, there it is an art. . . . Particulars of individual acts of corruption are not readily ascertained, are not always safe to publish; but the general fact that money is freely and uniformly expended by all successful applicants for Congressional favor, or even Congressional justice, is notorious.[90]

30

A scandalous Civil War incident involved a manufacturer who obtained the aid of Senator Simmons of Rhode Island in procuring a contract to manufacture rifles. Simmons' compensation was to be $50,000, and he had already received two $10,000 promissory notes when an inquiry was instigated. The Congressional Commission on Ordnance Stores concluded that the whole system of contract procurement then in effect "forces the citizen to seek the patronage of his government by purchase through mercenary agencies. . . ." [91] A resolution was submitted that Simmons be expelled from the Senate. A Senate committee reported that while such conduct was indefensible, it was not illegal or punishable at the time, and expulsion was not recommended. No further action was taken, but Senator Simmons thereafter resigned his seat. [92]

Although the Civil War scandals and abuses led to passage of new laws prohibiting Members of Congress from receiving compensation for such services, [93] the economic boom which followed the Civil War saw Congressmen finding ways to share in the new economic opportunities throughout the country. Legislative proposals to provide subsidies and land grants for railroads abounded in Congress. Not only were various Members identified as spokesmen for railroads in general, but each railroad had its own phalanx of Congressmen vying for the largest possible share of the public boodle. [94]

The biggest scandal of this period and perhaps in all of Congressional history was Crédit Mobilier, which came to light in 1872. It has been aptly summarized by author James Deakin:

> Crédit Mobilier of America was a joint stock company which . . . "owned nothing except a charter drawn in the widest possible terms." But it served a highly functional purpose for the directors and incorporators of the Union Pacific Railroad. With the aid of generous federal grants, the Union Pacific was engaged in building part of the first transcontinental railroad. The railroad promoters took over Crédit Mobilier and used it as the agency to pay themselves $93,000,000, most of it from the American taxpayer via the Union Pacific treasury. Their profit reportedly was $43,000,000. To protect this profit, it was necessary to insure that the federal subsidies kept coming. Washington was growing increasingly suspicious about the high cost of building the railroad. A good inside lobbyist was needed.

One was found. He was Congressman Oakes Ames of Massachusetts, who was given 200 unrecorded shares of Crédit Mobilier stock. Within a month, . . . Ames had entered in a small pocket book "the names of 12 of the most influential members of the House to whom he had given stock. . . ."

Among the 12 Representatives were Speaker Colfax, Blaine, Garfield, Boutwell of Massachusetts (later Secretary of the Treasury), and "Pig Iron" Kelley of Pennsylvania. Other Crédit Mobilier shares went to Representative Brooks of New York, Democratic leader of the House. "I placed it where it would do the most good," Congressman Ames later explained.

Once he had the stock distributed strategically, Ames relaxed, secure in the knowledge that there would be no embarrassing questions from Congress, "for I have found that there is no difficulty in inducing men to look after their own property." Speaker Colfax obligingly blocked a Congressional investigation.

The public, which had bought millions of dollars worth of Union Pacific stock, "was royally bilked," . . . "for the company could never hope to earn a return on the amount paid to the Crédit Mobilier." Ames and Brooks were censured by the House but not unseated.[95]

In the first decade of the twentieth century, roughly from 1902 to 1912, a number of writings publicized corruption in high places. The term "muckraking" came into vogue after Theodore Roosevelt used it to describe a series of articles which tackled the U.S. Senate. This was THE TREASON OF THE SENATE by David Graham Phillips, published in 1906 in COSMOPOLITAN MAGAZINE and subsequently as a book. The articles detailed scandalous and corrupt behavior on the part of twenty-one Senators then sitting. Hundreds of thousands of copies were sold as a result of the mass-promotion efforts of the magazine's publisher, William Randolph Hearst. The book undoubtedly advanced the movement for direct election of Senators. It also caused reduced public esteem for the Senate as a body and particularly for the subjects of the book. Some resigned or were defeated at the polls.[96]

The 1960's brought new and explosive ammunition to opinion-makers who wished to be critical of Congress. Drew Pearson's and

Jack Anderson's THE CASE AGAINST CONGRESS was a 1968 best-seller. The public scandals involving Representative Adam Clayton Powell, Senator Thomas Dodd, and Senate employee Robert G. (Bobby) Baker seriously damaged the public image of Congress and produced demands for ethical reform. Individual action, of varying degrees, was taken by the two houses of Congress, and permanent Ethics Committees and new Ethics Codes resulted. The contemporary successors to the Congressional critics of other days must be given substantial credit. Outraged public opinion is the single most effective pressure on Congress.

Our interviews revealed much resentment among Congressmen toward the press, occasioned by the manner in which the above incidents and others have been publicized. One hard-working Representative had become disillusioned with the job, saying, "I wonder if it's worth it. The press has really done a hatchet job on us." Some profess reluctance to move against unethical practices for fear that the press will unfairly distort or exaggerate them and leave the image of Congress in even worse repair than before.

That the press and the Congress are both allies and adversaries creates an ambivalent relationship. The press alone is rarely able to move Congress to act. In extreme cases, though, it can inspire voluminous Congressional mail, a manifestation of public opinion which Congressmen dare not ignore. This is illustrated by a response of a Southern Representative whom we interviewed. When asked why he voted to unseat Adam Clayton Powell, he said matter-of-factly, "It was either his seat or mine."

As educational levels and communications technology advance, an informed and demanding public should have an increasing influence on Congress collectively and on its individual Members. Ethical rules should enable both the institution and individual Members to dissociate themselves from the so-called "bad apples" who are occasionally exposed and generate bad publicity for the whole Congress. The rules should also be designed to reassure the public of Congressional good intentions and should aid Congress in assuring that public opinion is fairly and accurately informed.

CHAPTER TWO

CONFLICTS OF INTEREST

The most serious charge which can be made against a public official's ethics is that he betrays the public's trust in him by using the office to advance his own financial interests at the public's expense. Bribery and embezzlement are the most extreme forms of this and are covered by criminal statutes. A lesser form of the same evil, which may or may not be covered by statute, is the "conflict of interest." More accusations of official dereliction are lumped under this label than under any other. Much distrust of government flows from ambiguous circumstances where there is ground for suspicion that officials are promoting their own welfare rather than the public's. Our study has shown us that much can be done in the conflict-of-interest area to improve the Congressional image and enhance public confidence in Federal lawmakers.

THE FIDUCIARY CONCEPT

The term "conflict of interest" has widely varying connotations. This is especially true at the Congressional level because the Congress has never supplied a formal definition for its own guidance. Many different views flourish in the literature of the subject.

The broadest concept of Congressional conflicts of interest, and a valid one for many purposes, has been stated by Senator Wallace Bennett (R-Utah), a Member of the Senate Ethics Committee. He said:

> The legislator comes to office as the result of a struggle for power between groups of voters whose interests are in conflict, and he is elected because he is the choice of the larger number. . . .
>
> [Legislation], with its inevitable compromises, is produced by the clash of obviously conflicting interests; and to say that a legislator must avoid conflict of interests in that situation is to ask the impossible.
>
> . . . [A] legislator's own vote, in committee or on the floor, is usually arrived at through the same process of conflict, because all the people he represents are never in agreement. In fact, the list of potential types and sources of conflict in which he may find himself is long and fraught with inevitability. . . .
>
> For the record I should like to list these areas of conflict. It is not a complete list.
>
> First, there are interests represented by political entities. There is the national interest. There is the interest of the Senator's state. There is the interest of his political party. There is the interest of the "administration"—which controls the executive department. Then there is the interest of the Senate or the House, as the case may be, as an institution. And to assume or assert that all of these interests always line up in a parallel is, of course, ridiculous. . . .
>
> Then there are the interests that are represented by privately organized groups that from time to time and in various ways seek to influence Government policies for their private benefits. There are national organizations of citizens with a common purpose, such as labor unions, veterans' organizations, business associations, and so forth. There are similar groups operating within the Senator's State whose programs may not be exactly the same as their national counterparts.
>
> Then there are individual interests. There is the interest of an individual constituent. There is the interest of a group constituent formed as a corporation or organization. Then there is the interest of fellow legislators.

35

Then there are interests of each Senator that might be described as personal—his personal philosophy of life and government; his personal goals, political and in private life; the well-being of people and institutions in which he has a personal interest, such as his family, his friends, his church, the schools with which he or his family have been involved; other groups or organizations in which in private life he is a loyal and active member; his hobbies; and at the bottom of the list, his personal financial affairs.[1]

As an analysis of Congressional decision-making and the pluralistic qualities of legislation, Senator Bennett's thoughtful statement is very helpful; but, as he would doubtless agree, a more specific concept must be developed if conflict of interest is to be a guiding ethical consideration for Members.

Some narrower meanings of the term were suggested in 1964 by the Senate Rules Committee in the report of its investigation of former Senate Majority Secretary Robert G. (Bobby) Baker's financial activities. The Committee said:

The average citizen interprets the words to include any conduct of a public official which will or may impose any sort of restraint upon such official's complete freedom in performing all his official acts. For instance, if a public official engages in an outside private profit-making business, however legitimate or laudable the business may be, a conflict of interest arises if such official gives so much time and attention to it that his attention to his official duties is lessened.

Likewise, a conflict of interest is deemed by people generally to arise when a public official engages in private business for profit and uses the facilities of his office and his official position to promote and carry on such business.[2]

The Rules Committee characterized these as the "popular conceptions" of the term and concluded that Baker's outside activities[3] were within them. The Committee also noted as a "technical definition" the relevant Federal criminal statutes on conflicts of interest.[4] The Committee declined to judge Baker's guilt or innocence under these laws.

In our opinion, these statutes incorporate portions of the popular concepts identified by the Rules Committee. They are aimed at uses of public office for private economic gain and incorporate the fiduciary concept governing private trustees as the basic standard of conduct for public trustees in public office. This concept is very much applicable to Congressional office, although implementation must take somewhat different forms from that used for the Executive Branch.

The fiduciary nature of Congressional office was recognized by the United States Senate in 1968, when it adopted as the preamble to its Ethics Code:

> The ideal concept of public office, expressed by the words, "a public office is a public trust," signifies that the officer has been entrusted with public power by the people; that the officer holds this power in trust to be used only for their benefit and never for the benefit of himself or a few; and that the officer must never conduct his own affairs so as to infringe on the public interest.[5]

The Senate's admonition that a public official should never use his power for the benefit of himself states a basic fiduciary principle and holds the key to a workable system for regulating Congressional conflicts of interest. It is part of a pervasive legal concept that "the exercise of a granted power to act in behalf of others involves the assumption toward them of a duty to exercise the power in their interest and behalf. . . ." [6]

This duty prevents a fiduciary from acquiring any personal interest in the subject of the trust[7] because his sole motivation must be service of his beneficiary's interests. As stated by one expert:

> It is the duty of a trustee to administer the trust solely in the interest of the beneficiaries. He is not permitted to place himself in a position where it would be for his own benefit to violate his duty to the beneficiaries.[8]

Fiduciaries are never permitted to confuse their duty with their self-interest because:

> . . . when a conflict between duty and self-interest arises in the breast of a person holding a fiduciary relation, the only safe rule

37

to adopt . . . ascribes to self-interest rather than a sense of duty
the motive power of ensuing action.[9]

This principle accounts for much of the law governing public officials. Like private trustees, they can even be required to account for
personal profits earned from a breach of trust. In a leading English
case, the Crown was held to be entitled to money received by an army
sergeant for guiding smugglers past police inspectors in North Africa
during World War II.[10] The United States Supreme Court reached a
similar result in *United States v. Carter*,[11] an action against an army
procurement officer who received a kickback of half a million dollars
on contracts let for harbor improvements. Although several conflict-of-
interest statutes apparently were applicable, the Court mentioned
none of them and relied solely on the fiduciary principle to impose a
constructive trust on the tainted proceeds in the hands of the officer
and others.[12]

A lawsuit based on the same theory was brought by the United
States against Robert G. Baker in July 1969. A civil complaint filed by
the U.S. Department of Justice in the Federal District Court for the
District of Columbia alleged that Baker's net worth increased from
$11,000 in 1956, the year after he became Majority Secretary, to
$1,700,000 in 1963 ,when he resigned. An accounting was sought to
determine what portion of this increase resulted from Baker's
breaches of fiduciary obligation and exploitation of the influence and
confidences of his office. Recovery of this amount for the benefit of
the United States government is the ultimate relief sought.[13]

Conflict-of-interest rules governing public trustees reach corrupting
influences which stop far short of outright bribes and activity such as
Baker's. The controlling concept is considerably broader and ap-
pealingly simple. As our predecessor committee said when studying
these problems in the Executive Branch:

> The central conception of conflict of interest regulation is that an
> official should not act for the government where his private eco-
> nomic interests are involved.[14]

The evil is not only the possibility or appearance of private gain from
public office, but the risk that official decisions, whether consciously
or otherwise, will be motivated by something other than the public's

38

interests. The ultimate concern is bad government, which always means actual harm to the public.

That this is the basic thrust of conflict-of-interest laws governing the Executive Branch is shown by the decision of the United States Supreme Court in the famous Dixon-Yates litigation. A government contract for electric power was invalidated because the government had been represented in negotiations by a part-time financial consultant whose company could have been expected to profit from financing the construction of the contemplated power plants. In holding that a situation of such divided loyalty was an unlawful conflict of interest,[15] the Court said:

> . . . The statute does not specify as elements of the crime that there be actual corruption or that there be any actual loss suffered by the Government as a result of the defendant's conflict of interest. This omission indicates that the statute establishes an objective standard of conduct, and that whenever a government agent fails to act in accordance with that standard, he is guilty of violating the statute, regardless of whether there is positive corruption. The statute is thus directed not only at dishonor, but also at conduct which tempts dishonor. This broad proscription embodies a recognition of the fact that an impairment of impartial judgment can occur in even the most well-meaning men when their personal economic interests are affected by the business they transact on behalf of the Government.[16]

The evil, then, is risk of impairment of impartial judgment, a risk which arises whenever there is temptation to serve personal interests. The quality of specific results is immaterial. In this sense, conflict-of-interest regulation is true to the fiduciary principle. Like other fiduciaries, such as guardians, executors, lawyers, and agents, the public trustee has a duty to avoid private interests which cause even a risk that he will not be motivated solely by the interests of the beneficiaries of his trust. Properly conceived, conflict-of-interest regulation does not condemn bad actions so much as it erects a system designed to protect a decision-making process. It is preventive and prophylactic. Its aim is not detection and punishment of evil, but providing safeguards which lessen the risk of undesirable action.

The dangers controlled by other conflict-of-interest regulations exist at the Congressional level also. Members must act upon many matters in which they have private economic interests. But can regulation of Congressional conflicts be built upon the same basic concept: avoiding the risk of impairment of independent judgment?

Two main techniques of controlling conflicts of interest are used in the statutes governing officials in the Executive Branch and administrative agencies. The basic weapon is *disqualification*. Officials are forbidden to act on matters in which they have personal financial interests.[17] The disqualifying interest may be another's, like that of a relative or a law firm; or it may be prospective, like that of a possible employer. In either event, the decision-making process is protected by removing the decision from the interested official. This may have some utility in the Congressional context, but it also has obvious limitations. Constituents of the disqualified Member of Congress are denied their Constitutional right to representation in the particular legislation at hand.* There is no substitute or deputy who can act in his stead.

The second basic weapon is more promising. It is *interest avoidance*, which requires total abstention from particular holdings or relationships. Decision-making remains at its regular place, but its integrity is protected by mandatory prohibitions against certain interests which unquestionably have potential for impairing the judgment of particular officials. For instance, members and employees of the Interstate Commerce Commission are prohibited by law from any ownership interests in common carriers subject to their jurisdiction.[18] Cabinet members are similarly limited. The first Congress prohibited the Secretary of the Treasury from investing in government securities.[19] Interest avoidance is more commonly required of Cabinet members by non-statutory means. As conditions of Senate confirmation, they are normally required to divest themselves of certain holdings. Department of Defense appointees are generally required by the Senate Armed Services Committee to dispose of all stock in companies doing

---

* Former Senator Kenneth B. Keating of New York once announced that he might abstain from voting on a tax-relief bill which affected duPont stockholders because he personally owned such stock. Four stockholder-constituents wrote to praise him, but more than 100 wrote to criticize, one saying: "Your duty to represent me is preeminent to any incidental interest you might have because of duPont ownership." Keating voted for the tax relief and it became law. B. Bagdikian and D. Oberdorfer, *Conflict of Interest: Can Congress Crack Down on Its Own Members?* THE SATURDAY EVENING POST, Nov. 17, 1962, at 26–27.

substantial business with the Department of Defense. The Secretary of the Treasury is similarly limited with respect to bank holdings by the Finance Committee, and the Committee on Interior and Insular Affairs requires the Secretary of the Interior to give up oil investments.

This type of regulation also extends beyond present property interests to prospective opportunities. Executive officials are barred indefinitely from personally representing private interests against the government in specific matters in which they participated while in government,[20] and are barred for one year from matters which were under their official responsibility.[21] Our first and oldest conflict-of-interest limitation of this type is in the Constitution itself. During a term of office Members of Congress may not be appointed to any Federal office which was created, or whose emoluments were increased, during that term.[22] In all instances the purpose is the same: to eliminate a personal interest or opportunity which might subtly tempt the public official into subordinating the public interest to self-interest. Protecting the integrity of governmental decisions is again the key.

Interest avoidance obviously cannot be applied to Members of Congress as neatly as it is to administrators with limited spheres of responsibility. But this does not mean that it cannot be applied at all. Perhaps interests can be identified which have sufficiently close and recurring involvements in Congressional decisions, particularly at the committee level, so that it is reasonable to expect Members to avoid them.

In the previously quoted speech, after listing the various interests which compete in the decision-making process of a Senator, Senator Bennett said:

> Every important vote requires the resolution of conflicts in several areas, and among several groups, so who can say what interests were included in the combination that persuaded him to vote as he did? True, each interest that benefited from his vote can think he did it for them, and each of those on the losing side can assume that their interest alone was rejected, but none can say for sure, and if a personal financial interest were included in the combination, who can say it was the decisive one? I am always amused when a Senator is publicly given credit for great

virtue for voting against what seems to be his own financial interest and attacked when his vote seems to promise him some financial gain, however remote.[23]

The Senator's questioning that anyone could assess the decisiveness of personal financial interests goes to the key issue. Granting that no one can be certain that it *was* the decisive factor, the more pertinent question is: Who can say it *was not* the decisive factor. Granting the impossibility of probing a legislator's mental process, is it not a loss for citizens to be compelled to speculate whether their interest or the legislator's was decisive? Beneficiaries of fiduciary decision-making are not supposed to be left to such speculation. The fact that beneficiaries of Congressional trusteeship must sometimes be uncertain does not mean that such occasions should not be kept to a minimum. Reducing the causes for such speculation to the lowest possible level would inevitably bring gains in public confidence in Congress and, theoretically at least, it should improve the quality of legislative decisions.

Some may think it quixotic to attempt to move elected officials toward true fiduciary standards, arguing that the complexity of Congressional service and the multiplicity of interests and pressures operating on a Member make it unrealistic to deal simply with pressure from his personal *economic* interests. This could be said of any attempt to codify ethics for public officials. Our predecessor committee faced the same question in dealing with appointed officials in the Executive Branch. Despite other differences in our subjects, we can endorse their statement of the rationale for singling out economic interests for special attention:

> . . . [T]his inquiry is limited to conflicts between the official's duties and his personal economic interests. But man is driven by many motivations. What of conflicts between his official duties and, for example, his religious or family affiliations? In preference to his business associates, an official may choose to favor his old college roommate with a contract or his mother with a market tip. Job appointments in government are often made in accord with political debts; and intangible loyalties to an institution, such as a school, company, or law firm, may long survive resignation, sale of stock, or severance from a payroll. Then why single out simple economic ties for study and regulation?

The simplest reason is that it is better to control whatever fraction of improper behavior is attributable to economic motives than to control none. The second reason is that regulatory schemes have to be administered. Restrictions on outside economic affiliations can be written with reasonable particularity and enforced with moderate predictability; no one has yet devised a method for sorting out acquaintances, friends, relations, and lovers for purposes of a rule permitting official dealings with some and not with the others.[24]

Others may concede the manageability of the private-interest portion of the problem but question this as a means to the end of increasing the likelihood that Congressional decisions will serve the public interest and provide better government. What is "the public interest"?[25] And how can one be sure that it is served? We can add little to such customary terminology as "the general welfare" and "the greatest good for the greatest number." It must be conceded that reasonable men frequently differ on what serves the public interest in a given instance and that interested and disinterested men often agree. This makes our subject all the more important. Inherently difficult decisions should be as free as possible from unnecessary complication from decision-makers' private stakes in the outcome.

The term "unnecessary complication" is used advisedly. It must be conceded that the risk of selfish decision-making can only be controlled and reduced to some minimum, not totally eradicated. This does not frustrate our efforts. That some Congressional economic conflicts of interest are inevitable under our system does not mean that all such conflicts must be tolerated. Our inquiry accordingly turns to a search for conflicts which are not inevitable, those which may be called "avoidable conflicts of interest." If *unavoidable* conflicts can first be identified and separated from the total, those remaining can become the focus of attention. By definition, these will be *avoidable* and therefore regulable.

Unavoidable Conflicts of Interest

Conflicts of interest which must be endured for legitimate reasons and hence are unavoidable can be divided into three groups:

1. *Inherent Conflicts*

Since legislative bodies must be constituted from the general public, it is inevitable that legislators bring with them the interests of the economic groups to which they belong. As parents, homeowners, taxpayers, consumers, and representative members of their communities, legislators inherently have attributes which at various times produce some risk that their decisions may be made in the interests of something less than the entire public. Lawyers could not be expected to abstain from voting on bills regulating admission to practice before Federal agencies or requiring legal training for particular offices. If they did, there would be no quorum. Nor could homeowners and parents in Congress be disqualified on tax measures which benefit them. Such groups are quite large, however, and the legislator's interest is common to many persons. The potential for adverse effects from such conflicts is quite low.

Another type of conflict also inheres in legislative bodies. They have affirmative Constitutional duties to act upon some matters in which they are specially interested. No sharper conflict of interest can be envisioned than that which occurs when a Member of Congress votes upon his own salary. Distasteful as it is to most of them, this is a conflict which they and the public must accept. Political considerations and high visibility usually cause self-interest to be outweighed on this issue, but a Member's high sense of public duty can also control, as in 1933, when depression conditions moved Members to reduce their own salaries.

2. *Politically Dictated Conflicts*

A frequently cited example of the inevitability of conflicts of interest in Congress is the farmer elected from an agricultural district. His personal interest is shared by the dominant segment of his constituency, and he may well have been elected in large part because of his personal involvement with farm problems. The oil man from the Southwest and the textile man from the Carolinas may be comparable. Without suggesting fixed lines, however, one may question whether this over-all category includes many relevant groups, such as practicing lawyers, bankers, insurance agents, or real-estate developers. It is exceptional when a Member's business interests are a positive political asset.

3. *Personally Necessary Conflicts*

Although most Members give up active, compensated involvements in their businesses or professions when they enter Congress, some decline to do so for what they regard as reasons of personal necessity. Before the 1969 pay raise, the realities of Congressional campaign costs and levels of official salaries and allowances made it reasonable—perhaps in some cases essential—for a Member to have some source of outside income. Also, Members have personal assets which must continue to exist in some form. They cannot be expected to give them away. Whatever the size or form, such interests carry some potential conflict of interest. Typical income-producing investments can normally be managed so as to minimize the conflict problem. A difficult case is illustrated by the 1968 action of the Senate in allowing Deputy Defense Secretary David Packard to retain beneficial interests in a large defense-contracting firm. He was allowed to continue such holdings in contrast to the precedents of Charles Wilson and Robert MacNamara. Full divestment would have depressed the market and caused huge financial hardship to others.

Standards which required withdrawal from small, closely held family enterprises might similarly create hardships out of proportion to gains to the legislative process. This is a flexible area. Retention of particular holdings might be dictated for one Member but not for another, for a number of reasons related to their personal circumstances. What might be viewed as unnecessarily and unreasonably creating a conflict if voluntarily acquired by a Member after election to Congress might be reasonable for a Member who had owned it before his election. Representative Robert Taft, Jr. (R-Ohio) owned a large number of shares in Taft Broadcasting Company when

45

elected. He retained beneficial ownership, but placed the stock in trust for all purposes. He also continued to serve as trustee of several family trusts which held Taft stock. This seems reasonable, since he is not on the Commerce Committee and disqualifies himself on all communications legislation. It would seem very different for a member of one of the Commerce Committees to join in a new broadcasting venture which required a license from the Federal Communications Commission.

Avoidable Conflicts of Interest

The foregoing categories of unavoidable conflicts are believed to be all-inclusive. It is apparent from their narrowness that many economic interests of Members which risk impairment of their independence are neither inherent, politically dictated, nor personally necessary. It can therefore be concluded that many Congressional conflicts of interest are "avoidable."

For purposes of our analysis, an avoidable conflict of interest may be said to arise when a Member of Congress acts officially upon a matter in which he has a personal economic interest which is neither inherent in Congress, politically dictated, nor personally necessary. Since all three grounds of unavoidability can fairly be characterized as "necessary," avoidable conflicts of interest may then be further defined as those created by personal economic interests which substantially risk impairment of independence and are unnecessarily held by a Member.

Note that the interests in question are those carrying substantial risks to independence of judgment. As will be shown shortly, there are many investment alternatives which do not carry such risk. As for the fact of continued holding of the interest, the word "unnecessarily" is emphasized and intended to refer back to the three categories of unavoidable (necessary) conflicts.

This is not to say that Members are necessarily to be condemned for their avoidable conflicts. Whether these should be avoided or should require some sort of disqualification or merely be disclosed publicly raises a host of difficult questions. It is not necessary to quarrel with Members who feel they successfully subordinate their private interests to the public interest. Our concern is that their constituents be informed and allowed to judge whether a conflict is unavoidable because personally necessary to the Member, and whether it unduly affects his voting record.

The basic thesis of this Report and the opinion of this Committee is that an avoidable conflict of interest should normally be avoided. If not avoided, it should be disclosed to the Member's colleagues and to the public and perhaps should result in disqualification from voting or committee service.

THE SCOPE OF CONGRESSIONAL FINANCIAL INTERESTS

Throughout history, societies have differed on property rights and other economic interests of lawmakers. Plato prohibited his Philosopher Kings from owning property and made them wards of the state to secure them against criticism that they might be using their public offices for personal gain and to keep them from being distracted from public duties.[26] Solon and Augustus went to the opposite extreme and set high property qualifications for office,[27] apparently on the theory that such lawmakers would be more capable and less easily corrupted. It has never been seriously proposed in this country that the oath of Congressional office serve as a vow of poverty. To the contrary, property qualifications for these and other offices were common in the constitutions of the original states.[28] Theorists still differ on the political and governmental advantages of wealth among lawmakers, but democratic processes have caused Congress, economically, to become a diverse, pluralistic group representing many segments of society. This is indicated by Table 2.1.

In their various personal situations, Members of Congress are certain to arrive with some assets. They cannot be expected to fully strip themselves of worldly goods. Nor should the other extreme be tolerated: they can hardly expect to continue entrepreneurial enterprises on the same basis as other persons. Our research shows that Members have found a great variety of intermediate positions. Most have made considerable rearrangements of their financial affairs either to elimi-

47

nate threats to their independence or to free their energies for full-time Congressional involvement.

TABLE 2.1

Economic and Professional Backgrounds of Members of the 90th Congress

Background	House	Senate	Total
Agriculture	39	18	57
Business or Banking	161	23	184
Education	57	15	72
Engineering	6	2	8
Journalism	39	10	49
Law	246	68	314
Medicine	3	1	4
Organized Labor	2	0	2
Religion	3	0	3

Source: 1967 CQ ALMANAC 36. (Totals exceed the total membership because some members have multiple backgrounds.)

LEGAL LIMITS ON CONGRESSIONAL FINANCIAL INTERESTS

Except for serious restrictions on law practice, which are discussed separately, the law contains few obstacles for the Member of Congress who wishes to continue a particular property interest or business affiliation. The earliest limitation dates from 1808 and prohibits contracts between the Federal government and Members of Congress.[29] However, by its own terms, it is inapplicable to corporations of which Members may be stockholders and to sales of property if delivery is ready and payment is made when the contract is executed. Many other minor exceptions have been added over the years, most of them related to agricultural programs.[30] Another statute prevents contracts between Members and the United States for the acquisition of land for flood-control purposes.[31] An unusual limitation was included by Congress in the Merchant Marine Act of 1936; it forbids a contractor or charterer who receives subsidies under the Act from employing any Member of Congress as an agent, attorney, officer, or director.[32] Thus, legal barriers to outside business involvements of Members of Congress are indeed slight. Subject to political and ethical considerations, Members may now take advantage of business opportunities on substantially the same basis as other citizens.

Congressional Self-Limitation

In our interviews we attempted to learn something of the nature of Congressional business interests and the conflict-of-interest problems created for individual Members. We found early that questions which were phrased in general conflict-of-interest terms were not productive. Most Members view the suggestion of personal conflict of interest as equivalent to a charge of crime or corruption and were slow to attribute it either to themselves or to their colleagues. Few think the subject generally is much of a problem. However, many are sensitive to the fiduciary concept and go to considerable lengths to avoid personal financial interests which might impair their independence.

On two points Members were virtually unanimous. First, none felt that he had gained financially from holding public office. Many believed instead that they had served at a sacrifice and would be better off financially had they stayed in private life. This is undoubtedly true for the great majority; they are talented people who could have been successful in many walks of private life.

Second, nearly every Member told us that he had never experienced a personal conflict of interest. Setting his own salary and allowances was not even mentioned as a personal conflict of interest. Those who had affirmatively arranged their affairs to avoid conflicts felt they had fully succeeded. Those who retained holdings specially affected by Federal laws stated similarly that they had never found themselves in conflict situations. This shows that the term does not fully connote to them the true fiduciary concept which we have discussed. A Member could hardly feel that he had never voted on any matter which affected his own pocketbook. The broad sweep of Federal legislation on taxation, home ownership, social security, and veterans' affairs alone makes this impossible.

What the Members were telling us was that they felt they had never acted in their personal economic interest to the detriment of the public interest. Most can point to instances where they have voted against their economic interest. Each sincerely believes that any vote which happened to benefit him in some way would have been the same without his personal interest in the picture. This narrow view of conflicts of interest may be understandable, but it indicates a correspondingly narrow view of the fiduciary concept and falls far short of the conflict-of-interest thinking to be expected of a trustee.

On the positive side is the fact that so many demonstrate by their conduct that they sense the fiduciary concept. A majority keep themselves free from obvious and invidious conflicts of interest by abstaining from some type of interest. The interviews yielded a number of examples of Members who had either divested themselves of particular investments or abstained from them in order to avoid conflicts of interest.

Nine of the 23 Senators interviewed indicated that at some time they had imposed particular voluntary restrictions on their finances to avoid conflicts. Such restrictions included resignation from corporate directorships, divesting oneself of a business, placing assets in trust, and limiting investments to government bonds. In the House, 51 of the 97 Members interviewed mentioned some self-imposed restriction. Twelve abstained from particular investments or business affiliations. Thirty-five had divested themselves either of former business connections (21), particular investments (13), or corporate directorships (4). This does not necessarily include all self-imposed restrictions, since comments on Members' personal arrangements were not always elicited and were not necessarily complete when given. Nonetheless, enough instances and types of self-limitation were revealed to suggest norms which might be appropriate for all Members.

However, the interviews and other data make it clear that many Members have significant outside financial interests which must be classed as creating avoidable conflicts of interest. This is not necessarily a disparagement. The Member with no inducement to gain or preserve sources of income in addition to his salary is likely to be a rare, Spartan individual or a man supporting only his wife and himself after their children are grown. This was especially true before the 1969 pay raise.

Most Members interviewed revealed something of the nature of their outside incomes. Nineteen of the 23 Senators and 59 of the 97 Representatives mentioned investments in securities or in real estate other than personal residences. Twenty-nine Representatives, including a number who also rely on other investments, indicated an outside income from business or farming. Five Senators indicated income from operating a business or farm. Of those interviewed, no Senator and only 10 Representatives indicated a total lack of significant income other than their salaries.

Thus, the typical Member of Congress has financial interests with some potential for clouding his independence of judgment on legislation. Many have taken affirmative action to minimize this potential, but many others have done little in this direction. Without meaningful public financial disclosures, the full extent of avoidable conflicts of interest in the Congress must largely be left to speculation.

THE 1969 HOUSE FINANCIAL DISCLOSURES

The Ethics Codes adopted in 1968 required some measure of disclosure of investments and business connections of House Members. The Senate Code added nothing to public knowledge in this area because its public-disclosure rules apply only to contributions and honoraria. House Members were required to report capital gains netting $5,000, ownership interests worth more than $5,000 in businesses subject to Federal regulatory agencies or doing substantial business with the Federal government, and the receipt of income of $1,000 or more from corporate directorships and law firms. The first reports,[33] filed in April 1969, cast considerable light upon Representatives' holdings in defense-contracting firms, broadcasting, transportation, and financial institutions. Banking was shown to be the most popular field of Congressional financial activity, with 96 Representatives reporting interests in banks or savings-and-loan companies. This will be discussed later in more detail.

Sixty-one Representatives reported holdings in corporations ranked among the top 100 defense contractors. Many such holdings, however, are in such widely held companies as American Telephone & Telegraph Company, IBM, and General Motors—companies which have considerable operations beyond those supported by government contracts. Only a handful reported holdings in companies known to be almost totally dependent on such contracts. Only four of the 61 serve on the Armed Services Committee, while six are on the Appropriations Committee.

In the field of transportation, 16 Members reported stock in commercial airlines, while six reported railroad holdings, and five showed interests in trucking firms. Only three of the total reporting any transportation holdings serve on the House Interstate and Foreign Commerce Committee.

Twenty-three Representatives reported interests in radio or television stations. Much was already known in this area, and it, too, will be discussed separately.

A relatively low scale of general investment activity by Representatives is indicated by the capital-gains disclosures. If $5,000 in income resulted, the gain from any capital transaction other than sale of a residence was to be reported. Only 60 reported such income, and most of these showed but one or two transactions.

The most significant figure may be the number of Representatives who had neither transactions nor interests of the types required to be reported. Blank forms were filed by 155.

From the totality of the filings it appears that the great majority of Members have arranged their financial affairs so that there is little basis for suspicion of invidious conflicts of interest. However, enough have failed in this regard to provide continued ammunition for critics and to make the case for further reform.

SPECIFIC EFFECTS OF CONGRESSIONAL FINANCIAL INTERESTS

The fiduciary concept makes it unnecessary for our recommendations to be supported by evidence that identifiable harm to the public interest has resulted from past or present Congressional conflicts of interest. Nonetheless, in the interests of thoroughness and fairness we have examined material of public record in four areas for specific evidence that undesirable policy effects may actually flow from avoidable Congressional conflicts of interest.

Transportation

Congressional standards of ethics have improved immeasurably since Phillips' TREASON OF THE SENATE castigated Members for being financially tied to railroad interests. As shown earlier, personal ownership interests in air, rail, and trucking concerns appear now to be very few—indeed, so few that it appears that Members may deliberately avoid such interests.

The most notable recent charge that national transportation policy may have been affected for a time by personal interests of a Member involved former Senator John Bricker of Ohio. As Chairman of the Senate Commerce Committee, he fought the St. Lawrence Seaway while his Columbus law firm was retained by the Pennsylvania Railroad. The opposition of the railroads was a major factor in delaying Congressional authorization of the Seaway.[34] We have found no current evidence that Congressional financial interests in transportation are affecting the substance of legislation or agency administration.

Defense Contractors

The 1969 reports showed a high number holding stock in the nation's top defense contractors, but most of these are diversified and widely held corporations such as AT&T, General Electric, General Motors, IBM, Westinghouse, and others which would be represented in portfolios of many investors seeking merely to share in the capital growth of the country. Although a few report interests in companies which derive the bulk of their income from government contracts, such as Lockheed Aircraft, it is unlikely that Congressional financial interests deserve to be listed among the causes maintaining the military-industrial complex. Critics of this phenomenon usually cite the interchange of personnel between government and industry and the worth of government contracts to areas represented by powerful Members of Congress,[35] but do not mention ownership interests of Members. Those usually mentioned as Congressional friends of the military-industrial complex are conspicuously absent from those reporting ownership interests in it.

Broadcasting

A few publicized instances of Congressional ownership of radio and television interests may have caused this area to receive undue attention from Congressional critics. Since broadcasting licenses are so valuable and are solely dependent upon Federal largesse, it is easy for some to suspect that Members might attempt to use their office to obtain stations and favorably influence Federal laws and agencies.

Without deciding whether there may ever have been reason to suspect that those affected by FCC action were favored if a Member of Congress was included,[36] we are pleased to find that there is no basis to suspect this today. Congressional ownership of broadcasting interests has declined in recent years. In 1961, 1963, and 1965 BROADCASTING magazine's studies of FCC records showed that 23 Members had some such tie,[37] counting some who were on governing boards of noncommercial educational stations. In 1968 the magazine reported only commercial ownership interests and found the number to be only 15.[38] For some, the interest was quite remote; one Senator, for instance, was listed because his second cousin owned one of 1,643 shares of a corporate licensee.

CONGRESSIONAL QUARTERLY interpreted the 1969 House disclosures as showing 23 Representatives reporting requisite interests in radio or television stations or holding companies which control stations. The latter category included corporations such as Radio Corporation of America and caused the CQ figures to be higher than those of BROADCASTING magazine. Only two Members of the House Interstate and Foreign Commerce Committee reported such interests. One reported RCA, and the other a radio station owned before election to Congress. Under any theory the numerical extent of ownership of broadcasting interests by Members of Congress is quite low.

Whether the ownership which does exist affects communications policy-making is another question. Some Washington observers, usually after exaggerating the extent of Congressional broadcasting interests, go on to say that this contributes to an assumed Congressional "softness" toward the industry. We doubt this, and some reliable sources contradict it. They may feel that the broadcasting industry is somewhat overprotected and underregulated, both by Congress and by the FCC, but the best-reasoned analysis[39] attributes this to the

54

dependence of Congressmen upon broadcasters for publicity and free radio and television time. It is reported that 60 percent to 70 percent of Members of Congress receive free broadcasting time[40] for reports to constituents. Without deciding these questions, we say only that *if* Congress is overly friendly to the broadcasting industry, it is *not* because of Congressional ownership of broadcasting interests.

Banking

The only type of financial interest which can be said to be significantly overrepresented in Congressional portfolios is that in financial institutions, including state and national banks, savings-and-loan companies, and bank-holding companies. In the 1969 financial disclosures, 96 House Members reported ownership interests, and 43 reported either offices or directorships, or both. As high as it seems, this figure is actually lower than the true number because some did not report interests in state-chartered institutions. The House disclosure rule reaches these only if they are deemed to be "subject to Federal regulatory agencies." Although it was indicated once in the floor discussion of this provision that state banks would be covered if their deposits were insured by the Federal Deposit Insurance Corporation,[41] the Ethics Committee later interpreted the rule differently (and truer to its language) and advised Members that such holdings need not be reported.

Thirteen of the 96 who reported banking interests are Members of the House Banking and Currency Committee, and six sit on the tax-writing Ways and Means Committee. Seven who are members of these committees are directors or trustees of their institutions.

Here, those who seek a causal relation between Congressional business interests and Congressional decision-making may have more ammunition. Banks have played a role perhaps equal to that of law practices in generating Congressional scandal. We have previously mentioned personal speculation by Members of the 1st Congress in state-bank notes which were being refunded by the Federal government. In 1793 Thomas Jefferson complained of the high number of House Members with bank interests—approximately one half—and wrote of his wish to see both houses of Congress cleared of all such persons because of his belief that

. . . if the votes of those members who had an interest distinct from and contrary to the general interest of their constituents had been withdrawn, as in decency and honesty they should have been, the laws would have been the reverse of what they are in all the great questions.[42]

In the 1830's, during the fights over renewing the charter of the United States Bank, it was alleged that at times between 1831 and 1834 the bank had loans outstanding to as many as 59 Members (of a total of 243), in a sum greater than the combined salaries of all Members.[43]

In more recent years there have been occasional reports and rumors of individual Members of Congress being offered bank stock on bargain terms. One former Member tells privately how a banker in his district once solicited him to purchase stock in the bank and offered to have the bank lend him the necessary funds. The Member declined. Representative Wright Patman (D-Tex.), a vigorous critic of the banking lobby and Chairman of the House Banking and Currency Committee, once said on the House floor:

One clever means of antipublic action by the bankers' lobby is as subtle as a wart on a movie actress' nose. It takes the form of offering a Congressman bank stock either free or at a cost greatly under the market value.[44]

As an example, Patman then mentioned the disclosure by Representative Henry B. Gonzalez (D-Tex.), also a Member of the House Banking and Currency Committee, that a constituent banker had offered him $14,000 in stock as a gift while asking him to serve on the bank's board of directors. Gonzalez then confirmed Patman's statement and told how he had refused the offer in strong terms, telling the banker, "This would be more than just a conflict of interest, but at the least that is what it would be." [45]

There has been some reason to believe that applications for national bank charters were more likely to be successful when a Member of Congress was included among the incorporators.

As this report is written, a senior Member of the House Banking and Currency Committee, Representative Seymour Halpern (R-N.Y.) has been the subject of a WALL STREET JOURNAL article disclosing his heavy indebtedness to a number of banks. One debt of $40,000 was owed a New York City bank at a time when Halpern was allegedly voting in committee to advance bank-holding-company legislation favored by the bank.[46]

The Senate investigation of the activities of Robert G. (Bobby) Baker revealed some highly questionable mixing of Congressional influence, bank loans, and governmental favors. Baker was a subscriber to $25,500 of the initial stock of the District of Columbia National Bank when it was organized in 1962. In March 1963 he acquired a Washington, D.C., residence for the purchase price of $125,000 and applied to the bank for a loan of the entire cost. The application was granted, with the loan secured only by the property and without inquiry into Baker's grossly inflated financial statements. A memorandum in the bank's file recited:

> Mr. Baker's position with the United States Government recommends our serious consideration to the transaction, as he is a gentleman with innumerable friendships and connections whose good office in behalf of our bank could be very valuable in our growth.[47]

Officials of another national bank were implicated in the Baker hearings. This set of circumstances best speaks for itself in the following language of the Rules Commmittee:

THE REDWOOD NATIONAL BANK

The focus of this phase of the investigation was the chartering of the Redwood National Bank of San Rafael, Calif. It was suggested, once again, that Baker had feathered his own nest by abusing his public position. The founders of the bank were worried by a delay in granting them a charter. One of them, Sherman Leland, came to Washington in 1962 in search of a representative to handle their case. Through a network of friends and relatives, he was eventually put in touch with Wayne L. Bromley, legislative representative of the National Coal Policy Conference, and a friend of Robert Baker. It was repeatedly said in testimony, that one reason why Bromley was regarded as a good choice was the fact of his friendship with Baker. In September 1962, very shortly after Bromley had been hired, the charter was granted.

The committee's interest was directed to a $5,000 check paid by the Redwood National Bank to Bromley in March 1963. This fulfilled the terms of Bromley's employment by the bank, but the question was: How much of the money, if any, went to Baker? The question remains unresolved. It was established that the check was actually delivered to Baker, not to Bromley. It was claimed by Bromley in an interview, that, although he endorsed the check over to Baker, Baker gave him the full amount in cash in return.

Although Bromley was interviewed more than once by committee investigators, when subpenaed to testify under oath, he asserted his constitutional rights under the fifth amendment, and remained silent. Thus, lack of evidence made it difficult for the committee to make any firm determination on the disposal of the money, although it was established that Bromley paid a $2,500 hotel bill in currency on the same day the check was cashed. As for the granting of the charter, the Comptroller of the Currency testified that neither Bromley nor Baker appear in his office records as having taken any part in the matter. However, he later insisted on and obtained the resignations from the bank of Leland and other officers who had been party to the employment of Bromley.[48]

Evidence of the public concern in the banking area is the fact that Pearson's and Anderson's THE CASE AGAINST CONGRESS included a chapter entitled "Added Dividends: Bankers in the Cloakroom."

The disproportionate incidence of Congressional involvement in banks and bank stocks lends some support to the troublesome scattering of private and public accusations concerning the relation between Congress and the banking industry. Under all the circumstances, such a widespread community of Congressional interest must be deemed unfortunate. Reciprocal influence between banks and public officials and favoritism in the making and administration of the banking laws are not necessarily consequences. Nonetheless, a large number of conflicts of interest, mostly avoidable ones, are being maintained at a loss to public confidence in the Congress.

58

Conclusion

Except in banking, we have found virtually no evidence in these four areas that Federal policy or administration suffers substantially from Congressional business interests. Nonetheless, many Members continue business interests which must be classed as creating avoidable conflicts of interest. These Members presumably could do more than they have done to free themselves from actual or potential impairment of independent judgment. Those who studiously avoid financial holdings which might reduce their impartiality are doing their share to increase public confidence in the Congress, but the minority who cling to their avoidable conflicts are working against them.

REMEDIES FOR AVOIDABLE CONFLICTS OF INTEREST

Our primary purpose is to identify reasonable patterns of avoidance of conflicts which are followed by the majority of Members and to commend these as examples to all Members. A secondary goal is to increase the public's knowledge about those who maintain avoidable conflicts of interest.

Our definition of avoidable conflicts of interest included two basic elements: (1) unnecessary retention and (2) risk of impairment of independent judgment. The second element is present to some extent in any economic interest, but the degree of risk can vary widely, according to the size and nature of the interest and its relation to special responsibilities of the Member. Various means by which avoidable conflicts may be eliminated or minimized by altering either the interests or the legislative responsibilities will now be explored.

Rules Against Official Action for Personal Gain

It is generally taken for granted that a public official should never deliberately use his official position to enrich his purse. This is the most extreme form of fiduciary violation, and in its ugliest form—bribery—it is a criminal offense.[49] Rules of ethics and conflict-of-interest regulations are concerned with more subtle financial arrangements directed at the same end: impairment of official independence.

Rule 3 of the House Ethics Code is a good beginning point. It provides that a Member shall "receive no compensation nor shall he permit any compensation to accrue to his beneficial interest from any source, the receipt of which would occur by virtue of influence improperly exerted from his position in the Congress." This may appear to add little to the law of bribery, but it is nonetheless an appropriate code provision, because Congressional immunity precludes some criminal prosecutions for bribery. The *Johnson* case establishes such immunity if the bribed conduct is a vote or a speech on the floor of the House. Prosecution is possible, however, if a bribe is accepted for assistance with other government agencies. In *United States v. Burton*[50] the Supreme Court upheld a conviction of a Senator for bribed intervention with the Post Office Department. Johnson was accordingly held to be subject to prosecution for compensated assistance with the Department of Justice.[51]

The authors of the House Code view Rule 3 as going much further. The staff of the House Ethics Commmittee thus conducted an informal inquiry into LIFE's charges that Representative Cornelius E. Gallagher (D-N.J.) intervened with the Food and Drug Administration to expedite approval of a cancer drug in which he was financially interested. The theory was that if this enhanced the value of his drug interest, it would be viewed as "compensation" accruing to his "beneficial interest."

This is a very broad construction of these terms, but it is supported by their legislative history. Ethics Committee Chairman Price, in managing the House Code on the floor, responded to a question concerning this provision by saying:

> We could visualize instances where income could accrue to a Member as a result of proper business activities. If he used his political influence, the influence of his position as a Member, to make pecuniary gains, I believe that would be improperly done.[52]

Under this interpretation, the rule is a wholesome prohibition of the use of Congressional official power for financial gain.

There is no counterpart in the Senate substantive rules, but, as previously noted, their preamble states that a public official should never use his power "for the benefit of himself." This indicates a general Senatorial norm against use of office for private gain, as do the Dodd censure and the resulting rules against fund-raising for personal uses. Somewhat in point also is the 1967 investigation of charges that Senator Edward Long (D-Mo.) received payments from a fellow lawyer which were allegedly made to influence his conduct of committee hearings affecting a client.[53] The Baker investigation also presupposed some unwritten norms along these lines.

It can therefore be said that the written and unwritten rules of both houses now prohibit deliberate, purposeful use of Congressional office for private financial gain. However, such rules take in only a small portion of the full fiduciary concept developed in this chapter. The House rule also leaves much room for disagreement in particular cases by reaching only those instances where influence is "improperly" exerted to serve self-interest. A Member could easily claim, and understandably believe, that he was properly performing a duty for some group whose interests he happened to share.

The ambiguity created by Congressional self-interest causes unfortunate appearances in all such cases. Where the personal interest is avoidable, the Member unnecessarily creates grounds for suspicion of his motives. Accordingly, we recommend a broad rule which covers the situations reached by present rules but which goes further and reflects the concept of avoidable conflicts of interest:

Recommendation 2A
Each house should adopt the following rule: "A Member shall never use his official power for the purpose of economically benefiting himself and shall make every reasonable effort to avoid situations where it might appear that he is making such use of his office."

Interest Avoidance by Selective Investment

From a general rule we move to several more specific remedies. The first is one of self-limitation. Many conscientious Members have achieved a maximum of separation of self-interest from public duty simply by arranging their financial affairs to minimize the potential for impairment of independence. Senate Majority Leader Mike Mansfield (D-Mont.), for instance, follows the same practice as the late President John F. Kennedy and invests in nothing but government bonds. Although he must occasionally vote on legislation affecting himself and other government-bond holders, such issues are few and relatively non-controversial. Since the interest is a common one with a large segment of the public, the potential for advancing self-interest at the expense of the public interest is very slight.

All Members cannot reasonably be expected to follow this practice. Over 20 Senators are reported to be millionaires, and many Representatives obviously have large personal estates. For several reasons they might understandably object to converting all assets into this one type of security. Harsh and unnecessary divestments might exact an unduly high personal cost in some cases. Also, it would not be fair to expect Members of Congress totally to exclude themselves from participation in the capital growth of this country by self-limitation to fixed-return debt securities. These carry no hedge against inflation and do not appreciate in value with the growth of the economy.

This suggests an investment route which avoids one objection to government bonds. A Member can achieve similar purposes by investing in diversified mutual funds. The intervention of the fund's managers as investment selectors, the diversification of holdings, and the large number of persons with a community of interest carry advantages much like those of government bonds. Particular stocks held by the fund are quite remote from the mental processes of the individual investor and usually totally unknown to him. For this reason the Rules of Conduct of the Department of Defense expressly treat holdings of such funds as non-disqualifying financial interests[54] and exempt them under the *de minimis* provisions of 18 U.S.C. §208(b).

A closely related alternative used by some Presidents, many Executive Branch officials, and some Members of Congress is a blind trust arrangement. While it is not a full divestment of the assets involved, appropriate provisions in the trust instrument can advance the desired independence of official decision-making. Our predecessor committee strongly endorsed such arrangements for the Executive Branch, saying:

> Under this arrangement the appointee entering government puts the securities into a trust held by an independent trustee, the trust to terminate on the appointee's completion of his tour of government service. The appointee is not informed what securities are held by the trust, nor has he any power of control or

distribution or disposition over the properties in the trust so long as the trust continues. Properly set up and policed, and followed in good faith, this sort of plan offers an attractive adjustment between the frequently serious economic loss sustained by the appointee if he is required to divest himself of his securities and the public's need to protect itself against the use of public office for private gain. . . . The trust mechanism is healthy in appearance, protects the government since the trust beneficiary does not even know what securities he holds an interest in, and yet permits the appointee to enter government service without a complete disruption of his personal estate.[55]

A final possibility is to diversify investments so that all or most of them carry slight individual potential for either loss or gain. For this reason, under both the House Code and our recommended disclosure rules, Members may avoid public disclosure by spreading investments among units worth less than $5,000 each.

Combinations of the foregoing are available for all or part of Members' personal estates. The great majority should be able to reduce their avoidable conflicts to a handful. The appropriate recommendation is necessarily general:

Recommendation 2B

Each Member of Congress should make every reasonable effort to utilize available investment alternatives which minimize instances in which it may appear that his official decisions may be influenced by personal economic interests.

Avoidance of Corporate Offices and Directorships

When a Member accepts a corporate office or directorship, he takes on a whole new set of relationships and duties beyond those of a stockholder. Mere ownership of interests carries considerably less potential for impairing independence. As a director or officer, he actually becomes a fiduciary for the corporation and for its stockholders, charged with a duty to further their interests. He obviously will find it difficult to do this at times because he is also charged with the duty of furthering the public interest, and the two interests may well be in conflict. For much the same reasons for which we recommend normal abstention from law practice, we also believe Members should avoid corporate positions which create a fiduciary duty in the Member toward a particular business.

One of the leading figures in David Graham Phillips' 1906 attacks on the Senate was Senator Chauncey Depew of New York, who had risen to office by virtue of his relationship with Commodore Vanderbilt. He reportedly held more than 70 directorships and received more than $50,000 per year in director's fees alone. Refusing someone's demand that he resign from the Senate, he said: "Why should I resign? . . . As soon as I have completed my resignation from certain companies, I shall give all my time to my senatorial duties." [56]

We do not know what resignations occurred, but Senator Depew was defeated in the next election, and no Member of Congress is believed to have since approached his record in corporate directorships. Indeed, it is generally rare for public officials at any level to serve as directors of profit-making corporations. A 1967 survey of the boards of 436 manufacturing companies and 246 non-manufacturing companies found that only 20 of 5,324 outside directors came from an occupational group classed as "government and military." [57]

In contrast, a surprisingly large number of Members of Congress are directors, presidents, and board chairmen of corporations. Two Representatives are presidents of interstate trucking companies. Five are chairmen of the boards of financial institutions. Of the 96 Representatives who in 1969 reported banking or savings-and-loan interests, 39 reported directorships paying fees of $1,000 per year or more. Two held three such directorships, and four Members reported two. Several Senators are known to be actively involved in big businesses in which they hold executive offices.

The wisdom of Members holding corporate directorships can best be considered after examining their duties. For the guidance of bank directors, the American Bankers Association has published a well-written booklet entitled A Bank Director's Job. It first identifies a moral duty of the position:

There is first of all the moral responsibility a bank director assumes toward his fellow shareholders, the depositors, and the general public who are affected by the bank's soundness. Businessmen and others prominent in the community who serve as bank directors, having allowed the use of their names as assurance to the public that they are supervising and in fact directing the policies and activities of the financial institution, obviously are expected to use every care that the confidence placed in them is merited.[58]

The Association then discusses in detail the legal responsibility of bank directors under Federal and state law. They must regularly attend board meetings (which typically are held 10 or 12 times a year by banks[59]) and diligently assume many serious supervisory duties. Many derelictions are noted which might lead to personal liability of a director, such as approval of bad loans, slowness in loan collection, failure to establish committees required by corporate by-laws, permitting improvident expenditures, and so forth.

The bankers' booklet then emphasizes a practical business duty of all directors: bringing in new accounts. Of this duty it says in part:

The directors are in a position to help the bank get new business, although not all directors realize this. Occasionally some of those who do realize it nonetheless seem to regard it as beneath their dignity to seem to be selling the bank's services. Such an attitude is unjustified and unfortunate.

The first thing the directors can do to bring business to the bank is to bring in their own accounts and those of their businesses. This applies to the full range of banking, not overlooking safe deposit and trust matters. Nothing is more embarrassing to a bank than the disclosure, in case of death, that a director's will does not name the bank as trustee or co-trustee. The public will wonder in such a case why the director did not show more confidence in the institution to whose inner secrets he was privy.

Since most bank directors have to devote the larger part of their time to their personal business interests, they cannot be expected to make a career of acting as bank salesmen. However, directors who are constantly aware of the bank, can, in the course of their normal contacts, be ever watchful of opportunities for new banking business. Apart from being a bank booster among business and social acquaintances, a director can be extremely helpful to the bank's new business department by providing it with leads on prospects, giving introductions, and even using his influence with prospects in support of the bank's own efforts.

65

Such help need not be left entirely to the director's initiative. Members of the staff should be free to call upon the director for information, advice, and introductions in cases where the director, because of his acquaintance with the prospect, is in a position to be helpful.[60]

It is understandable that banks seek such directors among Members of Congress. The difficulty from the public's view is the possible effect of a loyalty like that described above on a Member when he must consider official action which might be adverse to his bank. We do not believe that Members should take on such outside loyalties.

If there is any difference between bank directorships and other corporate directorships, it is only in degree, not in kind. Where the added responsibilities of corporate officeholding are also assumed, the threat to Congressional time and independence is even greater. These relationships generally are avoidable conflicts and accordingly should be avoided.

The United States Judicial Conference for several years has prohibited Federal judges from serving as officers or directors of profit-making enterprises.[61] The considerations which moved the judges to insulate themselves from the potential which such fiduciary relations have for creating conflicts of interest also apply to Federal legislators. We therefore recommend a standard of self-limitation of business positions which is comparable to that proposed for lawyer-Members in the next chapter:

Recommendation 2C
Members of Congress should avoid serving as officers, directors, trustees, or partners in commercial enterprises.

Interest Avoidance Within Committees

Most Members follow some self-imposed rules of interest avoidance within areas of committee responsibility. It appears to be a common pattern to refrain from making particular types of investments in areas where they might profit from "inside information" or risk suspicion that official decisions might be made for personal gain. For instance, Representative Chet Holifield (D-Calif.), Chairman of the Joint Committee on Atomic Energy, totally refrains from investing in industrial stocks affected by defense or atomic programs. Senator Ste-

66

phen Young (D-Ohio) divested himself of his holdings in Pan American Airways when he became a Member of the Senate Commmittee on Aeronautical and Space Sciences. Representative Joseph Karth (D-Wis.) follows a strict rule of abstention from space and defense stocks because of his position on the House Science and Astronautics Commmittee, where he is Chairman of the Subcommittee on Space Sciences and Applications.

The most notable exceptions to such self-limitation occur in the respective Banking and Currency Commmittees. In the House financial disclosures of April 1969, interests in banks, savings-and-loan associations, or bank-holding companies were reported by 12 of the 35 Members of the House Commmittee. This figure is demonstrably low because reports of interests in state-chartered institutions were not required. Some Members of the Senate Banking and Currency Committee are also known to have banking interests, even though they are not yet required to report these to the public. One banker who formerly served on the Senate Commmittee was given much credit for delaying enactment of truth-in-lending legislation.

Needless to say, many actions of these committees affect the profitability of bank holdings. And it is not merely national banks or Federal savings-and-loan associations which are interested in these committees' work. State and national institutions compete for loans and deposits and are interested in each other's rates. State banks participate in the Federal Reserve System and insure their deposits with the Federal Deposit Insurance Corporation. Differing tax treatment of commercial banks and savings-and-loan associations,[62] although not handled by the Banking Committees, is another point of conflicting interests in Federal legislation.

Not all avoidable conflicts of interest arising from committee assignments are so easily identified or could be so easily avoided. Representative George Bush (R-Tex.) disposed of large holdings in oil businesses because of his membership on the Ways and Means Committee and its relation to oil-depletion allowances. He then bought a textile stock and soon complained that he then found that the Committee was confronted with voting on textile import quotas.[63]

While it seems fairly clear to us that a Member with current economic interests in broadcasting should not serve on the Commerce Committee, and a Member with such an interest in banking should

67

not serve on the Banking and Currency Committee, the issue is not free of debate. Opponents of such disqualification say that its logical extension would man the Agriculture Committee with lawyers, the Foreign Affairs Commmittee with farmers, the Judiciary Committee with businessmen, and the Banking and Currency Committee with schoolteachers.

This argument assumes that special expertise gained from personal interests has compensating advantages for the legislative process. We do not find this persuasive. Such expertise does not depend on current economic interests. Moreover, staff and other resources are amply available to assist Members with the issues before their commmittees.

The problem obviously varies widely, and no single mandatory rule can be uniformly applicable throughout the Congress. We therefore propose a discretionary rule for general application:

Recommendation 2D

Each house should adopt the following rule: "When a Member is appointed to a committee, he should, if reasonably possible, avoid all economic interests which may be specially affected by legislation within the jurisdiction of his committee."

It is implicit in the proposed rule that an alternative is service on committees where conflicts are not likely to occur. This seems to be the normal pattern.

While mandatory general rules of interest avoidance are not practicable for the entire Congress, this is not necessarily true at the committee level. It is not essential that individual Members' discretion determine permissible conflicts at the committee level.

Every Member of Congress has available to him a sufficient variety of investment opportunities so that he should be able to avoid investments and fiduciary relationships in industries regularly and specially subject to the jurisdiction of his legislative committees. We are confident that most Members practice some self-limitation, but find that the problems vary widely from committee to committee. Consider the following possibilities:

—a broadcaster on the Commerce Committee;
—an investor in defense industries on the Armed Services Committee;

68

—a bank director on the Banking and Currency Committee;

—an interstate trucker on the Commerce Committee;

—an oil-well investor on the House Ways and Means Committee, when it considers the oil-depletion allowance;

—an investor in a domestic industry protected by tariffs who serves on the Ways and Means or Finance Committee;

—a subsidized farmer on the Agriculture Committee.

While general rules are obviously inadequate for all these situations, it does not follow that all should be left to individual discretion.

An industry's dependence upon Federal legislative benefits may arise in a variety of ways, including direct agency regulation, special tax treatment, subsidy, or tariff protection. Also, the conflict-of-interest potential varies from time to time according to the directions of Congressional inquiries. A particular investigation could produce conflicts not regularly associated with a particular committee.

As one Member told us, "This is really a Congress of committees, not individuals." The power of having one vote in 100 or 435 on the floor is slight compared with an individual Member's power in committee. Congress therefore must deal with some of its diverse ethical problems at the committee level.

At this point Congress can profit from the experience of the Executive Branch in dealing with the differing conflict problems faced by the officials within different Executive agencies. An Executive Order[64] and Civil Service Commission regulations[65] set up basic rules applicable throughout the Executive Branch, just as each house of Congress uses general rules to establish certain norms of conduct which reasonably apply to all Members. However, the diversity in Executive agencies' ethical problems makes it necessary that each agency establish a sub-code of its own. Thus, employees of the Defense Department are freer to invest in mutual funds than are those of the Securities and Exchange Commission. Employees of both the SEC and the Internal Revenue Service are specifically prohibited from speculating in any securities. Employees of the Interstate Commerce Commission are forbidden to have pecuniary interests in regulated common carriers. Defense Department employees have many special rules on relations with government contractors.

In similarly dealing with conflicts of interest at the committee level, a particular committee might sometimes adopt the rule which Congress itself has imposed upon a corresponding agency that the committee oversees. Thus, just as 49 U.S.C. §11 forbids any member of the Interstate Commerce Commission to hold any interest in a "common carrier subject to the provisions of this chapter," Members of the respective Commerce Committees should impose a similar limitation upon themselves. Just as members of the Federal Reserve Board are made ineligible by 12 U.S.C. §242 to hold "any office, position or employment in any member bank," Members of Congress who have primary responsibility for banking legislation should similarly limit themselves by committee rules. Broadcasting holdings should be restricted for the Commerce Committees by rules following the Federal Communications Commission's enabling statute, which prohibits Commissioners from being financially interested in communication apparatus or holding any official relation to any person subject to the provisions of that law.[66] The two Armed Services Committees should adopt as self-limitations the rules they impose on Executive appointees and refrain from investments in companies which have annual defense contracts of more than $10,000. This list is regularly published in the Code of Federal Regulations and is equally appropriate as a guide both for Members of Congress and for Defense Department appointees.

In large part these proposals merely require committees to codify for all Members the unwritten norms of most ranking Members. They call upon Congress to require that some committees, such as Banking and Currency, observe the higher standards generally followed by other committees. Surely, for every committee there are some investments which should be off limits.

Some committees may find it appropriate to forbid certain investments only to members of particular subcommittees. This would incorporate the behavioral norm of Senator Thruston Morton (R-Ky.), who gave up membership on the Communications Subcommittee of the Senate Commerce Committee because of family broadcasting interests.

Committee members themselves can best deal with *ad hoc* problems temporarily caused by particular investigations. Suppose a Judiciary Subcommittee proposed to go into insurance rates or drug prices. Particular members might be relieved for this purpose, and all might be required to avoid new investments in the industry for some period.

Some committees' rules might be more liberal than others. In any event, neither the entire Congress nor an outside group can sort out the myriad of different situations and solutions. Accordingly, we recommend:

Recommendation 2E

Each house of Congress should adopt the following rule: "It shall be the duty of each committee to establish rules governing financial interests of its members and employees in matters coming before the committee."

Voting Disqualification

While interest avoidance is much the better tool for remedying Congressional conflicts of interest, the additional weapon of official disqualification may have some utility, particularly since the rules of both houses have some provision for it. Section 376 of JEFFERSON'S MANUAL, which is incorporated expressly by House Rule VIII, provides:

> Where the private interests of a Member are concerned in a bill or question he is to withdraw. And where such an interest has appeared, his voice has been disallowed, even after a division. In a case so contrary, not only to the laws of decency, but to the fundamental principle of the social compact, which denies to any man to be a judge in his own cause, it is for the honor of the House that this rule of immemorial observance should be strictly adhered to.

In addition, House Rule VIII provides that a Member shall not vote on a question if he has a "direct personal or pecuniary interest." Of this rule, the House Parliamentarian states:

> In the House of Representatives it has not been usual for the Member to withdraw when his private interests are concerned in a pending measure, but the House has provided by rule (Rule VIII, cl. 1) that the Member shall not vote in such a contingency. In one instance the Senate disallowed a vote given by a

Senator on a question relating to his own right to a seat; but the House has never had occasion to proceed so far.[67]

The House practice has official precedent in a famous 1874 ruling of Speaker James G. Blaine. It permitted three Representatives who held stock in national banks to vote on a bill to create a national currency and establish free banking. He ruled that a Member may vote on legislation that affects him only as a member of a class rather than as an individual. Only a private relief bill for a named Member could cause disqualification under this reasoning, and House Rule VIII is virtually a dead letter.

In the Senate there is no rule of mandatory disqualification for any circumstance, but Rule XII, Section 2, permits self-disqualification if reasons are stated and the Senate excuses the Member. It is occasionally invoked. However, the prevailing view in both houses is probably that stated by Senator Robert S. Kerr of Oklahoma, who justified his voting on farm and oil legislation by saying:

> Now wouldn't it be a hell of a thing if the Senator from Oklahoma couldn't vote for the things Oklahomans are most interested in? If everyone abstained on the grounds of personal interest, I doubt if you could get a quorum in the United States Senate on any subject.[68]

A Senator who regularly abstained on such issues would obviously arm his opponents with arguments that he was incompetent for his representative function.

Any rule of mandatory disqualification from voting is unworkable, but it would be a wholesome advancement if disqualification on a discretionary basis occurred more often. When Members vote despite conflicts of interest, they should do so for some valid overriding reason. Without attempting to codify the factors to be weighed by a Member,[69] we recommend a rule of discretionary self-disqualification:

Recommendation 2F

Each house should adopt the following rule: "When a Member must take official action on a matter in which he has a personal economic interest, he should consider eliminating the interest. If that is not feasible, he should consider abstaining from such official action. He need not abstain if he decides to participate in a manner adverse to the economic interest."

Public Financial Disclosure

The subject of disclosure also has its origins in the law of fiduciary obligations. A fiduciary frequently must affirmatively disclose relevant information to those to whom he owes a duty. Corporate insiders must disclose much to prospective investors, and lawyers must disclose conflicting client interests to the clients involved.[70] Since both houses have already adopted rules requiring a measure of financial disclosure, much of the debate over whether any degree of disclosure should be required has become moot.

Nonetheless, the legitimate functions of disclosure must be determined in order to delineate its proper scope. One value may derive from the mere fact of its occurrence. It dispels public suspicion engendered by past Congressional resistance to the measure. To a large extent, this advantage is symbolic.

A second purpose of disclosure is to deter some avoidable conflicts of interest. If a Member of Congress knows that he may have to justify his voting record alongside a particular investment, he may be deterred from holding it. There is reason to believe that the fact that BROADCASTING magazine began listing the names of Members of Congress who were interested in radio and television contributed to the decreasing representation of Members in this industry.

Finally, disclosure informs a Member's constituents and Congressional colleagues of facts relevant to decisions they must make. The public can judge whether a Member is reasonable in his retention of a particular holding which creates a conflict of interest that arguably is avoidable. Disclosure is the best means of policing avoidable conflicts which a Member may claim that he continues because to do otherwise would be a personal hardship. Other Members can better weigh his arguments and positions. To satisfy these purposes, disclosure must be public, but it need not be "complete" in the usual sense.

It is common for journalists and reformers in this area to call simply for "complete" or "full" financial disclosure, but few go on to say exactly what the terms mean. If such disclosure means Members should bare to the public every economic detail about themselves, their families, and their associates, then it is unprecedented and unnecessary. Such requirements now exist nowhere in our law and are not essential to conflict-of-interest regulation.

For instance, the securities laws require only that prospective investors be informed as to certain facts relevant to particular investment decisions. Stockholders do not receive "complete" disclosure of personal finances of officers and directors. Union officials are required to publicize financial data related to particular collective-bargaining relationships, but do not fully disclose the totality of their personal financial interests. Although judges are required to disqualify themselves if their personal pecuniary interests are involved in a case, this has been left largely to judicial self-enforcement. At the most, their duty is to divulge relevant facts on a case-by-case basis to enable possible challenge by the litigants.[71]

Recently adopted rules of the Judicial Conference of the United States moved toward *complete* disclosure, but stopped short of automatically publicizing the judges' reports. They must report income, assets, and liabilities to the Conference, but their reports are to be made public only as the Conference determines it to be in the public interest.[72] The disclosures required within the Executive Branch are fairly complete, but they are essentially confidential and internal. Presidential appointees file statements with the Civil Service Commission,* and disclosures by others are made within particular agencies. The aim of Executive Branch disclosure is to produce private counseling which may result in either divestment of particular holdings or disqualification from particular decisions.

The nearest thing to complete public disclosure is that made voluntarily by recent Presidential and Vice Presidential candidates. In both the 1964 and 1968 elections the nominees of the major parties published detailed financial statements.

The Congressional situation is more analogous to that of the President than to that of judges or Executive officials. Ideally, a public officer should make disclosure to some superior who is responsible for his conduct and then be required to disqualify himself or divest as the circumstances warrant. As in the case of the President, the only force superior to Congress is the public. This means disclosure must be public, but its scope may nonetheless be limited to that needed for the public intelligently to assess the trusteeship of Members. To go further than this merely to satisfy public curiosity would be burdensome for Members, and possibly embarrassing, without corresponding benefits to the public.

* Appointees subject to Senate confirmation also disclose to the appropriate committee, usually confidentially.

74

No public need requires complete inventories of everything of value owned by Members and their families. If the purpose is to inform the public of a Member's possible conflicts of interest, why should disclosure include his charitable contributions? These would appear on his Federal income-tax return, a common subject of complete disclosure demands, but hardly seem any business of his constituents. Such disclosure not only serves no conflict purpose, but might cause massive harassment by solicitors. Disclosure of total net worth likewise seems unnecessary, but would be reached by complete financial statements. We cannot see how disclosure of dollar values of such personal items as insurance, jewelry, furniture, clothing, furs, and bank deposits would bear on the relevant judgments. After thorough consideration, we have concluded that disclosure may appropriately be limited to the following:

Identity of Assets Worth More than $5,000. This minimum value figure embodies the same *de minimis* concept incorporated in the House Code of Ethics. Below it, an interest is too small to justify disclosure in the interests of the decisional process. A Member may avoid disclosure by diversifying his portfolio into small units of investment. Dollar amounts are not required, only the identity of the asset, which leaves a Member's exact worth undisclosed to the public. However, for whatever deterrent effect it might have and as an investigative aid to Ethics Committees, dollar amounts should be separately listed under closed seal. The Codes of both houses now require this.

Sources of Income Exceeding $1,000. This too adopts the *de minimis* concept incorporated in the House Code and protects dollar amounts. A source might be a capital-gains transaction, a law client,* director's fees, or corporate salary. As for assets, dollar amounts are not made public but are reported under seal, for possible later publication in the course of any Ethics Committee investigation.

On both assets and income, we cannot agree with the House's action in limiting disclosure to businesses regulated by the Federal agencies or doing business with the government. This has caused considerable confusion and fair criticism that many assets are omitted which might receive great benefits from Federal legislation such as tax

---

* The mere identity of a client is not protected by the lawyer-client privilege. 8 J. Wigmore, EVIDENCE §2313 (McNaughton rev. ed. 1961). As shown by the disclosure rules in Appendix B, we would require that a Member's law firm report the names of clients, whether such employment arose before or after the Member's election, and representation in matters involving the Federal government.

advantages, tariff protections, and Federal subsidies. We cannot imagine a business or asset which is not either governed by some Federal agency, doing business with the government, or affected by some Federal law. If there is slight risk of overdisclosure, it is preferable to the fact of great underdisclosure caused by the House's requirement of a special Federal connection.

Debts. Personal indebtedness played parts in both the Baker and Dodd cases, and the fact that a Member owes large sums may be as relevant to determining his conflicts of interest as is the nature of his investments and income. The debtor-creditor relationship can conceivably carry much greater influence than that between corporation and stockholder, especially if the debt is past due or based on a demand loan. The previously mentioned disclosure that a member of the House Banking and Currency Committee owed large sums to banks interested in current legislative issues dramatized the need for a measure of debt disclosure and should go far toward reducing Congressional resistance to it.*

As in the case of assets and income, it is not necessary that exact dollar amounts or relatively small debts be routinely publicized. Also, residential mortgage debts are so commonplace and innocent that their disclosure is unnecessary. All others should be reported. Accordingly, we recommend that the identity of creditors to whom more than $5,000 is owed be publicly disclosed and that exact dollar amounts be reported under seal. Members may find it to their advantage, however, to report the amount publicly, especially if it is low, and also to disclose any security of particular debts.

Honoraria Exceeding $300. This type of income deserves the special treatment which the Senate gave it. Although honoraria are not to be condemned on any absolute basis, they offer a convenient way for an interest group to pay substantial sums to a Member for relatively modest services. They are discussed in more detail in Chapter 6.

Interests of Spouses and Minor Children. A Member is as likely to be affected by such interests as by his own. Here, as in many other

---

* No disclosure whatever of debts is required by the House Code, and the Senate only requires sealed, confidential reporting of the identity of liabilities exceeding $5,000. On January 26, 1970, the House Ethics Committee recommended that the House Code be amended to require disclosure of the identity of creditors to whom a Member or employee had unsecured indebtedness of $10,000 or more for ninety days or longer during a calendar year. N.Y. TIMES, Jan. 27, 1970, at 25, col. 1.

76

areas of the law, the family unit should be treated as an economic unit.

Provision should also be made for disclosure by high-ranking Congressional staff. Both houses have already shown their readiness to require of such staff the same disclosure required of Members. The Baker case is sufficient proof of the need.

Unlike the present rules, our proposal requires reports to be filed both in Washington and in the Member's state or district. Difficulty of access has been one criticism of the present House financial disclosures;[73] constituents should not have to travel to Washington to learn such important information.

Although the Senate's disclosure rules apply to candidates as well as to incumbents, we do not recommend their inclusion. In our opinion, formal statutes would be necessary to compel action by non-Members. The Senate's theory was that a successful candidate who failed to disclose could validly be excluded as "unqualified" for violating a Senate rule. This issue was unsettled when the Senate Ethics Code was adopted, but it has since been resolved by the Supreme Court's decision on the exclusion of Representative Adam Clayton Powell (D-N.Y.), which is discussed in Chapter 7. Also, the political process is likely to produce some disclosure by challengers if incumbents have made disclosure.

The complete text of our proposed disclosure rules is set forth in Appendix B.

Recommendation 2G
Each house should adopt rules requiring public financial disclosure along the lines of the rules proposed in Appendix B.

CHAPTER THREE

CONGRESSIONAL LAW
PRACTICE

Although this topic is partly a branch of the larger subject of conflicts of interest, it is also considerably broader. It involves what is by far the largest occupational group in the Congress. Their numbers alone would justify special analysis because lawyers consistently account for about 60 percent of the Members of Congress. There were 314 lawyers among the 535 Members of the 90th Congress. Ethical advancements which improve the quality of Congressional service by the bar must inevitably result in considerable improvement of the group as a whole.

Some Historic Congressional
Law Practices

Most discussions of the ethics of public officials include a critical reference to Senator Daniel Webster's professional relationship with the Bank of the United States.[1] In a letter written "as a private one," the Senator first suggested on October 29, 1833, that Nicholas Biddle, president of the bank, might desire that Webster call Congressional attention to President Jackson's contemplated withdrawal of U.S. deposits from the bank. On December 21 Webster again wrote:

Sir

Since I have arrived here, I have had an application to be concerned, professionally, against the Bank, which I have declined, of course, although I believe my retainer has not been renewed, or *refreshed* as usual. If it be wished that my relation to the Bank should be continued, it may be well to send me the usual retainers.[2]

It would be naïve to speculate that Webster would have championed the bank's legislative causes with the same vigor had there been no lawyer-client relationship. It must be added, however, that neither the existence nor the success of the relationship was any secret, because Webster successfully represented the bank in forty-one cases before the United States Supreme Court.[3] Nonetheless, the misuse of the lawyer-client relationship revealed by the Webster-Biddle correspondence must be viewed as an unfortunate blemish on the career of one of the Senate's greats.

Webster's example was not universally followed. In 1845 John Quincy Adams was offered $5,000 to argue a Constitutional issue on separation of powers in the U.S. Supreme Court. He replied that he had long ceased to practice law in Federal courts, but as a Representative would give the prospective client his opinion on the question without charge. He recorded the incident in his diary and added:

It occurs to me that this double capacity of a counsellor in courts of law and a member of a legislative body affords opportunity and temptation for contingent fees of very questionable moral purity. Of one such transaction I had knowledge last winter, which in my mind was tainted with the vilest corruption; and I have heard of others, which I shall not specify, because they are familiarly spoken of as in no wise exceptionable, but for which the only palliation of which I deem them susceptible is that alleged by Lord Chancellor Bacon in his defence upon his trial before the English House of Peers—that there are 'vitia tem-

79

porum" as well as "vitia hominum." It is a sad contemplation of human nature to observe how the action of the members of legislative bodies may be bought and sold, and how some of the brightest stars in that firmament may pass in occultation without losing their lustre.[4]

As indicated earlier, it was not uncommon during the early nineteenth century for Members of Congress to represent claimants against the United States. The first statutory limits on such representation[5] grew from a public scandal created by the law practice of Senator Thomas Corwin of Ohio in the years following the Mexican War. He represented one Dr. Gardiner before the Mexican Claims Commission in a claim for damages arising from alleged destruction of a silver mine. The Senator's success in recovering $500,000 for his client received little notice until 1852, when it was revealed that both Dr. Gardiner and the silver mine were frauds. By then Senator Corwin had become President Fillmore's Secretary of the Treasury, and the incident became one of the major public scandals of the period.

A decade later Congressional practitioners were causing public debate by their representation of Civil War soldiers before U.S. Army courts-martial. The utility of being represented by a Member of Congress was obvious, and several Members took advantage of the expanded professional opportunities. Others declined and argued publicly that Congressional representation took unfair advantage of the power of individual Congressmen over the military judges before whom they appeared. This led Senator Foster of Connecticut to complain on the Senate floor that in one court-martial a Member of Congress serving as defense counsel had expressed dissatisfaction with a ruling and then said to a member of the tribunal, "You expect soon to be promoted, and I give you to understand that your confirmation will not get through the Senate without some difficulty." [6]

By the turn of the century the Populist and Progressive movements were producing widespread dissatisfaction with the power of corporate and moneyed interests in Congress. A part of this evil lay in the acceptance of legal retainers by lawyer-Members. The 1906 muckraking work TREASON OF THE SENATE by David Graham Phillips named 21 Senators in a polemic series which accused the Senate of betraying the people in favor of special interests. Sixteen of the 21 were lawyers (as were two thirds of the entire Senate), and the private practices of two, Senators Spooner and Bailey, were implicated dramatically by Phillips.

In 1886 Senator John C. Spooner of Wisconsin represented a railroad company in litigation before the United States Supreme Court concerning rights in public-land grants while he was allegedly seeking to obtain the same result by statute in the Senate. This caused Senator Beck of Kentucky to introduce a bill making it unlawful for a Member to represent a railway which had received a land grant from Congress. In the debates on this bill, Senator Beck said:

> Will any gentleman in either house insist that any man who is the attorney of either road, any man who is retained in any way by any of these roads, when these great questions involving perhaps fifty or one hundred million dollars to the tax-burdened people of this country come up for consideration, shall, without letting us know it, advocate the interests of the road whose money, in the shape of retainers or fees, he has in his pocket, keeping the fact concealed, professing all the time that he is acting and arguing in the interests of the United States? [7]

Beck's bill initially passed the Senate, but was killed on a motion to reconsider. Phillips gave the episode credit for causing Senators to become more secretive in their paid service of private interests.[8]

The other noteworthy law practice discussed by Phillips was that of Senator Joseph W. Bailey of Texas, who received more than $225,000 in legal fees from a single Texas oil man for services performed over a period of months. Bailey was the only one of Phillips' subjects to reply publicly. He challenged Phillips on several points, but conceded the charges concerning his law practice with a response which probably represented the prevailing Senatorial view of the ethics of accepting corporate legal fees. He said:

> He says that I practice law successfully, in that I make money. If he will ask my clients, he will also find that I have practiced law successfully in the way of protecting their interests. If that is a crime, it is time the country should know it. Mr. President, I despise those public men who think they must remain poor in order to be considered honest. I am not one of them. If my con-

stituents want a man who is willing to go to the poorhouse in his old age in order to stay in the Senate during his middle age, they will have to find another Senator. I intend to make every dollar that I can honestly make, without neglecting or interfering with my public duty; and there is no other man in this country who would not do the same, if he has sense enough to keep a church-yard.[9]

After Phillips' series had helped bring on direct election of Senators,[10] lawyers in Congress began to take a different view from that stated by Senator Bailey. By 1916 lawyers who did not practice had become more bold in denouncing their colleagues who accepted retainers from special interests. In that year Senator William E. Borah openly blamed Congressional law practice for the inadequacy of the legislation of the period. In a classic speech to the American Bar Association on the general subject of the responsibilities of lawyers in public office, he said:

> I do not believe that a lawyer has any more right, as a matter of correct public service, to hold a retainer while writing a law in the public interest and that a law which may affect his client adversely, than has a judge to hold retainers from those whose interests may be affected by the decisions which he renders. . . . Custom has inured us to a different code of ethics, but this custom has brought in its wake many inapt, inefficient statutes, timid and ineffective in their terms, shielding special interests and protecting private advantages . . . because of that timid, compromising spirit born of an effort to adjust conditions which cannot be adjusted. . . .[11]

Public condemnation of Congressional law practices subsided for a while, but one notable practitioner became a leading figure in H. H. Wilson's CONGRESS: CORRUPTION AND COMPROMISE, which appeared in 1951. A chapter on Representative Eugene Cox discussed events related to a 1948 disclosure by the Federal Communications Commission that a Georgia broadcasting company had issued stock and paid a $2,500 legal fee to Representative Cox after he had helped obtain its Federal license.

The most recent addition to the literature of Congressional criticism, THE CASE AGAINST CONGRESS by Drew Pearson and Jack Anderson, devotes an entire chapter to practicing lawyers.[12]

The Congressional scandals of the 1960's which contributed to this Committee's formation heavily involved Congressional law practices. In 1963 Representative Thomas F. Johnson (D-Md.) was convicted of accepting compensation for using his office to assist Maryland savings-and-loan institutions which were under Federal indictment for mail fraud.[13] After partial reversal on appeal, a new trial resulted in a second conviction. Johnson's main defenses were that payments which he admittedly received were either campaign contributions or legal fees. Testimony that he was paid for legal examinations of mortgage-loan papers was rebutted by the prosecution and apparently rejected by the jury.[14]

The revelations arising from Senate Majority Secretary Robert G. (Bobby) Baker's activities implicated both his law practice and his handling of campaign funds as conduits for improper payments by lobbyists. In one instance, cash payments to Baker from a lobbyist, made two days after passage of favorable legislation, were purportedly made for future legal services which were never actually rendered.[15] The Senate Rules Committee concluded that Baker's two-man Washington law firm was "an important factor in many of Baker's business and financial activities." [16]

The New York firm of Representative Emanuel Celler was mentioned in a different way in the Baker disclosures. In 1961 it had paid Baker's law firm* $2,500 as a "forwarding fee" for having referred a corporate client to it.[17] The client happened to be interested in government contracts and Federal legislation, but Celler's explanation that his firm received the $10,000 fee for examining New York real-estate matters was, in fact, established. However, a statement attributed in this context to Celler's law partner, Murray C. Spett, may have caused the public to speculate on whether Congressional law practices produce widespread referrals and "fee-splitting." Mr. Spett said:

> Whenever we have any matters in another state, we usually ask
> Mr. Celler to recommend a Congressman or a Senator lawyer in

---

* At Mr. Celler's request, we quote him as follows: "At the time, Mr. Baker was still Secretary to the Senate Majority, a respected and reputable public official and a trusted lieutenant of Vice-President Lyndon B. Johnson."

that particular state to handle it, and conversely Congressmen and Senators who have matters in New York and are not permitted to practice in New York refer matters to us.[18]

Fee-slitting of a more serious nature was involved in the case of Senator Edward Long (D-Mo.), who was embarrassed in 1967 by a series of apparent inconsistencies concerning his law practice, or lack thereof. The May 26, 1967, issue of LIFE quoted Long as denying that he had actively practiced law in recent years. He then reportedly explained some fees by admitting receipt of approximately $48,000 in "referral fees" * in two years from Morris Shenker, a St. Louis Teamsters' Union lawyer. He denied, however, LIFE's implications that this bore any connection to certain subcommittee investigative activities allegedly designed to benefit imprisoned Teamster leader James Hoffa. After closed hearings, the Senate Ethics Committee announced that Long had proved to its satisfaction that the payments represented his participation in fees paid by five named clients for whom both lawyers had performed services. A subsequent LIFE article stated that the Ethics Committee learned that Shenker had made payments totaling $160,000 to Long since 1961. This article also examined the legal work purportedly done for the clients and raised serious doubts that Senator Long had actually performed the claimed services for them.[19] These disclosures, combined with accusations that Long used his office to aid clients of the St. Louis labor lawyer, contributed to Long's defeat in the Missouri Democratic primary of 1968.

The public accusations made by the staff members who exposed Senator Thomas J. Dodd (D-Conn.) included charges that he used his Senatorial powers to aid private clients, although such charges were not the basis of the Senator's subsequent censure. In particular, Dodd was accused of helping a client obtain a loan from the Small Business Administration and of accepting both legal fees and loan-finder's fees from Hartford insurance companies while he was heading an inconclusive Antitrust and Monopoly Subcommittee investigation of the insurance industry.[20]

---

* Canons of professional ethics have long required that any division of fees be based upon a division of services or responsibility. "It hardly seems necessary to state that it is improper for an attorney to receive compensation for merely recommending another attorney to his client." ABA Comm. on Professional Ethics, OPINIONS, No. 97 (1933).

In 1968 LIFE turned to another lawyer in the Congress, Representative Cornelius Gallagher (D-N.J.). While he was accused primarily of misconduct unrelated to his law practice, it was also reported that Gallagher received $50,000 in legal fees in 1962–63 from Anthony "Tino" De Angelis, who was imprisoned soon thereafter for a notorious multimillion-dollar salad-oil swindle.[21]

We do not presume to judge the merits of the charges implicating law practices in Congressional scandals. Nor can we measure the actual harm done to the images of the Congress and the legal profession. It is hard to escape the conclusions, however, that law practice has demonstrated a special potential for actual and alleged Congressional improprieties, and that law practices have played a disproportionate role in the history of Congressional scandals. As further evidence of this, we refer to a cutting generalization recently made in a standard reference work by a veteran political writer:

> Foremost among these [political practices that raise ethical questions] is the mixed career of the lawyer-legislator. Lawyers lead all other professions in representation in the Congress and in the legislatures. It is accepted practice for a legislator to pursue his legal career and represent clients with a special interest in pending legislation—railroads, unions, manufacturing concerns, highway contractors, defense empires, vending machines, insurance companies. Such arrangements fairly shout "conflict of interest."
>
> The legislator who accepts a $20,000 bribe for pressing a special-interest bill faces a prison term if caught, but the legislator who receives a $20,000 legal fee from a company whose interests he champions in the legislature faces no penalty. He is doing what comes naturally in American politics.[22]

This statement is subject to challenge in one important respect. The conduct described does not "come naturally" for a lawyer in Congress. Receiving legal fees for any type of representation cannot be the Congressional norm because those who continue law practice are a small minority. That the practitioner has become a conspicuous exception, rather than the rule, will be shown in the next section.

WHO PRACTICES LAW?

This Committee found active law practice to be much more rare among lawyers in Congress than is generally assumed. Seventy-one lawyers were included in the 120 Members interviewed, a 59-percent representation which is identical to that of lawyers in the entire 90th Congress. Sixteen of the Senators interviewed were lawyers, as were 55 Representatives. Only 26 of these 71, or 37 percent, continued some form of law practice.

Our research also establishes that lawyer-Representatives account for a disproportionate share of Members who practice. A great majority of the Senate's 68 lawyers have completely terminated law practice, and it is safe to say that the fraction who continue any form of practice is no greater than one fourth. In a 1967 survey of lawyer-Senators, the ST. LOUIS POST-DISPATCH located only 17 with any practice involvement.[23] A survey of the listings of Senators in the Martindale-Hubbell Legal Directory also indicates this to be the maximum figure.

We are persuaded by information from several sources, some of them confidential, that no more than 10 or 12 of these Senators received substantial income from law practice. Some were allowing their names to be used for other purposes, such as retaining a place for the Senator's son. At least one had attempted unsuccessfully to halt the use of his name. We are also satisfied that even fewer actually performed legal services to any significant degree. We note too that 14 of the 17 practicing Senators are from states east of the Mississippi River.

Our interviews and the April 1969 financial disclosures in the House of Representatives both indicate a much higher incidence of law practice among Representatives than Senators. In the House, between 35 and 45 percent of the lawyers continue to practice.[24] This disparity calls for close analysis, which can be done empirically and which reveals two important variables that tend to cause law practice by Representatives.

The first relevant factor is length of service. The incidence of law practice according to terms of service is shown by Table 3.1.

86

TABLE 3.1

Practicing/Non-Practicing Lawyer-Representatives Interviewed by Terms of Service

	3 Terms or Less	More than 3 Terms	Total
Practicing	10 (63%)	14 (36%)	24 (44%)
Non-practicing	6 (37%)	25 (64%)	31 (56%)
Total	16 (100%)	39 (100%)	55 (100%)

Our first conclusion is that law practice by Representatives varies almost inversely according to length of service and is notably an attribute of juniority. Ten of the 16 Representatives who had served three terms or less, or 63 percent, continued to practice. At four terms the incidence of law practice drops sharply. Of the 39 Representatives who had served four terms or more, only 14, or 36 percent, continued to practice. Only one of the six most senior Representatives interviewed, all of whom had served 15 terms or more, continued to practice law.

It can thus be concluded that abstention from law practice is the behavioral norm of a majority of all Senators and of a majority of those Representatives who have begun to climb the seniority ladder. These presumably are beginning to find their Congressional work both more demanding and more rewarding. They also enjoy the advantages of incumbents against political defeat and are gaining in prestige and expertise which enhance their chances of profitable return to private life, if it becomes necessary.

In other words, Representatives whose situations have become comparable to that of Senators follow the Senatorial norm on law practice. Some of the junior Representatives who continue practice are only doing so on a tentative basis until they are re-elected once or twice. Others are gradually phasing out their practices. Unfortunately, a sizable group plans to continue indefinitely.

In addition to length of service, one other factor emerges as an explanation of continued law practice by Representatives: This is geography. Practicing lawyers are generally thought to account for much of the so-called "Tuesday to Thursday Club," which is said to consist of Members from Eastern states who historically have been enabled by proximity to spend long weekends in their districts. Although the jet age has made this fringe benefit available to more Members, differing travel costs and constituency demands and a greater tendency to leave families at home cause the Tuesday-Thursday phenomenon still to be largely a characteristic of Easterners.

The facts of law practice bear out the impression that proximity is related to continued law practice. Table 3.2 divides the lawyer-Representatives in our interview sample according to East-West locations of their districts and their incidence of law practice versus non-practice.

TABLE 3.2

Practicing/Non-Practicing Lawyer-Representatives Interviewed by Location of District

	East of Miss. R	West of Miss. R	Total
Practicing	21 (58%)	3 (16%)	24 (44%)
Non-practicing	15 (42%)	16 (84%)	31 (56%)
Total	36 (100%)	19 (100%)	55 (100%)

One salient fact emerges. Law practice in the House is a function of geography, just as in the Senate. If continued practice is a benefit either to the profession or to the public, it is a blessing which falls unevenly according to geography. Of the 24 practicing Representatives, only three come from states west of the Mississippi. If law practice is detrimental to efficient Congressional service, Eastern constituencies suffer disproportionately.

In another respect, the entire country may have cause for complaint. Easterners' law practices may help to limit Congress to a three-day legislative week. The Joint Committee on the Organization of Congress recommended in 1966 that both houses make special efforts to work a five-day week,[25] in the hope that sessions might then be completed by July 31, as required by law.[26] Nonetheless, a study of the first session of the 90th Congress showed that the difficulty of obtaining quorums on Fridays and Mondays caused the great bulk of House legislative activity to be scheduled for Tuesday, Wednesday, and Thursday.[27]

We have no doubt that Eastern Representatives' law practices are partly responsible for this shortened legislative week. Their added

88

capability of combining professional and Congressional careers may account for the unusually large numbers of practicing lawyers in the delegations from such states as New York, Connecticut, and New Jersey. New York's 41-Member House delegation includes 28 lawyers, slightly above the national average; and 17 of those 28 continue to practice, considerably above the national average. Similarly, Connecticut's 8-Member delegation is made up entirely of lawyers, of whom 5 continue to practice. Six of the 10 lawyers in the 15-Member New Jersey delegation have practices.[28] It is interesting, too, that 4 of the 6 Senators from these states are among the minority of lawyer-Senators who practice.

This suggests that some Members may be attracted to Congressional service because it permits outside law practice. The next question is whether discouraging such law practice might deter lawyers from seeking election. This can best be answered by comparing the number of lawyers in Western states' delegations, where there is little potential for continuing practice. Table 3.3 is helpful.

TABLE 3.3

East/West Distribution of Lawyer-Members of the 90th Congress

State	Senate Lawyers	House Lawyers	House Delegation	Percent of Total Delegation
East of Mississippi River				
Alabama	2	6	8	80
Connecticut	2	6	6	100
Delaware	1	1	1	67
Florida	2	9	12	80
Georgia	2	7	10	75
Illinois	1	9	24	38
Indiana	2	7	11	69
Kentucky	1	4	6	63
Maine	1	2	2	75
Maryland	2	2	8	40
Massachusetts	2	7	12	64
Michigan	2	12	19	67
Mississippi	2	4	5	86
New Hampshire	2	2	2	100
New Jersey	2	10	15	71

89

TABLE 3.3 Continued

State	Senate Lawyers	House Lawyers	House Delegation	Percent of Total Delegation
New York	2	28	41	70
North Carolina	1	8	11	69
Ohio	2	14	24	62
Pennsylvania	2	9	27	38
Rhode Island	1	2	2	75
South Carolina	2	4	6	75
Tennessee	2	2	9	36
Vermont	0	1	1	33
Virginia	1	7	10	67
West Virginia	0	2	5	29
Subtotal	39 (of 50)	165	277	62

West of Mississippi River

State	Senate Lawyers	House Lawyers	House Delegation	Percent of Total Delegation
Alaska	0	1	1	33
Arizona	0	2	3	40
Arkansas	2	3	4	83
California	1	14	39	37
Colorado	2	4	4	100
Hawaii	2	2	2	100
Idaho	1	1	2	50
Iowa	2	3	7	56
Kansas	1	3	5	57
Louisiana	2	5	8	70
Minnesota	1	2	8	30
Missouri	1	5	10	50
Montana	1	2	2	75
Nebraska	2	1	3	60
Nevada	2	0	1	67
New Mexico	1	0	2	25
North Dakota	1	0	2	25
Oklahoma	1	4	6	63
Oregon	1	2	4	50
South Dakota	0	1	2	25
Texas	1	15	23	64
Utah	1	1	2	50
Washington	2	4	7	67
Wisconsin	1	5	10	50
Wyoming	0	1	1	33
Subtotal	29 (of 50)	81	158	53
Total East and West	68 (of 100)	246	435	59

SUMMARY: LAWYERS ACCOUNT FOR THE FOLLOWING PER-
CENTAGES OF DELEGATIONS:

	Senate	House	Total
East (327 MC's)	78	60	62
West (208 MC's)	58	51	53
Total (535 MC's)	68	57	59

The disparity in lawyer-Members between Eastern and Western delegations is significant. Of the total delegations from the 25 Eastern states, 62 percent are lawyers, as compared to only 53 percent of the Western delegations. The possibility of conveniently continuing to practice law may be partially responsible for this difference. Of more significance, however, is the fact that a majority of the Western delegations are lawyers, despite their low potential for continued practice. This should establish that discouraging law practice by Members of Congress will hardly cause the profession to be underrepresented.

WHAT DO PRACTICING CONGRESSMEN DO?

The type of law practice available to a Member of Congress is severely limited by 18 U.S.C. §203(a). This statute had its origins in the previously mentioned Gardiner incident and prohibits a Member of Congress from receiving direct or indirect compensation for representation in "any proceeding . . . in which the United States is a party or has a direct and substantial interest, before any department, agency, court martial, officer, or any civil, military, or naval commission. . . ." More specific statutes prevent Members from practicing before the U.S. Court of Claims[29] or the Indian Claims Commission,[30] and from any employment by beneficiaries of maritime subsidies.[31] These laws should effectively insulate vast areas of typical law practice from any form of Congressional participation. The representation of clients before such Federal administrative agencies as the Securities and Exchange Commission, the Interstate Commerce Commission, the National Labor Relations Board, and the Federal Trade Commission is forbidden. More seriously, representation is precluded in tax matters before the Internal Revenue Service and all matters handled by the U.S. Department of Justice and other Executive Departments. A good part of the normal activity of most urban law firms is representation of the type forbidden to Members of Congress.

Is practice of law firms with Congressional membership actually so limited? Not necessarily. Among our interviewees we found that Section 203 is sometimes circumvented by the use of bookkeeping arrangements under which the firm accepts the prohibited Federal practice but the partnership agreement precludes the Member of Congress from participating in such income. Another has set up two firms under a "double door" or "dual partnership" arrangement so that the Member's name appears only in a firm which handles only the non-Federal matters permitted by Section 203. These arrangements apparently are inspired by a 1943 ruling of the Attorney General which indicated that if the Federal official personally receives none of the compensation, it does not violate Section 203 if his partners render the forbidden services.[32] The ethics of such arrangements are more doubtful and will be specifically discussed later.

In the absence of such arrangements, the Member and his firm are clearly limited to non-Federal practice and must decline such business and refer regular clients to other lawyers when Federal agencies become involved. Most claim to follow this procedure, although their professional notices in the Martindale-Hubbell Legal Directory do not so indicate. Most indicate "general practice," and a few specifically claim such Federal specialties as labor and tax practices. None disclaims Federal practice.

Where Section 203 is fully honored, the partial incompetence of such a firm might be expected to deter many clients, but there appear to be sufficient non-Federal areas for some lucrative Congressional law practices to flourish. They handle personal-injury litigation, probate and estate work, real-estate matters, and a variety of commercial representation. For instance, one Congressional law firm handles the real-estate problems of a national bank; another is counsel to a retail-trade association; a third devotes virtually all its time to the legal work generated by a savings-and-loan association's lending activities. The expertise which a Congressman develops in Washington obviously has little relation to the type of practice which the law permits him to pursue while in office.

Although most maintain their district Congressional offices separately from their law offices, a few have both at the same location. When our interviewer asked one such Representative what happened if someone seeking Congressional assistance turned out to need a lawyer instead, he was told, "Then he's referred to one of the other law-yers in the firm." Another sort of blending of the two occupations occurs in the law office of a Representative who carries two employees on his law-office payroll solely to handle Congressional case work.

Some key facts gleaned from our interviews with 24 practicing Representatives are shown in Table 3.4. It is considerably abridged to preserve anonymity.

TABLE 3.4

Tabular Analysis of 24 Practicing Lawyer-Representatives

Code	Senior/ Junior	Nature of Services	Practice Income	Other Income Above $5,000
A	S	"Occasional case for a friend"—deeds, wills	$2,000	No
B	S	None	Under $1,000	Undisclosed
C	J	None	$8,500 + %	No
D	S	"Very little" time	Undisclosed	Yes
E	S	Limited partner; occasional consulta-tion	Substantial	Yes
F	S	Estates, counseling—largely by telephone	$2,000	Yes
G	S	Non-court matters	Substantial	No
H	J	None	Undisclosed (10% of firm's net profit)	No
I	J	Referrals only	Substantial—draw + %	Undisclosed
J	J	Referrals only	Insubstantial—some referral fees	No
K	S	Counsel to family corporations	$20,000	Yes
L	J	None	$10,000–$15,000	Undisclosed
M	J	None	$8,000 + %	Yes
N	J	Of counsel; copyright opinions	Insubstantial	Yes
O	J	Estate work	$2,000	No
P	J	"Almost nil"	$2,000 + (Draw + %)	No
Q	S	Estate and real-estate work	Insubstantial	Yes

TABLE 3.4 (*Continued*)

Code	Senior/ Junior	Nature of Services	Practice Income	Other Income Above $5,000
R	S	Corporate and real-estate consultation	$9,000	Undisclosed
S	S	Senior partner in firm; probate; little time	$6,000	Undisclosed
T	S	No firm; minimal retainers for occasional advice	$2,500	Yes
U	S	No firm; estate and real-estate work; little time	Undisclosed	Yes
V	J	Sole proprietorship; "associates do all the work"	Substantial	Yes
W	S	Partner, "country-type practice"; little time	$3,500	No
X	S	Estates, "general retainers"; 1 day per week	$12,500	Undisclosed

SUMMARY DATA

S (4 terms or more)		14	Substantial ($5,000+)	13	Yes	10
J (3 terms or less)		10	Insubstantial	8	No	8
			Undisclosed	3	Undisclosed	6

[Substantial practice income without other income 2]

The first fact of importance is that many "practicing" Representatives perform no professional services whatever. When questioned about the nature of the services they personally render to their firms or to clients, some are quick to disclaim any drain on their time. These usually add that their names bring business to their firms or that they "refer business" to the firms in exchange for shares of the income. Among those who actually practice, estate and real-estate work accounts for the bulk of claimed actual services. The term "consultation" was sometimes used. Only one cited courtroom work; another said he would not dare appear in court for fear of offending local lawyers.

Those who actually perform some services almost uniformly claim that law practice is allowed to make only minimal demands on their time. One stated that he formerly went to his law office every Monday and Friday but can now give it only half a day every other week. Another goes to his law office every other Saturday. Two Members act as house counsel for family corporations but do not have their shingles out. They possibly should be placed in the category of corporate officers, rather than practitioners, for purposes of analysis. In sum, it appears that the quantitative diversion of Congressional manpower to actual law practice is relatively small.

REASONS FOR CONTINUING LAW PRACTICE

As previously indicated, junior Representatives who may be phasing out practice or clinging to a foothold until re-election gives them greater security account for the largest incidence of practitioners in the House. Senior Representatives and Senators who continue to practice usually assign one of two reasons: (1) a need for supplemental income; or (2) the security of having something to rejoin if they are defeated.

Prior to our interview program, little was known of the extent of income received by Members of Congress from law practice. One of the few lawyer-Members whose law-practice arrangements and income became public knowledge was former Senator John Bricker of Ohio. His firm's representation of the Pennsylvania Railroad while he opposed the St. Lawrence Seaway has been mentioned. He paid into the firm his entire Senatorial salary of $12,500 per year and received $24,000 from it. The firm was said to handle no Federal matters for the railroad, although public records showed that it earned $148,000 in fees from the railroad in a six-year period. Bricker insisted he shared in none of these fees.[33]

Our interviews included a sufficient number of practicing Representatives for useful generalization on their law-practice income. As indicated by Table 3.4, a substantial majority of practicing Representatives in the 90th Congress who were interviewed received annual income from law practice lower than the $12,500 salary increase voted early in the 91st Congress. Two of those interviewed later omitted law-practice income from their published financial disclosures because it was less than $1,000 for the previous year. One of these told us that his practice, a sole proprietorship with salaried associates, actually netted him a loss for the year. Most of those receiving substantial practice income had other sources also. Only two of the 24 interviewed indicated that law practice was both substantial and exclusive as a source of outside income.

It appears that very few of the present practitioners in the Congress can continue to justify it as a matter of financial necessity. A notable exception may be Senator Dodd, whose financial straits became a matter of public record. His 1961 income-tax return showed $61,434.33 received in legal fees during one year, but $50,000 of this total was a single fee which was spread over four years for tax purposes.[34] Another practicing Senator is known to receive substantial income from his firm but to spend a comparable amount from personal funds to supplement his Congressional office allowances. Increasing the latter would solve his problem.

The second reason—a need for a cushion against defeat—is more difficult to analyze. Some practitioners genuinely believe they would have difficulty in returning to law practice if they had not maintained a law-firm connection. This may be understandable in some cases, but experience is generally to the contrary. A 1954 study of the American legal profession included a survey of lawyers in politics by Professor Harry Jones of Columbia University, which found that lawyers' unique ease of re-entry to private life helps account for their large numbers in Congress. It said:

> A lawyer can leave his practice for two years or six, or for an even longer time, with some assurance that he can return to his practice with professional skills unimpaired and with the prospect of newly attracted clients to replace those that he might have lost during his years in Washington.[35]

The fact that most Members do not find it necessary to continue law practice is some evidence that it should not be necessary for a small minority. It is safe to say that the more typical case is that of the Midwestern Representative of medium seniority who said, "My old senior partner continues to offer me a home, and if I left Congress, I'd probably return to him." Talented people of the type who win election to Congress will always be in demand, and if they serve very long in Washington, they should gain Federal expertise and advantages unknown to most home-towners. Thus, the defeat-insurance argument is unpersuasive as a justification for indefinitely continuing Congressional law practice.

Why the Majority
Terminate Practice

Other than their generally being more senior and more Western, the non-practicing majority of lawyers in Congress have little in common on the surface. They are both liberal and conservative, Republican and Democratic, rural and urban. Some are wealthy, but many are of extremely modest means. A senior Representative who abandoned private practice when he was first elected from a rural district said, "In a rural district, if a Member continued his law practice, he would probably practice himself right out of Congress." Political considerations unquestionably influence many Members. It can possibly be a liability and never a political asset for a Congressman to be practicing law. Lawyers who lose business to him and laymen whose interests conflict with those of the Congressman's clients might understandably complain. Representative Thomas Steed (D-Okla.) indicated an even higher level of such political sensitivities when he told us that he did not allow his lawyer son to take cases involving the Federal government. He feared that it might cost him the good will of lawyers in his home town if they had reason to suspect that a member of the local bar was receiving business because his father was a Congressman.

Apart from political considerations, many Members of Congress genuinely believe they cannot practice law without raising insurmountable conflict-of-interest problems. A veteran Senator, who has never practiced, said in his interview:

I don't think a Senator or Congressman should practice law, whatever the protective arrangements. There is a threat of conflict of interest every day. You can't even probate an estate now without some Federal involvement.

A letter of March 5, 1968, to this Committee from Representative David Henderson (D-N.C.) included similar judgments:

> In the second place, with the Federal government these days doing business or otherwise acting in a way that affects virtually every phase of commerce, business, and even our everyday lives, how can a member of Congress possibly be free of conflict of interest if he is practicing law? And what does he do in case of conflict of interest? Obviously, he cannot decline to vote on an issue or decline to participate in committee consideration of an issue if he represents a client who has a direct or indirect interest in the subject matter, and if he turns away every prospective client who may or might possibly some day have an interest in a matter before the Congress, I simply do not see how he can practice law.

The reason most frequently cited by non-practitioners is the full-time nature of Congressional service. Many point to the increasing demands of Congressional service upon their time and profess inability to understand how any Member of Congress can actually practice law while doing justice to his Congressional duties. Such Members frequently go on to state personal objections to trading on the office by allowing a law firm to use a Member's name without the Member actually practicing.

This leads to a final reason which was rarely mentioned but which seems to us to underlie the feelings of many non-practitioners. They do not want to endanger their effectiveness with Congressional colleagues, and they sense something important which our interviews disclosed: Other Members are surprisingly suspicious and resentful of those who have law-practice arrangements. Few believe that they are actually practicing, and many characterize Congressional law firms as influence-peddling or improper trading upon their public office.

The disabling effect of law practice upon a Member's effectiveness was stated eloquently by Senator Borah in his 1916 condemnation of it. He said:

> If a legislator should feel that the rights of some great corporate interests were being unjustly assailed, if he should feel that some law which seemed to favor interests then under public censure was entitled to his support, he would be perfectly powerless to be

of any service to them if it was known that he held a retainer from those engaged in a similar kind of business. In other words, it is just as important that the legislator be free from entanglements and those associations which seem to direct his actions in order that he may do justice to the business and corporate interests of the country as that he may do justice to the public. If he feels called upon to make a fight for the rights of those under public censure I cannot imagine his being fitted for that fight unless he is wholly disengaged in every conceivable way from any business or personal interest in the result.[36]

The practicing lawyer is inescapably suspect when he champions legislative interests of a client. His colleagues understandably cannot know whether he is motivated by the public interest or the client's interest. This alone is sufficient reason for most Members to avoid most law practice. Also, the majority who terminate law practice set persuasive examples for the others, and some are disturbed that the minority does not follow.

THE ETHICS OF FAÇADE PRACTICES

The bulk of Congressional law practice falls under what one non-practicing Senator has called a "façade." When the commission method of setting Congressional salaries was being debated, Senator John Pastore (D-R.I.) said in its defense:

> Let me say that many Senators have to depend upon their Senate salary to live. They have to maintain two homes. They cannot practice law, if they are lawyers, because that would subject them to conflict of interest.
>
> We can go around making speeches and lectures. That gives us a little money. Or we can get tied up with *a law firm where we would not do any work, but just have our names on the door, and receive some form of compensation.* Those who are lawyers but do not choose to do this have a right to stand up and say, "This is what I think we are worth". . . .
>
> The idea seems to be prevalent that we have got to make big money in order to stay in the Senate with all its demands, unless we happen to come in here as wealthy men, unless we happen to

have oil wells, or own a television station, or a radio station, or *a law practice which is only a façade. . . .*[37] [Emphasis added]

One Senator interviewed receives $12,000 per year from a firm for which he no longer does anything, but whose practice he helped build in his pre-Congressional career. Six of the 24 practicing Representatives listed in Table 3.4 performed *no* services, and two reported "referrals" as the only basis for their income. We have the strong impression that no more than four of the 24 can fairly be said to furnish professional services in any substantial amount. The basic element of "façade"—receipt of income without performing services—is present to some degree in most practices and is frankly admitted by most who engage in it. They consider it a redeeming factor that their practices distract them so little from their official duties.

The difficulty with façade practice is identifying the *quid pro quo* received by the law firm or its clients. Some façade practitioners frankly admit they are paid for the prestige their names add to the firms. Referrals of prospective clients is a similar consideration. This was identified as a problem of Congressional ethics by the Douglas subcommittee in 1951. After discussing the inadequacy of Congressional salaries and allowances and the need for supplemental incomes, it said:

> The upshot is that a majority of the Members of Congress find it necessary to supplement their salary in some way. Were Congress meeting but 6 months or less a year, as it once did, there would be no serious difficulty, but membership is now practically a year-round activity, which, with the duties of campaigning, leaves little time to engage in business or professional activities. Members who are lawyers may accept fees or retainers for giving advice and counsel or for other legal services. But they have little time for very extensive service and if their duties become perfunctory, the question always arises, are they being paid for their influence and to influence their perspective. Men who pay legal retainers expect to get something for their money.[38]

Another justification for receiving income without performing services was disclosed by some of our interviews and by the 1967 survey reported in the St. Louis Post-Dispatch. It concluded:

The most common pattern found in a survey of Senators who maintain a connection with a law firm provides for regular payments, usually of a fixed amount, from the partnership, with little or no work by the Senator. Characteristically the arrangement was justified on grounds that the Senator, before his election, had been the founder or leading member of his law firm and had devoted many years to building up its clientele. The payments being received now were seen by most members as nothing more than compensation for their hard-earned interest in the firm. . . .[39]

Such arrangements assume a *sale* of the inactive partner's interest in the practice, with the consideration to be paid in installments over a period of years. If it is truly a sale, it is a peculiar one. The "sales price" is open-ended and bears no logical relation to the subject of the "sale." It becomes greater as Congressional service, which occurs *after* withdrawal from practice, grows longer. The worth of the asset sold, the Member's pre-Congressional contribution to the firm, should vary according to his professional services *before* withdrawal from practice.

More important from an ethical viewpoint is the simple fact that to sell a law practice violates the professional canons. Although lawyers hear of this occasionally, and one Representative publicly reported income from such a sale in the House's 1969 financial disclosures,[40] the nature of the lawyer-client relationship is supposed to preclude its transfer for a price.

This was made clear in 1945, when a law firm applied to the Ethics Committee of the American Bar Association for approval of the proposed purchase of the practice of a deceased solo practitioner. The prospective purchasers would have paid his heirs either a lump sum or an agreed percentage of future fees received from the deceased's clients. The Committee ruled negatively for a number of reasons.

Canon 34, on fee-splitting, was held to prohibit such payments from future fees because the payees would not be lawyers and could not possibly have rendered services or responsibility to the clients involved, an ethical prerequisite for fee-sharing. Canon 27's prohibition of solicitation would preclude the purchasing lawyers and the estate from asking the deceased's clients to employ the purchasers. Also, the requirement of Canon 37 that a lawyer preserve his client's confidences beyond the period of his personal employment was viewed as inconsistent with sale of a law practice as a going business. Finally, the nature of the lawyer-client relation itself was invoked, with a basic admonition:

> Clients are not merchandise. Lawyers are not tradesmen. They have nothing to sell but personal service. An attempt, therefore, to barter in clients, would appear to be inconsistent with the best concepts of our professional status.[41]

This is squarely at odds with the thinking of a Senator who told us that he receives a large annual stipend for "having founded the firm and having brought it most of its present clients."

Since a salable asset cannot be found from past endeavors, can a valid *quid pro quo* be found in the subsequent business produced by the mere presence of the Congressman's name in the law firm? The legal profession again says, "No!" Although the question may have previously been debatable, the profession's present answer is emphatically negative.

The earlier canons of ethics were silent about a law firm's continuing to use the name of a full-time public official, except for the superfluous admonition of ABA Canon 33 that a firm could not continue to use the name of a judge if he was "precluded from practicing law." The relevant opinions of ethics committees were understandably vague and permissive. The leading statement was OPINION 192 of the ABA Committee on Professional Ethics and Grievances, issued in 1939. It approved, if permitted by law, a full-time public official's continued firm membership and participation in earnings so long as the public was not misled and conflicting interests were not served. It reaffirmed, however, an oft-stated principle:

> . . . [A]n attorney holding public office should avoid all conduct which might lead the layman to conclude that the attorney is utilizing his public position to further his professional success or personal interests.

While it can be argued that the reasoning of OPINION 192 never validated what we call façade practices, it must nonetheless be conceded that the profession's pre-1969 position was essentially permissive in this whole area.

When the American Bar Association Canons were revised in 1969, the profession dealt expressly with the ethical fallacy of permitting law firms to display the names of full-time public officials. The risk is unavoidable that the public will be misled either as to the performance of legal services by the official or as to special influence which the firm and its clients may be presumed to have with him. The new Code of Professional Responsibility deals effectively with the façades in Disciplinary Rule 2–102(B), which provides:

> . . . A lawyer who assumes a judicial, legislative, or public executive or administrative post or office shall not permit his name to remain in the name of a law firm or to be used in professional notices of the firm during any significant period in which he is not *actively and regularly* practicing law as a member of the firm, and during such period other members of the firm shall not use his name in the firm name or in professional notices of the firm.[42] [Emphasis added]

By definition, façade practice is neither "active" nor "regular." The new rule goes so far as to reach professional notices which may attempt a measure of disclosure of the Congressman's limited participation. Such terms as "of counsel," "retired," and "inactive" can no longer be used with the names of inactive Congressional lawyers. *Active and regular practice* is a condition of *any* use of a Member's name in professional notices of a firm.

Now that the canons of ethics are clear on this, façade practitioners must either terminate their relationships or escalate their levels of practice activity. Otherwise they risk disciplinary action by the bar. Those who actually engage in active practice and risk its political dangers have already been shown to be few in number. Compliance with the new ethical code should eliminate the great bulk, perhaps 80 to 90 percent, of Congressional law practices. Those which remain will also fail to pass muster, but for different reasons to be developed in the next section.

THE ETHICS OF ACTUAL PRACTICE

We concur in the judgments of the large number of Senators and Representatives who refrain from law practice because of its inherent conflicts of interest. As developed in the previous chapter, the conflict-of-interest concept seeks to prevent a public official from acting upon matters in which he has a personal pecuniary interest. Should a lawyer in Congress be allowed to legislate upon matters in which his clients are interested? Stated differently, is the relationship between lawyer and client such that the two should be treated as having a community of interest? If so, the lawyer-Member should not be allowed to act upon his client's interests and should avoid the relation creating the conflict of interest.

One of the Representatives interviewed has been publicly accused of serving legislative interests of corporate clients. He acknowledged that he was retained by a national business concern as its local counsel, largely for real-estate matters, and that he worked in Congress for legislation protecting it from import competition. He added, however, that the company had a big payroll at a plant in his district and that its welfare was important to many of his constituents. In other words, he would have pursued the same Congressional course without the retainer because client interest and constituent interest coincided. This is exactly the sort of blending of personal interest and public duty which the fiduciary concept forbids. Both his legislative efforts and the public's confidence would be enhanced if there were no grounds for suspicion that the corporate retainer might have motivated his actions. This Representative unnecessarily placed his voting record within what has been called an area of "invited distrust" by former American Bar Association President Ross L. Malone. He once said of lawyer-legislators in general:

> Inevitably, however, the legislature is going to consider proposed legislation affecting clients represented by the lawyer-legislator. Some of them will be regular clients of his office. He may have accepted an annual retainer from others. While accepting a retainer in no sense involves a surrender of independence of either thought or action on the part of a lawyer, it is not realistic to say that he has the same freedom of choice on matters affecting the client that would exist in the absence of such an arrangement. Regardless of the subjective effect upon him and his vote as a legislator, it is certain that the public would never believe— nor could it be expected to believe—that his vote would not be affected by his relationship with his client. A lawyer voting as a

legislator on matters affecting the interests of a retained client invites justified criticism, if not distrust, not only of the lawyer but of the legal profession itself.[43]

Malone's analysis is addressed largely to appearances and to the possibility for impairment of legislative judgment. The point can be carried an important step further—to actual, as opposed to merely potential, subordination of the public's interest to client's interests by lawyers in public service.

Senator Borah did this with considerable professional insight when he said:

The relationship of client and attorney is the closest. Consciously or unconsciously he comes to feel that his client's demands are wholly just. Yet men will argue that a lawyer with a thirty or forty thousand dollar retainer from some client is perfectly fitted to shape legislation which his client will argue is all wrong, wholly unjust and vitally injurious to his business interests. I am not speaking now of a conscious corruption which some people assume to take place in legislation more often, perhaps, than it does. There is no occasion for conscious, open, affirmative corruption for which some one may be sent to the penitentiary when the same thing can be accomplished by that unconscious and subtle influence for which there is no punishment and which may even be justified by good people. Suppose every lawyer in the legislatures of the country or in Congress were in the employ of those great business interests engaged in interstate commerce. What do you think would be the necessity of employing lobbyists in order that no laws seriously affecting interests might be passed? A member of Congress is in an indefensible position who is called upon to legislate concerning those matters in which his clients may have an interest and which may concern them vitally.[44]

In all professional candor, we must agree. Both the theoretical and the actual nature of the lawyer-client relationship are such that it is totally unrealistic to expect lawyers to subordinate their clients' interests when they make decisions as trustees of the public's interest. Temporarily removing the lawyer's hat to put on a public-service hat cannot eclipse the lawyer's duty of loyalty to clients. We can virtually take professional notice that lawyers almost invariably become identified with their clients' interests and view public issues accordingly.

One of the few instances where this has been publicly stated by a lawyer is in an article by Randolph Paul, former General Counsel to the Treasury and a leading tax lawyer, who was writing about the public responsibilities of tax advisors. After first pointing out that in representing a client a tax lawyer properly argues for official decisions in the interests of his client, not the public, Paul then noted how such advocacy is invariably continued when the lawyer works on public issues on his own time. In the voluminous published writings of tax advisors he found a uniform tendency to present the taxpayer viewpoint and concluded:

> . . . [O]ne type of suggestion is made conspicuous by its absence. Their writings consistently fail to espouse amendments of the statute which will operate in favor of the government. Their silence about flagrant loopholes is unrelieved. . . . [M]any tax advisers would like . . . to spend part of their time working for a better tax system, but . . . honestly think that they cannot afford that luxury. They have accepted the doctrine that they will attract and hold tax business only if they remain completely conventional, voicing opinions that will be popular with taxpayers. . . . They have become mental prisoners of the views and interests of clients.[45]

In the past, the ethical relativism of some lawyers on this point may have been partly due to an inadequate statement of conflict-of-interest rules for the guidance of practitioners. Empirical studies show this to be an ethical value to which lawyers as a group have a low sensitivity.[46]

Before 1969 the Canons contained a rather narrow provision which stopped short of true fiduciary concepts. Canon 6, by its terms, prevented a lawyer from representing multiple interests only where it was his duty in behalf of one client to contend for a result which duty to another client required him to oppose. This is an adversary concept aimed only at immediate clash of clients' interests in the particular matters entrusted to the lawyer. A leading expert thus concluded: "Where there is no real conflict of interest, the canon does not apply, as where the two matters are wholly unrelated to one another." [47]

This indicates that a lawyer may concurrently work both for and against the same client in unrelated cases. Clients understandably might object to this, and the profession sometimes took a broader view. As stated by one ethics committee,

> . . . despite the absence of any conflict of interest, maintenance of confidence in the Bar requires an attorney who has accepted representation of a client to decline, while representing such client, any employment from an adverse party in any matter even though wholly unrelated to the original retainer.[48]

The confusion over whether actual collision of client interests was essential to an ethical violation doubtless helped to cause the ABA to drop the term "conflicting interests" in its 1969 Code. The new rules are directed at service of "differing interests," which are defined broadly to include "every interest that will adversely affect either the judgment or the loyalty of a lawyer to a client, whether it be a conflicting, inconsistent, diverse, or other interest." [49]

The new rules state broad principles aimed at preserving independence of professional judgment. By focusing on the lawyer's independence of professional judgment and forbidding arrangements which threaten this independence, the new canons essentially incorporate the traditional fiduciary concept. This leaves no room for inquiry as to whether there is actual conflict between the interests of the fiduciary and his beneficiary, but instead prevents the possibility of conflict. As stated by the New York Court of Appeals:

> . . . [T]he question of bad faith or damage is irrelevant to our inquiry. . . . Measured by these standards, we think it clear that these attorneys placed themselves in a situation wherein their own personal purposes *might* well conflict with the purposes of the trust beneficiaries. . . . The basic vice is the existence of a personal interest, entangling their private claims with those of their beneficiaries, thus creating the danger of biased judgments. . . .[50]

As developed in Chapter 2, public officials should generally be held to fiduciary standards under the "public office–public trust" concept. This precludes official action where the circumstances even risk impairment of impartial judgement. Under this test a Member of Congress should never be heard to say that he can subordinate clients' interests to the public interest.

The American Bar Association's new Code of Professional Responsibility is something of an improvement in this regard. Lawyers in legislative office, state or Federal, may be subject to disciplinary proceedings for grievous misuse of their public offices to aid professional clients. Disciplinary Rule 8–101 reads:

> DR 8–101   Action as a Public Official.
> (A)   A lawyer who holds public office shall not:
>> (1) Use his public position to obtain, or attempt to obtain, a special advantage in legislative matters for himself or for a client under circumstances where he knows or it is obvious that such action is not in the public interest.
>> (2) Use his public position to influence, or attempt to influence, a tribunal to act in favor of himself or of a client.
>> (3) Accept any thing of value from any person when the lawyer knows or it is obvious that the offer is for the purpose of influencing his action as a public official.

The greatest significance of this rule may be that the profession has moved significantly to regulate actions of lawyers in other capacities which are not held exclusively by lawyers. The effect is to hold lawyers in public office to a higher standard than non-lawyers. A retailer-legislator, for instance, unlike a lawyer, can advance legislation which aids a customer without risking loss of his occupation as a retailer.

Nonetheless, the prohibitions of DR 8–101 fall considerably short of fully incorporating the fiduciary principle. The main provision, subsection 8–101(A), appears to be somewhat subjective. The implication is that a legislator is free to serve self-interest when he personally believes that the public interest coincides and is not obviously mistaken in this belief. However, the Disciplinary Rules are not the entire code, but only its mandatory provisions. They state "the minimum level of conduct below which no lawyer can fall without being subject to disciplinary action." [51] So viewed, 8–101(A) may be an acceptable statement of the point at which a lawyer-legislator's misuse of legislative office becomes intolerable to his fellow lawyers.

For those lawyers concerned with more than the possibility of disciplinary proceedings against them, the Ethical Considerations underlying Rule 8–101 supply a higher standard than the Rule itself. These are "aspirational in character and . . . constitute a body of principles upon which the lawyer can rely for guidance in many specific situations." [52] The relevant Ethical Consideration, EC 8–8, states that a lawyer in public office "should not engage in activities in which his personal or professional interests are or foreseeably may be in conflict with his official duties." The official footnote to this Ethical Consideration reaffirms a principle asserted under the old canons: that a lawyer in public office "should avoid all conduct which might lead the layman to conclude that the attorney is utilizing his public position to further his professional success or personal interests." [53]

We believe that the Ethical Considerations dictate against continued law practice by Members of Congress. Disciplinary Rule 8–101 necessarily deals with all legislators, state and Federal, and understandably attempts to do so with a single mandatory admonition. Its permissiveness was doubtless motivated by the fact that practicing lawyers in part-time state legislatures cannot practically be expected to avoid all conflicts between client interests and legislative duties. The high salary and the full-time nature of Congressional service make it unnecessary similarly to dilute the fiduciary principle at the Federal level. This is not to say, however, that the ABA, in stating broad principles applicable to lawyers generally, should have dealt explicitly with the few, though exceptionally important, lawyers who practice while serving in Congress.

Can it be said that all law practice conflicts with the public duty of a Member of Congress? Since Federal-agency practice is now precluded by law, some may argue that those areas of practice legally available to a lawyer-Member have little potential for conflict with his Federal legislative decisions. Probate, negligence, real estate, and state trial work are said by some practicing Members to pose no conflicts with their Congressional duties. This overlooks the fact that it is not the nature of the practice, but the mere existence of the lawyer-client relationship with its duty of loyalty, which risks conflicts. These result from the pervasive scope of Congressional power. All clients are interested in the legislative work of Congress. As in our conclusions on financial disclosure, we can delineate no Federal nexus for separating interests which create avoidable conflicts of interest. Just as we decided earlier that Federal legislative jurisdiction is so broad that no asset or activity is insulated from it, the same must be said of clients and law practice.

THE PRACTITIONER'S ETHICAL DILEMMA

Those who seek to justify Congressional law practice face a dilemma. If the practice is only nominal, it violates the new ABA Disciplinary Rule requiring "active and regular" practice by public officials whose names are used by law firms. If his practice is in fact active and regular, the Member encounters the full-time nature of Congressional service and a fair inference that truly active practice is at its expense. In both instances, his loyalties to clients impair his independence and thus create avoidable conflicts of interest.

Since the 1969 salary increase, few can validly claim economic justification for law practices. The need for cushions against defeat is outweighed by the incumbency advantage and the success of ex-Members in resuming private practices. The right to continue practice is not essential to recruitment of lawyers for Congressional service. All of this is clearly demonstrated by the examples of most Senators and senior Representatives who are lawyers. Add to these considerations the historic record of law practice by legislators in generating public scandals, and the case for continued law practice by Members of Congress approaches the vanishing point.

In terms of our analysis in Chapter 2, law practice raises avoidable conflicts of interest. It could be reasonably argued to be unavoidable only under the "personally necessary" classification and here only for junior Members who have not yet obtained a measure of job security. After a Member of the House is re-elected twice or a Senator to a full term, his chances of continued re-election are so great that he can reasonably be expected to abstain from law practice. Also, he should be sure by then which of the two conflicting careers he chooses to pursue.

Preferably, all Members should terminate practice upon taking office. On balancing the equities, however, it must be conceded that a junior Member's personal circumstances sometimes cause the economic advantages to him of briefly continuing practice to outweigh the advantages to the public which would accrue from total and immediate termination. A short period of transition between careers is tolerated in many other circumstances and appears to be both reasonable and normal for newly elected Members of Congress.

Our recommendation that Members voluntarily refrain from law practice accordingly excepts Senators filling a vacancy for an unexpired term and Representatives in their first two terms. This strikes a reasonable balance and approximates the behavioral norm of the great majority of lawyer-Members.

Those who continue practice for any period should be subject to the client-disclosure rules proposed in Chapter 2 and expressly stated in Appendix B. This will fully inform their constituents of the relevant facts so that they may judge the effects upon official performance.

Some may contend that our position is an unfair singling out of the legal profession from other occupations. Lawyers should be the last to claim this because they are generally supposed to hold themselves to higher standards than those of the market place. This is especially true where the legal system itself is involved. The work of the Congress is one of the fundamental parts of our legal system, and a lawyer's participation should not be ambiguous. Finally, the number of lawyers in Congress and their unique relation to political and governmental processes make it appropriate to hold lawyer-Members to special standards.

Recommendation 3A

All Senators, after election to one full term, and all Representatives, after election to a third term, should thereafter totally refrain from any form of law practice.

FEDERAL PRACTICE BY PARTNERS OF MEMBERS

This aspect of the over-all subject merits special treatment. Federal-agency practice by partners of Members of Congress occurs under a form of Congressional law practice which is of doubtful propriety under any circumstances. The resulting avoidance of a Federal conflict-of-interest statute defeats an important national policy.

As previously indicated, 18 U.S.C. §203 prevents Members of Congress from compensated representation before governmental agencies in matters in which the United States is interested. For this reason a Member who wishes to continue law practice sometimes resorts to a dual-partnership or "double door" practice. Two law firms are created, one with and one without the Congressional participant. The firm to which the Member belongs takes no cases within the purview of Section 203, but may have a flourishing state and local practice. On the same premises is the firm to which he does not belong and which freely handles the Federal business declined by the other firm because of Section 203.

Although the device appears to be diminishing in use, such dual partnerships have been utilized by several New York City Representatives in recent years, including Representatives Emanuel Celler* (D-N.Y.) and Jacob Gilbert (D-N.Y.) and former Representatives Paul Fino (R-N.Y.) and Abraham J. Multer (R-N.Y.). In other regions the desired result is sometimes achieved by bookkeeping arrangements without ostensibly separate firms. Most practicing Members state that their firms accept no business involving Federal agencies and hence have no need for any sort of dual arrangement.

While the use of two firms allows a Member's partners to accept Federal matters without violating Section 203,[55] the ethics of such arrangements pose a different question. For conflict-of-interest purposes, it is well settled that neither a firm nor any member may accept employment which any member of the firm cannot properly accept. Thus a member of a law firm may not represent a defendant in a criminal case which is prosecuted by another member of the firm.[56] Where one member of a firm was attorney for a drainage district, his partner could not accept employment by a taxpayer who wished to bring a suit which would injuriously affect the district.[57] Nor could a partner of a special master accept employment in a subsequent proceeding in which the master's findings might be questioned, because the master himself would have been disqualified under the prohibition of then Canon 36 against employment in any matter previously acted upon in a judicial capacity.[58]

This principle has been applied in cases of overlapping partnerships

---

* The Celler firm has occasioned adverse press comment, some of which describes in detail the two firms' physical arrangements.[54]

under reasoning which appears to be applicable to dual Congressional partnerships. For instance, a partnership of X and Y once obtained annulment of a marriage on ground of their client's imbecility. Subsequently X and Y ended their relationship, and X formed a new partnership with C. The former client then brought suit to annul a deed on grounds of her imbecility, and the defendant employed X and C, with C actually trying the case. In holding that the prior employment of X and Y barred a subsequent conflicting employment of X and C, the ABA Committee said:

> A firm of which X was a member, having acted for A, in an action to procure relief on the ground of her imbecility, all the members of that firm and of every other firm of which any one of them may become a member are prohibited by *Canon 6* from subsequently accepting employment to maintain that she was not an imbecile at the time of the first suit, or to affect the decree obtained in the first suit adversely to the interest of their client therein. *The relations of partners in a law firm are so close that the firm, and all the members thereof, are barred from accepting any employment, that any one member of the firm is prohibited from taking.*[59] [Emphasis added]

Under this reasoning, individual partners of a Member of Congress and other firms to which they belong should be precluded from any employment forbidden to the Member as a conflict of interest. Federal law supplies the conflict rule which disqualifies the Member, and the legal profession, basing its attitude upon its knowledge of the partnership relation, follows a principle which disqualifies his partners.

It must be admitted, however, that the legal profession has never moved against such dual arrangements of lawyers in Congress. They do not raise the sort of ethical issue which causes aggrieved individuals to file formal complaints with bar associations. Indeed, the only formal ethics opinion on the subject which has come to our attention was favorable to dual partnerships. It was issued in 1964 by the Committee on Professional Ethics of The Association of the Bar of the City of New York as an advisory opinion rendered at the request of a Congressman's law firm. In an earlier 1938 opinion,[60] the same committee had held it to be improper for two firms with overlapping partners to practice from one office because of the danger of confusing and misleading clients as to the responsibilities of the various lawyers involved. This reasoning suggests that all clients of both firms in a double-door arrangement might be led to think they had employed the Member of Congress. Nonetheless the 1964 opinion viewed the Congressman's inability to engage in Federal practice as an "extenuating circumstance" not present in the 1938 case and approved the arrangements.[61]

We do not agree with this ruling and hope it will be reconsidered and overruled in an appropriate proceeding. The ruling considered only the possibility of confusion of clients as a basis of ethical violations and was not concerned with the ethical principle which disqualifies all partners in a firm from any representation which one of them cannot accept. The ethical issue which we have discussed arises not upon the simple fact of holding out a confusing dual arrangement to the public but upon subsequent appearances before Federal agencies by partners of the Member of Congress, a separate substantial issue.

One cause of the professional confusion on the propriety of such dual arrangements is the fact that the controlling principle was not explicitly stated in the pre-1969 Canons of Ethics. The rule of vicarious disqualification of partners developed as one of interpretation in the application of the old skeletal and inadequate rules. The new Code of Professional Responsibility now explicitly contains it. Disciplinary Rule 5–105(D) provides:

> If a lawyer is required to decline employment or to withdraw from employment under DR 5–105, no partner or associate of his or his firm may accept or continue such employment.

Although DR 5–105, the rule referred to as causing the primary disqualification, involves the representation of other clients, secondary disqualification should also occur when the primary disqualification results from an even higher law against divided loyalty—such as the statute forbidding Federal-agency practice by Members of Congress. Although a breach of confidences of another client may not be possible, the intimacy of the law-partner relation is the same in either case, and the interests and disabilities of one partner should be imputed to all others.

114

Whether or not such dual arrangements technically comply with formal rules of ethics, their appearances are damaging to the public, the Congress, and the legal profession. Under the higher-than-marketplace standards which lawyers and Members of Congress should follow, we strongly recommend that those law firms which include Members of Congress who continue to practice for any reason terminate any such dual arrangements and accept no employment forbidden to the Member of Congress.

Recommendation 3B

Partners of a Member of Congress should not accept employment forbidden to him, and dual arrangements used for this purpose should be terminated.

Since a Federal statutory policy is at stake, elimination of dual partnerships should not be left solely to ethical self-limitation by Members and their law partners. The current loophole in Section 203 should be filled by statutory amendment.

The Federal agencies before which a Congressman's partners practice are creatures of Congress. The Member of Congress votes on their appropriations and writes the statutes they administer. Federal officials may be influenced by a Congressman's partner's appearance in much the same way they would be influenced by the Member himself.

To meet the possibility that ethical considerations will not suffice to correct this situation, we recommend an appropriate statutory amendment.

Recommendation 3C

18 U.S.C. §203(a)(1) should be amended to forbid Federal-agency practice by partners of Members of Congress as well as by Members themselves.

COURT APPEARANCES
AGAINST THE UNITED STATES

Both the text and legislative history of Section 203 make it clear that Congress intended to permit its Members to practice in courts, even where interests of the United States were at stake. Although the predecessor to Section 203 was enacted in response to a Congressional scandal (Senator Corwin's prosecuting a fraudulent claim before the Mexican Claims Commission), the legislative response was narrowly tailored to meet the evil which produced it. The rationalization for excluding courts apparently was that non-judicial agencies are susceptible to pressure from individual Members of Congress but that Federal judges are surrounded by protections to assure their independence and would be indifferent to the fact that lawyers appearing before them happen to serve in Congress.[62]

Another law soon came to prohibit Congressmen from practicing before the U.S. Court of Claims,[63] and it could well have been thought that Congressmen were left with no significant areas in which to oppose the Federal government in their law practices. The recent proliferation of Federal administrative agencies whose decisions are judicially enforced in Federal courts has altered this. Fortunately, no major scandals have erupted in this area to produce a demand for appropriate statutory amendment.

In any event, Section 203 deals with only a portion of the problem which produced its original enactment. Ideally, the statute should guard all Federal officers from undue Congressional influence and should equally protect all matters in which the United States is interested. There are always employees of the United States representing the government on the opposite side from the Member, and their vulnerability to Congressional influence is the same in judicial and non-judicial proceedings. Also, it is the duty of a Member of Congress to approach all Federal matters from the public's interest; he should never allow legal fees to put him in the position of representing individual private interests against the government of which he is an officer.

No widespread abuse is claimed to have resulted from the continued omission of courts from Section 203. Political and ethical considerations prevent most lawyer-Congressmen from opposing the government in court for fees, and the recent public record has very few instances to the contrary. One involved former Representative Earl Chudoff of Pennsylvania. His efforts to appear in a United States District Court on behalf of a criminal defendant charged with sending obscene materials through the mails produced an inconclusive suit for mandamus when the Federal District Judge initially refused to permit such representation on grounds that it was forbidden by Section 203.[64]

A more recent instance of a Member practicing in court against a Federal agency occurred in 1964. Senator Sam Ervin (D-N.C.) represented for compensation[65] a North Carolina textile company against the National Labor Relations Board in the United States Supreme Court.[66] Under Section 203, a Senator could not have represented such a client against the General Counsel in proceedings before the Board itself; but when agency procedures ended and judicial enforcement proceedings became necessary, the ban of Section 203 lifted and the Senator was free to oppose the Board in the Federal courts. Senator Ervin subsequently conducted an investigation of the NLRB in hearings conducted by his Judiciary Subcommittee on Separation of Powers.[67]

Section 203 is deficient in several respects, and wholesale revision would be appropriate. We propose amendments to remedy two narrow defects. On a broader scale, it has been called the "bar sinister" of the 1962 statutory recodification that Section 203 was not combined with Section 205, which deals with uncompensated representation, into a single statute on Federal practice by Federal officials.[68] When Congress next revises the laws governing Congressional conflicts of interest, it should examine all of these defects; but, considering Section 203 alone, we recommend, in addition to the previous proposal, that courts be included among the tribunals protected by it. This too can be accomplished very simply.

Recommendation 3D

18 U.S.C. §203 should be amended to provide that Members of Congress may not engage in compensated representation against the United States before courts as well as other agencies and tribunals.

CHAPTER FOUR

CAMPAIGN FINANCING

Campaign financing involves perhaps the most difficult problem in the entire field of Congressional ethics. Although the problem remains unsolved, its existence and the seriousness of it have been well recognized. As Congressman James Wright (D-Tex.) wrote in March 1968, "In the grey area of campaign finance lie the most subtle tendencies to unsavory influence."[1] These "subtle tendencies" were brought into the open by the late Senator Francis Case of South Dakota, who reported that he had been tendered a $2,500 campaign contribution by oil and gas lobbyists to influence his vote on the 1956 natural-gas bill. Rarely is the attempt to influence legislative behavior so transparent. But inevitably a community of interest tends to arise between contributor and candidate which may conflict with the public interest. The successful candidate may tend to identify his own interests with those of the contributor, and the result can be an impairment of independent judgment similar to those created by personal financial interests of the officeholder.

The most fundamental fact about campaign financing is the murkiness of public knowledge of the subject. As one scholar observed,

[T]here is an incredible lack of data, mountains of misinformation, and a large measure of just plain nonsense about congres-

118

sional campaign costs. . . . There are few topics in American politics about which less is actually known than congressional campaign finance. . . . Campaign cost data exist, of course, but they are almost impossible to collect for the record.[2]

The potential of large contributions for corruption of the political and legislative process is aggravated by the secrecy, subtlety, and subterfuge surrounding present campaign-financing practices. Nonetheless, it is a matter of public record that many millions of dollars are contributed to Congressional campaigns. Our grossly inadequate Federal laws on reporting of campaign costs and a scattering of more effective state laws produce enough figures to establish a disturbingly high level of total spending. Candidates in Congressional elections reported 1968 expenditures of $8.5 million to the Clerk of the House and Secretary of the Senate.* A leading expert on campaign costs, Herbert E. Alexander, guesses that the true costs of the 1968 elections may have been as high as $50 million.

PUBLIC FINANCING
OF CONGRESSIONAL CAMPAIGNS

The Rising Level of Campaign Spending

In 1846 friends of Abraham Lincoln gave him $200 to run for Congress. He returned $199.25. His only campaign expense was 75 cents for a barrel of cider. There are still a few seats which involve minimal expense because they are uncontested, but even a $5,000 or $10,000 campaign is rare today. This is especially true in the Senate, where a relatively greater number of seats are contested [3] and all campaigns are statewide.

In 1873 Senator James Harlan of Iowa was censured by a Senate committee, though the entire Senate failed to act, for accepting a campaign contribution of $10,000 from an officer of the Union Pacific

---

* Congressional Quarterly, WEEKLY REPORT, Dec. 5, 1969, at 2433, 2445–2456. One example of the greater effectiveness of state reporting laws is Pennsylvania, where figures filed with the state showed that Senator Richard S. Schweiker (R) spent $664,614 in defeating former Senator Joseph S. Clark, who reported $425,000 in spending. The total reported to the Senate by both candidates was $6,236. *Id.* at 2437.

Railroad—a "corporate creation of Congress, which would probably be again the subject of legislation." [4] The Senate Committee did not spare its language:

> The use of large sums of money to influence either popular or legislative elections strikes directly at the fundamental principle of a republican government. It excludes merit from public place and undermines the public and private virtue upon which alone republican institutions can stand.[5]

Not many persons would be surprised today to learn of a contribution this large. Indeed, many Members of Congress receive sizable contributions from individual executives of corporations which have recurring legislative interests before the Congress.

Another historic contrast with contemporary standards is the 1921 case of Senator Truman H. Newberry. He spent $195,000 in his primary-election campaign and was convicted of violating the Corrupt Practices Act. The conviction was reversed, however, by the United States Supreme Court;[6] and the Senate voted 46 to 41 to seat him. But when a fellow Michigan Senator, who had led the fight to seat him, was defeated in the following election, Senator Newberry announced his resignation, feeling that further service by him in the Senate would be futile.

Five years later, in 1926, two Senators-elect, William S. Vare and Frank L. Smith, were denied their seats by the Senate because of excessive spending. Vare had spent $786,000 in a Pennsylvania race,[7] and Smith, $458,000 in Illinois.[8] These exclusions represent the high-water mark of Congressional discipline for excessive spending.

Senatorial campaigns today in states such as Michigan, Illinois, and Pennsylvania frequently cost more than $1 million. Allowing for the changed value of the dollar, there still can be no doubt that campaign costs have risen greatly in recent years. Nonetheless, campaign spending has not been the subject of a serious election challenge since 1926, and the exclusionary power of Congress is little deterrent, if any, to heavy spending to gain election.

Tables 4.1 and 4.2 are based on our interviews with Members of Congress and show current levels of campaign spending.

The Federal Corrupt Practices Act limits personal spending by candidates to $5,000 in House elections and $25,000 in Senatorial cam-

TABLE 4.1

Amount Spent on Last Campaign (Senate)

SENATE	$100,000 or Less	$100,101– $200,000	More than $200,000
Party			
Democrats (16)	31.3%	31.3%	37.5%
Republicans (7)	28.6	28.6	42.9
Seniority			
Senior* (12)	33.3	33.3	33.3
Junior (11)	27.3	27.3	45.5
Population of Home State			
Over 5 million (4)	25.0		75.0
Under 5 million (19)	31.6	36.8	31.6
Region			
West (9)	33.3	22.2	44.4
Midwest (5)		40.0	60.0
South (6)	33.3	16.7	50.0
East (3)	66.7		33.3
Total (23)	(30.4)	(30.4)	(39.1)

* In this and the other tables in this chapter, Senators whose present service commenced prior to April 1957 are classified as senior. Representatives elected to five or more terms (including the 90th Congress) are classified as senior.

paigns.[9] But such major items of expense as travel, stationery, postage, most printing costs, distribution of letters and circulars, and telephone costs are excluded from the limitations. Even with these exclusions, the amounts have come to be too low as permissible figures for total spending and are unrealistic for today's typical media-oriented campaign. In other words, the economic necessities of present campaigning for Congress invite evasion and circumvention of the law. Conveniently for candidates, these figures are not the effective limits. Unlimited totals may be spent by collections of committees which act in behalf of a candidate but are organized ostensibly "without his knowledge and consent," and unlimited individual contributions to a campaign may be made by giving to numerous committees. The law does not restrict the number of committees that may be formed in behalf of a candidate and is inapplicable to committees organized within a single state.

The legislative purposes of the Corrupt Practices Act—to prevent

TABLE 4.2

Amount Spent on Last Campaign (House)

HOUSE	$30,000 or Less	$30,001– $60,000	More than $60,000
Party			
Democrats (50)	50.0%	34.0%	16.0%
Republicans (41)	48.8	36.6	14.6
Seniority			
Senior* (49)	69.4	22.4	8.2
Junior (42)	26.2	50.0	23.8
Type of District			
Large Metropolitan Area* (16)	50.0	25.0	25.0
Other City (29)	44.8	41.4	13.8
Rural (46)	52.2	34.8	13.0
Region			
West (14)	35.7	42.9	21.4
Midwest (25)	64.0	32.0	4.0
South (24)	33.3	41.7	25.0
East (28)	57.1	28.6	14.3
Total (91)	(49.4)	(35.2)	(15.4)

* In this and subsequent tables in this chapter, "Large Metropolitan Area" is defined as comprising more than three Congressional districts.

the concentration of undue influence in the hands of a few large contributors, as well as to impose campaign-fund restrictions—have been evaded and ignored virtually from the outset. This prompted President Johnson to refer to the Corrupt Practices Act as "more loophole than law." [10]

A leading authority in the field of campaign financing, Alexander Heard, believes that dollar limits on spending are unenforceable.[11] Since costs continue to rise, any limit, however generous, must soon become obsolete and invite circumvention. In the heat of a campaign, candidates are likely to spend whatever sums they think are necessary to win election, if they are able to raise such amounts.[12]

Campaign costs are impossible to stabilize. The cost of postage alone has doubled since 1958. Postage for one letter to each of the 200,000 adult citizens in an average Congressional district is $12,000, to which must be added the costs of stationery, duplication, and addressing. The mushrooming costs of campaigning are also attributable to large outlays for travel, the growing use of public-relations firms, and, most importantly, increased reliance on expensive broadcasting. In 1960 then-Senator John F. Kennedy said of television costs:

> If all candidates and parties are to have equal access to this essential and decisive campaign medium, without becoming deeply obligated to the big financial contributors from the worlds of business, labor or other major lobbies, then the time has come when a solution must be found to this problem of TV costs.[13]

Candidates find it convenient, efficient, and often essential to use television. While large audiences may not choose to watch programs denominated as political, they are compelled to watch spot announcements of one minute or less worked into their favorite entertainment programs. These "spots" can be very costly, although it is generally acknowledged that they are not very informative. Between 1962 and 1966 the amount of money invested in spot announcements increased by 85 percent. Six times as much money in 1966 was spent on spots as on program time.[14]

In the view of one observer, the high costs of television may disqualify poor candidates from the start.[15] He observed that television "has created an entirely new syndrome of campaign costs" and explained that because of television, larger sums are now spent on "advertising firms, opinion surveys, film and video tape productions, and —recently—computers." [16]

Under present law, candidates, poor or rich, can themselves bear as much of the costs of their own campaigns as they care to, subject to the partial legal limits already mentioned. However, the astronomically high expenses of modern campaigns compel candidates to depend on other sources. Representative Wright has written of numerous instances of individuals who sought public office unsuccessfully and thereafter spent years retiring their debts.[17] This could mean that financially disadvantaged candidates are tempted to make compromising arrangements for campaign funds in order to gain public office.

Campaign costs often are underwritten by representatives of special interests. This may take the form of a large cocktail party or other fund-raising event to which representatives of trade associations buy $10, $25, $50, or $100 tickets to support candidates with whom they share a community of interest. Special interests have been involved in campaign politics in more notorious ways. Recent newspaper and magazine articles have, for example, detailed the extensive involvement of the maritime industry and maritime unions in support of many political candidates.[18] Shipbuilding and operating subsidies now total $400 million annually. The relevant Congressional committees are manned by Members who represent ports and shipbuilding centers and who receive generous campaign support from the maritime industry and unions.

The generous political spending of the Seafarers' Union has been widely reported. Among the principal beneficiaries of this spending have been influential members of committees with jurisdiction over maritime interests. One source indicates that 72 cents of every dollar earned by seamen on an American subsidized ship is paid by the taxpayers.[19] It has been charged that the intimate relationship between the maritime community and Congress has led to inadequate Federal regulation of the industry, resulting in maladministration and deterioration of the maritime fleet.[20]

Another frequently mentioned example of heavy union financing of campaigns is the Steamfitters' Union. It was reported recently that a 1,200-member Midwestern unit of this union paid out at least $1,082,761 through its political arm to candidates for Federal, state, and local office between 1963 and 1966. Among the recipients were 32 candidates for Congress.[21]

In our interviews Members asserted that communities of interest exist between particular Members and the oil industry, the tobacco industry,[22] and the medical profession. In 1954 a Federal nickel contract was awarded to a company whose officers increased their contribution to the party in power from an average of $636 per year in the seven previous years to $7,500 in 1954.[23] A recent NEW YORK TIMES story indicated that a brokerage firm channeled contributions up to $5,000 to a number of Members whose committee responsibilities touched on the interests of the firm. One recipient of such a contribution ran unopposed.[24]

Rationale for Public Financing
of Congressional Campaigns

The present system of financing campaigns exclusively from private funds works against the public interest in two important ways. First,

candidates without personal wealth frequently must rely on large contributors, a fact which may tend to foster compromising obligations.
Contributors have understandable expectations which officeholders
may try to evade, but evasion is difficult because an appreciative
officeholder is constrained at least to grant access to generous contributors.

In our staff interviews with Members of Congress and in the 1967
Senate debates on Senator Russell Long's (D-La.) "Presidential Election Campaign Fund Act," the general view that campaign money
buys influence was frequently affirmed. Officeholders should neither
be subject to undue influence nor be tainted by its appearance. The
actual or apparent impairment of independent judgment is similar to
that caused by conflicts of interest, and the public confidence suffers
comparably.

Second, candidates have unequal access to public office because of
unequal access to campaign funds. A man should not have to mortgage his home and spend his savings to seek public office effectively.
Many capable men are prevented from seeking office by the realities
of political fund-raising.

In 1967 President Johnson, in a message to Congress, recognized
the inherent threat to legislative integrity in the present system and
said of campaign financing:

> I believe that our ultimate goal should be to finance the total
> expense for this vital function of our democracy with public
> funds, and to prohibit the use or acceptance of money from pri-
> vate sources.[25]
>
> Competitive elections are essential to our political life and to the
> legitimate exercise of government power by officeholders. The financ-
> ing of such elections serves a public purpose of the highest order in a
> democratic system. The use of public funds for such purposes is easily
> justified.[26]

In the 90th Congress, the Senate Finance Committee held extensive hearings on the proposed Honest Elections Act of 1967, which
provided for public subsidies of Presidential and Senatorial general-
election campaigns. The amount of public funds required if this bill
were extended to cover elections to the House also would total approximately $100 million.[27] This stands in ratio of 1:6,000 when com-

pared with total government spending at current levels for a two-year period; in terms of the gross national product the ratio is 1:18,000. It about equals the estimated cost of one supersonic transport; it is half the 1969 Federal subsidy for merchant-ship construction, and one fourth the total support for the maritime industry. Subsidized biennial elections under this scheme could take place for the next 100 years at a cost of less than the Space Agency's budget for 1968.

Support for a Public Subsidy

Two of President Johnson's predecessors proposed a Federal campaign subsidy before he did. President Theodore Roosevelt proposed government subsidies of political campaigns in 1907. Under his plan, the amount of the fund would be determined by multiplying the number of voters by 10 cents. A special Congressional committee in 1936 proposed payments from the public Treasury to subsidize campaigns.[28] As practical a politician as former President Truman also lent support to the public-subsidy proposal.[29] Japan and France are among the foreign countries with one type of subsidy or another; in France the government pays for television, printing, postage, gasoline, and bill-posting.[30] In Puerto Rico political parties are partly financed by government subsidy.*

In 1956 the late Senator Richard L. Neuberger proposed legislation for a sizable Federal government subsidy to the national committee of each major party to support the campaigns of Federal candidates.[31] Senator Neuberger stated that his plan would discourage fraud in elections, lessen the dependence of candidates on interested contributors, and equalize candidates' access to communications media.[32]

The public-subsidy plan has received support from Representative Wright, who says that his modest means twice prevented him from running for the Senate in Texas because he was not personally suited for the role of "[meeting] with affluent individuals . . . to discuss what [he] could do for them." [33]

The "drinking at the public trough" argument against subsidies has been anticipated by Representative Morris K. Udall (D-Ariz.), who said:

---

* The main problem with the Puerto Rican law is that the fund has been too small to be of much use. See H. Wells & R. Anderson, GOVERNMENT FINANCING OF POLITICAL PARTIES IN PUERTO RICO: A SUPPLEMENT TO STUDY NUMBER FOUR (Citizens' Research Foundation, 1966).

[T]he public already pays—and it is a staggering price, in terms of legislative and administrative actions that serve the interests of big contributors and lobbyists.[34]

The public now pays for the many official and semi-official resources available to incumbents which may be used for political purposes. Among these resources, discussed more fully in Chapters 1 and 5, are: the frank, used to send out press releases, newsletters, and speeches; service to constituents through case work; radio and television tapes produced in the subsidized House and Senate studios and used to inform one's constituents; and Congressional staffs.

Of the Members of Congress interviewed who expressed any opinion on public subsidies, Members of the House were opposed to it by about 3 to 1. Since a public subsidy would undermine the incumbent's normal advantages of visibility, recognition, and ability to attract private campaign funds, this opposition is understandable. However, the number of Senators who favored public financing of campaigns equaled those who opposed it. This suggests that in addition to being persuaded of the merits of a subsidy, Senators find the problem of fund-raising so massive that many would support a public subsidy and take their chances on the aid it might give to their opponents. A subsidy would also spare them the burden, anxieties, and potential conflicts of interest inherent in private campaign financing.

How Much Subsidy?

Ideally, any public subsidy should be large enough to make private contributions unnecessary. Achieving the goal of effectively reducing private contributions depends partly upon the marginal utility of privately raised dollars—viz., the return in political value from each dollar spent above those provided by the subsidy. There is presumably a point of diminishing returns for election spending as for other spending. At some point dollars spent yield so low a return that such spending will be thought wasteful or even damaging. It may produce undesirable obligations or embarrassment, or bore or annoy the electorate. If campaign spending had been fully reported and disclosed over the last several years, a more accurate estimate could be calculated and the public subsidy pegged to that level, making due allowance for rising costs. But wherever the additional spending is considered politically valuable by candidates and campaign managers, any attempt to totally prohibit private spending is likely to be evaded.

Consultations with advertising agents, media time-buyers, and professional campaign consultants* persuade us that the advertising industry already possesses sufficient skill to predict fairly accurately how much it costs to publicize a candidate in a given area to the point where most voters are aware of his candidacy. The estimates of media experts tend to show that the costs of such advertising are within the range of politically feasible public financing.

Even if the subsidy were not high enough to discourage private spending, such spending probably would be reduced because solicitors of private funds would be hard pressed to convince many donors that their contributions were necessary and would be well spent. In any case, a subsidy designed to cover the key expenses needed to put a campaign before the public, such as media, travel, and postage, would help the candidate of modest means to hold to a minimum his obligations to interested contributors.

Alternatives to a Direct Subsidy

The direct-subsidy plan has only recently been seriously explored. Another form of public subsidy, however, has engendered broad support. It uses tax incentives for political contributions to divert public funds to political campaigns. The principal incentives suggested are a tax credit, under which taxpayers would receive a small credit against Federal income taxes for political contributions † (proposed limits range from $5 to $50), and a tax deduction, which would allow deductions from taxable income (proposed limits range from $100 to $1,000). The President's Commission on Campaign Costs, chaired by Alexander Heard, recommended in 1962 that individuals be given either a credit of 50 percent of contributions up to $10 or a deduction

* These consultants, who all had several years of experience in media advertising, assisted our staff in learning about the vagaries of political-broadcasting policy and practice.

† In the debates on the Tax Reform Act of 1969 (H.R. 13270) the Senate tabled by a 50–45 vote an amendment offered by Senator Edward M. Kennedy (D-Mass.) which would have allowed a tax credit of one half of a taxpayer's political contributions to all candidates up to a maximum credit of $25. 115 CONG. REC. S16237 (daily ed. Dec. 9, 1969). A similar proposal by Senator Howard W. Cannon (D-Nev.), limited to contributions to candidates for Federal political office, was tabled by a 55–26 vote. 115 CONG. REC. S16399 (daily ed. Dec. 10, 1969).

128

for contributions up to $1,000. The approach was apparently a compromise between Republican suggestions for a deduction alone and labor-union proposals for a tax credit alone. President Kennedy sent bills to Congress incorporating these provisions, except that the maximum deduction was set at $500 per year.[35] The only contributions eligible for benefits under the Heard Commission's recommendations would be those made to national committees of parties whose Presidential candidates got on the ballot in 10 or more states, or to a single political committee in each state designated by such national committees.

Senator Howard W. Cannon (D-Nev.), Chairman of the Privileges and Elections Subcommittee of the Senate Rules Committee, reintroduced in the 91st Congress the substance of the proposed Election Reform Act of 1967,* adding a new provision for a tax credit of up to $20 or a deduction of up to $100.[36]

The amount and direction of the subsidy resulting from tax incentives is determined by citizens according to their voluntary contributions.† Tax incentives might broaden public participation, and if sufficient money were generated, candidates' dependence on large contributions would probably be reduced. It would be a wholesome result if such government encouragement caused small and moderate contributors to bear the bulk of the costs of Federal elections.

This Committee prefers a direct subsidy to that which would result from tax incentives, primarily because such devices would be complex and administratively expensive without necessarily increasing the amounts of money available to candidates. Tax incentives might mean only that the government would share in providing money at the level now contributed and that tax windfalls would come to those who now contribute. The possibility that new political giving would be greatly stimulated by tax incentives is thought by Treasury officials to be very doubtful.[37] Candidates could not know in advance what new funds would flow from tax incentives and would undoubtedly still seek contributions from previous sources at the same levels.

The level of funds that incentives would generate is speculative at best. Senator James B. Pearson (R-Kans.) presented figures in the

* The provisions of this bill are discussed below at p. 149.
† Alexander Heard notes, however, that if contributions only to *Federal* candidates entitled the contributor to a tax benefit, local candidates would be placed at a fund-raising disadvantage.

CONGRESSIONAL RECORD on the growth of small contributors which led him to believe that a $500 deduction and a $10 credit would motivate a quarter to a third of all Americans to contribute a maximum of $190 million[38] for political campaigns, but we doubt that the figure would approach this level. The Teamsters' legislative director, testifying at the Senate Finance Committee hearings, said he did not believe that the average workingman would contribute anything, notwithstanding any tax credit.[39] Moreover, lower-income contributors generally lack sophistication about tax options. Others might falsely claim the credit. And enforcement would be both difficult and costly. Concern has also been expressed about erosion of the tax system:[40] Credits might open the door to similar treatment for other socially desirable programs.

The deduction has less to recommend it than the credit, since it disproportionately favors those at higher income levels and is unlikely to broaden the base to include non-wealthy givers. Herbert Alexander reports that five states—Minnesota, Hawaii, Missouri, Arkansas, and California—have experimented with allowing tax deductions for political contributions.[41] None has reported much success thus far in expanding the volume of political giving.

A final argument against both the credit and the deduction is that 25 to 30 percent of American voters do not pay income taxes, and no tax incentive will increase their involvement in campaign financing. The only practical way to involve the public as a whole is by subsidy from public funds. Such spending is for the general welfare, and all citizens should share in it.

Other proposals for indirect public financing include "matching funds" plans and Senator Lee Metcalf's (D-Mont.) "voucher" plan. Under the matching-funds plan, individual contributions up to a small amount, probably $5 or $10, would be matched by an equal amount from the U.S. Treasury. The Treasury would presumably disburse matching funds upon presentation by candidates or their representatives of some receipt or certificate verifying the private contributions.

The plan has these virtues: Each matched contribution is increased by 100 percent, ensuring more money to candidates than tax incentives can guarantee. If, for example, $200 million is contributed to political campaigns, a tax incentive could cost the government $20 to

$30 million in tax revenue with no benefit whatever to the candidates. Under the matching plan, however, this same $20 to $30 million would be paid to candidates as additional funds. According to Treasury officials, problems of false claims could more easily be handled under the matching plan because only committees and candidates need be policed, not taxpayers as well.

Critics of the matching-funds plan, on the other hand, argue that the plan invites abuse and fraud. Opponents also claim that the plan would involve many people and much paperwork, which would reduce its economic utility. Finally, the plan may place too great a premium on skill in fund-solicitation by parties and candidates. The likelihood that the small contributor would be stimulated to give because his contribution would be doubled is not great. Nonetheless, if Congress rejects a public subsidy, this matching-funds plan seems preferable to other public-financing proposals. It would broaden the base of political contributions, make some public money available to candidates, and reduce candidates' dependence on large contributors.

Under Senator Metcalf's voucher proposal[42] every taxpayer would receive contribution vouchers redeemable by the Treasury. Each voucher would be worth $1, and the taxpayer would receive a voucher every second year which he could donate to a Congressional campaign, and an additional voucher every fourth year for a Presidential campaign.

This plan appears likely at least to broaden the base of political contributions. The costs of administration, however, would probably be high. If costs were reduced by distributing vouchers with tax materials, many vouchers might be lost or forgotten between January and the campaign season. It seems preferable to put the money directly into campaigns through a public subsidy, particularly since the main purpose is to make untainted funds available to political candidates rather than simply to increase citizen participation in the electoral process.

Some Congressional critics of the plan noted also that vouchers would have to be returned to candidates long before the election to be of much use to the candidates, and donors may not decide whom to support so early in the campaign.

If all of these public-financing proposals are viewed side by side, the direct Federal subsidy seems preferable to the other choices. It is the one most capable of coping adequately with the ever rising costs of campaigning.

The most vigorous opposition to the Federal subsidy is based not on its cost but rather on an assumed American tradition of voluntarism. Otherwise untraditional Members sometimes defend this tradition on the theory that an officeholder is more likely to be responsive to public wants and needs if he must appeal to his electorate for money as well as for votes. Others see a man's fund-raising ability as a measure of public approbation. The main difficulty with the traditional method, however, is that it has not met, nor does it seem likely to meet, the problem of making adequate and untainted funds available to candidates for public office.

A small proportion of the American people now contributes to campaigns. None of the plans for broadening the base is likely to increase this percentage more than marginally, and even at that, the administrative cost of doing so is likely to be very considerable.

Voluntarism has been used as a slogan to conceal the troublesome problem of candidates' dependence on specially motivated contributors. Voluntarism has allowed ethically ambiguous relationships with such contributors to flourish, giving rise to the conflicts of interest which are at the core of this Committee's concern. Without some public intervention, candidates will continue to be dependent on voluntary contributions from the interested few.

Increased awareness of the merits of candidates and election issues can come about not primarily through campaign contributions to a candidate but rather through exposure to him on television, in his campaign literature, and in his personal appearances. It is toward these avenues of communication that the public subsidy is directed.

Some contend that if public subsidies are allocated to candidates directly, party cohesion will be undermined since candidates will be less dependent on parties for funds. There is no doubt that candidates would be less dependent on parties for funds if they received a direct public subsidy. But there are other motivations for party organization and party loyalty, of which probably the most important is mutual self-help among candidates and officeholders from the same party. Candidates and their friends today are generally responsible for raising their own funds. The era of the party machine seems to be passing, and if anything, there is a trend toward identification with individual candidates rather than with parties. Television and other modern campaign techniques are undermining party organization by stressing the individual candidate and his views.

Some have suggested that the subsidy be granted to parties rather than candidates. If public money were granted to party officials for distribution by them, parties might well develop a more cohesive operational structure, but the cost in independence of individual officeholders would be too great.

The Honest Elections Act of 1967 as a Model for a Direct Subsidy

The Honest Elections Act of 1967 was the first legislative proposal for a direct Congressional campaign subsidy to be voted out of a Congressional committee. The bill was favorably reported by the Senate Finance Committee on September 14, 1967, by a 10-to-7 vote. It never reached the floor of the Senate, nor was it the subject of hearings in the House. Extensive hearings, however, were held in the Senate, and on the basis of the expertise thereby accumulated by the Senate Finance Committee, the broad outlines of the bill can be accepted as a starting point for advancing our subsidy proposal.

The Honest Elections Act of 1967 is a revised and considerably improved substitute for the Presidential Election Campaign Fund Act of 1966.[43] The latter measure originated as an amendment to the so-called "Christmas Tree Bill," thus known because of the unexpected tax gifts which flowed from it; attached by Senator Russell Long as a rider to a tax bill, it was accepted in the adjournment rush by House-Senate conferees. Under the plan, taxpayers could choose each year to have $1 of their income tax allocated for expenses of the next Presidential campaign. Contributions were to be divided evenly between the two major parties, and each national party could have received a campaign fund as large as $30 million for the 1968 Presidential election.

Senator Albert Gore (D-Tenn.) led the successful fight to suspend this Act at the start of the 90th Congress. The measure was objected to on various grounds: It placed "too much power in the hands of the national political leaders who would distribute the funds," permitted "commingling of public funds with private contributions," "hindered the development of third parties," "provided no guidelines on how the money could be spent," and "violated the American tradition of voluntarism." [44]

Whatever its shortcomings, Long's original proposal reshaped administration and Congressional thinking on campaign financing. As indicated earlier, President Johnson identified himself strongly with the Federal subsidy in his Message to Congress entitled "The Political Process in America." [45]

In spite of his opposition to the Presidential Election Campaign Fund Act, Senator Gore became a staunch advocate of public financing of campaigns. He joined Senator Long in co-sponsoring the subsidy proposal which was to replace the 1966 Act.[46] The new bill extended public subsidies to U.S. Senatorial candidates,[47] relying on direct appropriation rather than a tax check-off. It made funds available to candidates directly, set minimum guidelines for using the subsidy, and adopted other electoral reforms. The Republican members of the Finance Committee opposed the bill,[48] citing most of the same objections that had been raised against the earlier measure. In addition, they noted the program's expense,[49] and its failure to cover primary elections.

These objections seem unpersuasive, particularly in the face of the strong public purpose served by public financing. We have already dealt with objections based on voluntarism. "Commingling of private and public funds," while conjuring up an image of abrogation of fiduciary obligation, is actually nothing more sinister than raising and spending all lawfully collected funds.

In drafting their bill, Senators Gore and Long attempted to protect minority parties. Under the proposed Honest Elections Act, minor parties—those receiving 5 percent of the vote in either the previous election or the current election—receive twice as much per vote as do the major parties. If the minor party's subsidy is determined by the current election, reimbursement obviously must await the outcome.

For political considerations, the authors of the Honest Elections Act preferred that the question of subsidies for Representatives' races be left to the House. The subsidy should be extended to include candidates for the House as well as the Senate. Primaries present very difficult problems involving candidate eligibility and party politics. There is no doubt, however, that in many situations winning the primary is equivalent to winning the general election. If the subsidy should prove workable for general elections, perhaps at some future time a method of primary subsidy could be devised.

One feature of the bill—the public/private option—seems to have dubious justification and ought to be eliminated. Under this provision, each eligible candidate chooses either to accept the public subsidy and forgo all private contributions for 60 days preceding the general election and 30 days following it, or to forgo the public subsidy and rely totally on private funds, which he could raise without restriction. The 90-day limitation seems to invite evasion. The whole public/private option seems to be tenuous, and, accordingly, it would seem more desirable for every candidate to be entitled to the public subsidy as a "floor" with which to commence his campaign.

We propose that if a public subsidy is enacted, there should also be enacted a $1,000 limitation on individual political contributions to, or for the benefit of, any candidate. With full public disclosure, contributions and spending from private sources should be automatically and substantially reduced. There are also other reasons for believing that the level of private contributions would be reduced and that total spending levels would not be substantially increased. First, most candidates have a real interest in being independent of large money-givers and in being relieved of some of the pressures of campaign fund-raising. Many do not now raise all they can from private sources. Some candidates turn down what they regard as tainted contributions, and others refuse to accept contributions above a certain amount. Many regard heavy campaign spending as politically distasteful and even harmful. Second, since candidates' needs for funds would be reduced, the incentive to contribute and to approach specially interested contributors should be correspondingly reduced. Finally, as we have already noted, there is a point of diminishing returns in campaign spending beyond which additional spending is inefficient or wasteful.

One objective of the public subsidy is to enable all candidates to wage an adequate, competitive campaign. In most campaign situations a large guaranteed amount with which to start would enable candidates to contract for space and time in the media and plan and organize their campaigns in a rational way. The subsidy should be high enough for most candidates to run without private financing if they so choose.

135

A full public subsidy, coupled with a prohibition on private fundraising and spending by the candidate,[50] does not seem practical or politically feasible at this time. Campaign situations vary widely. There will always be some candidates who will not need the full amount of a subsidy and should, of course, turn back any excess. However, a subsidy adequate for every Congressional race would be too large for many of them. Any further limitation on private financing should await accumulation of data indicating the actual spending needs of candidates. The contemplated Federal Elections Commission* would undertake serious and constant review of election finance, which should yield these data; and on that basis the public subsidy could in later years be fixed at a level which would enable private spending to be further reduced. It is most important at this time to take the initial steps toward public financing and to modify afterward with the benefit of experience.

Table 4.3 shows the amounts which would have been available to each major-party candidate, assuming there was a Senatorial election in each state in 1968, under the Honest Elections Act of 1967. Subsidies for House candidates could follow a similar formula. In the course of hearings on the merits of the direct subsidy to candidates, the subject could be more fully explored and more appropriate formulas might be developed.

The public-subsidy scheme could be administered by the Federal Elections Commission, the new agency which would be brought into being under the set of election-reform proposals discussed later in this chapter.

Recommendation 4A

Congress should provide by statute for direct public subsidy of all general election campaigns for seats in the House and Senate along the lines of the public subsidy approved by the Senate Finance Committee in 1967. Such enactment should be accompanied by a reduction to $1,000 of the limitation on individual contributions to, or for the benefit of, any candidate.

A Postage-Free Mailing for All Candidates

It is generally acknowledged that one of the principal advantages of incumbency is the use of the frank.[51] Although Members are not per-

---

* See pp. 150, 277–79 below.

TABLE 4.3

Application of Subsidy Formula for Senatorial Candidates*

State	Payment	State	Payment
Alabama	$251,000	Montana	$128,000
Alaska	100,000	Nebraska	207,000
Arizona	186,000	Nevada	100,000
Arkansas	202,000	New Hampshire	130,000
California	1,500,000	New Jersey	659,000
Colorado	245,000	New Mexico	145,000
Connecticut	334,000	New York	1,523,000
Delaware	100,000	North Carolina	375,000
Florida	461,000	North Dakota	121,000
Georgia	318,000	Ohio	884,000
Hawaii	103,000	Oklahoma	276,000
Idaho	132,000	Oregon	247,000
Illinois	1,031,000	Pennsylvania	1,054,000
Indiana	508,000	Rhode Island	167,000
Iowa	327,000	South Carolina	195,000
Kansas	262,000	South Dakota	133,000
Kentucky	299,000	Tennessee	319,000
Louisiana	269,000	Texas	615,000
Maine	163,000	Utah	170,000
Maryland	313,000	Vermont	100,000
Massachusetts	559,000	Virginia	298,000
Michigan	731,000	Washington	342,000
Minnesota	401,000	West Virginia	248,000
Mississippi	172,000	Wisconsin	428,000
Missouri	454,000	Wyoming	100,000

* Table adapted from Congressional Quarterly, WEEKLY REPORT, September 22, 1967, at 1856, citing Senate Finance Committee. Amounts were rounded to the nearest $1,000 and computed on the basis of votes cast in Senatorial elections in 1964 and 1966.

A "major party" is defined as one whose Senatorial candidate in either of the two preceding Senatorial elections in the state received at least 25 percent of the total vote for the office; a "minor party" would have received between 5 percent and 25 percent; and any other candidate would have to receive at least 5 percent in the current election in order to qualify.

Federal payments to Senatorial candidates would be based on population differences in the various states. Generally, the cost to the government would be somewhat more than 20 cents per vote cast for Federally financed candidates. Based on the number of votes received by all Senatorial candidates in whichever of the two preceding Senatorial elections produced the largest vote, a Senatorial candidate of a major party would be eligible to receive a Federal payment of 50 cents per vote for the first 200,000 votes, 35 cents per vote for the next 200,000 votes, and 20 cents per vote for each additional vote, with a minimum of $100,000. A Senatorial candidate of a minor party would be eligible to receive a Federal payment of $1 per vote for the first 100,000 votes, 70 cents per vote for the next 100,000 votes,

mitted to use the frank for mailing campaign literature, in practice this is not much of a barrier. Until the few weeks before Election Day a Congressman can, with impunity and usually without criticism from colleagues or constituents, send a virtually unlimited amount of franked mailings to his constituents. With such a strong advantage ranked opposite him, the newcomer needs all the help he can get to present his case to the electorate.

To reduce the disadvantage of non-incumbent candidates who have no costless way of reaching the voters, we propose that each candidate for Congress be entitled to at least one mailing to every voter at public expense in both primary and general elections. This scheme is in force in Great Britain, where each candidate for office is allowed one free mailing of up to two ounces of informational literature.[52] State law on ballot qualification would determine a candidate's entitlement to the mailing. The relatively modest costs that the government would assume are justified in terms of the benefits of a better-informed citizenry and a reduced disadvantage among non-incumbent candidates competing against incumbents.[53]

A free mailing could easily be put into effect. Representative Jonathan Bingham (D-N.Y.) has pointed out that Members-elect are given franked envelopes carrying the designation "Member-elect." Candidates for Congress could be given franked envelopes similarly identified.

Recommendation 4B

Title 39 of the U.S. Code, §416, should be amended to add: "B. Every legally qualified and nominated candidate for Congress may send through the mails, postage free, one letter or printed matter not to exceed 2 ounces in weight, contained in one envelope, to every registered voter in his state or district, within 30 days preceding the date of his primary and/or general election."

---

and 40 cents per vote for each additional vote. This same scale of payments based on a current election applies also to a Senatorial candidate of a party which did not receive enough votes in the preceding elections to qualify as a minor party, but which does receive the requisite 5 percent of the vote in the current election.

Reducing the Costs
of Political Broadcasting

The sharp rise in campaign costs during the past decade is due more to television than to any other single factor. How to deal with this is one of the most vexing public issues of the day. A variety of remedies has been put forward, but none has been adopted by Congress, the Federal Communications Commission, or the broadcasting industry, except for the network-sponsored Great Debates between the 1960 Presidential candidates. Financing of political broadcasting is probably the thorniest problem in the whole area of campaign costs.

It is often argued that the public franchise given broadcasters justifies requiring them to offer candidates free broadcast time.[54] This overlooks the fact that licensees incur risks as well as benefits and does not justify requiring broadcasters to sustain the full burden of subsidizing a worthwhile public function.

At the same time, private enterprise—especially when using public resources under licenses[55]—should not be in a position to profit unduly by meeting the public's need for information about political candidates and issues. Public subsidies could funnel more money to broadcasters than ever before and would make it all the more appropriate that political broadcasting rates be reduced.

At present, broadcasters, licensed to serve "the public convenience, interest, [and] necessity," [56] are under no requirement to accord any air time to the political process. They may sell, give, or withhold access as they please, subject only to the requirement of Section 315 of the Federal Communications Act and the Fairness Doctrine. Section 315, generally known as the equal-time provision, requires that if a broadcaster gives or sells air time to one candidate, he must afford equal opportunities to competing candidates to use or buy equivalent air time.[57] The Fairness Doctrine requires broadcasters "to afford reasonable opportunity for the discussion of conflicting views on issues of public importance." [58] Opposing views must be presented at the broadcaster's own expense and initiative if other sponsorship is unavailable.[59]

An appreciable amount of free time for campaign appearances is now provided by some television-station owners. FCC figures show, however, that in the primary and general elections of 1966 four times as much television time was bought by candidates and their supporters as was provided free of charge to them.[60] In our interview program a majority of Senators reported heavy purchases of television time, and all junior Senators but one reported heavy use. Nearly half of the senior Senators, however, got by on only "some" TV use. Other variables are also shown in Table 4.4, but in several cases the numbers are too small for meaningful generalizations.

TABLE 4.4

Use of Television in Last Campaign (Senate)

SENATE	Heavy* TV	Some* TV	No TV
Seniority			
Senior (11)	54.5%	36.4%	9.1%
Junior (11)	90.9		9.1
Population of Home State			
Over 5 mill. (3)	66.7		33.3
Under 5 million (19)	73.7	21.1	5.3
Region			
West (9)	88.9	11.1	
Midwest (5)	80.0	20.0	
South (5)	60.0	20.0	20.0
East (3)	33.3	33.3	33.3
Cost of Campaign			
$0–$100,000 (7)	28.6	42.8	28.6
$100,001–$200,000 (7)	85.7	14.3	
$200,001 or more (8)	100.0		
Total (22)	(72.7)	(18.2)	(9.1)

*These are relative terms based on interview responses. A Member who indicated, for example, that he spent more than half his campaign funds on paid television time was classified as a "heavy" user of TV.

Only one fourth of Representatives interviewed reported heavy use of television in their most recent campaign. Almost half reported no use of TV at all. Senior Members used less television than junior Members, but the discrepancy is not wide. Many junior Members come from large cities where television use is uneconomical because their constituents account for only a fraction of the total viewing audience. Table 4.5 shows clearly that virtually no Member from a large metropolitan area resorted to television, whereas the majority of other Members used TV to some extent. Most Eastern Representatives used no television, but that is a function of the urban character of their districts, not geography.

TABLE 4.5

Use of Television in Last Campaign (House)

HOUSE	*Heavy TV*	*Some TV*	*No TV*
Seniority			
Senior (52)	19.2%	30.8%	50.0%
Junior (42)	33.3	23.8	42.9
Type of District			
Large metropolitan area (17)	5.9	11.8	82.4
Other city (29)	27.6	24.1	48.2
Rural (48)	31.3	35.4	33.3
Region			
West (13)	38.5	15.4	46.2
Midwest (28)	25.0	32.1	42.9
South (24)	41.7	37.5	20.8
East (29)	6.9	20.7	72.4
Cost of Campaign			
$0–$30,000 (45)	13.3	24.4	62.2
$30,001–$60,000 (32)	34.4	25.0	40.6
$60,001 or more (13)	53.8	30.8	15.4
Total (94)*	(25.5)	(27.7)	(46.8)

* Four respondents for whom campaign expense figures were unavailable are not included in the campaign cost section.

The law applicable to political buyers of television time, as promulgated and interpreted by the FCC,[61] attempts to require that TV stations charge political customers no more than they charge commercial customers. The FCC does not presently go into media economics, and it might raise a political storm if the Commission changed this policy. According to FCC Commissioner Nicholas Johnson, "The FCC has never imposed any regulation which interfered with a broadcaster's ability to make the maximum profit." [62] The Commission is not concerned with stations' diverse rate structures. Consequently, there are both local rates and national rates. Some stations give volume discounts for conglomerations of commercial products but not for comparable groups of political candidates who pool resources.[63] All this is beyond the scope of the FCC's present scope of inquiry.

The relations between broadcasters and political candidates vary all the way from deep suspicion to intimacy and mutual support. Broadcasters are fearful that Congress may someday limit their profits, and Congressmen are fearful that somehow they will incur the displeasure of broadcasters and lose favorable publicity advantages. A broadcaster can have considerable power over individual Congressmen. He might treat a Congressman's every utterance as newsworthy or he might find ways to favorably publicize his opponent. The broadcaster may even own the local newspaper as well [64] and may or may not support the Members' re-election with either organ.

Relationships between broadcasters and Congressmen can be as troublesome as those between Members and their campaign contributors, as illustrated by the following instance cited by news correspondent Robert MacNeil:

> [I]n June, 1967, WNBC-TV, NBC's New York station, gave a dinner party in Washington for Congressmen from the New York, New Jersey and Connecticut area. After the dinner, the Congressmen were given RCA tape recorders and their wives transistor radios. Only a few of the Congressmen did not think it proper to accept the tape recorders, and left them behind.[65]

Moreover, a station which gives free time to a politician outside of the campaign period, either for personal appearances or for taped reports to constitutents, places him under an obligation comparable to that which arises from a generous campaign contribution. While making information available to the public, the station confers a political benefit upon a Member through such free exposure.

In practice, candidates are charged a higher rate than virtually all commercial advertisers, particularly by local stations. The rate structure is designed for commercial advertisers, not political uses. Most commercial advertisers are quite content with the fact that spots purchased at reduced rates are subject to pre-emption. Political advertisers, however, operating within strict time constraints, must pay premium rates to avoid pre-emption. Also, spots tend to cost more in the fall, which is the political season, because the new shows are beginning and audience interest is at a peak. In our interviews several Congressmen insisted that they are charged inflated rates for their political advertising, both on television and in newspapers.[66] They are correct in one sense at least. In terms of "cost per thousand viewers," a media measurement, there is no question that large advertisers pay considerably less than one-time or two-time political advertisers.[67]

Political broadcast rates could be reduced in various ways:

1. Political advertisers could be charged the most favorable volume rate available to commercial advertisers.

2. Non-preemptible spot time could be provided for political uses at preemptible time rates, which amounts to an effective reduction of one third.[68]

3. Where stations have both a local and a national rate, the FCC by ruling, or Congress by statute, could require them to charge Congressional candidates the lower local rate.

4. Stations could be required to allow political advertisers to buy a specific amount of advertising or program time at a specific percentage of the single fixed prime-time rate.

The National Committee for an Effective Congress favors this last approach, and has proposed legislation* which is being sponsored in the House by Representative Torbert MacDonald (D-Mass.) and in the Senate by Senators James B. Pearson (R-Kans.) and Philip A. Hart (D-Mich.) and a large number of co-sponsors. In broad terms, this bill requires area stations as a group to make available to each legally qualified general-election candidate† for the Senate a total of 120 one-minute prime-time spots at 70-percent discount, and each station to make available one 30-minute program for each candidate at 80-percent discount. In elections to the House, 60 one-minute prime-

* H.R. 13721 and 13722 and S. 2876, 91st Cong., 1st Sess. 115 Cong. Rec. H7762–63, S10352–56 (daily ed. Sept. 10, 1969).

† Although the bill does not differentiate between "major" and "minor" candidates, §315 could be amended to afford minor candidates some fraction of the time afforded to major candidates. A minor candidate could, for example, be entitled to purchase time at reduced rates in the proportion that his party's vote in the previous election bears to the votes cast for the losing major candidate at that election, with all candidates having a minimum entitlement to purchase 5 percent or 10 percent of the time afforded to major candidates. See S. 2090 (90th Cong., 1st Sess., 1967). Differential equality of access is also discussed by Barrow, *The Equal Opportunities and Fairness Doctrines in Broadcasting: Pillars in the Forum of Democracy*, 37 U. Cin. L. Rev. 447 (1968). See also House Special Subcomm. on Investigations of the Comm. on Interstate and Foreign Commerce, The Fairness Doctrine and Related Issues, H.R. Rep. No. 257, 91st Cong., 1st Sess. (1969).

time spots at 70-percent discount and one 30-minute program at 80-percent discount would be required.*

Some of our consultants have advocated a totally new rate structure for political broadcasting. They argue that the present rate structure, particularly when applied to political uses, is archaic, unfair, easily manipulated, enormously difficult to comprehend, and possibly subject to legal attack as an unreasonable restraint on trade. They urge that a Federal unit be established, either independent of or subordinate to the Federal Communications Commission, to promulgate and enforce a new political rate structure.

Our consultants also agreed on the strong desirability of Congress setting precise limits on the minimum and maximum time which television stations should be required to make available for paid political advertising.[69] The amount of time should be generous enough to inform the citizenry but not so generous as to give an unconscionable advantage to rich candidates[70] or to permit saturation advertising. Challengers generally need more exposure than incumbents, and any limit is likely to disadvantage some challengers, particularly if incumbents spend up to the limit. But this price seems worth paying for the advantages of equalizing access to the media and reducing reliance on large contributors.

Free Television Time?

Although free television time for political broadcasting has been[71] advocated by so diverse a group as an editor of THE NEW REPUBLIC, Mayor John Lindsay of New York City (who would also prohibit the purchase of additional time),[72] and President Eisenhower,[73] as well as the British government (which prohibits paid political broadcasts), it is reasonably clear that a program of compulsory free television time for *all* Congressional candidates would be administratively unworkable. The sizes of constituencies and the number and radii of television stations vary too greatly.†

* A combination of public subsidy, blanket coverage by all stations, and reduced rates for television in Presidential campaigns has since been proposed by a special commission headed by former FCC Chairman Newton N. Minow. N.Y. TIMES, Oct. 1, 1969, at 1, col. 2.

† Here are some of the questions which come to mind: What time would be made available? Only prime time? Only in peak hours? How much time? Who would do the allocating? Which stations would forgo time? Would stations be compensated if the burden of providing free time fell unevenly on them? How

As indicated, not all Congressional candidates use television. Since the media market is tailored entirely to commercial uses and does not coincide with political subdivisions, an appreciable amount of political television is wasted on viewers who cannot vote for the candidate.[74] It is therefore unsuited to a candidate who is "merchandisable" only within a small portion of a station's viewing area. Free-time proposals would then burden some stations much more than others. Glaring inequities could result.

It is clear from our interviews that if free time were made available, an artificial incentive to use it would be created. Virtually everyone would want to take advantage of the opportunity without regard to economic feasibility.[75] The resulting traffic in the large metropolitan stations might be excessive.[76] Payment of some kind probably acts as a screening device to keep non-serious candidates out of the market and helps ensure the most economical uses of campaign resources.

In the foreseeable future, cable television may be more fully developed and widely used than at present. It may become feasible to beam a program on cable television to individual Congressional districts, which would be particularly helpful to candidates in large metropolitan regions. If television markets were broken down, television would become more available to more campaigns. At that juncture free television time should be re-examined to determine whether it would be administratively feasible for each Congressional candidate to be given free time on the cable TV system in his district.

Section 315—the Equal-Time Provision

Closely tied to the question of free television time is the equal-time provision of Section 315 of the Federal Communications Act.[77] Broadcasters frequently point to the possibility that if they make time available to the two major candidates, they may be confronted with countless small-party candidates demanding equal time.[78] Their resolution of this apparent dilemma is to make free time available to no one. According to R. Peter Straus, President of Radio Station WMCA in New York, "315 is the greatest excuse in the world for not giving any time to anything." [79] The FCC's latest Survey of Political

---

would the Congressman or Senator be compensated who either has no television in his district or state or cannot use it efficiently? Who would qualify as a bonafide candidate? Who would determine format?

Broadcasting[80] shows that the average amount of free program time reported for major-party candidates was about the same, whether or not there was a third-party candidate. The stations reporting that they provided time for third-party candidates simply provided more total time for all candidates for the given office. It thus appears that Section 315 is not so great a barrier as many broadcasters contend.[81]

Some broadcasters and other observers[82] have urged that the equal-time provision be permanently suspended and that the Fairness Doctrine extend to all cases now covered by Section 315. In spite of the recent strengthening of the Fairness Doctrine by the Supreme Court,[83] it is still somewhat vague and subjective and is hardly adequate as the sole guiding rule for broadcasters' treatment of political candidates. Suspension of the equal-time law would not provide free time for Congressional candidates and would relieve none of their financial pressures.

The FCC should be encouraged to clarify candidates' rights under both the equal-time provision and the Fairness Doctrine. For example, it seems reasonably clear that a station cannot, consistent with this provision, sell to one candidate all the available advertising spots on a particular program which has a large and specialized audience, such as the World Series or the Olympic Games. Election Eve is another situation in which there is no comparable time. The equal-time provision requires the station to make available comparable time, but in some cases there is really *no* comparable time.

Reduced Rates for Political Broadcasting

In our interviews, Members were asked their opinions on various proposals designed to reduce rates, or to make free time available for political broadcasts. The proposals included free time, limits on total purchasable time, "broadcaster-subsidy" by rate reductions, and a government subsidy for political broadcasting. The overwhelming majority favored some plan which would cause some financial detriment to broadcasters by incorporating either free time or reduced rates.

Of all the proposals reviewed herein, the proposals for across-the-board percentage reductions in political broadcast rates embodied in the Pearson-Hart and MacDonald bills seem to us most promising.[84] In view of the complexity of the subject, precise details of the plan should await legislative hearings. In any case, we lack the information

TABLE 4.6

Attitudes Toward Political-Broadcasting Proposals According to Seniority, Party, and Use of TV in Campaigns

SENATE	Would Put Burden on Broadcasters	Would Put Burden on Government	No Change
Seniority			
Senior (8)	62.5%		37.5%
Junior (8)	75.0		25.0
Party			
Democrats (9)	55.6		44.4
Republicans (7)	85.7		14.3
Use of TV			
Heavy TV (12)	66.7		33.3
Some TV (2)	100.0		
No TV (2)	50.0		50.0
Total (16)	(68.8)		(31.3)
HOUSE			
Seniority			
Senior (29)	65.5	6.9%	27.6
Junior (31)	67.7	16.1	16.1
Party			
Democrats (33)	75.7	6.1	18.2
Republicans (27)	55.6	18.5	25.9
Use of TV			
Heavy TV (17)	64.8	5.8	29.4
Some TV (17)	70.6	17.6	11.8
No TV (25)	64.0	12.0	24.0
Total (60)*	(66.7)	(11.6)	(21.7)

* One respondent for whom data on TV usage was unavailable is not included in the last section.

and expertise to be certain of specific recommendations which will be fair to all concerned. We recognize that any rate-reduction plan may substantially affect the broadcasting industry, and that complete legislative hearings should precede it. We concur, though, in the language of Judge (now Chief Justice) Burger in a recent Court of Appeals decision: "Broadcasters are temporary permittees—fiduciaries—of a great public resource, and they must meet the highest standards which are embraced in the public interest concept." [85]

147

Recommendation 4C*

We urge that Congress consider† and act upon pending proposals for reducing political broadcast rates. We specially commend for their favorable consideration the reduction formula embodied in the Hart-Pearson and MacDonald political-broadcasting bills.

LIMITS ON CAMPAIGN CONTRIBUTIONS AND SPENDING

In 1907 the Tillman Act prohibited corporations and national banks from making money contributions for elections. The first Federal Corrupt Practices Act was passed in 1910, modified in 1911, and refined in the Corrupt Practices Act of 1925, which is the major Federal control on campaign spending in effect today.[86] The Act requires candidates and national political committees operating in more than one state to report campaign receipts and expenditures in general elections to the Clerk of the House and the Secretary of the Senate. It also sets unrealistic spending limits which are easily evaded by having funds channeled through multiple committees.

The Hatch Political Activity Act, passed in 1939, limited to $5,000 the amount any individual may lawfully contribute to Federal political campaigns.[87] An individual may, however, contribute to as many committees as he wishes and hence circumvent the law. Moreover, contributions to state, local, or District of Columbia committees need not be reported under the law, even though the committees may support Federal candidates.

The Labor Management Relations Act of 1947 extended to labor unions the prohibition on political contributions by corporations.[88] It also brought primary campaigns within the law's coverage.

Two Election Reform Acts proposed in the 90th Congress, S. 1880 and H.R. 11233, would bring much-needed overhauls of the present law governing the reporting and disclosure of spending and contributions in connection with campaigns for Federal office. The Corrupt

---

* Committee member Samuel I. Rosenman did not participate in the deliberations of the Committee on this particular Recommendation.

† On October 21, 22, and 23, 1969, hearings on the Hart-Pearson Bill were held by the Subcommittee on Communications of the Senate Commerce Committee.

Practices Act is ineffectual. Hardly anyone has ever been prosecuted for not complying with it, in spite of the fact that virtually every candidate has been forced to circumvent the law with one subterfuge or another. This situation breeds hypocrisy, conceals vitally important information, and fosters public cynicism.[89]

The Senate and House election-reform bills in the 90th Congress represented the furthest either house had ever gone toward comprehensive election reform. These are the principal features of the bills:

1. Federal requirements of reporting and disclosure requirements are extended to cover all primary campaigns and conventions for selecting Congressional and Presidential candidates. Moreover, all political committees are required both to register and to report, whether they operate within the borders of one state or not.[90] Present law exempts committees which operate solely within one state, and this has become the most common way to circumvent the law in Presidential campaigns. The reports require considerably more detail than the present law, including full names and addresses of all contributors of $100 or more.

All fund-raising activities, except those conducted by exempt state or local committees primarily supporting state or local candidates, are to be reported. Candidates and committees are required to file detailed contribution and spending reports four times a year and also on the fifteenth and fifth days preceding an election. A fund-raising event held in a non-election year to pay for political expenses or to pay off a deficit* would be reportable. Any person, other than a political committee or candidate, whose political expenditures in a year exceed $100 must file a similar report.

2. The House bill requires reports to be filed not with the Clerk of the House and the Secretary of the Senate, as provided by present law and the Senate bill,[91] but rather with a new, independent Federal

---

* Rule XLIII(6) of the House Code of Ethics expressly permits fund-raising to pay off campaign deficits. The language of the Senate Code is ambiguous, but during the Senate debate on the Code's adoption Senator John Stennis (D-Miss.), Chairman of the Senate Ethics Committee, declared that the Code did not permit deficit financing. 114 CONG. REC. S3237 (daily ed. Mar. 22, 1968). This interpretation seems to reflect the Ethics Committee's sensitivity to any device that carried a potential for misappropriation of campaign funds. The House rule seems more realistic, since deficit financing seems more the rule than the exception among candidates. Under existing law, if a deficit fund-raising event is held later than 30 days following an election, it escapes reporting. This is further evidence of the need for election reform.

Elections Commission. The Clerk and Secretary have shown little interest in ensuring the filing of reports, checking their accuracy, or prosecuting violators.[92] A Federal Elections Commission would have rather extensive responsibilities under the House bill, including registering and publicizing facts about political committees, receiving and publicizing reports of campaign contributions and expenditures of candidates and committees, and conducting appropriate audits.* It could also serve as the administering agency of the public subsidy recommended above.

3. The present statutory ceilings on total spending by individual candidates and political committees[93] are repealed altogether by both the Senate and House versions. Both bills, however, retain and tighten the $5,000 limit on contributions by individuals to any Federal candidate or political committee. Present law permits many separate gifts of up to $5,000 each to ostensibly separate committees working in behalf of a candidate; both the Senate and House versions limit to $5,000 the contribution to any candidate or to all political committees substantially supporting him.† The Senate version specifies that a contribution made by a person's spouse or minor child shall be deemed to be made by him.

Although members of a candidate's family are subject to the general limitation on contributions in both bills, neither measure limits the amount a candidate may spend on his own campaign. We believe that the bills are deficient in this respect. If a wealthy candidate may spend without limit, a less affluent opponent may be at a great disadvantage and be driven to incur compromising obligations in order to raise enough funds to compete. Accordingly, this Committee believes that a reasonable limit should be imposed on all candidates' spending from personal funds; $25,000 is recommended.

---

* The only other appropriate administering body would be a unit functioning under the supervision of the Comptroller General. Senators Hugh Scott (R-Pa.) and Joseph Clark (D-Pa.) unsuccessfully sought to have the Comptroller General rather than the Clerk of the House or Secretary of the Senate administer this law. The Comptroller General has, however, indicated reluctance to assume any such responsibilities. He pointed out that his office is a creature of Congress, and it might be inappropriate for him to police his employers. While we recognize that many may validly question the creation of another new Federal agency, we believe that the importance of the proposed Commission's task overrides this objection.

† We recommended earlier that if a public subsidy is enacted, the limitation on individual contributions should be lowered to $1,000.

Recommendation 4D

Congress should, by legislation, limit to $25,000 the amount a candidate for Congress may spend during any calendar year in connection with his own campaign for nomination or election.

The removal of limits on total spending is generally regarded as a sound feature of the bills. It is widely believed that limits are unenforceable[94] and invite circumvention. The President's Commission on Campaign Costs (the Heard Commission) recommended that the present "meaningless" ceilings on contributions and on expenditures by political committees be abolished.[95] The Commission felt that statutory ceilings do not really limit spending or contributions. They may give a false impression that spending or contributing is controlled and discourage complete reporting. In addition, ceilings cause proliferation of bogus political committees and invite other forms of evasion.

President Eisenhower favored the elimination of spending ceilings on the theory that the vast disparity in campaign conditions throughout the country makes it impossible to devise fair ceilings.[96] There is a great difference in the costs of campaigning between urban and rural constituencies. One Member estimated that the median costs of a campaign might be as much as ten times as high in a city as in a rural area. Moreover, he said, costs go up so rapidly that proper ceilings soon become unrealistic, and the law is unlikely to change accordingly.

Perhaps the best reason of all for removing spending ceilings is that it would give an added incentive to individuals, candidates, and committees to disclose fully their contributions and spending.[97] With full disclosure, fairly complete data on the sources and objects of campaign spending could be gathered. These data would help determine how much it costs in different parts of the country to conduct an effective campaign. Such knowledge might make it possible to set Federal subsidies at levels generally adequate to cover essential campaign costs.

One of the principal features of both versions of the Election Reform Act is the requirement that political committees primarily supporting Federal candidates must report their donors. The practice of corporate executives contributing to political candidates through groups whose names do not reveal the actual source of the campaign

funds is known to be widespread.[98] The requirement that all committees register with the Federal Elections Commission and file detailed
statements of organization is intended to disclose such committees.*
These regulations are desirable because, among other reasons, committees are not subject to the $5,000 limit on contributions. No work-
able plan for limiting group financial support has yet emerged from
any source.

Two additional features of the Election Reform Act are worth noting. First, the officers charged with receiving reports must make copies
available at the cost of reproduction to anyone interested in seeing
them.[99] Also, copies of the statements must be filed not only in Washington but also with the Clerk of the U.S. District Court for the
district in which the candidate's residence is located. In the case of
incumbents we would further require reports to be made available for
public inspection in Members' state or district offices.

The subterfuges that have grown up under the Corrupt Practices
Act would not all be swept away by the Election Reform Act, but
many of them would. The knowledge that all facts of campaign
finance will be matters of record will in itself tend to curtail excesses
and promote circumspection among candidates, political parties, and
their supporters. In the words of one observer, "the knowledge that
the candidate's financial backing is a matter of public record will tend
to inhibit the contributor's expectation of favors and the legislator's
willingness to bestow them." [100] The bill gives candidates no incentive
to be dishonest and enables those interested in campaign finance to
find out amounts and donors of contributions, and how the moneys,
goods, and services are used.

Although all Senators apparently agreed with Senator Cannon's assertion that the existing law was "antiquated, meaningless and totally
ineffective," [101] there was considerable disagreement over how far reform should go. Nevertheless, S. 1880 passed the Senate by an 87-to-0
roll-call vote.

The House bill was buried by the Rules Committee and, in fact,
had great difficulty getting out of the House Administration Committee because of the combined opposition of (a) Southern Democrats
who preferred no change at all; (b) Northern Democrats who did not
want to risk the reinstatement on the House floor of the prohibition
on union political-action units (such a provision was in the original

* See Sections 203–05 of the proposed Election Reform Act in Appendix E.

152

House bill, but was deleted by a majority vote of the committee); and (c) one Representative who claimed that the removal of spending limits would eventually make Congress a "rich man's club."

The reluctance of the House of Representatives to act, notwithstanding the strong support for the Election Reform Act from editorial writers,[102] then-President Lyndon Johnson, and individual Members of Congress, is regretted by this Committee. We believe firmly in the necessity of a strong election-reform act with effective reporting and disclosure provisions. We believe further that the removal of secrecy from campaign financing of Congressional candidates will effectively reduce the potentially corrupting influence of large contributions.

Recommendation 4E

Federal law should impose strict limits on campaign contributions and require full reporting of contributions and spending by all primary and general election candidates for Congress, and all committees supporting them. A Federal Elections Commission should be established to administer this law. Congress should enact an election-reform bill along the lines set forth in Appendix E. (This model is identical to S. 1880, 90th Cong., except that Title II of H.R. 11233, 90th Cong., is substituted for Title II of S. 1880. Such substitution would transfer to a Federal Elections Commission the duties and powers entrusted to the Clerk of the House and Secretary of the Senate by S. 1880.)

CONCLUSION

For many years the campaign-finance laws have given committees and candidates a powerful incentive to withhold information. The proposed election-reform bills remove much of the incentive for dishonest or incomplete reporting by removing spending limits. Accurate reporting should enable the new Federal Elections Commission to accumulate heretofore unavailable election-finance information and share it with the electorate. Even with the enactment of a comprehensive Election Reform Act, only careful monitoring of elections and election reports will yield this information.

Elections are at the core of the American system of free government, and their reform has been neglected for too long. We are aware that the questions raised and directions outlined in this chapter may not immediately lead to effective solutions. But we are certain that reforms are much overdue. What is needed is to begin with new techniques, and to learn, modify, and refine those techniques from experience. Public financing of campaigns, reduced television costs, limits on individual contributions, and comprehensive reporting are the most promising legislative program with which to begin.

CHAPTER FIVE

SALARIES AND
ALLOWANCES

Congressional salaries and allowances are vital to our subject. In the past, their inadequacy has caused many Members to seek or retain outside sources of income with consequent risk of conflicts of interest. Also, the Members' personal economic interest in determining their own salaries creates an unavoidable conflict of interest to which both Congress and the public are highly sensitive. Historically, the ethical considerations have caused Members of Congress to be self-conscious and defensive about the subject. If the public thinks a particular Congress is overly generous with itself, the ethical issues quickly become potent political issues.

In the first Congress, Members received *per diem* allowances of $6 as their only compensation.[1] This was unchanged until the famous salary-increase episode of 1816. A bill providing an annual salary of $1,500 for each Member was reported. John Randolph spoke for the bill, saying that the $6 *per diem* made Members work for less than a dollar an hour, "which is something more than you pay a man for sawing wood."[2] John C. Calhoun favored an even higher salary of

$2,500 on the theory that "[t]he sole check on an undue executive power is an able, intelligent, and experienced House," [3] and to get such a House, it would be necessary to pay men of ability enough to attract and keep them there. The bill quickly passed both houses and was made retroactive to the beginning of the session.

The Members who voted for this measure were denounced from one end of the country to the other. According to one account,

> Grand juries presented the conduct of the supporters of the law as deserving universal detestation, and called on the voters to return no man to Congress who was not hostile to the measure. Effigies meant to represent its supporters were burned. Mass meetings demanded that members who had voted for it should instantly resign. "Wherever I went," said Henry Clay to the House some months later, "I do not recollect to have met with one solitary individual who was not opposed to the act; who did not, on some ground or other, think it an improper and unjust law." [4]

The measure resulted in the defeat of all the Members from Ohio, Delaware, and Vermont and most Members from Georgia, Maryland, and South Carolina, and the increase was repealed the following year.[5] The next substantial adjustment in salary did not occur until 1856, when Congress voted itself a $3,000 annual salary. This increase passed with hardly a ripple. "[M]oney was plenty . . . times were good . . . the slavery issue was engrossing attention," observed an historian.[6] The amount was increased to $5,000 in 1866 and to $7,500 in 1873. Times were hard, and the response of the voters was again irate; the $5,000 salary was restored in 1874. Congress did not return to the $7,500 level until 1907.

The salary was next increased in 1925 to $10,000 and remained there until 1946, except for percentage cuts caused by general government-economy legislation during the period from 1932 to 1935 (15 percent, 10 percent, and 5 percent in each year, respectively; full compensation was not restored until April 1, 1935). In 1946 the salary was raised to $15,000, which included a $2,500 tax-free expense allowance. In 1955 the salary was raised to $22,500, but the expense allowance was dropped. In 1965 the salary was increased to $30,000. On March 1, 1969, during the course of our study, the salary was raised to its present level, $42,500 per year.

156

When the salary question came before the Congress, this Committee sent telegrams to selected Members expressing our strong support for the increase and indicating a belief that it would reduce Members' dependence on outside income and thereby reduce their exposure to conflicts of interest. We concurred also in the considerations which had moved the Commission on Executive, Legislative and Judicial Salaries to recommend an even larger figure, $50,000,[7] and which led President Johnson to recommend the 41-percent raise which was enacted.[8] The Commission had urged that Members' salaries be adjusted "to compensate for the substantial and unique responsibilities they bear, to meet the cost peculiar to elective rather than appointive office, and to minimize the need to rely on other means of augmenting income." [9]

The Salaries Commission was established pursuant to Public Law 90–206, for the purpose of assisting in setting top-level salaries in all three branches of the Federal government. It was composed of nine members, of whom three were appointed by the President, two by the Vice President, two by the Speaker of the House, and two by the Chief Justice of the United States.* The enabling legislation provided that the recommendations of the President transmitted to the Congress would become effective at the beginning of the first pay period following transmittal unless Congress specifically disapproved all or part of these recommendations or passed a superseding statute. This "commission method" of raising salaries was chosen by Congress to remove itself from an active role in recommending its own salary increases and thereby avoid the adverse publicity normally accompanying salary increases. Moreover, in a straight bill there undoubtedly would have been bargaining back and forth as various interested persons and groups attempted to place certain jobs at certain pay levels.

The Salaries Commission report included several important comparisons of top Federal salaries with salaries of private executives and

---

* Appointed by the President: Frederick R. Kappel, Chairman (retired Chairman of the Board, American Telephone and Telegraph Co.), John J. Corson (consultant and corporate director), George Meany (President AFL-CIO). Appointed by the Vice President: Stephen K. Bailey (Dean, Maxwell School), Sidney J. Weinberg (investment banker). Appointed by the Speaker: Edward H. Foley (attorney and former Under Secretary of the Treasury), William Spoelhof (President, Calvin College). Appointed by the Chief Justice: Arthur H. Dean (attorney and Chairman, U.S. Delegation, Nuclear Test Ban and Disarmament Conference), William T. Gossett (attorney and President of the American Bar Association).

officials of state and local governments. It was found that 2,316 state, city, and county officials, including 37 state Governors, received annual salaries of $30,000 or more.[10]

The majority of Members of Congress whom we interviewed found the $30,000 salary inadequate and drew upon personal resources to supplement salaries. Slightly more than half the Senators interviewed (12 of 22) said the salary was adequate for them at $30,000. In the House, however, almost twice as many (60) Representatives found the salary inadequate as found it adequate (34). In both chambers junior Members more often found the salary inadequate than senior Members. Junior Members, less secure in their seats and likely to come from competitive districts or states, feel the need to spend more money politicking and have less access to committee staff and other resources. Tables 5.1 and 5.2 summarize these findings.

We learned from our interviews that the adequacy of the Congressional salary varies with the needs, tastes, habits, and family size of a Member; the expectations of his constituents; the proximity of his district or state to Washington; whether his constituency is urban or rural; and many other factors. One Member mentioned that several of his fellow Californians arrived in Congress in mid-career with a growing family and without having had time to build an estate. Such a man typically is 35, has three children, and generally assumes a heavy mortgage on the house he buys in Washington. Members who arrive later in their careers, after their children have grown, are more likely to find the salary adequate.

About half of the interview sample rely on $5,000 or more outside income to supplement their salaries. More than one quarter mentioned the need for an increased cost-of-living deduction or an expense account. Nine of the 17 Senators (52.9 percent) who acknowledged outside income received over $10,000 from all sources; fewer Members of the House (23 of 90, or 25.6 percent) indicated outside income over $10,000.

The 1969 pay increase became law without a vote in the House, but was debated extensively and put to a roll-call vote in the Senate, where it was approved by a vote of 47 to 34. Senators supporting the increase justified it on the basis of the increased cost of living, maintaining two homes, and services to constituents. Other views expressed during the Senate debate were that the Senate owed a duty to

TABLE 5.1

Senators' Opinions on Salaries
(Prior to 1969 Salary Increase)

Region	Adequate	Inadequate
West (9)	77.8%	22.2%
Midwest (5)	60.0	40.0
South (5)	20.0	80.0
East (3)	33.3	66.7
Seniority*		
Senior (12)	66.7	33.3
Junior (10)	40.0	60.0
Population of Home State		
Over 5 million (3)		100.0
Under 5 million (19)	63.2	36.8
Total sample (22)	(54.5)	(45.5)

TABLE 5.2

Representatives' Opinions on Salaries
(Prior to 1969 Salary Increase)

Region	Adequate	Inadequate
West (14)	35.7%	64.3%
Midwest (27)	48.1	51.9
South (24)	33.3	66.7
East (29)	27.6	72.4
Seniority*		
Senior (51)	41.2	58.8
Junior (43)	30.2	69.8
Total sample (94)	(36.2)	(63.8)

* In these and the other tables in this chapter, the 46 Senators in the 90th Congress elected before 1957 are classified as senior. Representatives elected to five or more terms (including the 90th Congress) are classified as senior.

the entire Federal salary structure to raise salaries; responsibility of the office justified the increase; too many good people were being lost by the government; higher salaries were necessary to recruit able and talented men into politics; Members could, if they chose, earn a great deal more money in private industry; and younger Members with families could not get by on the old salary.[11]

Members interviewed after the increase took effect were generally of the view that the $42,500 salary made it more likely that they could depend exclusively on their Congressional salaries. One has publicly announced that the increased salary was adequate and enabled him to terminate his law practice.[12]

At the conclusion of our study this Committee felt even more strongly than it had in early 1969 that the salary increase was fully justified. The difficulty of recruiting able and talented men into government at 1968 salary levels had become clear. The $42,500 salary puts Members of Congress in the upper 0.6 percent of the country in terms of individual income.[13] They can live comfortably, though not necessarily luxuriously, and ought to be able at this salary level to raise and educate their children as do men of comparable station in private life. The risks of political life are indeed considerable, and it seems appropriate to afford Members an income at least commensurate with that of a corporate vice-president.

The high responsibility and dignity of the office of a Member of Congress justify the increase. Most Members of Congress work long hours and are subject to great pressure and demands. They have unique financial burdens. Their expenses include, for many Members, the maintenance of two residences and large unreimbursed travel expenses.[14]

The increased salary is consistent with the fact that Congress is now a full-time job. It will be seen in this chapter that for those who remain in office the Congressional service carries the traditional benefits of a full-time career, such as insurance, health care, pension rights, and survivor benefits. Finally, and most importantly to this Committee, the salary increase will make it possible for more Members to avoid outside activities. Members should be able to live comfortably without having to practice law, accept corporate directorships, seek out honoraria, or operate businesses.

FRINGE BENEFITS

Several other benefits accrue to Members of Congress as part of the emoluments of office which may properly be regarded as part of their monetary compensation.[15] Such benefits include the opportunity to purchase life and health insurance at reduced premiums, with the government paying part of the cost of the insurance;[16] hospital care in military hospitals in the Washington area at reduced rates (the 1968 rate was $49 per day);[17] retirement and death benefits;[18] and for House members, a cash refund of the unused portion of yearly stationery allowances.*

A Member of Congress who elects to participate contributes 7.5 percent of his annual salary to a retirement fund. At age 62, if he has served in Congress a minimum of five years, he may retire and draw a lifetime pension equal to 2.5 percent of his annual salary multiplied by the number of years he has served (up to a maximum of 32 years).[19] The cost of pensions for more than 200 former Members of Congress now comes to nearly $2 million a year.[20] Before the recent salary increase, a Member with five years of service at $30,000 and 32 years of Congressional service could have retired at a pension of $24,000. A number of Members whom we interviewed indicated that they could gain financially from retiring, since they had accumulated so many years in office; but they chose to remain for reasons of public service. Surviving wives of Members are now paid benefits equal to 55 percent of the annuities earned by their husbands.[21]

---

* The Senate had the same right until it was taken away as a result of an amendment to the Legislative Appropriations Bill of 1969 sponsored by Sen. John Williams (R-Del.). Senators must now return to the Treasury the unused portions of their stationery allowances. 114 CONG. REC. S8319 (daily ed. July 9, 1968). The same proposal was defeated two years earlier by a Senate vote of 61 to 16. 112 CONG. REC. 20,056 (1966). In the House, the unused stationery allowance may be accumulated, and if the amount is so accumulated, it is due the Member when he retires, or his estate when he dies. In 1968 one Representative received an unused balance of $2,870 from his original $3,000, and several Representatives were able to receive $2,500 or more. In all, 179 Representatives claimed and received refunds in 1968. See Committee on House Administration, 90th Cong., 2d Sess., DETAILED STATEMENT OF DISBURSEMENTS, JULY 1 TO DECEMBER 31, 1968, at 153–55 (Comm. Print 1969). Numerous Senators also received refunds in 1968. The highest refund was $2,587. See Secretary of the Senate, REPORT FROM JULY 1, 1968 TO DECEMBER 31, 1968, S. DOC. No. 91-6, 91st Cong., 1st Sess. 437 (1969).

TAX TREATMENT
OF MEMBERS' EXPENSES

According to Internal Revenue Service officials,[22] one IRS agent is assigned the year round to assist Members with personal tax questions. Between December 15 and April 15 of each year this agent is joined by three others, and they occupy offices on Capitol Hill provided them by the Sergeants-at-Arms. Two take up stations in the House and two in the Senate. A third agent is added on the House side for the final five weeks of the tax season.[23] This unit assists about half the Representatives and about four fifths of the Senators in completing their income-tax returns. Members have not always been aware that this service was available to them. Last year a Member who had been in Congress for ten terms learned of it for the first time.

At the beginning of each Congress this Capitol Hill unit of the IRS participates in two tax seminars for new Representatives, organized, respectively, by House Republicans and House Democrats. The IRS agents explain what expenses may be deducted and what may not. The main deductible items are expenses incurred in travel to and from a Member's state or district; entertainment of constituents; communicating with constitutents through newsletters, questionnaires, and CONGRESSIONAL RECORD reprints; and subscriptions to newspapers and periodicals. The costs of radio and television tapes appear less frequently on Members' returns than in the past, and it seems to be common for stations to assume the cost of producing such tapes. Telephone and postage costs rarely appear as out-of-pocket expenditures. Salaries and reasonable expenses of staff paid out of a Member's pocket are deductible when the range of constituency business justifies it. An extra state or district office would be similarly treated.

No Senator assisted by a member of the IRS Capitol Hill unit has claimed more than 19 trips home in any recent year. If a Member returned home more often than twice a month, the agent might question whether the trips were really official. If so well-traveled a Member had no Washington residence, the agent might tend to infer that some of his trips home were personal and non-deductible. But if a

Member's family resided with him in the Washington area, the agent would tend to infer that the trips were official. He would also tend to treat as official all travel, however frequent, of Members to distant districts. The agents use their own best judgment in passing upon travel deductions, taking into account the number of trips and the amounts of money involved.

As a general rule, Members are advised not to deduct the cost of a trip if the primary purpose was to address a political gathering. Members are also strongly advised not to deduct *any* expenses incurred during the period extending from one month before a primary election to one day after the general election. Clearly personal expenses are always regarded as non-deductible.

In addition to business-expense deductions analogous to those allowed in the private sector, the Internal Revenue Code recognizes the special situation of Members brought about by their need to maintain two residences. Section 162(a) of the Internal Revenue Code[24] provides, *inter alia*, that amounts expended by Members of Congress within each taxable year for living expenses (in metropolitan Washington) "shall not be deductible for income tax purposes in excess of $3,000." Since 1960 it has been IRS policy not to require specific verification for this deduction. Members need only to state that they spent the statutory amount on living expenses away from home.

Members with access to outside funds to defray office expenses are advised to report such funds as income and then deduct payments from the fund as expenses. In this way no tax is paid, but the Member stays above reproach. It is assumed that the Member has effective control over such supplemental funds even if formal control lies elsewhere. A similarly cautious approach is taken toward reimbursement of travel expenses in connection with speeches to private groups. Members are advised to list all reimbursements as income and then to deduct actual expenses. Refunds from stationery allowances are treated as ordinary income. The agents report that their advice is almost invariably followed.

In his message to Congress transmitting the recommendations for salary increases, President Johnson recommended that the maximum Federal-tax deduction for Congressional living expenses be raised from $3,000 to $5,500 for each Member of Congress.[25] This was beyond the scope of the Salaries Commission, whose charge was to set "rates of pay" only,[26] and hence could not be incorporated in the Commission's recommendations. In the view of this Committee, the increased costs of living and of maintaining two residences justify the recommended increase in the cost-of-living deduction.

Recommendation 5A
Congress should amend the final clause of Section 162(a) of the Internal Revenue Code to read "Amounts expended by such Members within each taxable year for living expenses shall not be deductible for income tax purposes in excess of $5,500."

It has already been noted that the Salaries Commission was allowed by law to examine "rates of pay" only. This Commission will reconvene every four years, and it would be desirable for it to be empowered to look into all matters closely related to salaries, such as Members' cost-of-living deduction, retirement rights, and other fringe benefits. Congressional diffidence is as great for these items as for salaries, and the insulating effects of the Commission are equally needed. In time there should emerge a more rational and integrated system of compensation for Congressional service.

Recommendation 5B
Congress should empower the quadrennial Federal salary commission to make recommendations with regard to Members' cost-of-living deduction, retirement rights, and other fringe benefits, in addition to salaries.

OFFICE ALLOWANCES*

Congress is becoming increasingly liberal in authorizing office allowances for its Members. Virtually every Legislative Branch appropriations bill in the last several years has stepped up existing allowances in the areas of staff, postage, stationery, telephone and telegraph,

---

* Figures in the balance of this chapter may not reflect changes made by the legislative appropriations for the fiscal year ending June 30, 1970 (H.R. 13763). While this manuscript was being processed, Senate amendments were adopted which increased staff, travel, communications, stationery, and other allowances. 115 CONG. REC. S12958–83 (daily ed. Oct. 25, 1969).

office expenses outside the District of Columbia, district-office rental, and travel.[27]

The House, where all Members now represent districts approximately equal in population, has been particularly generous recently in its allowances, notably in the areas of staff and travel allowances. Most Senatorial allowances are under the jurisdiction of the Legislative Appropriations Subcommittee of the Senate Appropriations Committee. That subcommittee is traditionally run by Senators from small states whose responsibilities in the area of constituency service are easily manageable and whose seats are relatively secure.[28] They have taken little initiative in expanding Senatorial allowances, which may explain why Senators long were provided with fewer trips home than Representatives.

STAFF ALLOWANCES

Some of the Members whom we interviewed and some of their staff expressed the belief that there is a "critical mass" of staff above which a Parkinsonian effect sets in and a large staff, particularly when it exists in cramped quarters, becomes counterproductive. Others express amazement that some staffs, working under extremely adverse and crowded conditions, can turn out such good work. A well-managed large staff in which particular tasks are assigned to each member and responsibility and authority are carefully delineated could be highly effective because of its expanded resources and capabilities. In general, however, Congressional work is such that it is difficult to organize efficiently.

Each Member of the House of Representatives is entitled to an allowance for staff of $34,500 a year "base," to be distributed among as many as 12 staff members.[29] The figures are misleading. The staff-allowance "base" was established in 1944. Since then Congressional employees have received a number of pay increases according to various formulas, each of which must be applied consecutively to the employee's "base" pay rate to determine his actual annual pay. Each Administrative Assistant to a Member is equipped with elaborate tables converting the "base" figure into actual salaries, since only the base rate is shown on the employee's official employment form.[30] Depending on how the Member distributes the "base" allowance among his staff, the gross amount can be considerably over $100,000. This confusing and complicated structure for calculating staff allowances and staff salaries should be revised and modernized.* The House should follow the Senate's recent example and eliminate the base-pay formula.

Staff allowances in the Senate depend upon the population of the state. States are divided into 12 groupings: If the population of a Senator's state is less than 3 million, he receives a total of $240,000 for staff salaries; if the population of the state is 17 million or more, the Senator receives a staff allowance of $402,000. There are 10 intermediate groups. Only one employee on a Senator's staff may be paid the maximum annual salary of $31,317, and there are similar limits on the number of employees who can be retained at other top salary levels.[31]

Many Senators from the most populous states find their allowances to be inadequate, and it takes only a superficial examination to find that there is a bias against them in the staff-allowance structure. The Senator from New York receives less than twice what is allowed the Senator from Alaska, even though New York has almost 75 times Alaska's population. No one contends that the New York Senator should have a staff 75 times greater, but the current table of compensation for Senate staff (Table 5.3) shows substantial discrimination against the more populous states in the additions of staff above the minimal base. At four population levels the allowance increases are no greater for an additional two million persons than they are for one million. The cumulative result for the largest states is that for four million of their total population there are no commensurate increases in staff allowance. This discrimination should be removed, and the entire schedule, above the base, should reflect adequate, uniform increments in staff allowance for each million population. Such revision would substantially aid those large-state Senators whose existing staffs are now overburdened by constituents' demands.

---

* In general, Congress does not make it easy for anyone fully to know Members' financial arrangements and consequently their financial needs. One can learn the salaries paid House staff members only by inspecting the books at an office in the Cannon House Office Building and taking notes in longhand. The Senate is somewhat more helpful, since it publishes salary figures twice a year. Both House and Senate publish full statements of disbursements without much attempt to classify or categorize disbursements. To find out what was spent, one must go through these statements line by line.

TABLE 5.3

*Senate Staff Allowances**

Population	Amount	Increment per million over Prior Category
Less than 3 million	$239,805	
3 to 4 million	255,135	$15,330
4 to 5 million	268,275	13,140
5 to 6 million	280,320	12,055
6 to 7 million	280,320	0
7 to 8 million	293,460	13,140
8 to 9 million	293,460	0
9 to 10 million	308,790	15,330
10 to 11 million	324,120	15,330
11 to 12 million	339,450	15,330
12 to 13 million	354,780	15,330
13 to 14 million	370,110	15,330
14 to 15 million	370,110	0
15 to 16 million	385,440	15,330
16 to 17 million	385,440	0
17 million or more	401,865	16,425

* The Senate amended the legislative appropriations for the fiscal year ending June 1970 to increase each Senator's clerk-hire allowance by $23,652. Otherwise the schedule shown above was unchanged. 115 CONG. REC. S12958, 12979–83 (daily ed. Oct. 21, 1969).

Recommendation 5C

The schedule of compensation for Senate employees contained in 2 U.S.C. §60(f) and in the Legislative Branch Appropriations Act of 1968, as amended, should be amended to reflect adequate increments in staff allowance for each million population above 3 million.

STAFF MISUSE
AND PAYROLL PADDING*

Occasionally a Member demonstrates that his staff allowances exceed his needs by employing persons who perform little or none of his

* Nepotism would have been included in this section a few years ago, but this issue became moot at the Federal level with the enactment of Public Law 90–206, 5 U.S.C. §3110 (1969). Since December 16, 1967, all Federal officials have been barred from employing or appointing relatives.

official workload. Rule 8 of the House Code prohibits a Member from having employees who do not perform duties "commensurate with their compensation." This apparently resulted from the Powell case and seems to be a worthwhile codification of basic requirements of good government and proper use of public funds. One may suppose that it is also among the unwritten rules of the Senate.

Such a rule should make it clear that the "commensurate duties" to be performed should be those for which the person is officially employed, thus reaching such things as the use of a secretary as a maid as well as payment for incommensurate services. This suggests another situation: What of the use of staff for political campaigning? Senate Rule XLIII deals with one aspect of this problem. It stems from Baker's diversion and misuse of Congressional campaign contributions,[32] and, as originally proposed by the Ethics Committee, it would have prevented Senate employees from soliciting campaign funds or serving as more than mere conduits for them. By a floor amendment which was opposed by the Ethics Committee and supported by both parties' Senatorial campaign chairmen, the Senate voted 43 to 37 to except Senatorial assistants publicly designated as authorized to solicit and distribute campaign funds.[33]

This amendment was unfortunate but not a major ethical setback. If it is construed as stating the sole permissible use of staff in campaigns, the rule may actually be an advancement. It might reduce the amount of use of official staff in campaigns for re-election. Public employees should not be paid to serve as campaign workers, including the staff "treasurers" permitted by the Senate rule. We accordingly recommend a broadened version of the House rule on staff services, which should promote integrity in the use of personnel:

Recommendation 5D
Each house should adopt the following rule: "A Member shall employ with public funds no one who does not perform duties commensurate with his compensation and shall utilize such persons only for the official purposes for which they are employed."

POSTAGE

Members may use franked envelopes (envelopes with the Member's facsimile signature in the upper right-hand corner) for all official mail,[34] which is postage-free. Official mail may also be circulated to constituents in envelopes addressed simply "Postal Patron [City, State]." The theory of the frank is that the expense of public business should be borne by the public.

This privilege of sending letters postage-free is of English origin.[35] In 1660, when it was proposed in the House of Commons formally to recognize the privilege, Sir Heneage Finch (later Lord Nottingham) called it "a poor mendicant proviso, and below the honour of the House." The Speaker, Sir Harbottle Grimstone, was unwilling to put the question, saying he was ashamed of it. During the next hundred years the privilege gained full acceptance. Some Members of Parliament did not confine themselves to sending mail. One historian tells of Members of Parliament sending "hampers of game, baskets of fish . . . even in some cases girls and able-bodied men . . . at His Majesty's expense." [36] In the United States the frank has been confined to more conventionally mailable matter, although, according to one report, more than ten times as many franked packages as letters passed through the Washington, D.C., Post Office in 1841.[37] Even today a major portion of all franked mail consists of books and publications.

In addition to the frank, all Senators are given an annual air-mail and special-delivery postage allowance of $960 which is raised to $1,200 if their state lies partially or wholly west of the Mississippi River. Representatives are entitled to a $700 postage allowance.[38] These allowances may be used only for official mail. Postage for political mail is expected to come out of the Member's own pocket.* It is likely that the Post Office Department will soon be sending all first-class mail to distant places by air, thus eliminating any additional post-

---

* Since December 1968 the position of the Post Office Department has been that it would no longer review franked material and bill Members in individual instances of abuse. Its General Counsel was quoted as saying: "The use of the franking privilege for correspondence on official business is a matter strictly between the Member and his conscience." Congressional Quarterly, WEEKLY REPORT, Nov. 14, 1969, at 2284.

age costs presently borne by Senators and Representatives from distant districts.

STATIONERY

In addition to generous annual paper and envelope allotments from
the Government Printing Office, Senators and Representatives receive $3,000* a year in stationery allowance for their Washington
office.[39] Representatives may draw the unused portion in cash or accumulate it; any refund is subject to income tax.[40] The House should
abolish this windfall as the Senate already has done.

TELEPHONE

The House and Senate each have separate complicated unit systems
by which telephone allowances are calculated.[41] In interviews, Members generally regarded present telephone allowances as adequate.
After five P.M. all Members of Congress may use the Federal telecom-
munications system to make long-distance calls without charge. The
government also pays telephone bills up to $1,200 a year for calls out-
side Washington, generally from Members' district offices. Presentation of bills is required only in the House, and most Senators receive
quarterly checks for the full amount of $300.[42] Senators are also enti-
tled to an additional yearly "communications allowance" † of $150,
which is also normally disbursed in full amounts.[43]

DISTRICT OFFICE

Senators and Representatives are entitled to rent-free office space at
no more than two locations in their districts or states in Federal facilities acceptable to them.[44] If no Federal facilities are used, the Member

* Increased to $3,600 for Senators by the fiscal 1970 legislative appropriation.
See footnote, *supra* p. 164.

† The Senate also amended the fiscal 1970 legislative branch appropriation to
authorize a WATS line for each Senator who surrenders 50 percent of his long-
distance allowance. See footnote, *supra* p. 164.

is entitled to a rental allowance of up to $300 a month, generally paid directly to the landlord.* [45] If one Federal office is used, the Member may still use his entire $300 on a second office.[46] Also, every Representative is given an allowance of $1,200 per year and every Senator $1,600 for expenses in such offices.[47]

OFFICE EQUIPMENT

House Members are entitled to a specified total value of $2,500 in office equipment, or $3,000 if their constituencies exceed 500,000.[48] This includes mimeograph, duplicating, addressing, and dictating machines, and automatic typewriters. Automatic, electric, or mechanical equipment to facilitate correspondence in a Senator's office may be purchased without dollar limitation by a charge against the Senator's clerk-hire allowance, subject to approval by the Senate Rules Committee. All Members are additionally entitled to a specified number of electric typewriters. Also the Senate Rules Committee makes available to every Senator upon request a large photocopying machine for use in his Senatorial office.

SUBSIDIZED SERVICES

Other perquisites of Congressional office include the use of subsidized recording studios, which enable Members to produce radio and television broadcasts at the film and tape cost, and the use of folding rooms, which enable them to send out volume mailing to their constituents without charge. All employees of the House and Senate folding rooms are paid by their respective chambers. Members may use the services of Majority and Minority printers who conduct their operations from the basements of the House and Senate office buildings. These shops print Members' newsletters, questionnaires, and other bulk mailing items. They provide automatic typewriting services, pre-

---

* It is apparently permissible, though certainly politically unwise, for a Member who cannot find suitable office space in a Federal building to rent himself the space—from his law or business office. In one notorious instance, a Representative rented himself as a district office the front porch of his home. He gained the nickname "Front Porch" and served only one term in Congress.

pare addressing-machine plates, and address envelopes in bulk. Services are billed to Members at cost of materials.

TRAVEL

When the first Congress in 1789 set the pay of Members at $6 a day, it granted an equal amount for every 20 miles of travel going to and returning from the "seat of Congress." [49] Since 1866 this basic mileage allowance has been fixed at 20 cents per mile.[50] Using modern rail or air transportation, Members may stretch this basic amount to cover two or three trips home. Senators are entitled to be reimbursed for six additional round trips to their home states each fiscal year.[51]

Representatives are entitled to reimbursement for one trip each month Congress is in session, payable upon presentation of receipts. In lieu of reimbursement for actual expenses, if a Representative drives to and from his district he can be compensated at the rate of 12 cents per mile.[52] Representatives may also elect a lump-sum reimbursement of $750 per year for travel. Those whose districts lie close to Washington and who claim the lump-sum reimbursement of $750 may be able to travel home several more times a year than more distant Members. A New York City Member, for example, may stretch his lump-sum to pay for 18 round trips by air.

Two employees in a Representative's office may each be reimbursed for one round trip a year to the Member's district upon presentation of actual receipts, or, alternatively, one employee may be reimbursed for two trips. A Senator's staff is entitled to similar reimbursement at 10 cents per mile for not more than four round trips if the state has less than 10 million inhabitants or six round trips if the state is more populous.[53]

During the last 15 years House travel allowances have been increased four times, from one trip to three, to five, and finally to the present provision of one trip for every month Congress is in session, in addition to the one 20-cents-a-mile basic round trip.

While the House has shot forward in adjusting its travel allowances, the Senate allowance has leveled at six trips a year.[54] Most Senators travel home as often as most Representatives (see Tables 5.4 and 5.5) and have to travel throughout their states and deal with a diverse constituency. Moreover, Senators from distant states are at an obvious disadvantage if they wish to travel home more often than every second month because traveling costs are so great.

TABLE 5.4

Interviewed Senators' Annual Trips to Constituencies

	7 or less	8–12	13 or more
Region			
West (9)	33.3%	33.3%	33.3%
Midwest (5)	20.0		80.0
South (5)	40.0	20.0	40.0
East (2)			100.0
Seniority			
Senior (10)	50.0	20.0	30.0
Junior (11)	9.1	18.2	72.7
State Population			
Over 5 million (4)	25.0	25.0	50.0
Under 5 million (17)	29.4	17.6	52.9
Total sample (21)	(28.6)	(19.0)	(52.4)

TABLE 5.5

Interviewed Representatives' Annual Trips to Districts

	12 or less	13–24	25 or more
Region			
West (8)	37.5%	50.0%	12.5%
Midwest (27)	14.8	37.0	48.1
South (22)	18.2	22.7	59.1
East (28)	3.6	14.3	82.1
Seniority			
Senior (44)	25.0	27.3	47.7
Junior (41)	2.4	26.8	70.7
Total sample (85)	(14.1)	(27.1)	(58.8)

Not surprisingly, Representatives from the Eastern states travel home appreciably more often than do Representatives from other less proximate regions. Still, the majority of Members interviewed indicated that their travel needs exceed their travel allowances, as shown by Tables 5.6 and 5.7.

TABLE 5.6

Senators' Opinions on Travel Allowance

	Adequate	Inadequate
Region		
West (9)	66.7%	33.3%
Midwest (5)	20.0	80.0
South (6)	50.0	50.0
East (3)	33.3	66.7
Seniority		
Senior (12)	75.0	25.0
Junior (11)	18.2	81.8
Population of State		
Over 5 million (4)	25.0	75.0
Under 5 million (19)	52.6	47.4
Total sample (23)	(47.8)	(52.2)

TABLE 5.7

Representatives' Opinions on Travel Allowance

	Adequate	Inadequate
Region		
West (13)	53.8%	46.2%
Midwest (26)	42.3	57.7
South (22)	36.4	63.6
East (29)	31.0	69.0
Seniority		
Senior (48)	54.2	45.8
Junior (42)	21.4	78.6
Total sample (90)	(38.9)	(61.1)

These tables show that once again senior Members differ markedly from junior Members in both chambers. One may suppose that these senior Members are more secure, need to travel home less frequently, may have access to committee travel funds, and thus find it easier to stay within their allowances. Fifteen of 21 Senators exceed their travel allowances, as do 73 of 85 Representatives. Two thirds of these pay for this extra travel from personal resources. Yet even among those who believe travel allowances to be inadequate, a moderate number (8.7 percent in the Senate and 13.3 percent in the House) would not support an increase, believing that it would increase absenteeism and arouse public criticism.

Some Members suggested that every certified trip by a Member to his district should be presumed to be on constituency business and be reimbursed as such. Others indicated that travel allowances ought not to be increased because that would encourage additional, unnecessary travel and would put pressure on non-traveling Members to go home more often.

One House Member observed that most of these trips, especially in a campaign year, were politically motivated. He mentioned that the Republican Campaign Committee in the Senate gives every Republican Senator standing for re-election an airline credit card for his unlimited use, and suggested that the two political parties ought to underwrite the unreimbursed travel expenses of their Members.

Two Congressmen drew attention to the inefficient work schedule of Congress, which has the effect of encouraging extra travel. If Congress is not conducting significant legislative business on Friday and Monday, Members are given an incentive to go home and use their free time to political advantage or to attend to their business or personal affairs. Both of these Members urged that Congress work five days a week and that Members return home only when Congress is not in session.

Recommendation 5E *

Senators as well as Representatives should be entitled to one trip home for every month Congress is in session. The statute 2 U.S.C. §43(b) should be amended to read: "The Contingent Fund of the Senate is hereafter made available for reimbursement of transportation expenses incurred by Senators in traveling, on official business, by the nearest usual route, between Washington, District of Columbia, and any point in their home States, for not to exceed one round trip for each month the Congress is in session. . . ."

* Senate amendments to the fiscal 1970 legislative appropriations go further than this recommendation by authorizing 12 round trips per year for Senators. See footnote, *supra* p. 164.

What Are Adequate Allowances?

Our interest in Congressional allowances stems from the assumption that adequate allowances make it less likely that Members will incur obligations to special interests in order to meet the expenses of the office. The question of adequacy of allowance differs with each Member, depending, as noted by the Senate Ethics Committee, on such factors as his methods of communicating with his constituents; his personal habits of frugality; and the distance, population density, and degree of urbanization of his constituency.[55] A Member from a distant state, for example, may well find one trip a month adequate, whereas a Member from a nearby state may feel called upon to return home two or three times a week. Scholar Charles Clapp notes that

> there are sharp differences in needs between offices, and it is virtually impossible to establish a reasonable standard that will not restrict some members unduly and provide so much aid to other legislators that it cannot possibly be used efficiently.[56]

In the Senate, seven of the 23 Senators interviewed found their allowances adequate. All seven, however, were senior Senators. In the House 40 of 94 found the allowances adequate, but 31 of those 40 were senior Members. Many senior Members, particularly in the Senate, have committee resources available to them that are generally unavailable to their more junior colleagues. Tables 5.8 and 5.9 are illustrative.

Junior Members apparently use up their allowances more rapidly than their more secure senior colleagues. They have smaller support staffs because they are not committee or subcommittee chairmen. They also tend to come from the more competitive constituencies, which gives them an added incentive to exhaust their allowances in maintaining close contact with constituents.

Among those Members who found their allowances less than adequate, some were reluctant to raise allowances because they prefer to subsidize some of their semi-official expenses out of pocket (which will be easier on a $42,500 salary than before); or they recognize that some of their travel expenses are incurred for unofficial purposes. A

176

TABLE 5.8

Senators' Opinions on Allowances for Official Expenses
(Excluding Travel Allowance)

	Adequate	Inadequate
Region		
West (9)	44.4%	55.6%
Midwest (5)	60.0	40.0
South (6)	83.3	16.7
East (3)	66.7	33.3
Seniority		
Senior (12)	83.3	16.7
Junior (11)	36.4	63.6
Population of Home State		
Over 5 million (4)	50.0	50.0
Under 5 million (19)	63.2	36.8
Total sample (23)	(60.9)	(39.1)

TABLE 5.9

Representatives' Opinions on Allowances for Official Expenses
(Excluding Travel Allowance)

	Adequate	Inadequate
Region		
West (15)	66.7%	33.3%
Midwest (27)	81.5	18.5
South (24)	54.2	45.8
East (28)	67.9	32.1
Seniority		
Senior (52)	78.8	21.2
Junior (42)	54.8	45.2
Total Sample (94)	(68.1)	(31.9)

few Members, however, consider that all their expenses are for the benefit of constituents and should be reimbursed. One suggests that Members be reimbursed for such items as the cost of entertaining constituents, all travel, and all newsletter and public-relations costs. Another former Member believes that anything tax-deductible by a Member as a business expense should be fully reimbursed.

A reasonable compromise would seem to be an allowance structure adequate for a typical, conscientious Member to serve his constituents effectively, though perhaps insufficient to meet the needs of the most ambitious or free-spending Member. There is always likely to be a gap between what is appropriated and what some very active Members believe they need to serve their constitutents well and to stay in office. Those Members who feel the need to spend more than is appropriated must resort to other means to supplement funds. This subject is treated in the section on supplemental office funds in Chapter 6.

CHAPTER SIX

GIFTS, SUPPLEMENTAL FUNDS, AND HONORARIA

GIFTS AND TESTIMONIALS

Treatment of gifts to public officials is essential to any discussion of governmental ethics. The greatest single Congressional scandal, Crédit Mobilier, resulted from gifts of stock by corporate promoters to Representative Oakes Ames, with Ames in turn giving stock to 12 fellow Members. The purposes of the gifts were well summarized in Ames' own words: ". . . I have found that there is no difficulty in inducing men to look after their own property." [1]

This illustrates one class of improper gifts: those designed to create a conflict of interest in the recipient. On rare occasions, public officials still receive stock either as an outright gift or at bargain rates. The giver's purpose is usually to create a situation in which the Member has a personal economic stake in common with the giver. Self-interest can then take its course.

The more typical gift raises different ethical issues. The problem arises not from the nature of the item given, but from the normal

sense of appreciation in the donee and subtle expectations which tend
to arise in donors. Presents to government officials from their subjects
have long troubled political philosophers. In SPIRIT OF THE LAWS,
Baron de Montesquieu strongly expressed the view that they should
be absolutely prohibited. He said:

> In a republic, presents are odious, because virtue stands in no
> need of them. In monarchies, honour is a much stronger incen-
> tive than presents. But in a despotic government where there is
> neither honour nor virtue, people cannot be determined to act
> but through hope of the conveniences of life.
>
> It is in conformity with republican ideas that Plato ordered
> those who received presents for doing their duty to be punished
> with death. "They must not take presents," says he, "neither for
> good nor for evil actions."
>
> . . . They who receive nothing expect nothing; they who re-
> ceive a little soon covet more, till at length their desires swell to an
> exorbitant height. Besides, it is much easier to convict a man who
> knows himself obliged to accept no present at all, and yet will
> accept something, than a person who takes more when he ought
> to take less, and who always finds pretexts, excuses, and plausible
> reasons in justification of his conduct.[2]

Our present system of financing political campaigns makes Montesquieu's views incapable of perfect implementation. Since Members of
Congress must necessarily accept many donations of money as campaign contributions, it is unavoidable that they are subject to some
risks of influence caused by their gratitude for donations from friends.
However, campaign contributions are tolerated because they are a
necessary incident of our present electoral system. Acceptance of gifts
beyond the requirements of campaign necessities cannot be similarly
justified. Nonetheless, attitudes caused by dependence of Members
upon campaign contributions have produced considerable confusion
and Congressional disparity in the general area of personal gifts.

A chapter of H. H. Wilson's CONGRESS: CORRUPTION AND COM-
PROMISE was devoted to former Senator A. B. (Happy) Chandler of
Kentucky, who was given a swimming pool by a government contractor. A Senate committee investigated the matter and dismissed it as a
gift from a friend.[3]

Although swimming pools are unusual subjects for gifts, the Chandler incident illustrates a major problem. Members of Congress understandably expect to continue normal incidents of friendship and social relations enjoyed by private citizens. A Member may feel that he becomes a sort of second-class citizen if he must shun gifts which would have been received whether or not he was a Member of Congress and which are not accompanied by special expectations in the donor.

In 1951 the Douglas Subcommittee on Ethics in Government discussed the gift issue:

> The line between the proper and improper begins to be less certain when one looks for a consensus of opinion as to favors, gifts, gratuities, and services. The exchanging of gifts and favors is reported to be rather general in the business community. What is it proper to offer public officials, and what is it proper for them to receive? A cigar, a box of candy, a modest lunch (usually to continue discussing unfinished business)? Is any one of these improper? It is difficult to believe so. They are usually a courteous gesture, an expression of good will, or a simple convenience, symbolic rather than intrinsically significant. Normally they are not taken seriously by the giver nor do they mean very much to the receiver. At the point at which they do begin to mean something, however, do they not become improper? Even small gratuities can be significant if they are repeated and come to be expected. But here, too, convention must be considered: gifts to school teachers are now generally forbidden by law, but a Christmas-time present for the postman, usually on engraved green paper, is almost as well established as holly.
>
> Expensive gifts, lavish or frequent entertainment, paying hotel or travel costs, valuable services, inside advice as to investments, discounts and allowances in purchasing are in an entirely different category. They are clearly improper. On this, there is substantial agreement in the governmental community, and anyone who thinks them proper must have already lost his perspective. The difficulty comes in drawing the line between the innocent or proper and that which is designing or improper. At the moment a doubt arises as to propriety, the line should be drawn. Innocence is perhaps lost when one is conscious that it exists.[4]

181

The 1967 Senate debates on the censure of Senator Thomas Dodd (D-Conn.) revealed significant disagreement on whether a Senator's friends should be allowed to supplement his income by money gifts in order to relieve personal financial problems. Senator Dodd wrote to Senators in his defense:

> In my home state of Connecticut testimonials are exceedingly commonplace affairs, and it is universally known by those who are in the habit of attending political functions that the proceeds of testimonials are intended as personal gifts.
>
> The sum I am alleged to have used improperly is $116,000. The total raised at the testimonial affairs held in my honor on four separate occasions in 1961, 1963, and 1965 (which of course were not campaign years) amounted to about $170,000. My position is that substantially more than $116,000 was intended as a gift to be used at my discretion.[5]

In defense of Dodd, Senator Russell Long (D-La.) frequently referred to the late President John F. Kennedy's discussion of Senator Daniel Webster in his famous work PROFILES IN COURAGE. After mentioning Webster's receipt of legal retainers from the Bank of the United States, Kennedy added:

> But Webster accepted favors not as gifts but as services which he believed were rightly due him. When he tried to resign from the Senate in 1836 to recoup speculative losses through his law practice, his Massachusetts businessmen friends joined to pay his debts to retain him in office. Even at his death bed, legend tells us, there was a knock at his door, and a large roll of bills was thrust in by an old gentleman, who said that "At such a time as this, there should be no shortage of money in the house."[6]

Those who disagreed with Dodd and Long were able to point to Kennedy's further description of this feature of Webster's career as a "flaw in the granite" which evidenced a moral weakness and Webster's unawareness that he had, in Kennedy's words, "sold his services and his talents, however extraordinary they might have been, to the people of the United States, and no one else. . . ."[7]

Nonetheless, several Senators indicated that they saw no wrong in the Webster gifts, and Dodd's censure was based essentially on factual findings that the purpose of his testimonial dinners was represented to be campaign fund-raising and that he converted political funds to personal uses.* Other Senators disagreed and indicated that they did not consider the element of misrepresentation to be essential to Dodd's ethical violation. In their view, it would be improper for a Senator to use his title or office to solicit constituents' donations for personal uses even if such purposes were fully disclosed. Senator Monroney of Oklahoma forcefully stated this position when he said in the Dodd debates:

> Our sanction of this system of fund-raising occasions—whether they are called deficit lifting banquets, campaign expense banquets or testimonial dinners—where the funds in whole or in part are eligible for personal expenses of the honoree—to be spent as he chooses—leads us down a dangerous path for democracy.

> The dangers of giant corporations with special interests corrupting State legislatures—and even some few in the Congress as happened in the earlier days of our Nation—would again be possible under this system, if we adopt an ethical standard that sanctions the raising of any amount of funds, from any source, at any time, for any purpose the honoree of a testimonial wants to use them for.

> Such testimonial funds would be unreportable in the regular accounting of campaign expenditures—particularly if they were used for the betterment of the candidate's personal living. They would, I believe, be nontaxable as income on the basis that such subscriptions are "gifts." They would be legal and thus their receipt in any amount, high or low, would put their acceptance by a sitting Member or a candidate beyond the reach of the Corrupt Practices Act.[8]

After Dodd's censure, the Senate Ethics Committee returned to drafting its Ethics Code and attempted to settle the uncertainty surrounding testimonial events openly designated as personal. Those Senators who agreed with Senator Monroney and disapproved of all testimonial fund-raising for personal uses undoubtedly reflected the

---

* All Senators, including Dodd, agreed that this was improper if factually established. The Ethics Codes of the House and Senate and our recommended Model Code include rules to this effect.

dominant ethical values of the country. A veteran political writer had commented on the theory of Dodd's defense:

> . . . [I]f it is both moral and legal for a Senator to collect large sums from interested citizens, pocket those sums, and pay no income tax on them, a seat in the Senate is potentially worth more than several oil wells. A really enterprising and influential Senator should be able to collect at least six million tax-free dollars in his six years in office, and even a Representative should be able to pile up a modest competence.[9]

The Senate Ethics Code reflects the prevailing view and forbids testimonials for personal uses. Rule XLII limits the use of such funds to campaigning or office expenses. The rule also closely regulates such events when used for permissible political fund-raising. A Senator may accept contributions from fund-raising events only if he gives advance approval and receives an accounting of the sources and disposition of the funds. This accounting must be publicly reported under Rule XLIII.

The House Code's provision on fund-raising events is less stringent. Rule 7 requires that a Member treat such proceeds as campaign funds if "the sponsors of such affairs do not give clear notice in advance to the donors or participants that the proceeds are intended for other purposes." [10] This permits testimonial dinners of the type claimed by Senator Dodd and which are known to have been held for at least one Representative.[11] It requires only that the advance notices state that the proceeds of the event are for a Member's personal use. This could have been thought to be a sufficient deterrent. At present Congressional salary levels, the public will probably take a very dim view of fund-raising beyond that required for campaigning.

Our interviews and other sources of information indicate that purely personal testimonials are rare, but, for the reasons which produced the Senate's Rule, we do not believe they should ever be tolerated. We accordingly recommend as follows:

Recommendation 6A

Each house should adopt the following rule: "A Member shall not conduct or permit to be conducted fund-raising events which seek to provide money for his personal uses."

The direct individual gift to a member differs in both form and substance from the testimonial. It is less offensive in that it is unsolicited, but it is more conspicuously associated with the person of the donor. It can range from the Christmas or birthday token from a friend or relative to something akin to the gifts of stock in Crédit Mobilier. In the field of foreign affairs the Constitution expressly protects the Congressional process from the potentially corrupting effects of gifts. It prohibits officials of the United States from accepting "any present . . . from any King, Prince, or foreign State." [12]

The dangers inherent in other gifts to officeholders from persons in need of their favor are taken for granted in most contexts.* In the 1940's and 1950's no one defended White House aides who accepted freezers and vicuna coats from businessmen with Federal problems. In one such case a House subcommittee found that the giver had also paid hotel bills for an Executive Branch official who later resigned because of the scandal. At the same time it found that the donor had similarly paid hotel bills totaling $1,200 for three Senators,[13] but no disciplinary proceedings were seriously suggested for these Senators. Comparable "hospitality" is still believed to be fairly common, particularly at resort facilities and at hotels in home districts.

Gifts of free transportation pose similar problems. They can significantly enrich the Member and create the appearance of unseemly obligations. For example, several Members are said to fly regularly to their districts in company planes of concerns that do business with the government.[14]

Many individual Members, of course, have strict standards governing their acceptance of gifts. Former Senator Paul Douglas refused to accept any non-family gift greater than $2.50 in value.† Such members presume that any donor has some interest in his official duties and commendably refuse to allow their relationship to be clouded by gratuities.

The House and Senate Ethics Codes differ sharply in their treat-

---

* As this Report is completed, two Justices of the Illinois Supreme Court have resigned after an investigation disclosed their acceptance of bank stock, one by gift and one upon favorable sales terms, while an officer of the bank was the defendant in a pending criminal case. N.Y. TIMES, Aug. 3, 1969, §1 at 66, col. 6.

† When our predecessor committee sent a copy of its book, CONFLICT OF INTEREST AND FEDERAL SERVICE, to each Member of Congress, one Senator returned his copy, citing a similar rule of self-limitation.

ment of individual gifts. Rule 4 of the House Code bans acceptance of any "gift of substantial value, directly or indirectly, from any person, organization, or corporation having a direct interest in legislation before the Congress." The Senate rules deal explicitly with gifts only by requiring confidential disclosure. Rule XLII (4) requires sealed reporting to the Comptroller General of gifts worth $50 or more. However, the Senate Ethics Committee indicated an interpretation which implies a broad prohibition of gifts. It said of Rule XLII:

> . . . [T]he rule would permit a Senator to accept a personal gift if he reports the source and value. This exception was made to avoid imposing an unfair hardship on a person who is offered a genuine personal gift, which, but for being a Senator, he could accept. In framing this section, the Committee had two types of gifts in mind. The first is a gift from a member of the Senator's family, which does not have to be reported. The second is a token of sentiment of nominal value, such as a portrait of the Senator. A gift might also include a testamentary devise or bequest, or inter vivos gift from an older relative who is trying to simplify his estate. Any attempt to use this provision as an evasion of the limitations on contributions will amount to a violation of the rule, which is presented as an ethical standard and not as a police measure.[15]

This analysis indicates that "gifts" which do not satisfy either the very limited familial or nominal tests stated in the report are "contributions" within the meaning of Rule XLII and therefore must be publicly disclosed and used only for the political and semi-official purposes specified by that rule. All other gifts, if worth $50 or more, must be reported under seal, and the rules "permit" them only if they are innocent sentimental or familial items of a sort which might have been given to the donee if he were not a Senator. The Senate Rules reflect the experience of the Dodd case and intend that gifts be treated much the same as funds raised by testimonial events.

Under this interpretation, the Senate's rule on gifts is much more restrictive than that of the House. Rule 4 of the House code only forbids gifts from persons "directly" interested in legislation "before the Congress." Those interested "indirectly" or without interests in particular pending legislation may make gifts to Representatives without restriction. We doubt the wisdom and workability of these exceptions. Indirect effects of legislation are sometimes more important than direct effects. In our conflict-of-interest discussion, we concluded that disclosure rules and law-practice limitations should not depend upon other Federal involvements of those in a financial relationship to Members of Congress. Finally, improper gifts can be envisaged where the donor did not happen to be interested in legislation pending at the time.

Neither rule defines "gift" or deals expressly with gifts of services or hospitality. Precision of language is very difficult in this area. Broad, sweeping prohibitions may necessitate long lists of exceptions if the entire rule is to be literally applied. For example, the Defense Department[16] prohibits its personnel from accepting "any gift, gratuity, favor, entertainment, loan or any other thing of monetary value" from any person or entity doing business with or regulated by the Defense Department. The prohibited items are defined to include "any tangible item, intangible benefits, discounts, tickets, passes, transportation, and accommodations or hospitality. . . ." The Directive then uses three pages to list 15 exceptions to the rule.

Such specificity would be impossible in rules for Congress. Problems of specific application are best left to interpretation and to common-sense self-implementation. For instance, the general term "gift" in a rule should be interpreted to include such things as airplane rides and unusual hospitality without their being specifically mentioned. These should not be accepted by Members when cash would not be taken for the purpose of purchasing the services offered.

We prefer the wider scope of the unstated Senate rule, but have difficulties in attempting to codify it in simple form for literal application. A broad prohibition aimed at substantial gifts from all but relatives is chosen as the least objectionable alternative. The term "personal gift" is used to describe all gifts other than contributions to political campaigns and office funds. The term "substantial" permits customary wedding, birthday, and Christmas presents among friends. All others should be declined. We therefore recommend as follows:

Recommendation 6B
Each house should adopt the following rule: "No Member shall accept a substantial personal gift from anyone except a relative."

187

As a deterrent and procedural sanction against improper gifts, we also propose a rule requiring public disclosure of personal gifts worth more than $25:

Recommendation 6C

Each house should adopt a rule requiring public disclosure of all personal non-family gifts worth more than $25, along the lines of the Model Disclosure Rules set forth in Appendix B.

SUPPLEMENTAL FUNDS

In contrast to gifts, where the donee's use is unrestricted, supplemental funds are sometimes collected by or on behalf of a Member for a specific purpose, that of meeting unreimbursed expenses related to his office. These funds are akin to personal gifts if they enrich the Member by subsidizing expenses he would otherwise bear personally. They also resemble campaign contributions in that they enable a Member to better perform his job and thus enhance his chances of staying in office.

The expenses which supplemental funds underwrite are neither clearly legislative nor clearly political. They include the costs of publication and distribution of newsletters,* production of radio and television tapes, travel by a Member or his staff in excess of the allowed quotas, entertainment of constituents, flowers for constituents' funerals, contributions to charities, newspaper subscriptions, additional staff, and district-office, telephone, and stationery expenses over and above official allowances.

Sources of Supplemental Funds

These semi-official expenses do not seem to be ones which the public treasury should bear. Who, then, should pay for them? A number

---

* See Tacheron & Udall, THE JOB OF THE CONGRESSMAN 286–7 (1965), citing a study of operations in 158 Congressional offices. 121 Members indicated they sent a newsletter to constituents on a regular basis. 98 Members distributed newsletters by mailing list, 12 by mailing to all postal patrons, and 14 by both methods. In response to the question, "Does your office allowance cover the cost of your newsletter operation?" 31 Members replied "Yes" and 89 replied "No." See also *Campaign Brings on a Flood of Newsletters*, N.Y. TIMES, Oct. 18, 1968, at 35.

of Members use their own personal resources, as shown by Table 6.1:

TABLE 6.1

Does Member Use Personal Resources to Defray Official Expenses?**

	Yes	No
SENATE		
Senior (11)	36.4%	63.6%
Junior (7)	85.7	14.3
Total (18)	(55.6)	(44.4)
HOUSE		
Senior (35)	48.6	51.4
Junior (34)	85.3	14.7
Total (69)	(66.7)	(33.3)

* Responses were obtained before the salary was increased to $42,500.

One Senator from a large state told us that he invariably puts his entire salary into office-related expenses.† Another Member attempts to earn $1,000 a month in honoraria to cover such expenses. A third indicated that he had for eight years gone into debt $2,000 to $3,000 each year to cover the costs of being a Congressman. And another Member was able to claim $14,000 as deductible expenses on his 1968 income-tax retrn; he had no outside income and relied exclusively on his salary, although, unlike most Members, he maintains three offices in his district. Clearly, a Member without independent means should not have to go into debt to give his constituents adequate service.

Several Members of Congress whom we interviewed indicated that they usually had "modest" campaign surpluses which they used for political expenses between formal campaigns.‡ This suggests that

† In the Senate vote on the increase of Members' salaries to $42,500, 23 of 28 Senators (82.1 percent) from large states (over 4.5 million people) favored the increase, whereas only 31 of 68 Senators (45.5 percent) from small states favored it. Presumably the disparity is accounted for by the costs of meeting the greater volume of constituent demands on large-state Senators.

‡ Other dispositions of campaign surpluses include returning money to contributors; transferring the surplus to the state or local party treasury; and banking the money for use in the Member's next campaign.

campaign contributors should be allowed to supplement office funds as well. It is debatable whether there is a logical distinction between a supplemental fund resulting from a campaign surplus and one which is raised specifically to defray intra-term political expenses. If the view is taken that a Member may properly begin running for re-election the day after he is elected, the distinction between campaign funds and office funds is totally obscured.

A number of Members indicated in interviews that party organizations ought to pay these expenses. The Republican Congressional Campaign Committee already subsidizes all Republican Representatives in amounts ranging from $2,000 (for Members from "safe" districts) to $3,500 (for freshman Members and those from "marginal" districts) for office expenses and publicity. The use of these funds is restricted by the Committee. They may be used for public relations and "informational services," including newsletters, questionnaires, and other frankable matter; radio and television tapes; and reprints from the CONGRESSIONAL RECORD. We are informally advised that they may *not* be used for campaign expenses, staff salaries, professional-service fees, advertisements, travel and entertainment, postage, telephone, office equipment and supplies, Christmas cards, or gifts.[17] Thus the Republican fund seems designed to stay in the gray area of constituency service and to avoid both the "white" of official allowances and the "black" of campaign expenses.

The Democrats have no such fund. This may help to explain the fact that seven of the nine House Members interviewed who maintain office funds were Democrats. This leads to the final alternative means of raising such funds. A Member may call upon his supporters to pay his intra-term expenses by asking them to contribute to a supplemental office fund.

Prevalence of Supplemental Office Funds

Information gathered from our interviews on the prevalence of office funds is not conclusive, largely because many Members who do not have office funds as such nonetheless use surplus campaign contributions or testimonial-dinner proceeds to meet intra-term political expenses. Thirty-nine Representatives reported some outside source of funds for intra-term expenses, with surplus campaign funds cited most frequently as their source.

Forty-six Members of the House indicated that they use personal funds to subsidize official and semi-official expenses, as opposed to 23 who do not. Of those Members who responded to the question "Do you have an office expense fund?" three Senators and nine Representatives said they did.[18] Ten of these 12 were junior Members.

The first office expense fund to arouse public attention was established for the benefit of then-Senator Richard M. Nixon of California, who was reported in 1952 to have received an $18,000 fund to defray office expenses. Nixon answered demands for an explanation by appearing on nationwide television to reveal the nature of the fund. He contended that the fund was perfectly proper, that he used it for postage for mail "on which [he did] not choose to use the much-abused Senatorial franking privilege," for travel expenses, for printing speeches and documents "which otherwise might have been printed at the taxpayers' expense," and for extra clerical help needed to answer California mail.[19] The public appeared to forgive the fund when it became clear that Nixon had not profited personally.

Whether or not office expense funds were uncommon in 1952, they have become more prevalent in recent years. But they continue to be dangerous politically. Most officeholders, recalling Nixon's difficult experience, have either avoided establishing such funds or have avoided publicizing them.

In 1967 a newly elected Senator decided to establish an office expense fund and make it public, presumably in the expectation that such openness would disarm critics and redound to his credit. He sought to differentiate between campaign and office expenses and indicated that his supporters sought funds only for the latter. Those who contributed $500 or more were reportedly told by the fund-raisers that they would serve as "unofficial advisors" to the Senator and have "immediate mail access" to him. They reportedly were also promised social contacts with him in the form of cocktail parties, luncheons, and breakfasts at which they would be given "off-the-cuff" briefings. There was no indication that the Senator had approved these representations. Less than three months after the fund was first announced, it was officially dissolved, and the Senator, responding to press and public disapproval, returned the collected funds to the donors.

A freshman Senator announced in 1969 that a special fund had been set up by his supporters to pay for extra trips home, his wife's and aides' travel in his home state, and occasional newsletters. He hoped that by announcing the fund publicly he would avoid criticism, especially since it was made clear that he would have no control over the funds and that contributions to the fund could not exceed $100 nor would they be accepted from persons having business with the Senator. His only alternative to a fund, he said, was to "hit the honorarium trail hard," and he believed that individual $100 contributions presented fewer potential conflicts than honoraria from special-interest groups. The fund was later abandoned, presumably because of public criticism.

Shortly after Senator Charles Goodell (R-N.Y.) moved to the Senate from the House, he was quoted in a story in THE NEW YORK TIMES as saying: "You have nearly 50 times as many people to represent with three times the staff [that a House Member has] and twice as much money." Senator Goodell indicated that when he was a Representative a committee had solicited in his behalf small contributions totaling $8,000 or $9,000 each year for the costs of producing newsletters and unreimbursed travel. Goodell expressed his desire to "work out a completely circumspect, clean and open trust-fund . . . , where the money would not go into my hands but would pay these expenses, with a large base of contributors." [20] After a thorough study, however, he decided against establishing such a fund.

Office expense funds seem to be particularly popular among Members from the Southwest. In the 1968 debates on the Senate Ethics Code, Senator Ralph Yarborough (D-Tex.) led the move to restore the authorization of such funds after it had been removed by a close vote.[21] In 1969 one Texas Representative published in the CONGRESSIONAL RECORD a full disclosure of his office expense fund, showing that roughly $12,000 had been contributed to the fund and expended from it for newsletters and unreimbursed travel expenses. Another Texas Representative has a fund in the form of a club.* The club has 200 members, each of whom annually contributes $100, for a total of $20,000. This amount is used to defray office and campaign expenses.

---

* The "club" technique seems to be patterned after the Kennedy and Johnson "President's Club," which extended membership to those who contributed $1,000 or more to the Democratic Party. One Senator has "Senator's Clubs" in large cities in his state and extends membership to contributors of $100 or more. Club "dues" are used for constituency communication.

In return for his contribution, a club member has the privilege of attending dinners with VIP's brought by his Congressman. Through this quid pro quo the Member hopes to avoid having contributors believe that he is under any special obligation to them. Some of the Southwesterners with office expense funds are generally regarded as Members who are highly sensitive to ethical considerations. Their constituencies' distance from Washington causes additional travel and communication costs which they are unable to meet except through a supplemental fund.

House and Senate Ethics-Code Provisions

Nowhere in the House Ethics Code is there any language which applies specifically to supplemental office funds, but two provisions bear tangentially on the subject. As mentioned earlier, Rule 4 disallows the acceptance of gifts of substantial value from any person, organization, or corporation having a direct interest in legislation before the Congress. The other relevant provision, Rule 6, requires Members to keep campaign funds separate from personal funds and forbids conversion of campaign funds to personal uses. Reimbursement for legitimate and verifiable prior campaign expenditures is permitted. No reporting, disclosure, or specific enforcement mechanism attaches to it. We are advised by responsible sources that the House Ethics Committee regards supplemental office funds as equivalent to campaign funds.

The Senate Ethics Committee's Report accompanying its proposed Code of Ethics contained a detailed justification of supplemental office funds and observed:

> It is general knowledge that the expenses of conducting the office of a Senator have risen steadily over the years. The increasingly better informed public is taking a greater interest in public affairs. This brings about more communication between the public and the Senator, with consequent rising costs of correspondence, telephone and telegraph, radio and television broadcasting, quasi-official entertainment, and travel for a Senator. . . . Dedicated and efficient Senators, both in the past and at present, have found it necessary to accept funds from private sources in order to fulfill their responsibilities.[22]

193

As originally reported by the Ethics Committee, the Senate Code specified that a Senator might use contributions from fund-raising events or from individuals or organizations not only to influence his nomination or election but also to defray the "reasonable expenses . . . of his office." [23] The Committee Report contained an interesting statement about the difficulty of distinguishing between political campaign contributions and contributions to office expenses:

Although making a distinction between [these two] contributions . . . , the Committee agrees that a strong argument can be advanced that supplementary office expenses may be political expenses.[24]

The Report went on to conclude on the subject:[25]

After a thorough consideration of all of the ramifications, the committee decided to recommend the approval of office funds, subject to the following controls:

(a) Advance approval by the Senator of fund-raising events;

(b) complete and accurate accounting;

(c) use for political or office purposes only;

(d) office expenses must be reasonable; and

(e) public disclosure.

During the floor debate on adoption of the Code, Senator Clifford Case (R-N.J.) offered an amendment to delete its sanctioning of supplemental office funds. Senator Case advanced three arguments. First, he thought the Senate should not give color of official approval to what he regarded as a potentially corrupting practice. Second, if office expense allowances were inadequate, as Case conceded they were, they should be re-examined and increased by recommendation of the Rules and Administration Committee. Third, since public officials in the Executive Branch may not accept funds from private sources to finance performance of public duties,[26] the same rule should be followed in the Legislative Branch.

A principal difficulty of Case's position, according to Senator James B. Pearson (R-Kans.), is that it is nearly impossible to separate office expenses from campaign expenses. Newsletters, questionnaires, speeches and reports, and radio and television tapes all have an informative as well as a political purpose. Senator Pearson summarized the dilemma in the following excerpts from the Senate debate:

> . . . There is an annual reporting [of political contributions to Senators]. It is consistent, perhaps, with the ruling of the Bureau of Internal Revenue which declares that the day after U.S. Senators are elected, they are deemed to be candidates for reelection 6 years hence; so that funds which may be left over from a campaign may be used. That is how the ruling came up. Funds left over from a campaign, and so forth, should they be used, as they are used, in the operations of his office, and, incidentally, expenses which pertain to a campaign, are not deemed to be income.[27]

Later in the debate Senator Pearson continued:

> . . . [I]f this amendment [the Case amendment] is adopted the result will be that those who are able to and have the means to do it will pay for it out of their own pocket. Those who do not have the means will go without, until the campaign period, when money comes in under those auspices that are used for the office of a Senator.[28]

Senator Case acknowledged that Senators are running for re-election the day after they are elected and, accordingly, can regard all office expenses as political expenses payable from campaign funds.[29] This suggests the issue may be only a matter of labeling and book-keeping, not substance. Also, the substantial increases in allowances which Senator Case would support could, under the umbrella of "office expenses," include some which taxpayers have never borne, such as newsletters and recording tapes. These expenses unquestionably have a political flavor. To pay them from official allowances would, among other things, substantially increase the disadvantage of challengers.

In opposing the Case amendment, members of the Senate Ethics Committee argued further that the area of supplemental expenses was not subject to a uniform rule of prohibition since conditions vary so greatly from one state to the next. Some Senators observed that even with the office-fund section deleted, Senators could use surplus campaign funds for office expenses. The Committee indicated that it would rather deal with the problem directly than encourage circumventions.

The Case amendment was adopted by a vote of 41 to 40. The next day, however, the Senate reversed itself, in large part, when it voted 43 to 28 to adopt the Yarborough-Javits amendment.[30] This is now Senate Rule XLII (3) and reads:

> Nothing in this Rule shall preclude the use of contributions to defray expenses for travel to and from each Senator's home State; for printing and other expenses in connection with the mailing of speeches, newsletters and reports to a Senator's constituents; for expenses of radio, television and news media methods of reporting to a Senator's constituents; and for telephone, telegraph, postage and stationery expenses in excess of allowance; and for newspaper subscriptions from his home State.

Apparently the main rationale for sanctioning office funds was to avoid discriminating against poorer Senators. So long as Senators with private means could pay for office expenses out of pocket, Senators of modest means would be disadvantaged if denied such funds.

The amendment omitted certain expenses that would have been permitted by the rule as originally proposed, such as additional staff, uncompensated travel for staff, and constituent entertainment.[31]

Disclosure of Supplemental Funds

Senate Rule XLIV (3) (a) requires Senators to disclose annually all contributions received by them during the preceding year. The 1968 public disclosures[32] showed that eight Senators not up for reelection received amounts up to $13,000. Some Senators, known to have office funds, nonetheless reported no contributions, possibly because such funds are under the control of an independent committee. While control by an independent committee seems eminently sound, it should not serve to frustrate the public's interest in identifying the sources of a Member's financial support. Our Model Disclosure Rules in Appendix B attempt to remedy this omission.

In summary, supplemental funds tend to create ambiguous relationships between contributors and recipient Members of Congress. Although in many respects they are fraught with the same ambiguities as campaign contributions, the donor may be even more likely to believe that the recipient is under a special obligation to him. These office contributions are not *prima facie* essential to a Member's re-election, as are campaign contributions. A Member accepting these contributions may become beholden to a limited number of individuals who, according to one newspaper editorial, "may look . . . for special consideration from [the Member] to whom they have given special largesse." [33] Moreover, public disclosure of such funds does not fully remove the appearance of impropriety. Accordingly, this Committee proposes:

Recommendation 6D

Members of Congress should avoid establishing supplemental office funds. Members who establish such funds should publicly disclose all contributions and expenditures pursuant to rules along the lines of the Model Disclosure Rules set out in Appendix B. Individual contributions to such funds should be counted toward the legal limitation on the contributions made to an incumbent candidate during the term preceding his campaign for re-election, as recommended in Chapter 4.

HONORARIA

The term "honorarium" is defined by the Senate Ethics Code[34] to encompass fees received not only for speeches but also for "written articles, television appearances, participations in discussion groups, and similar paid services."

83.3 per cent of the Senators and 77.3 percent of the Representatives whom we interviewed reported earning honoraria income. A number of Members apply their honoraria to pay for intra-term political expenses of the sort borne by other Members' office expense funds. Some years ago one Senator was quoted:

> To do my duty as a Senator, I have to go back home and talk to people at least once a month. Each trip costs $200 to $250, and every time I go, I have to scrounge the countryside like the Russian Army making speeches and lectures along the way.[35]

Thirteen of the 15 interviewed Senators who accept honoraria receive over $1,000 annually from this source. In the House, 22 of 58 Representatives receive over $1,000.

TABLE 6.2

Amount of Yearly Honoraria Income

	Less than $1,000	$1,000 or More	$5,000 or More
SENATE			
Senior (5)	40.0%	60.0%	40.0%
Junior (10)	0	100.0	50.0
HOUSE			
Senior (34)	52.9%	47.1%	11.8%
Junior (24)	75.0	25.0	0

Complying with Senate Rule XLIV (3) (b) requiring annual public reporting of the amount and source of all honoraria of $300 or more, 61 Senators reported having received honoraria totaling $302,-920[36] in 1968.* The top earner reported six-month honoraria earnings totaling $18,158. The Senator second in earnings reported $21,556 for the full year. Thirty-one Senators reported no honoraria income. The highest single honorarium was $3,500, paid by the Savings and Loan League to a candidate running for re-election in 1968.

The main ethical problem involved in honoraria arises when a group with legislative interests within a Member's committee's jurisdiction invites that Member to speak for a fee, or when a union or corporation, otherwise prohibited from contributing to a Member's campaign, invites a Member to give a speech for a handsome honorarium. One Senator confided to us that certain groups paid him inflated honoraria to mask campaign contributions.

During the 1954 Senate debates on the motion to censure the late Senator Joseph R. McCarthy, it came out that McCarthy received $10,000 from a company whose affairs were within his committee's jurisdiction.[37] The money was paid for an unfinished manuscript.[38]

A number of Members acknowledged in our interviews that their

---

* Most reports covered the full 1968 calendar year, but several Senators accounted only for July 1 through December 31, 1968, since the new rules took effect on July 1, 1968.

speaking invitations arose from their committee positions. One Senator told us of a large communications company paying him and another Senator $2,000 each and expenses to Florida while both were on the Commerce Committee. Another Senator reported in the 1969 public disclosures a $1,000 honorarium received from the National Forest Products Association contemporaneously with his sponsoring legislation and conducting hearings in which it was vitally interested.[39]

Examination of the public disclosure of Senators' honoraria also bears out the connection between committee duties and honoraria.[40] One Member noted that certain members of the Banking and Currency Committee were well traveled on "the banking and savings and loan honorarium circuit."

The banking and merchant-marine communities appear from the Senate disclosures and from news reports to be the most active and most generous sources of honoraria. The National League of Insured Savings Associations paid an honorarium of $1,000 to a member of the Senate Banking and Currency Committee. Another Senator on the same committee received $1,200 for a speech to the National Mortgage Banking Association.[41]

It has been reported that several members of the House Merchant Marine, Education and Labor, and Appropriations Committees received honoraria as high as $1,250 for delivering speeches in Washington prepared for them by their hosts, the Maritime Trades Department.[42] According to this report, 55 fees were paid in a recent 12-month period to strategically placed Members of Congress for speaking to Maritime Trades Department lunches, breakfasts, and seminars.

From our interviews and from the 1969 Senate honoraria disclosures, we have developed skeletal data on the market in Congressional speaking fees. Senators who are both powerful and eloquent command honoraria as high as $2,500. A number of Members were asked whether they had any limit on the amount they would accept for a speech. One Senator replied that he was quite sure $1,500 was not too much, but $5,000 might be excessive. No Representatives other than a few committee chairmen are in such demand. One Senator, when asked whether he earned in the range of $5,000 in honoraria per year replied, "Even in a lean year, it doesn't get as low as *that!*"

Another Senator follows four rules with regard to honoraria: (1)

He speaks for pay only to organizations which normally have outside speakers. (2) He speaks only on his legislative specialties (conservation and environmental control). (3) He watches amounts to be sure he stays within the norms of the particular organization and never accepts more than $500. (4) He refuses a fee if the theme of his speech coincides with the inviting organization's legislative interests. Many Members indicated that they refuse honoraria from groups within their states or districts. One Member donates his honoraria to charity.[43]

It is believed that most Members are sensitive to excessive honoraria and can recognize the situation when one is used as a device to tender money for collateral purposes. What is not known is how often the excess is nonetheless accepted and whether the recipient is influenced. In any case, the most appropriate regulation of honoraria income seems to be full disclosure.

The 1969 Senate disclosure was fairly complete and revealing, except in the case of a few Senators who named lecture bureaus rather than principals as the sources of honoraria. According to one Senator, these bureaus generally initiate contact with better-known Members and offer their promotional and managerial services in exchange for a percentage of honoraria received. Members whose engagements are arranged by lecture bureaus may not only speak more often and earn more money than they otherwise would, but they are spared the demeaning and potentially embarrassing task of negotiating speaking fees. As a matter of interpretation, the Senate rule should be construed, however, to require reporting of original sources rather than agents through whom honoraria may be channeled and sources concealed.

Rule 5 of the House Code prohibits acceptance of an honorarium "in excess of the usual and customary value for such services." The obvious question is what are the criteria for determining "usual and customary value." The House Report indicates the test is to be what another person "of equal public importance" [44] could command. Honoraria disclosure is required of House Members only if a single source produces honoraria exceeding $5,000 in one year—a figure considerably higher than the arguably fair value in almost any case.

Senators now disclose to the public honoraria over $300, and there is no reason why Representatives should not do so as well. While disclosure is probably a sufficient remedy, the Senate should also adopt the House rule against acceptance of excessive honoraria. The formal rule may have some deterrent effect by expressly reminding the Member that a fee which appears excessive might invite investigation by the Ethics Committee.

Recommendation 6E

The House of Representatives should adopt the Senate rule requiring public disclosure of each honorarium of $300 or more, as provided in the Model Disclosure Rules set forth in Appendix B.*

Recommendation 6F

The Senate should adopt the House rule prohibiting acceptance of an honorarium "in excess of the usual and customary value for such services."

* On January 27, 1970, the House Ethics Committee recommended that the House Code be amended to this effect. N.Y. TIMES, Jan. 27, 1970, at 25, col. 1.

CHAPTER SEVEN

CONGRESSIONAL SELF-DISCIPLINE: ETHICS CODES AND COMMITTEES

Constitutional Provisions

Article I of the Constitution of the United States provides in Section 5, Clause 1, that each house of Congress "shall be the Judge of the Elections, Returns and Qualifications of its own Members." Clause 2 then confers additional powers:

> Each House may determine the Rules of its Proceedings, punish its Members for disorderly Behavior, and, with the Concurrence of two thirds, expel a Member.

There are basically two reasons why each house must have these powers over its own Members. First, they have been historically demonstrated to be necessary for the proper functioning of the legislative process. The authority to make rules governing its proceedings and to discipline Members for misbehavior is essential to the effectiveness of each house as a deliberative lawmaking group.

Secondly, each house was given those powers and privileges necessary to constitute Congress as a separate, independent, co-equal branch of the Federal government. Among these are the Congressional-immunity provisions, the principal one being the Speech and Debate Clause, which protects Members from being "questioned" elsewhere about their official conduct.[1] This was intended to free the Congress and individual Members from possible harassment and usurpations by other branches of the government. However, each Member of Congress would enjoy full license to misuse his Congressional immunity if each house were not given correlative powers and responsibilities to police Members' behavior. For instance, the previously mentioned action of former Representative Thomas Johnson of Maryland, who allegedly accepted a bribe for delivering a speech on the House floor, was immune from criminal prosecution.[2] Such conduct is not absolutely privileged, but lies instead within the jurisdiction of Congress itself to punish. Bribery has been the basis for Congressional discipline on several occasions.[3] The duty of each house to discipline its Membership is a burden made necessary by the prerogatives of high office. If Congress did not police itself, its Members would be above all law in the areas protected by Congressional immunity, a concept alien to our legal system and never intended by the framers of the Constitution.

The power of the voters to deny re-election to a Member is another and perhaps more important form of discipline, but it cannot be exclusive. Suppose a stubborn constituency was fully aware of gross misconduct but nonetheless re-elected a Member? The Constitution empowers his colleagues to deal with this situation. The continued presence in Congress of a dangerously errant legislator was not intended to be solely a matter for his own constituents. At some point the entire nation, as represented by the total membership of the House or Senate, has an interest which may override the wishes of a single constituency.

The three Constitutional sanctions for Congressional self-discipline are expulsion, exclusion, and punishment. We shall take them in the obviously descending order of seriousness.

Expulsion

Each house may expel a duly elected and seated Member by two-thirds vote. No express limits or qualifications are placed upon the power to expel, and it was apparently intended that it could be exercised for any reason sufficient to a particular house. This is one of several areas where the Constitution places ultimate power in two-thirds majorities in the Congress. By two-thirds votes of both houses, Congress may override Presidential vetoes. By such votes it also may remove an incapacitated President or propose Constitutional amendments. Upon impeachment charges initiated in the House, the Senate may by a two-thirds vote remove Federal executive or judicial officials, including the President or the Chief Justice. Impeachment was not provided for Members of Congress, apparently because the plenary power of expulsion was regarded as its equivalent.

As the framers doubtless contemplated, Congress has been extremely reluctant to use its power of expulsion. Except during the passions generated by the Civil War, when 22 Senators were expelled for disloyalty, the Senate has expelled only one duly elected Member. This occurred in 1797, when Senator William Blount of Tennessee was expelled for his extra-Congressional activities in scheming with British agents and dealing with Indians. The Supreme Court later referred to the Blount action as illustrating the scope of the expulsion power, noting that Blount's misconduct involved neither a "statutable offence" nor any official conduct, and concluding generally:

> The right to expel extends to all cases where the offence is such as in the judgment of the Senate is inconsistent with the trust and duty of a member.[4]

The House has used the power of expulsion even more guardedly. All three expulsions of Representatives were on grounds of treason and occurred at the beginning of the Civil War.

Exclusion

In adjudging a Member-elect to be unqualified and then excluding him, both houses have occasionally used this power as the equivalent of expulsion. In so doing, they sometimes achieved by simple majority vote what the Constitution framers intended to be reserved for a two-thirds majority. Exclusion of a prospective Member is not listed in the Constitution with the disciplinary powers of Congress and is incidental not to Congressional discipline but to the final authority of Congress over the process of its Members' elections.

204

The exclusion issue arises most frequently in the resolution of election contests, where a house acts as a supreme board of elections, not a guardian of Congressional ethics. On rare occasions, however, both houses have used the power to reject Members-elect adjudged to be unfit to serve in the body. Such exclusions are based on ethical determinations and serve obvious disciplinary functions. They also carry serious implications for traditional concepts of representative government. The most recent such exclusion, that of Representative Adam Clayton Powell (D-N.Y.), produced the decision of the United States Supreme Court in *Powell v. McCormack*.[5]

Both the holding and the background of the *Powell* case merit close study. The history of Mr. Powell's various encounters with Congressional self-discipline illustrates the range of institutional sanctions available for use against an errant Member.

Representative Powell entered the House from the Harlem district of Manhattan in 1945, was regularly re-elected thereafter, and rose by virtue of seniority to chairmanship of the Education and Labor Committee. In time an accumulation of charges of indiscretion in his private life, excessive absenteeism and junketing, contempt of New York courts, and misuse of public funds brought him under widespread public and Congressional criticism.

Powell's downfall within the Congress probably dates from February 5, 1963, when Senator John J. Williams (R-Del.) delivered a speech on the Senate floor which raised several charges against him and challenged Powell's fitness to conduct a proposed House investigation of juvenile delinquency.[6] Powell soon answered charges based upon his wife's being on his office payroll and his personal use of overseas counterpart funds by saying that other Members did the same things. He also attributed Senator Williams' charges to the fact that Powell was black.[7]

The House then began a unique series of disciplinary steps against Powell. On March 6, 1963, it cut Powell's committee's funds from a requested two-year grant of $697,000 to a one-year figure of $200,000. In an even more extraordinary move, $150,000 of this sum was made directly available to subcommittees and placed beyond Powell's control.[8]

In the succeeding Congress a bipartisan revolt against Powell arose within the Education and Labor Committee. Frustrated by his absenteeism and erratic actions in handling particular labor and poverty legislation, the Committee, by a 27-to-1 vote, adopted new rules which stripped Powell of much of his power. It empowered subcommittee chairmen to take bills directly to the House floor under certain circumstances, thus depriving Powell of the traditional ability of a chairman to delay legislation. Severe restrictions were also placed on Powell's power over funds and staff.[9] An unidentified member was quoted as saying that "the rules leave Powell nothing but his gavel." [10]

In the same month, September 1966, an official investigation was begun of alleged misuse of committee funds and personnel of Powell's committee. It was conducted by the House Administration Committee's Special Subcommittee on Contracts, chaired by Representative Wayne Hays (D-Ohio). The subcommittee reported on January 3, 1967, and made several findings adverse to Powell. It condemned his misuse of public funds, and recommended that Mrs. Powell be discharged from her $20,578-a-year position.[11] She had disregarded a subcommittee subpoena, but there was nonetheless sufficient evidence to raise a strong presumption that her employment was illegal because she resided in Peurto Rico and apparently did not work for Powell either in Washington or in his Congressional district.

Powell had met the Hays subcommittee's invitation to testify by offering to prove nepotism and junketing by other Members,[12] and the 90th Congress convened on January 10, 1967, amid widespread public and Congressional demands for punitive action. On January 9 the House Democratic Caucus stripped Powell of his party seniority and deprived him of his chairmanship of the Education and Labor Committee. Proponents of this move deemed it a pro-Powell measure, arguing that otherwise the House would not seat him. Nonetheless, by a 363-to-65 vote, the House moved against Powell the next day and required him to stand aside without being seated while a select committee investigated him. By denying Powell his seat pending the investigation, the House departed from its own precedents. Normally, a challenged Member-elect who has been duly certified is seated provisionally pending resolution of the issue bearing on his qualifications or election. The regular procedure was followed on the same day in the case of Representative Ben Blackburn (R-Ga.), who was challenged because of alleged irregularities in his election.[13]

A committee of nine lawyer-Members, headed by Judiciary Committee Chairman Emanuel Celler (D-N.Y.), proceeded to investigate Powell's qualifications. This committee was carefully chosen from Members who could not be charged with racial bias and included one black Representative. Nonetheless, Powell angered his House colleagues by public statements that the movement against him was racially motivated, calling it a "lynching Northern style," and himself a "black Dreyfus." [14] Powell may have further alienated House Members by then refusing to answer any questions unrelated to his age, citizenship, and inhabitancy, contending that the committee lacked jurisdiction beyond the three stated grounds of Constitutional eligibility for the House.*

When it reported on February 23, the committee agreed with Powell that he possessed the requisite Constitutional qualifications and could not be excluded. However, it found punishment to be warranted and recommended that Powell be seated but then censured, denied seniority,† and fined $40,000.[15]

The committee stated four specific categories of Powell's misconduct: (1) contumacious conduct toward New York courts, which reflected discredit on the House of Representatives; (2) maintaining his wife on the Congressional payroll while she performed no services and was not located where she could lawfully be employed to perform services; (3) expenditure of government funds for private purposes; and (4) refusal to cooperate with the two Congressional committees which had investigated his activities.

The House's response had probably been predestined since January 10, when Powell had virtually dared it to go through with punitive action. When temporarily denied his seat, he told the House, "[H]e who is without sin should cast the first stone. There is no one here who does not have a skeleton in his closet. I know, and I know them by name." [16] As though it were proving its collective courage and integrity by accepting Powell's dare, the House did much more than

---

* Article I, Section 2, of the Constitution provides that no person shall be a Representative "who shall not have attained to the Age of twenty-five Years, and been seven Years a Citizen of the United States, and who shall not, when elected, be an Inhabitant of that State in which he shall be chosen." Otherwise identical language in Section 4 requires that a Senator be 30 years of age and have been a citizen for nine years.

† This refers to general seniority in the House itself, not the party seniority which determines committee chairmanships. Only room assignments depend on House seniority as such.

cast a stone. It rejected the committee's recommendations as inadequate by voting 222 to 202 against a motion to bring them to a vote. The committee's resolution was then amended to require Powell's exclusion and passed by a final vote of 307 to 116.[17] This was done despite express recognition in the resolution that Powell possessed the requisite qualifications of age, citizenship, and inhabitancy.*

Powell was overwhelmingly re-elected in the special election which was held to fill the vacancy, but did not present himself again to the 90th Congress. Instead, he relied solely on a lawsuit brought in the District Court for the District of Columbia against Speaker John W. McCormack, Majority Leader Carl Albert, Minority Leader Gerald Ford, and two Members of the select committee which had investigated him. The Clerk of the House, the Sergeant-at-Arms, and the Doorkeeper were also named as defendants. Powell alleged that the House's action was unconstitutional on its face and that its Members were lawfully obligated to seat him. The House employees were therefore alleged to be wrongfully denying to Powell the perquisites of membership. Declaratory and injunctive relief were sought, including an order to the Sergeant-at-Arms to require payment of his Congressional salary.

The District Court granted the defendants' motions to dismiss, and the Court of Appeals for the District of Columbia Circuit affirmed. The United States Supreme Court reversed, in an opinion which, while indeed historic, is not as broad in its holdings as some may have thought.

A fact which is missed in many discussions of the *Powell* litigation is that the Supreme Court affirmed the dismissal of Powell's action against the five named Members of the House of Representatives. Although the case will historically be styled *"Powell v. McCormack,"* the Court held that Powell had no case against the Speaker. The Speech and Debate Clause was held to render the Members immune from the action because it was based upon their official legislative conduct. However, the lower courts were reversed as to the three employees of the House, and the case was remanded for favorable declaratory relief and further proceedings against them.

---

* The Speaker had ruled that a majority vote of the House would be sufficient for final passage. This indicated that the House was acting under the exclusion power rather than the power to expel and implicitly included a ruling that the House could exclude on extra-Constitutional grounds.

The money involved turned out to be the grounds of judicial jurisdiction. The Court accepted Powell's contention that the framers of the Constitution gave the people the right to be represented by whomever they choose, subject only to the mandatory qualifications of age, citizenship, and inhabitancy, which are the sole criteria to be judged by the House in a duly elected Member. The basis for withholding Powell's salary was therefore unconstitutional and he asserted a valid property right against the Sergeant-at-Arms. The decision can result in no court orders against the House or its Members, but it could possibly lead to a painful dilemma for the Sergeant-at-Arms if he is faced with conflicting orders from Congressional superiors and a Federal judge. The section of the Court's opinion on the merits of the exclusion issue is included in Appendix F. It fully treats the history of the subject in England and this country, including the Constitutional background and Congressional precedents. It is recommended reading for close students of our subject.

The *Powell* case's reasoning leaves unaffected the ultimate power of Congress to dissociate itself from an errant Member. The Court wisely confined itself to the case at hand and emphasized that it was not passing upon the power of a house to expel a seated Member. In the highly unlikely event that a house is ever driven to an irrational use of the expulsion power, the Supreme Court will then be compelled to face this more difficult question. Short of this, all concerned should follow the admonition of Mr. Justice Miller, who said in a similar context:

It is not necessary to decide here that there may not be things done, in the one House or the other, of an extraordinary character, for which the members who take part in the act may be held legally responsible. If we could suppose the members of these bodies so far to forget their high functions and the noble instrument under which they act as to imitate the Long Parliament in the execution of the Chief Magistrate of the nation, or to follow the example of the French Assembly in assuming the function of a court for capital punishment we are not prepared to say that such an utter perversion of their powers to a criminal purpose would be screened from punishment by the constitutional provision for freedom of debate.[18]

209

In the meantime Powell had been elected to the 91st Congress. This time the House seated him and imposed punitive conditions comparable to those recommended in the 90th Congress, but with only a $25,000 fine and without censure.[19] This action is probably unassailable as an exercise of the House's power to punish, rather than an attempt to require extra-Constitutional qualifications under the power to exclude.

Censure and Other Punishment

Although the power to "punish . . . for disorderly behavior" has usually taken only the form of censure, the *Powell* case shows that the House, in both the 90th and 91st Congresses, did not doubt its power to impose a fine as well. Traditional forms of punishment used in criminal law were probably within the contemplation of the framers when they used the term "punish" and gave Congress adjudicative functions over matters insulated from the courts. The Supreme Court has even indicated that imprisonment of a Member is a possible punishment.[20]

Censure is not an innocuous sanction, and Congress has been very sparing in its use. Fifteen House Members have been censured; the latest instance, in 1921, was for placing obscene material in the CONGRESSIONAL RECORD.[21] The Senate has resorted to censure on seven occasions, the most recent being those involving Senator McCarthy in 1954 and Senator Dodd in 1967.

Analyses of the records of the two houses show differing patterns in their use of the censure power.[22] In each case of Senate censure the offender was guilty of some conduct which may not have been unlawful but which went against generally accepted norms of Senatorial behavior. In each instance some written or unwritten standard of the Senate was violated by such conduct as fighting on the Senate floor, publicizing confidential information, or verbally abusing Senatorial colleagues. In contrast, the House has sometimes punished conduct which could have been the basis of criminal prosecution. In several nineteenth-century cases Representatives were censured for indictable instances of bribery.[23] When Powell was excluded in 1967 and seated with punishments in 1969, the fact that criminal prosecutions were also possible for some of the alleged misconduct was not considered to preclude punitive action by the House.

The appropriateness of Congressional discipline for criminal mat-

210

ters will be considered in evaluating the present codes of Congressional ethics. As will be shown there, investigative action short of discipline and the forwarding of evidence of criminal violations to appropriate law-enforcement officials can occur and has occurred in both houses.

REASONS FOR CONGRESSIONAL RELUCTANCE TO DISCIPLINE MEMBERS

The historical record compels one conclusion: Congress is reluctant to police its Members' ethics by formal discipline. Expulsion is virtually non-existent. Exclusion has properly been reserved largely for election contests. Although the Senate has used censure twice in the last fifteen years, it can hardly be said that censure is invoked in all circumstances for which it might be appropriate. (However, it must be added that the salutary effects of unused Congressional disciplinary power are much greater than is shown on the surface of the record. Several Members have resigned or declined to seek re-election because of pending or potential disciplinary proceedings.) The reasons for the reluctance of Congress to discipline itself are quite complex. Since they account for its long delay in adopting codes of ethics and could still affect the level of ethics enforcement, the causes of Congressional restraint merit close analysis.

Two political scientists who reviewed the Congressional disciplinary record to the early 1950's reached conclusions unsympathetic to Congress. Both largely attributed Congressional reluctance to discipline Members to a "club spirit" or institutional self-protectiveness which causes Members of Congress either to ignore misconduct or to close ranks in defense of an impugned Member. One was H. H. Wilson, whose CONGRESS: CORRUPTION AND COMPROMISE has already been mentioned. The other was George A. Graham, who wrote MORALITY IN AMERICAN POLITICS.

Graham's views have since been provocatively woven into a broader evaluation by scholars Rogow and Lasswell:

Although there was some corruption in the Senate and House during the years preceding the Civil War, it was political ambition rather than opportunities for corruption that attracted most men to legislative careers. Indeed, the prestige of the House of Representatives was such as to make a number of congressmen, notably Henry Clay, reluctant to leave the House for a seat in the Senate. Membership in the House, and especially the speakership, were regarded as providing more certain access than a Senate seat to higher positions in the government, including the presidency. During the era that closed with the Civil War three speakers of the House were nominated for the presidency, and one of them, James K. Polk, was subsequently elected president. In the one hundred years since the election of Abraham Lincoln only one speaker, James G. Blaine, has been nominated—unsuccessfully—for the highest office.

The declining prestige of Congress after the Civil War, however, provides only one part of the explanation for the prevalence of legislative corruption in the so-called "Gilded Age." In the House of Representatives, especially, corrupt behavior owes a good deal to the failure of both the leadership and membership to enforce rectitude standards. Although the leaders of the Senate and the House after the Civil War were not, for the most part, less able or capable than their pre-War predecessors, unlike them they were largely passive in the face of widespread evidence that much legislative business was transacted in a corrupt fashion. Moreover, an indifferent attitude toward corrupt behavior of members remains characteristic of both houses. As George A. Graham has observed, the Senate and House have taken disciplinary action "chiefly when issues have been forced upon them by publicity or other outside pressure, and punishment has been meager." No senator or congressman "has been expelled or disciplined in any way for receiving money, gifts, services, swimming pools, lakes, or anything else from contractors doing business with the government." In fact, according to Graham, "no member has been expelled for violation of the law even when indicted, tried, and convicted of crime." The "implication" of such inaction "is that according to Congressional standards anything goes, not only everything the law allows, but also what it does not allow." Unable or unwilling to enforce rectitude standards with regard to its own membership, the legislative branch is hardly in a position to establish itself as a moral model for behavior at executive and administrative levels.[24]

In reaching similar conclusions, Wilson cited a statement of former House Speaker Champ Clark, who likened the "House spirit" to the morale of a military unit, saying, "Men who fight together in this legislative body have a feeling approximating that of soldiers' feeling for one another." [25]

Institutional loyalty undoubtedly plays a part, but it can be exaggerated. Writing in 1966, Professor Robert Getz criticized Graham and Wilson for overemphasizing club spirit and offered as an additional cause of Congressional reluctance the historic fact that individual uses of the disciplinary power are likely to become overly political.[26] He concluded that Congress' long delay in establishing an effective Congressional code of ethics resulted partly from the legislators' belief that "an objective setting for the enforcement of such a code cannot be achieved within the halls of Congress." [27] In support of this doubt, Getz documented evidence of political partisanship in several disputes over disciplining Members. For instance, in 1967 a much higher proportion of Republicans than Democrats cast anti-Powell votes, with only 11 of 184 Republicans opposing exclusion on the final vote. In the Senate, both the Rules Committee and the Senate itself split along party lines in holding the Baker investigation within narrow limits which minimized possible political repercussions upon other Senators, President Johnson, and the Democratic Party. On several key votes, Republicans were unanimous in their unsuccessful efforts to broaden the Baker investigation, while Democrats were opposing them with near unanimity.[28]

Another oft-cited justification for Congressional inaction in this area is the belief that the electoral process should be the exclusive discipline and that fundamental rights of people to choose representatives of their choice might be imperiled by regular Congressional discipline of Members. Former Senator Glenn H. Taylor was quoted as stating this view in these words:

. . . [N]othing is more sacred than the right of the people to choose their own Representatives and Senators. If a legislative body could, on flimsy pretext, eliminate men whose politics are distasteful, democracy would become a meaningless word.[29]

This view has considerable appeal in terms of democratic theory, but our system contemplates some limits on voters' free choice and makes a measure of self-discipline one of the duties of Congressional service. Taylor's reasoning justifies caution but not abdication of Congressional responsibility for its Members' ethical standards.

Another reason which motivates some Members to move slowly is the fear that repercussions from individual cases may produce more harm than good in over-all effects upon public confidence in the Congress. Many Members harbor genuine distrust of the press and fear that zealous newsmen may mislead the public into thinking that an aberrant Member is typical of the group. They fear that any praise of Congress for taking disciplinary action will be lost in the sensational features of a case. This view was reflected somewhat in a letter written by Representative Celler to H. H. Wilson:

> There is no doubt that an esprit de corps does exist among members of Congress and they do their best to protect each other. This is not, of course, without its unfortunate aspects, but it must be remembered that members of Congress are assailed more often for their shortcomings than they are praised for their good work. It is natural, therefore, for them to fly to each other's defense. It must be remembered too that very often the whole body is condemned for the misdeeds of one. When one is guilty or allegedly guilty of misconduct, it is not unusual to find that Congressmen generally are assailed. . . . I am not attempting to defend this "esprit de corps"; I am merely explaining it.[30]

A further reason for Congressional reluctance to discipline its Members stems from its general need for harmony among Members if it is to function effectively. Testifying before the Douglas Subcommittee on Ethical Standards in Government in 1951, Senator William Fulbright (D-Ark.) noted the competing interests and resolved the conflict in favor of harmony. He said:

> I see this in the press very often: "Why does not the Congress clean its own house? Why do they not discipline their own Members? Why do they not do so-and-so?"
>
> I simply do not agree that it is the proper function of the Congress. I think it is extremely difficult to make 96 people from

divers parts of the country get along in some harmony. If we undertake to discipline our own Members and that sort of thing, we will really bog down in recrimination and not accomplish anything. The greater purpose of making the Government function far outweighs these individual delinquencies. . . .[31]

In 1963, after Senator Williams denounced Representative Powell on the Senate floor, Senator Wayne Morse (D-Ore.) challenged the wisdom of Williams' course of action and sought to have his remarks stricken from the record. Morse thought the prohibition of Senate Rule XIX, which precludes one Senator from imputing unworthy conduct or motives to another, should be extended to cover similar imputations of Representatives. In Morse's view, the legislative effectiveness of the entire Congress was imperiled by such unusual use of floor privileges as Williams' criticism of Powell.[32] Obviously, the need for Congressional harmony and a spirit of good will works against any ambitious program for Congressional self-discipline. The acrimony and trauma which are suffered in heated disciplinary cases should be reserved for compelling circumstances.

This leads to a final reason for the relative disuse of Congressional disciplinary powers. Most Members understandably regard it as a diversion from their main business. When it was suggested to one veteran Senator who has been active in the field that the Senate Ethics Committee should take on a responsibility comparable to that of a grievance committee of a bar association, he quickly retorted: "Then who's going to take care of their constituents?" The Dodd case occupied the Senate Ethics Committee for 16 months and required 10 days of public committee hearings which filled 1,164 printed pages. It was the principal business of the entire Senate for nine legislative days, and the debate filled 300 of the Congressional Record's copious pages. The Senators who were actively involved can look back on many long hours of strife-ridden work. For many reasons, busy legislators want very few repetitions of their experience in the Dodd case.

Despite these negative considerations, both houses now have standing ethics committees and written codes of conduct. In the light of the understandable Congressional reluctance of the past, one may well wonder how such developments came about. A brief survey of their legislative history may suggest some answers.

HISTORY OF THE SENATE ETHICS
COMMITTEE AND CODE

The Senate Ethics Committee had its origins in the Rules Committee's investigation of Robert Baker. Baker resigned his position as Secretary to the Democratic Majority following initial revelations of misuse of his office for personal financial gain. The Senate then unanimously authorized the Committee on Rules and Administration to investigate financial interests of any Senate employee or former employee.[33] On July 8, 1964, the Rules Committee reported its first round of findings and recommended passage of a resolution requiring limited disclosure of assets and income by employees and Senators. Although the Committee divided along party lines on the adequacy of the Baker findings, it was unanimous on the disclosure recommendation. In supplemental views Senator John Sherman Cooper (R-Ky.) asserted the additional need for a permanent bipartisan Senate committee for investigating ethical charges. Cooper took as his example the special temporary committee which had investigated Senator Joseph McCarthy in 1954, and said of the role of a permanent committee:

> Such a committee, unhampered by other legislative duties which are in the jurisdiction of every committee, including the Rules Committee, would be able to deal with actual breaches of rules and standards with dispatch and firmness. The equal division of membership between the majority and minority parties would tend to remove any element of partisanship. I do not believe such a committee would be considered as a policing body in the narrow sense of the term, but as a group of distinguished Members of the Senate, its existence would have great influence in deterring violations of rules or standards of conduct that would reflect upon the U.S. Senate.[34]

It should be noted that Senator Cooper's main argument was that the mere *existence* of such a committee would deter unethical conduct.

After an amendment was approved giving the Rules Committee compulsory jurisdiction over ethical charges, Senator Cooper then introduced a substitute amendment which embodied his proposal for an ethics committee. The debate and legislative action which followed have been aptly summarized by Professor Getz:

> While the overwhelming majority of the Democratic Senators sat silent, a small group of Republicans, led by the three-man minority of the Rules Committee, urged that the Select Committee be created. They were abetted by Senator Mundt who noted that the unhappy experience of the Rules Committee was the result of too much politics. He added that he was not criticizing the majority members, because it was probably too much to expect them to damage their own party in an election year.
>
> The voice of dissent was raised primarily by Senator Spessard L. Holland (D, Fla.) and Senator Dirksen. The former stressed the affront to the Rules Committee; the latter expressed the Senate's traditional reluctance to question a fellow member's conduct or his concept of his congressional responsibilities.
>
> With his usual eloquence and sarcasm, Dirksen probably spoke for more of his compatriots than the voting would indicate when he said:

> "I shall be happy to vote for the Cooper substitute, because it is fair and impartial, it is an objective, non-political way of going about the job of snooping on one another, if there exists a prevailing opinion that this should be done to make the U.S. Senate appear decent and honorable and respectable. . . .
>
> ". . . This is no way to build up mutual respect and amity within a legislative body. If we do not trust each other, let us then adopt the amendment . . . , and at least keep the process clean and equitable insofar as politics are concerned."

Mr. Dirksen followed up his remarks by joining 32 of his compatriots in a vain attempt to defeat the Cooper substitute. Among those casting negative votes were Senators Mansfield, Clark, Morse, and Neuberger. The last three legislators are among the chief exponents of strong disclosure legislation. Their action may be interpreted as a reflection of their well-founded fears that the disclosure motion would be scuttled. They, along with Dirksen, cast their lot with the majority to pass the amended resolution, 61–19.[35]

Although the Ethics Committee was authorized on July 24, 1964, it was not until July 9, 1965, that Members were appointed to it,* and the Committee did not organize itself and set up a staff until October 21, 1965. The Committee announced at the time that it accepted

the duty of attempting to express its understanding of the standards of conduct in the field of senatorial responsibility which the people of the United States are entitled to expect of Senators and their staffs, and the officers and employees of the Senate.[36]

The Committee viewed as its main responsibility the establishment of rules to govern the gray areas in which Baker had operated. That its jurisdiction was considerably broader is shown by its enabling resolution (Appendix D). The investigation of Senator Dodd intervened soon after the Committee was organized and became its first order of business. The Dodd matter preoccupied the Committee and its staff until June 1967. The Committee then resumed its study of a code of ethics and reported to the Senate on March 15, 1968.

As Senator Stennis stated at the time, the Senate Code did not purport to be complete. It dealt mainly with the issues raised by the Dodd and Baker cases and stopped considerably short of the public disclosure recommended earlier by the Rules Committee. The Senate approved the Code without major changes other than some dilution of its provisions on office expense funds and solicitation of political funds by staff. A proposed amendment calling for greater financial disclosure was defeated 44 to 40.[37]

HISTORY OF THE HOUSE ETHICS COMMITTEE AND CODE

On July 28, 1966, the Joint Committee on the Organization of the Congress recommended that the House follow the Senate's example by creating its own ethics committee.[38] Moved by this and the begin-

* Majority Leader Mansfield stated at the time that appointments to the Committee were deliberately delayed until the Rules Committee completed the Baker matter so that there would be no problems of overlapping jurisdiction between the two committees. N.Y. TIMES, July 10, 1965, at 8.

nings of internal sanctions against Powell, the House Rules Committee voted out a resolution late in the 88th Congress which established a Select Committee on Standards and Conduct. It was sponsored by Representative Charles Bennett (D-Fla.), who had long been in the vanguard of House efforts at ethical reform. A committee of six Republicans and six Democrats was proposed to investigate allegations of conduct which might reflect upon the House or which violated applicable rules or laws.

Bennett's resolution met vigorous opposition from Representative Wayne Hays, who referred to it as suicidal "self-immolation." House Members first appeared to agree with Hays, because a voice vote quickly tabled Bennett's resolution. But on a roll-call vote the House reversed itself and kept the issue alive by a vote of 238 to 24. The resolution was then amended to merely create a study committee charged with recommending a code of ethics to the House. This was approved by a vote of 256 to 0.[39]

This committee, headed by Representative Bennett, had only two and one-half months to function because its life was limited to the balance of the 89th Congress. It was able to do nothing more than to recommend re-establishment of the committee in the 90th Congress. This was achieved by a vote of 400 to 0 on April 13, only six weeks after Powell was excluded.[40]

In the Powell debates several Members had called for a permanent ethics committee to ensure due process in future disciplining of Members and to counter the charge that other Members could commit similar offenses with impunity. One of the more eloquent statements to this effect was made by Representative Hervey Machen (D-Md.):

> Now that the difficult decision has been made to exclude a Member who had served in these Halls for over 22 years, the House cannot quickly turn its back and pretend as though nothing has happened.
>
> The Nation and the world have watched our actions closely and I know that there is a question in many quarters as to why Representative Powell's behavior went on so long. The actions of Adam Clayton Powell were deplorable but they were tolerated by this House for a long period of time.
>
> The formation of a strong Committee on Ethics is the best

answer to that question. I believe that support for such a committee is the moral obligation of every Member who voted against the select committee report. The Powell case must provide the catalyst for the establishment of such a body that would not only have the authority to investigate but the power to enforce its sanctions.

There was much reference in the debate to the damage done to the reputation of the House by the behavior of the Harlem minister. We do not wipe out this stain by one moralistic act. We must be consistent, just and firm. We will only play into the hands of the more emotional opponents of punishment unless we demonstrate that they are wrong when they argue that Powell only did what others do, or that his punishment was related in any way to his race.

We have nothing to fear from the formation of such a committee. Let us not permit the American people to think we do.[41]

A new study committee was then appointed and given ample time and resources to write an ethics code. It conducted public hearings in August and September of 1967 and reported to the House on March 14, 1968. It proposed that it be made a permanent committee to police a recommended code and disclosure rules. With one dissenting vote, the resolution was adopted on April 3, 1968, and an Ethics Committee and an Ethics Code became permanent features of the House of Representatives.[42]

Thus, by early 1968 both the House and the Senate had created permanent watchdog committees on ethics and had written ethics codes. It had been less than four years since the Senate Rules Committee had made its first report in the Baker investigation and Senator Cooper had first called for such a committee. The course of events surrounding the Baker and Dodd cases in the Senate and the Powell case in the House had made major corrective measures essential. Despite many Members' misgivings and objections, new systems of self-discipline, designed to overcome the historic inertia of Congress, had become facts of Congressional life.

To a great extent Congress embraced such codes and committees under the force of public opinion. They would not have arrived without the impetus of the Baker, Powell, and Dodd cases. The general reluctance to use self-discipline is still in the background and could be a key factor in the effectiveness of the new codes and committees.

EFFICACY OF ETHICS CODES AND COMMITTEES

Codes of ethics and committees charged with their enforcement are generally associated with the professions. They represent self-imposed limitations by which a group engaged in a high calling sets forth standards which it observes above and beyond those imposed by law. Here lies the principal meaning of the term "ethics." In one sense, law is a codification of ethics, but "ethics" is generally intended to encompass standards which are norms of conduct, not because of the coercive command of law, but because of inner values and assumption of responsibilities which exceed legal requirements. As former Chief Justice Earl Warren once said, "Law floats in a sea of Ethics." At the same time he added:

> Not everything which is wrong can be outlawed, although everything which is outlawed, is, in our Western conception, wrong. For many years, legislatures and courts have endeavored to define for corporate and Government officials what constitutes a conflict between their public responsibilities and their private interests. None has yet been able to state in legal terms rules that will at the same time afford both freedom of dynamic action by the individual and protection of the public interest. Every law designed for such purpose has presumed, and I must necessarily presume, that such laws cannot be effective unless there is law behind the law; i.e., an ethical concept on the part of all who accept public responsibilities.[43]

Extra-legal codification of ethics by groups engaged in high callings goes back 2,500 years to the medical profession's classic statement in the Hippocratic Oath.[44] The spread of ethical codification to other professions is a relatively recent development. Although lawyers' professional canons are traceable in unwritten form to the customs and practices of the Inns of Court in London in the twelfth and thirteenth centuries, written codes of the organized bar date from the code of the Alabama Bar, adopted in 1887. This was based largely on Judge Sharswood's lectures on professional ethics, delivered at the University of Pennsylvania in 1854, and on the 50 Resolutions in Regard to Professional Deportment published by David Hoffman of the Baltimore Bar in 1834.[45] More recently, ethical codes have been developed by teachers, accountants, architects, engineers, and other groups. There is increasing evidence that formal rules of ethics for business management are emerging.[46]

Can Congressional service be viewed as a "profession" for purposes of analyzing its Members' duty to codify their ethics? The fact that governmental office is involved is certainly no barrier to professionalism. Since 1958 a general code of ethics, without enforcement machinery, has been in existence for the guidance of all in Federal government service.[47] Judges have long had their special written codes.[48] Federal Executive Branch officials are now subject to separate ethical rules contained in an Executive Order,[49] Civil Service Regulations,[50] and individual agency and departmental codes of conduct.[51] Municipal employees are increasingly governed by such codes,[52] and there is a mounting trend toward ethical codes for state legislators, some 16 states having enacted them in the past two decades.[53]

A more difficult question is whether the political component of Congressional service is consistent with a truly professional code of ethics. Scholars Eulau and Sprague recently assessed political careers as professions after reducing the tests of professionalization to three criteria: (1) professional independence; (2) professional ethics; and (3) orientation to public service. Of the second criterion, they said of politicians:

> This is not to deny that the development of a voluntary code of ethics for politicians presents difficulties that may be *sui generis*. What is and what is not permissible conduct in politics is likely to be more ambiguous than in other areas of social life precisely because politics, by definition, operates in a twilight zone of behavior where disagreement over acts of omission and commission makes the problem of sanctions in the case of breakage of norms particularly subtle, and where the relationship between means and ends is always a matter of continuing formulation rather than of definitive settlement. But efforts to establish

codes of ethics for both the executive and legislative branches of government, often including prohibitions that already have legal sanction, suggest that politics is not immune to this aspect of professionalization.

Perhaps more telling than these formal attempts to bring norms of professional ethical conduct to politics is the discovery that there exist, in fact, numerous informal rules of behavior—often called "rules of the game" and sometimes "folkways"—that are more or less specific concerning what is and what is not proper political behavior. Particularly in legislative bodies, as recent research, including this study, shows, there can be found many unwritten and even unspoken norms whose influence on conduct must not be underestimated. Moreover, all indications are that these "rules of the game" are viewed as being of great functional value to political success. Just why these rules of the political game have not as yet been formalized in a code is an interesting question. . . . It would seem that, even though a professional ethics of politics is underdeveloped, there is enough consensus among politicians as to what is proper conduct in office to suggest that, from this point of view, politics may partake of more professionalism than is often assumed.[54]

The trend toward professionalization of Congressional service is evidenced by the emergence of the full-time-job concept, the increased salary, and the mushrooming literature on Congressional methods and behavior. While the electoral process—the means of obtaining the job—may be less subject to ethical codification,* the legislative function of Congress is a profession by almost any test. Codification of its ethics can be achieved by simply identifying the unwritten rules or norms observed by most Members.

Congressional ethics committees could function without written codes, as did the Senate Ethics Committee in the Dodd case. Committees could be viewed merely as investigative aids to the self-disciplinary powers of each house. The standing ethics committee can function like other committees, merely as a repository of investigative and

---

* The political campaign has matured considerably in this regard, and significant ethical limits are emerging. Basic norms of fairness are policed by a watchdog citizens' committee called the Fair Campaign Practices Committee. For its origins see B. Felknor, DIRTY POLITICS 10–12 (1966).

recommending authority in one portion of Congressional jurisdiction. If this were done on a systematic basis merely for accusations of conduct generally conceded to be improper, it would be a vast improvement from the level of self-discipline which existed without permanent committees. This would increase the likelihood of discipline, serve as a deterrent, and be preferable for many reasons to *ad hoc* committees or summary chamber action without committee investigation and findings.

Codes are worthwhile, though, and do more than merely provide substantive rules for committees to apply. The Douglas subcommittee's 1951 report, in endorsing the concept of ethical codes for all public officials, aptly summarized the arguments for written codes:

> The testimony [before the committee] brought out a number of arguments for codes . . . : (1) They would clarify new or complex situations where the application of basic moral principles is far from obvious; (2) they would anticipate issues so that difficulties could be foreseen and basic policy decided when rational consideration is possible (i.e., the rules of the game must be approved before play begins); (3) the enhancement of the influence of the more progressive elements of the group who will tend to bring the whole group up to higher standards; (4) they would be a basis for discipline if the group had enough leadership and pride to act; (5) they would furnish a basis for instructing new members of the group as to their professional obligations (Hippocrates required all of his disciples to take the oath); and (6) they would instruct the public as to what it should expect of the principal elements in the realm of public affairs.[55]

A skeptic might point to the fact that Congress and the entire Federal service had a code starting in 1958 and that its existence had little practical significance. This is probably true, but it is largely because no one was charged with the responsibility of enforcing the 1958 code. This points up the necessity that ethics codes be coupled with ethics committees. If there is a permanent committee, there is someone *to whom* complaints of individual violations can be made and *against whom* complaint can be made if ethical rules generally go unenforced.

Fortunately, each house of Congress now has both code and committee. These codes and the resolutions governing their jurisdiction and procedure are set forth in Appendix D. However, neither code should be regarded as the final word on the subject. In support of the Senate Code, Ethics Committee Chairman Stennis has referred to it as "not a finished product . . . but a substantial beginning." [56] The Senate Code is deliberately incomplete. The resolution by which it was adopted stated in its preamble that its rules "complement the body of unwritten but generally accepted standards that continue to apply to the Senate." [57] The House Ethics Committee's report referred to its code as "a meaningful beginning . . . subject to revision and refinement." [58]

EVALUATION OF PRESENT ETHICS CODES

In evaluating formal rules of Congressional ethics, one must bear in mind both the "ambiguous" nature of political activity mentioned earlier by Eulau and Sprague and the fact that group ethical norms must depend upon group sanctions to be effective. This latter carries inherent limitations suggested in the following statement by Professor Phillip Monypenny:

> Ethics as a system of control also deals with groups, not with isolated individuals. Particular individuals may be capable of very high standards of performance, but it is large groups which must be moved in all social endeavor. Groups impose their own standards on the individuals who join them; they develop their own standards out of their own experience. A man in isolation may change his own conduct radically. It is difficult for a group to develop new standards in relation to the activity which makes it a group.
>
> The standards for groups are therefore likely to be more modest than those which a dedicated individual may embrace. They will also be partial in relation to the whole life of man, covering the aspect of affairs which are common to the group. They must grow out of present practices and standards. They must be capable of relatively easy application to the events of the day: they must not be so general that a long and sophisticated chain of

225

reasoning is necessary to relate the standards and the action required at the moment; in this respect they are the opposite of constitutional law. The standards developed for governmental employment will probably be various, developed separately for the many different kinds of work which is done by governmental employees.[59]

In earlier sections of this Report we have proposed a number of specific rules for adoption by the Congress. They have dealt with financial disclosure, gifts, honoraria, office expense funds, voting disqualification, interest avoidance, and misuse of staff. In Appendix A we include a complete Model Code of Conduct which contains these rules and two which are yet to be proposed. Disclosure rules are stated separately in Appendix B. We now consider some provisions of a more general nature.

Discrediting Conduct

Rule 1 of the House "Code of Official Conduct" requires that a Member conduct himself so as to "reflect creditably on the House of Representatives." No such provision is contained in the substantive Senate Rules, but S. Res. 338 of the 88th Congress, which defines the jurisdiction of the Senate Ethics Committee, directs it to investigate allegations of "improper conduct which may reflect upon the Senate."

Conduct which discredits the Senate undoubtedly violates the unwritten rules which are complemented by its Code. As previously noted, Senate disciplinary actions from the 1797 expulsion of Blount through the 1967 censure of Dodd have been based on conduct which was unbecoming but not necessarily unlawful. In each instance the conduct involved was viewed as indefensible under any reasonable standard and was properly condemned under such labels as "unbecoming" or "dishonorable." In Senator Dodd's case the censure resolution recited that Dodd's conduct "is contrary to accepted morals, derogates from the public trust expected of a Senator, and tends to bring the Senate into dishonor and disrepute." [60]

While such general condemnations have been appropriate in censure cases, the aberrant conduct has always been subject to narrower specification too. For instance, Senator Dodd was specifically cited in the same resolution for "exercising the influence and power of his office . . . to obtain, and use for his personal benefit, funds from the public through political testimonials and a political campaign. . . ."

Some may question whether a formal rule against "discrediting" conduct supplies a sufficiently definite standard that proceedings based on it satisfy due process of law, but such a broad standard has its counterparts in other areas of both ethics and law. Federal judges may be impeached under a Constitutional clause which simply provides that they shall hold office "during good behaviour." [61] Rule 8 of the Rules of the United States Supreme Court calls for discipline of attorneys guilty of conduct "unbecoming a member of the bar of this Court." Article 133 of the Uniform Code of Military Justice prohibits officers from "conduct unbecoming an officer and a gentleman," and Article 134 outlaws all "conduct of a nature to bring discredit on the Armed Forces." The term "due process" is itself a vague catch-all which takes on real meaning only if precedents applying it are examined. Such general terms tend to develop a specific content from experience and have proven their utility in areas where particularized codification is difficult. They connote underlying values and principles which are generally accepted.

Even if such a general term amounted to no rule at all, it would still serve a valuable due-process function by placing Members on notice that they are subject to discipline for conduct which their colleagues may find after the fact to have discredited the body. By our proposed code much unethical conduct is left for treatment under this rule, but the traditional restraint of Congress on the subject makes it unlikely that the rule will be used against any conduct which is not generally agreed to be improper. The absence of a more specific rule will be no more of a defense in the future than in the past, when Senator Monroney rebutted such a position in the Dodd debates as follows:

Are there special standards of conduct which Senators must meet? A Senator must, of course, obey the laws of the land and abide by the rules and regulations of the Senate. Beyond this there are now no specific, written standards that have been adopted by the Senate which would apply to the charges made against the senior Senator from Connecticut.

But I firmly believe there is a higher standard of conduct which must guide us as individuals, as well as in our role as Senators—a standard accepted and expected by society. It exists and, nebulous though it may be, we must pay the price when we breach it.

* * *

Does the lack of any specific, written standard covering the conduct of the senior Senator from Connecticut mean that the Senate should take no action? I think clearly not. For an affirmative answer to that question would mean that the very persons responsible for writing a code of conduct could evade punishment for clearly unethical actions merely by failing or refusing to adopt rules of ethical conduct. If that were the case, we would be a law unto ourselves. As the lawmakers in our society, we would be above any law, above any mores, above any reproach for our actions. We cannot adopt such an attitude.[62]

While such a general rule may add little to the explicit guides for Congressional conduct, it will aid in answering *ex post facto* defenses in situations comparable to the Dodd case. Accordingly, our model code incorporates Rule 1 of the House and we recommend as follows:

Recommendation 7A
Each house should adopt the following rule: "A Member shall conduct himself at all times so as to reflect credit upon the Congress."

Obedience to Laws and Rules

Rule 2 of the House Code requires adherence to Rules of the House, and the procedural rules governing the House Ethics Committee authorize it to investigate violations of any law, rule, or regulation applicable to the official conduct of a Member. They also authorize the Committee, with approval of the House, to report to appropriate Federal or state authorities evidence of violations of laws applicable to such official conduct.

The Senate substantive rules contain no counterpart to House Rule 2, but Section 2(a)(1) of S. Res. 338, its procedural resolution, authorizes the Senate Ethics Committee to investigate "allegations of . . . violations of law, and . . . rules and regulations of the Senate, relating to the conduct of individuals in the performance of their duties. . . ." Section 2(a)(4) then requires the Committee, without

Senate approval, to report evidence of violations to Federal and state authorities. It is noteworthy that the House reserves to the full body control over the referral of investigative results to law-enforcement agencies, while the Senate vests in its Ethics Committee both the power and the duty to make such reports. In the Dodd case, the Senate Ethics Committee referred to the Attorney General the matters of a cash corporate contribution and automobile loans and to the Internal Revenue Service the matters of taxability of funds raised by Dodd for personal purposes.* It also referred to the Attorney General the matter of unauthorized removal of papers from Dodd's office by former members of his staff.[63] After investigating Powell's handling of committee funds, the Hays subcommittee sent its evidence and hearings record to the Department of Justice without recommendation.[64]

Formal requirements that Members of Congress obey applicable statutes and Congressional rules may appear to be mere truisms or surplusage. Nonetheless, such provisions serve a valuable function by providing a basis for exercise of investigative jurisdiction by the respective Ethics Committees.

These provisions indicate that both houses contemplate that normal law-enforcement procedures will be used to prosecute Members' criminal offenses. It is best for Congress generally to let its Members be answerable initially to judicial proceedings and to withhold exercising any overlapping disciplinary jurisdiction until court actions have run their course. While this may frustrate some purists, it is consistent with the general concept that codes of ethics serve primarily for enforcement of extra-legal norms.

As indicated earlier, however, this custom has not been universally observed by Congress. Where misconduct severely discredits the institution and violates Congressional norms as well as criminal statutes, circumstances may move a house to act earlier, as in the Powell case. Just as deference to the political process is a general rule subject to exceptions, normal deference to judicial processes on criminal matters need not be followed in exceptional cases. Suppose a Member and the local prosecutor were allies in corrupt conduct. Inaction should not

---

* On December 23, 1969, the Department of Justice announced that it had concluded that criminal prosecution of Dodd was not warranted. N.Y. TIMES, Dec. 24, 1969, at 1, Col. 1.

bar Congressional discipline. Also, the evidence of guilt may be so indisputable and the damage to public confidence in a house so great that speedy dissociation by the body is in the public interest.

Accordingly, our proposed model code of conduct contains an appropriate rule, and we recommend as follows:

Recommendation 7B
Each House should adopt the following rule: "A Member shall obey all rules of the [House/Senate] and all laws relating to his conduct in the performance of his duties." *

Enforcement Mechanisms

The great value of permanent ethics committees has already been shown. Despite a few points where draftsmanship could be improved,† the procedural rules of both committees appear to be adequate, and no recommendations are made on this subject.

Each committee seems sufficiently empowered to receive and investigate complaints and to make recommendations to the full body. No Member has yet filed a formal complaint against another Member in either house, but each committee nonetheless has some tangible achievement, and the staffs of both committees have conducted numerous informal inquiries based on press reports, letters from Members, and complaints from the public. The equal representation of parties on the committees and the requirement that a majority of members is necessary for action make it unlikely that insubstantial or politically motivated charges will result in formal investigations.

In major cases the Committee is likely to proceed on something of an *ad hoc* basis whatever its rules provide. Also, flexibility has great value in this field, as evidenced by the manner in which the Senate Ethics Committee proceeded in the case of Senator Edward Long (D-Mo.). Closed sessions produced Committee findings favorable to Long, but they were accompanied by a Committee press release dis-

---

* Since this rule is limited to law violations which are office-related, allegedly unlawful conduct concerning the private life of a Member could be the basis of discipline only if it came within the broader rule against discrediting conduct.

† For instance, the House Committee must "investigate" a private citizen's complaint only if three Members refuse *in writing* to refer it to the Committee, conditions precedent obviously beyond the citizen's control. Nonetheless, private accusations can cause "preliminary inquiries" to be conducted informally by staff and may lead to formal investigations initiated by majority vote.

closing the names of alleged clients. This led to a further article in LIFE which severely undermined Long's claim that shared legal services were performed for these clients. The entire sequence undoubtedly contributed to Long's defeat at the polls. A combination of the electorate, the press, and limited use of formal ethics machinery achieved effective disciplinary results.

The only formal action* of the House Ethics Committee since its permanent establishment concerned revelations that absent Representatives were sometimes recorded by clerks as present and voting. The Committee recommended installation of electronic voting devices[65] after an investigation which was accompanied by resignation of a House employee responsible for the situation.

It appears that neither Committee is likely to render and publish many formal advisory opinions. It is feared that anonymity would be impossible and that the press might unduly magnify the scope of questionable activity revealed by such opinions. However, both receive many private inquiries from Members, and the Committees and staffs are furnishing informal equivalents of advisory opinions.†

In fairness, it should be said that neither committee has yet functioned long enough to be closely evaluated. The mere formation of the Committees has been a great step forward, and the level of ethical sensitivity in the Congress has risen appreciably because of their existence. Considering the scarcity of formal disciplinary actions in the past, it seems safe to say that Congress has entered a historic new phase of ethical self-discipline. The number of instances of formal action seems certain to increase even though the occasions when such action is appropriate should decrease markedly.

The public should be properly appreciative of the ethics advance-

* While this Report was being printed, on January 26, 1970, the House Ethics Committee issued its Advisory Opinion No. 1 on the role of a Member in communicating with executive and administrative agencies. The Committee stated guidelines covering the type of alleged activity which had caused the January 12 indictment of Speaker McCormack's administrative assistant, Dr. Martin Sweig. For details of the indictment see Congressional Quarterly, WEEKLY REPORT, Jan. 23, 1970, at 239–43.

† The Chairman of the Senate Ethics Committee recently announced that its staff was conducting a preliminary inquiry into reports of abuses in the area of private immigration bills for the relief of "Chinese ship-jumpers." The Committee also announced that it interpreted Senate rules to require that Senators personally sign and present all private relief bills sponsored by them, procedures not generally followed in the past. 115 CONGRESSIONAL RECORD S11515 (daily ed. Sept. 29, 1969).

ment in Congress over the past few years. Nonetheless, much remains to be done to perfect the infant ethics systems. Also, it is sadly true that in government the mere existence of a code and an agency responsible for enforcement does not guarantee compliance. The press and the public must continue to be vigilant.

SUMMARY OF
RECOMMENDATIONS

I. SUMMARY ACCORDING TO SUBJECT MATTER

Conflicts of Interest (Chapter 2)

Finding that many Members of Congress have *avoidable* conflicts of interest (those which are not inherent, politically dictated, or personally necessary), the Committee recommends seven remedies to minimize such conflicts and their effects:

1. Rules against Members' official action for personal gain (p. 61).
2. Selective investment policies which minimize the risks that Members' official duty may conflict with private interest (p. 63).
3. Voluntary abstention from serving as officers, directors, trustees, or partners in commercial enterprises (p. 66).
4. Voluntary avoidance of economic interests specially affected by the work of committees upon which a Member serves (p. 68).
5. A requirement that Congressional committees adopt mandatory rules governing financial interests of Members in matters within committee jurisdiction (p. 71).

6. Discretionary self-disqualification from voting on matters in which a Member has a personal economic interest (p. 72).

7. Broader public financial disclosure of Members' financial interests, under recommended Model Disclosure Rules (p. 77, Appendix B).

The Committee surveyed four selected areas of Congressional financial involvement in an effort to determine whether Members' personal interests cause any specific effects upon national policymaking. In three—transportation, defense contracting, and broadcasting—the Committee finds no such evidence. However, in the fourth area—banking—the Committee is uncertain on this point. It notes a number of publicly reported instances of impropriety and a disproportionately high incidence of Members' ownership of bank stocks and serving as bank officers and directors. The community of Congressional and banking interests is concluded to be unfortunate under all the circumstances, in terms of lending grounds for public suspicion. The Committee's recommendations on Members' holding corporate offices and directorships and investing in areas of committee responsibility were in part based upon, and directed toward, the extensive banking involvements of Members.

Law Practice (Chapter 3)

Because of the high numbers of lawyers serving in Congress and the historic potential of law practice by Members for causing Congressional scandal, this topic is specially considered. It was found that the overwhelming majority of all lawyer-Senators and of all lawyer-Representatives except the most junior ones totally abstain from any form of law practice. Concluding that lawyer-client relationships produce avoidable conflicts of interest, the Committee recommends:

1. Members should totally refrain from any form of law practice, except possibly for a relatively brief initial period of transition during an incomplete Senate term or the first two terms as a Representative (p. 111). The legal profession's Code of Professional Responsibility now forbids law firms from using the names of public officials unless they are *actively and regularly* engaged in the actual practice of law, a condition which the Committee feels can rarely be satisfied by a Member doing justice to the full-time demands of Congressional service (p. 103).

2. All lawyer-Members should avoid "double door" or dual-partnership arrangements under which the Member's partners engage in Federal-agency practice prohibited by law to him. It is recommended that this be done voluntarily for ethical reasons (p. 115), but further recommendation is also made that the federal statute on law practice by Members be appropriately amended (p. 115).

3. The statute on law practice by Members should also be amended to forbid compensated court appearances against the United States (p. 117).

Campaign Financing (Chapter 4)

Describing this subject as "perhaps the most difficult problem in the entire field," the Committee proposes public financing of campaign costs, reduced television rates, stringent regulations on contributions, and broader public reporting. In particular, the Committee recommends:

1. Direct subsidies in general elections to candidates of major parties and qualified minor parties, along the lines of a bill approved by the Senate Finance Committee in 1967 (p. 136).

2. A postage-free mailing for all qualified candidates in both primary and general elections (p. 138).

3. Legislation requiring television stations to sell time to candidates at substantial discounts (p. 148).

4. Enactment of a law combining features of two election-reform acts, one which passed the Senate in 1967 and one which was approved by a House Committee in 1968, which would expand reporting requirements, tighten limits on individual contributions,* and establish a Federal Elections Commission (p. 153, Appendix E).

Salaries and Allowances (Chapter 5)

The Committee had already endorsed the 1969 legislation which raised Congressional salaries from $30,000 to $42,500 a year. This Re-

---

* Our proposals differ from both bills by placing a $25,000 gross limit on the amount an individual candidate can spend from his own funds (p. 150). Also, the limit on a single individual contribution should be reduced from $5,000 to $1,000 if the Federal-subsidy proposal is adopted.

port justifies that position and makes several further recommendations:

1. The Federal Salaries Commission, whose recommendations led to the 1969 salary increase, should also be authorized to act in the areas of such fringe benefits as retirement rights and tax deductions (p. 164).
2. The present cost-of-living tax deduction of $3,000 per year should be raised to $5,500 (p. 164).
3. The Senate formula for staff allowances should be modified to eliminate its discrimination against Senators from the most populous states (p. 167).
4. Each House should adopt proposed rules against misuse of staff and padding of payrolls (p. 168).
5. Senators should be reimbursed for one trip to their home state per month while Congress is in session, thus equalizing travel allowances of Senators and Representatives (p. 175).

Gifts, Supplemental Funds, and Honoraria (Chapter 6)

1. A general rule against accepting substantial personal gifts is recommended, along with public disclosure of gifts worth more than $25 (p. 188).
2. The use of testimonial dinners and other fund-raising events to secure funds for a Member's personal uses are specifically prohibited under a recommended rule (p. 184).
3. Members are urged to avoid privately financed office funds, and full public disclosure is proposed for those which are maintained (p. 197).
4. The Senate is urged to adopt the present rule of the House of Representatives forbidding excessive honoraria (p. 201), and the House is urged to adopt the Senate's rules requiring public disclosure of any honorarium exceeding $300 (p. 201).

Congressional Self-Discipline:
Ethics Codes and Committees (Chapter 7)

A model code of conduct is recommended for adoption in the rules of each House (Appendix A). It consists of the various rules suggested under specific topics, plus a rule prohibiting discrediting conduct by Members (p. 228) and a rule requiring obedience by

Members to the laws and regulations and rules governing their official conduct (p. 230).

The Committee found understandable reasons for Congressional restraint in formal discipline of Members, noted the work of the relatively new House and Senate Ethics Committees, and concluded generally that it was too early to evaluate their effectiveness. No recommendations were made concerning their jurisdiction and procedures (p. 231).

II. SUMMARY ACCORDING TO FORM

Recommendations for Changes in the Rules of Each House

Ten of the Committee's recommendations are incorporated in its proposed Model Code of Conduct (Appendix A). One other proposed rule would require Congressional committees to adopt their own rules on conflicts of interest (p. 71).

Proposals for public disclosure of financial interests, gifts, honoraria, and supplemental office funds are incorporated in the recommended Model Disclosure Rules (p. 77 and Appendix B).

Recommended Legislation

Eleven of the Committee's recommendations call for statutory enactments. They are:

1. Prohibition of Federal practice by partners of Members (p. 115).
2. Prohibition of Members' court appearances against the United States (p. 117).
3. Public subsidies for general elections (p. 136).
4. Postage-free mailings for all candidates (p. 138).
5. Reduced rates for political broadcasting (p. 148).
6. A $25,000 limit on candidates' individual personal spending (p. 150).
7. Comprehensive election reform governing reporting and limits on campaign contributions and establishing a Federal Elections Commission (p. 153 and Appendix E).

8. Expanding the jurisdiction of the Federal Salaries Commission (p. 164).
9. Raising Members' tax deduction for cost of living from $3,000 to $5,500 (p. 164).
10. Removal of discrimination in staff allowances of large-state Senators (p. 167).
11. Increased travel allowances for Senators (p. 175).

Voluntary Self-Limitations

A number of the Committee's recommendations state its collective opinion on certain standards of conduct which Members of Congress should normally follow, whether or not required to do so by rule or statute. They are:

1. Selective investment policies which minimize conflicts of interest (p. 63).
2. Avoidance of financial interests in areas of committee responsibility (p. 68).
3. Disqualification from official action on matters affecting personal interests (p. 72).
4. Total abstention from practice of law, except possibly for a transitional period (p. 111).
5. Avoidance of "double door" law-practice arrangements (p. 115).
6. Avoidance of supplemental office funds (p. 197).

MODEL CODE OF CONDUCT

(With parenthetical references to relevant pages of this Report)

1. *Discrediting conduct.* A Member shall conduct himself at all times so as to reflect credit upon the Congress (p. 228).

2. *Obedience to rules and laws.* A Member shall obey all rules of the [House/Senate] and all laws relating to his conduct in the performance of his duties (p. 230).

3. *Official action for personal gain.* A Member shall never use his official power for the purpose of economically benefiting himself and shall make every reasonable effort to avoid situations where it might appear that he is making such use of his office (p. 61).

4. *Committee conflicts of interest.* When a Member is appointed to a committee, he should, if reasonably possible, avoid all economic interests which may be specially affected by legislation within the jurisdiction of his committee (p. 68).

5. *Abstention from official action.* When a Member must take official action on a matter in which he has a personal economic interest, he should consider eliminating the interest. If that is not feasible, he should consider abstaining from such official action. He need not abstain if he decides to participate in a manner adverse to the economic interests (p. 72).

6. *Staff Misuse.* A Member shall employ with public funds no one who does not perform duties commensurate with his compensation and shall utilize employees only for the official purposes for which they are employed (p. 168).

7. *Campaign funds.* A Member shall keep his campaign funds separate from his personal funds. He shall convert no campaign funds to personal use in excess of reimbursement for legitimate and verifiable prior campaign expenditures. He shall expend no funds from his campaign account not attributable to bona-fide campaign purposes (p. 183).

8. *Testimonials.* A Member shall not conduct or permit to be conducted fund-raising events which seek to provide money for his personal uses (p. 184).

9. *Gifts.* A Member shall not accept a substantial personal gift from anyone except a relative (p. 188).

10. *Honoraria.* A Member shall accept no honorarium for a speech, writing for publication, or other similar activity, in excess of the usual and customary value for such services (p. 201).

MODEL DISCLOSURE RULES

1. On or before May 1 of each year, every [Representative/Senator] and every officer and employee of the [House/Senate] compensated at a gross rate in excess of $18,000 per annum shall file with the [House/Senate Ethics Committee] a statement showing the following:

a. The identity of each interest in real or personal property having a value of $5,000 or more which he owned at any time during the preceding calendar year, except bank deposits, insurance policies, household furnishings, personal effects, and principal residence.

b. Each source of any income, including capital gains, aggregating $1,000 or more during the preceding calendar year.

c. The identity of any creditor to whom he owed debts aggregating $5,000 or more during the year, except a debt secured by mortgage upon his principal residence.

d. The source and value of all non-family gifts in the aggregate amount of $25 or more received from any single source during the preceding calendar year.

e. The amount or value and source of each honorarium of $300 or more received during the preceding calendar year.

2. For purposes of these rules, a person required to report is deemed to be the owner of the following:

a. Assets of a spouse or minor child of such person.

b. Assets of corporations in which such person or his immediate family owns 50 percent of the outstanding stock.

c. A proportionate share of assets of a partnership of which he is a member.

d. Assets of trusts and estates in which such person has a vested beneficial interest, except that

(i) such interests may be actuarily apportioned for purposes of valuation; and

(ii) they need not be reported if the terms of the applicable trust instrument preclude such person from knowledge of the identity of such assets.

If such person holds a power of revocation of a trust, its assets shall be deemed to be owned by him.

3. For purposes of these rules, a person required to report shall be deemed to have received the following:
    a. Income received by a spouse or minor child of such person.
    b. Legal fees aggregating more than $1,000 received from a single client during the year by a law firm with which such person has any professional relationship. The names of such clients shall be reported, together with an indication of whether the firm was initially employed before such person became an officer, employee, or Member of Congress, and the identity of any litigation or administrative proceedings in which the firm represents the client and in which the United States is an interested party.

4. A Member shall report amounts and sources of all contributions received by him or by others on his behalf, including political committees, to defray official or semi-official expenses related to his office, including, but not limited to: travel to, from, and within each Member's home state or district; printing and other expenses in connection with the mailing of speeches, newsletters, and reports to a Member's constituents; expenses of radio, television, and news-media methods of reporting to a Member's constituents; telephone, telegraph, postage, and stationery expenses in excess of allowance; newspaper subscriptions from his constituency; and staff compensation and travel in excess of allowances. If funds for these purposes are collected and expended by others for the benefit of the Member or his staff, so that the Member has no knowledge of an original donor's identity, he shall cause the person having such knowledge to file the reports required herein.

5. Such reports shall be public documents and shall be made reasonably available for copying by any person.

6. Copies of such reports filed by Members shall also be filed with the Clerk of the United States District Court of the judicial districts in which their home residences are located, and shall be made available to the public on the same basis as other public documents. A copy shall also be maintained in the principal office of the Member in his state or Congressional district and shall be made reasonably available to the public for copying.

7. The dollar value of interests reported under 1a and dollar amounts of items of income and indebtedness reported under 1b and 1c shall be filed separately under seal with the [House/Senate Ethics Committee] and shall not be opened except in the course of an official investigation by such committee and pursuant to a majority vote of its members.

APPENDIX C

THE RESEARCH PROGRAM

The research program of the Committee was divided into eight steps:
1. Review of existing historical and reference material;
2. Discussions with key observers;
3. Acquainting the Congressional leadership with the Committee's mission;
4. Letters to all Members of Congress;
5. Construction of the interview sample and questionnaire;
6. Pre-testing and periodic revision of the questionnaire;
7. Interviews with sampled Members;
8. Coding, analysis, and interpretation of interview data.

1. REVIEW OF EXISTING MATERIAL

Initially, a careful review was conducted of the material pertaining to Congressional ethics in CONGRESSIONAL QUARTERLY magazine since 1945; recent literature on campaign financing; press and periodical clippings, primarily from the files of reporters for the WASHINGTON POST, WASHINGTON STAR and WALL STREET JOURNAL; and materials of the Legislative Reference Service of the Library of Congress bearing on Congressional ethics.

Martindale-Hubbell proved a useful index of the professional associations of lawyer-Members of Congress.

Throughout the two years of the study, the daily editions of the CONGRESSIONAL RECORD, NEW YORK TIMES and WALL STREET JOURNAL, and the weekly edition of CONGRESSIONAL QUARTERLY were culled for pertinent material.

2. DISCUSSIONS WITH KEY OBSERVERS

Through the fall of 1967 and the winter of 1968 discussions were held in Washington and elsewhere with about 150 journalists, political scientists and other academicians, members and former members of Congressional staffs, and members or former members of the Executive Branch who have a special knowledge of Congress. In the case of journalists, the discussions focused on the general ethical climate of Congress, with an attempt to get a feel for the nature and scope of ethical problems on

243

Capitol Hill and the people about whom conflict-of-interest questions have been raised. The academics served primarily to refer our staff to other key informants and observers and to share with us their knowledge of the literature on Congress and their experience in talking with Members. Other Legislative and Executive Branch informants generally spoke in areas in which they had particular expertise. Consultations with professionals in the advertising and broadcasting industries served to assist our staff in learning about policies and practices relating to political broadcasting.

Government Officials

Manuel F. Cohen
Phillip Elman
Wilfred V. Gill
E. William Henry
Nicholas Johnson
Frederick J. Lawton
Saul Lindebaum
M. Cecil Mackey

Timothy J. May
Frank McCulloch
Robert J. Rosthal
Stuart Siegal
Elmer B. Staats
Stanley Surrey
Lee C. White
Jerre Williams

Samuel Zagoria

Congressional Staff and Former Staff

William Allen
Richard Aurelio
John Blair
Jack Blum
Kurt Borchardt
James Boyd
Robert Burt
Charles Caldwell
John P. Coder
Wilkes Coffey
Larry Conrad
Ted Crolius
James Duffy
Milton Eisenberg
Bernard Fensterwald
Benjamin Fern
Charles Ferris
Clyde Flynn
Gerald Grinstein
Bailey Guard

Gordon Harrison
Stephen Horn
W. Pat Jennings
Erwin G. Krasnow
Julian Langston
Daniel M. Lewis
John McEvoy
Marcia McNaughton
Jerry Manges
Nicholas Masters
John Martiny
Roy Millenson
W. DeVier Pierson
Thomas J. Scott
Stuart Siegal
Charles P. Sifton
Michael Spence
John Swanner
Thomas Vail
Richard Wallace

Paul Wilson

Social Scientists and Professors of Law

Marver Bernstein
Elliott Cheatham
Charles Clapp
Richard Fenno
Ralph Huitt
Leslie Kish
Kenneth Kofmehl
Andreas Lowenfeld
Bayless Manning
Frank Newman
L. Ray Patterson

Robert L. Peabody
Nelson W. Polsby
H. Douglas Price
James A. Robinson
Howard R. Sacks
William Spurrier
John Steinbruner
Donald Stokes
Lawrence Stone
Edward Tufte
Raymond E. Wolfinger

Journalists

John Berry
Milt Britten
Turner Catledge
Roan Conrad
Joe Foote
Fred P. Graham
Richard Harwood
John A. Hamilton
Edwin Kenworthy
Jerry Landauer

Clark Molenhoff
Neil MacNeil
Robert Novak
Neil R. Pierce
Walter Pincus
James B. Reston
Eileen Shanahan
John Simonds
Richard Strout
Robert Walters

Tom Wicker

Lawyers

Joe Borkin
John E. Bryson
Herbert Brownell
Jean Camper Cahn
David Ellenhorn
John M. Foley
Marion E. Harrison
Max Kampelman

Jerome Medalie
Lee Mitchell
Stephen D. Potts
Frank Reeves
John Ritchie
Charles Sommers
John Trubin
Milton C. Weisman

Media Professionals

Mary Lou Benjamin
Fred Friendly
James Hagerty
Richard Heffner

Sheila Kelley
Herman W. Land
William Murphy
Ed Peter

Mary Schoonmaker

Others

Hale Champion
Bruce Felknor
Russell Hemenway

Wesley McCune
Maurice Rosenblatt

State Legislative Consultants*

CALIFORNIA

Robert Burton
Robert Fairbanks
Sen. Donald Grunsky
Frank Mesple
Sen. George Moscone
George Murphy
Tom Purcell
Alan Post
Jerry Rankin
Sen. Albert Rodda
Assem. Jesse Unruh
Sen. Howard Way

NEW YORK

David Beetle
Sen. Jeremiah D. Bloom
Assem. Albert H. Blumenthal
Assem. John Buckley
Assem. Harold W. Cohn
Harold Fisher
Sen. Harrison Goldin
Sen. John H. Hughes
Assem. Daniel M. Kelly
Sydney Schanberg
Sen. Whitney N. Seymour, Jr.
Donald Zimmerman

ILLINOIS

Rep. George M. Burditt
John Dailey
Sen. James P. Loukas
James B. Moran
Dawn Clark Netsch
Rep. Bernard B. Wolfe

Research on state legislative developments was conducted in Illinois in 1967–68 by Mr. Lawrence Burick and in New York by Miss Josephine Gittler, both senior students at Northwestern University Law School. Each wrote an individual paper on the state involved, and the two co-authored a general summary of state codes of legislative ethics. Copies of these three useful papers have been deposited in the libraries of the Northwestern University School of Law and The Association of the Bar of the City of New York.

* The Committee thought it desirable and instructive to examine the experience of a number of states in dealing with conflicts of interests and related ethical questions in the legislative branch. New York, California, and Illinois were singled out for special study for two reasons: (1) each of them recently had enacted new conflict-of-interest legislation, and (2) as they are the three largest states in population, their legislatures seemed most nearly comparable with Congress. Ultimately it was concluded that the full-time nature of Congressional service makes Congress *sui generis*. Notwithstanding new salary increases designed to make possible full-time state legislative service, most state legislators view their work as part-time.

During its early meetings the Committee met informally with a number of men with special knowledge of one or more of the subjects of our study: former Senators Paul H. Douglas and Kenneth Keating, who vigorously supported higher ethical standards during their Senate careers; Mayor John V. Lindsay, a prominent supporter of ethics legislation when he was a Member of Congress and a member of our predecessor committee; James B. Reston, Vice President and former head of the Washington bureau of THE NEW YORK TIMES; Stephen K. Bailey, Dean, the Maxwell School of Public Administration, Syracuse University, and author of THE NEW CONGRESS; Bayless Manning, Dean, Stanford Law School, and director of our predecessor committee's study; and Stanley Surrey, former Assistant Secretary of the Treasury.

Political scientists Robert Peabody of Johns Hopkins University, John Steinbruner of Harvard University, and Herbert E. Alexander of the Citizens' Research Foundation; and Dean Howard Sacks of the University of Connecticut Law School served the Committee as professional consultants. John Berry, a free-lance journalist, assisted the Committee as a researcher during the early stages of our work.

3. Visits to Congressional Leadership

In February 1968 various members of the Committee and staff met informally with the House and Senate leadership and the Ethics Committee chairmen to acquaint them with our project and to enlist their good will.

4. Letters to All Members of Congress

Shortly thereafter (March 1, 1968) a letter was sent by Mr. Loeb to every Member of the 90th Congress (see page xxiv). The letter explained the Committee's objectives and indicated that interviews would be sought with a broad cross-section of the Membership to guarantee a reliable factual basis for our ultimate recommendations.

5. Construction of the Interview Sample and Questionnaire

The interview sample was constructed with the assistance of two professional statisticians, Irving Roshwalb, Senior Vice President of Audits and Surveys, Inc., in New York, and Leslie Kish, the chief statistician of the Survey Research Center at the University of Michigan. It was decided that Congress be divided into three categories:

Category One: Leaders and Committee Chairmen in both houses.
Category Two: Two groups of ethically concerned Members:
  A. Members of the House and Senate Ethics Committees and the Special Committee to Investigate Adam Clayton Powell (the Celler Committee); and

       B. Members about whom conflict-of-interest questions had been
raised in the press.
Category Three: A random sample of all remaining Members.

We decided to attempt to interview all Members of Congress who fell
into Categories One or Two and randomly sample one third of the remainder (Category Three). Moreover, we decided to stratify Category
Three by party, seniority, and membership or non-membership in the
legal profession. This yielded eight strata, and we then randomly sampled one third of each stratum, using a table of random numbers. This
procedure yielded a total sample of 182 Members of Congress.

    A large index card was prepared for each Member of the 182 in the
sample, indicating the reason he was chosen for the sample, salient bio-
graphical information obtainable from the Congressional Directory, a
record of any correspondence on file with our Committee, his votes on
the Powell or Dodd case, a note of any public disclosure of his income
and assets, and, if a lawyer, a summary of his listing in Martindale-
Hubbell.

    The interview questionnaire was constructed with the advice and as-
sistance of various political scientists who had had extensive interviewing
experience. It was decided that a mixture of short-answer and open-
ended questions would be used. The questionnaire went through six drafts.
The first three reflected revisions and criticisms from staff, Committee,
and outside experts and were developed before any interviews were conducted.

6. Pre-Testing and Periodic
Revision of the Questionnaire

For about a month the questionnaire was used in test interviews with
about a dozen key persons, including three Members of Congress, to determine whether and to what extent the questions yielded pertinent and
candid responses. Appropriate modifications were then made.

    The questionnaire was revised three times after interviewing began, to
reflect the experience gained from early interviews. At first the questionnaire contained virtually every question the staff could devise which related to the various fields of our study—viz., salaries and allowances, the
ethical problems of Congressional staff, campaign financing, conflicts of
interest, the Dodd and Powell cases, executive-agency relations, and practice of law. The questionnaire was then refined, and less-relevant or ex-
traneous questions were eliminated so that the interview would take no
more than one hour. The order of the questions was designed to sustain
maximum interviewee interest and cooperation. Questions which yielded
specific data (*e.g.,* "How much did your last campaign cost? Are you
richer or poorer now than when you entered Congress?") were preferred
over merely attitudinal questions. The final form of the questionnaire

was developed after 53 interviews. (The final questionnaire is reprinted at the end of Appendix C.)

7. INTERVIEWS WITH SAMPLED MEMBERS

From April 23 to October 2, 1968, and from January 27 to February 28, 1969, extensive interviews were conducted by the staff in Washington during visits ranging from three days to two weeks. Ninety-four interviews were conducted by Mr. Rosencranz and twenty-six by Mr. Kirby.

Preceding the staff member's trip, a letter was sent to each prospective interviewee, explaining our Committee's purpose and asking the Member to set time aside for an interview. Normally, two or three days before the staff member's visit, the Committee's Administrative Assistant telephoned the offices of Members with whom interviews were sought, and upon arrival in Washington the staff member telephoned each such Member to arrange or confirm a meeting time.

A typical schedule entailed three to five interviews per day (three in 1968, when the legislative calendar was crowded and a campaign was imminent; five in 1969, when Members seemed to have more time to spare). Interviews generally took place in Members' offices, although a number were conducted in the Rayburn Room off the House floor, the Senate Reception Room off the Senate floor, and the Members' Dining Room in the Capitol. Tape recorders were not used, but extensive notes were taken in the course of the interviews. These notes were transcribed into memorandum form, usually during the week following the week of the interview, labeled "Confidential," and distributed only to Committee members. The interviews averaged 45 minutes in length (somewhat longer with lawyer-Members). In general, Members were refreshingly candid, although the degree of candor varied. It is safe to say that virtually all were candid on one or more topics, either about themselves or others. A letter was sent to Members after the interviews, thanking them for their cooperation.

Those Members who were unavailable upon initial approach were called again during one or more of a staff member's subsequent visits to Washington. Of the 120 Members interviewed, 80 were seen after the first contact, 32 after the second, 6 after the third, and 2 after the fourth.

One third of the original sample, 62 of 182, were never interviewed. Fifteen of these retired or were defeated before we could interview them. Most of the others said that the pressure of legislative or constituency commitments prevented them from receiving our interviewer during a given Washington visit. Undoubtedly some of these would have declined an interview under any circumstances, although only 10 flatly refused to be seen at any time. Among sampled Members whom we did not see were those whose conduct has been the subject of a recent formal investigation within Congress. Nonetheless the final sample resembled the original sample in every stratum except one: Of 29 Senators with twelve or more years of service, we were able to interview only 12. Table C.1 gives a profile of the interview sample.

TABLE C.1

Comparative Profile of Interviewed Sample

CHAMBER	SENATE		HOUSE	
	Sample	90th Cong.	Sample	90th Cong.
Total	(23)	(100)	(97)	(435)
Party				
Democrats	16	64	54	248
Republicans	7	36	43	187
*Seniority**				
Senior	12		54	
Junior	11		43	
Occupation				
Lawyers	16	68	55	246
Non-lawyers	7		42	
Status				
Committee chairmen	9	17	12	21
Leadership	1	5	4	4
Ethics Committee	3	6	8	12
Celler Committee			8	9
Controversial	2	8	11	14
Random sample	8		54	

* The 46 Senators in the 90th Congress elected before 1957 were classified as senior. Representatives elected to five or more terms (including the 90th Congress) were classified as senior. This division placed approximately half the membership of each house in each category.

8. CODING, ANALYSIS, AND INTERPRETATION OF INTERVIEW DATA

As position papers were prepared, preliminary compilations and tabulations were made of pertinent responses of all Members interviewed to that date. After all the interviews had been completed, a re-evaluation of the questionnaire and responses was made. Some of the questions were eliminated because they seemed to produce irrelevant or unreliable responses. New categories were added where the data warranted it. All responses were then categorized and coded from interview memoranda by the committee's two able research assistants, G. William Sisley and Robert N. Chester, who played crucial parts in this stage of the research program. A keypunched card was prepared for each Member.* These

* A computer could as easily have been used, but that entailed the use of a programmer, and it was decided that the counter-sorter system would allow for more flexibility in aggregating and charting the data.

cards were fed into a statistical counter-sorter, and results were recorded. Multiple "runs" were made on all questions to attempt to isolate the relevant variables, such as party, seniority, and region.* Selected questions were cross-run with other relevant questions to analyze the relationship between them.† The whole mass of raw data was tabulated and aggregated for purposes of evaluation and interpretation, and various hypotheses were tested against the refined data.

These data are summarized at the end of this appendix. For comparison, committee chairmen and members of the leadership in both houses are presented separately from the total sample, as are the members of the Senate and House Ethics Committees and the Celler Committee, although both groups are included in the total sample. To arrive at the total figures for each house, the sample was divided into four groups: (1) committee chairmen and leadership; (2) Ethics Committee members (including members of the Celler Committee in the House); (3) randomly sampled Members; and (4) members about whom conflict-of-interest questions had been raised in the press. Each of the first three groups was then weighted according to the proportion it bore to the total membership in the respective chambers. For example, since approximately half the committee chairmen were interviewed, each interviewed chairman was given a weight of two. Members in the House random sample were one seventh the total House membership not specially sampled, and were weighted accordingly. Members in group (4) above were not weighted (each received a weight of one) because individuals within this group could not be presumed to be representative of the whole group.

The tables in the text are not similarly weighted. The random sample and special sample were treated equally for ease of statistical presentation, for more refined analysis and cross-tabulation within a manageable number of tables, and because it was concluded that there would be no gain in information if the random and special groups were presented separately. We examined and compared the weighted sample against the non-weighted sample and found no substantive differences in results. In several cases the results produced by the weighted sample strengthen our observations. For example, Table 5.6 showed that 52 percent of all Senators and 61 percent of all Representatives said their travel allowances were inadequate. These figures are even higher—65 percent of Senators and 72 percent of Representatives—in the weighted sample. In all cases the weighted sample fully supports our factual findings and conclusions.

* It was shown, for example, that the majority of practicing lawyers in Congress come from states east of the Mississippi and have been in Congress for less than eight years.

† For example, the cost of a Member's campaign was correlated with his use of political broadcasting.

TABLE C.2

Interview Response Data

	Total SENATE (100)	Total HOUSE (435)	L+CC* (47)	EC† (27)
Salaries, Allowances and Expenses				
Salary opinion (pre-1969 increase):				
Salary adequate	52.0%	28.7%	48.9%	78.3%
Inadequate compared with private industry		7.3	4.3	4.3
Inadequate due to extra costs of being a Member (*e.g.*, Washington cost of living, cost of maintaining two homes, travel, entertainment)	38.0	61.0	38.3	17.4
Inadequate due to extra demands for charitable contributions	1.0	2.1	4.3	
No answer	9.0	0.9	4.3	
In discussion on allowances, Member mentioned:				
Inadequacy of Congressional tax deduction for living costs	2.0	18.9	8.7	4.3
Need for an expense account	16.0	11.5	8.7	8.7
Both		5.3		4.3
Neither mentioned	82.0	64.4	82.6	82.6
Allowances for official expenses are:				
Adequate (no specific complaint)	20.0	29.7	67.4	56.5
Adequate except for travel	20.0	28.0	23.9	21.7
Less than adequate	60.0	38.9	8.7	21.7
No answer		3.4		
Opinion on travel allowance:				
Adequate	35.0	27.8	60.9	56.5
Inadequate; supports increase	54.0	53.3	19.6	30.4
Inadequate; opposes increase because of public opinion	11.0		4.3	
Inadequate; opposes increase because it might encourage absenteeism		2.3	4.3	
Inadequate; opposes increase for some other reason		13.1		4.3
No answer		3.4	10.9	8.7

* Committee chairmen and leadership in both houses.
† Ethics Committees in both houses plus Celler Committee in the House.

	Total SENATE (100)	Total HOUSE (435)	L+CC* (47)	EC† (27)
Number of trips to home district per year:				
7 or less	17.0	2.8	19.1	8.7
8 through 12	15.0	6.0	17.0	
13 through 24	35.0	24.1	23.4	34.8
25 or more	29.0	59.4	14.9	39.1
No answer	4.0	7.8	25.5	17.4
Member's travel above allowances (if any) is paid by:				
Personal resources	13.0	48.5	14.9	31.8
Office expense fund		1.6		
Surplus campaign fund	11.0	2.3	10.6	
Honoraria	22.0	0.7	12.8	4.5
Political party campaign committee		3.2		
Combination of above sources	31.0	9.9	8.5	22.7
Some other source		1.8		
No answer	23.0	32.0	53.2	40.9
Does Member use personal resources to defray official expenses?				
Yes	46.0	59.7	23.9	27.3
No	24.0	18.4	39.1	50.0
No answer	30.0	21.9	37.0	22.7
Does Member use an office expense fund to defray official expenses?				
Yes	27.0	10.6	4.3	8.7
No	63.0	49.0	57.4	69.6
No answer	10.0	40.5	38.3	21.7
To finance intra-term political expenses such as newsletters and radio-TV tapes, Member relies on:				
Personal resources		10.6	4.2	8.9
Office expense fund	9.0	6.7		4.3
Surplus campaign fund	11.0	8.0	8.3	13.0
Honoraria	11.0	3.2		8.7
Political party campaign committee		6.4		
Testimonials		4.8		
Combination of above sources	18.0	4.2	4.2	
Some other source	11.0	0.5	8.3	
No answer	40.0	55.7	75.0	65.2
Information on honoraria:				
Accepts less than $250 per year	4.0	30.8	25.5	13.6
$251 through $1,000 per year	9.0	4.8	4.3	9.1

	Total SENATE (100)	Total HOUSE (435)	L+CC* (47)	EC† (27)
$1,001 through $5,000 per year	40.0	18.6	10.6	27.3
More than $5,000 per year	33.0	2.5	19.1	4.5
Opposes acceptance of honoraria in principle	2.0	5.5	4.3	9.1
Accepts no honoraria within home district		3.2		
Accepts expenses only	3.0	12.0	8.5	4.5
No answer	9.0	22.5	27.7	31.8

Campaign Financing

Amount spent on last campaign:

	Total SENATE (100)	Total HOUSE (435)	L+CC* (47)	EC† (27)
$0 through $15,000	2.0	18.6	27.1	22.7
$15,001 through $30,000	2.0	22.2	8.3	31.8
$30,001 through $45,000		17.7	4.2	9.1
$45,001 through $60,000	11.0	22.2	8.3	4.5
$60,001 through $75,000	2.0	6.4		9.1
$75,001 through $100,000	4.0	6.2	12.5	9.1
$100,001 through $150,000	17.0		12.5	9.1
$150,001 through $200,000	3.0	1.6	4.2	
$200,001 through $300,000	27.0	1.6		
$300,001 through $500,000	32.0		8.3	
More than $500,000				
No answer		3.4	14.6	4.5

Communications media used in last campaign:

	Total SENATE (100)	Total HOUSE (435)	L+CC* (47)	EC† (27)
Heavy use of television	9.0	5.8	4.2	4.5
Moderate use of TV	2.0	9.7	14.6	4.5
Heavy use of radio		6.9	4.2	
Moderate use of radio		15.7	4.2	9.1
Both used heavily	44.0	13.6	12.5	13.6
Both used moderately	6.0	14.5	14.6	18.2
Heavy radio; moderate TV		0.7	4.2	4.5
Heavy TV; moderate radio	34.0	7.1	12.5	9.1
None (used neither)	4.0	25.1	25.0	27.3
No answer	1.0	0.9	4.2	9.1

Opinion on placing a limit on total campaign spending:

	Total SENATE (100)	Total HOUSE (435)	L+CC* (47)	EC† (27)
Desirable	35.0	27.5	19.1	40.9
Undesirable and/or unenforceable	27.0	48.5	25.6	36.2
No answer	38.0	23.9	55.3	22.7

Attitude toward public financing of campaigns:

	Total SENATE (100)	Total HOUSE (435)	L+CC* (47)	EC† (27)
Strongly positive	21.0	6.5	4.3	
Positive	15.0	12.7	17.4	13.0
Equivocal	11.0	14.1	10.9	4.3
Negative	23.0	51.8	26.1	52.2
Strongly negative	4.0	6.0	15.2	8.7
No answer	26.0	9.0	26.1	21.7

Attitude toward television campaign cost proposals:

	Total SENATE (100)	Total HOUSE (435)	L+CC* (47)	EC† (27)
Free time should be available to candidates	36.0	19.8	10.6	45.5
Candidates should be entitled to reduced rates	9.0	14.3	4.3	9.1
Television costs should be subsidized		8.3		4.5
Allowable expenditures for TV should be limited	2.0	5.5	8.5	
Free time plus a limit on additional purchases	11.0	11.8	8.5	
Reduced rates plus a limit on additional purchases		1.6		
Subsidies plus a limit on additional purchases		0.2		
Some other change	2.0	2.1	8.5	
Member favors no change	17.0	11.5	23.4	9.1
No answer	23.0	24.9	36.2	31.8

Conflicts of Interest

Present economic position compared with position before entering Congress:

	Total SENATE (100)	Total HOUSE (435)	L+CC* (47)	EC† (27)
Richer from savings from salary	4.0	7.1	23.4	4.3
Richer from other sources	58.0	25.7	31.9	17.4
Richer as a result of both		4.4	10.6	
About the same	20.0	20.4		52.2
Poorer due to extra expenses of Congressional service	3.0	28.4	4.3	17.4
Poorer due to some other cause	4.0	11.2	8.5	
No answer	11.0	2.8	21.3	8.7

Does Member rely on outside income for living expenses?

	Total SENATE (100)	Total HOUSE (435)	L+CC* (47)	EC† (27)
Yes	23.0	19.1	4.3	13.0
No	25.0	37.2	19.6	39.1

	Total SENATE (100)	Total HOUSE (435)	L+CC* (47)	EC† (27)
No answer	52.0	43.7	76.1	47.8
Amount of outside income:				
Less than $1,000	18.0	7.3	4.3	8.7
$1,000 through $5,000	4.0	4.1	14.9	4.3
$5,001 through $10,000	20.0	6.9	4.3	8.7
More than $10,000	37.0	26.4	23.4	8.7
Some unspecified amount	2.0	34.4	21.3	47.8
None		18.6		8.7
No answer	19.0	2.3	31.9	13.0
Sources of outside income:				
Business	11.0	10.1	10.6	13.6
Investments	39.0	25.1	27.7	36.4
Law practice		12.2	4.3	4.5
Business plus investments	8.0	11.3	17.0	13.6
Business plus law practice				
Investments plus law practice		17.7	6.4	9.1
Business, investments and law practice	2.0	0.2	4.3	4.5
Other	36.0	0.7	4.3	4.5
No answer	4.0	22.8	25.5	13.6
Time spent on outside occupation:				
Two days per month or less	95.0	77.9	80.4	87.0
More than two days per month		13.8	4.3	4.3
No answer	5.0	8.3	15.2	8.7
Has Member ever made a financial disclosure statement?				
Yes	36.0	20.5	15.2	34.8
No	7.0	32.6	41.3	17.4
No answer	57.0	46.9	43.5	47.8
Member's attitude toward disclosure:				
Favors full public disclosure	50.0	25.5	22.9	54.5
Favors limited disclosure (*e.g.*, as provided in House Ethics Code)	20.0	15.2	14.6	4.5
Neutral; but would not resist greater disclosure	1.0	19.5	4.2	13.6
Opposed in principle; but finds present code acceptable		8.7	4.2	4.5
Opposed on grounds of privacy or second-class citizenship	6.0	15.2	27.1	4.5
Opposed; fears demagogic use of disclosed information	2.0	5.3	8.3	
Opposed; some other reason	10.0	1.8		4.5
No answer	11.0	8.7	18.8	13.6

	Total SENATE (100)	Total HOUSE (435)	L+CC* (47)	EC† (27)
Lawyer-Member Responses				
Lawyer-Member's handling of professional affiliations: ‡				
Maintains some connection with private practice and				
Contributes no service	4.6	17.4	6.7	12.5
Contributes minimal service		37.5	10.0	12.5
Contributes substantial service		6.7		6.3
Has totally severed all ties with past practice	95.4	37.5	83.3	56.3
Has officially severed ties but handles infrequent cases		0.4		6.3
No answer		0.4		6.3
Lawyer-Member's income from legal affiliation:				
Less than $500	95.4	46.0	80.6	76.5
$500 through $5,000		10.6	6.5	5.9
$5,001 through $10,000	3.1	19.0	6.5	5.9
More than $10,000	1.5	23.9	6.5	5.9
No answer		0.4		5.9
Lawyer-Member's income from sources other than salary and legal services:				
Less than $1,000	15.4	35.4	9.7	25.0
$1,000 through $5,000	20.0	7.1	19.4	
$5,001 through $10,000	30.8	4.0	6.5	12.5
More than $10,000	7.7	3.5	12.9	
Some unspecified amount	26.2	49.6	51.6	56.3
No answer		0.4		6.3

QUESTIONNAIRE

Salaries, Allowances, Aids

1. Do you think the salary of a (Representative/Senator) is adequate? Is your salary adequate? If not, what would be adequate?
2. Some Members (especially Senators from large states) say their office and staff allowances are inadequate to deal with their large

‡ Responses of lawyer-Members only are included in this and the next two questions.

volumes of constituency business. Do you think these allowances should be raised?

Are your office allowances (stationery, equipment, etc.) adequate? Do you have as much staff as you need?

Do you draw on personal resources to pay official expenses? To what extent?

3. Is your telephone allowance adequate?
4. How often do you travel to your home district?

Do you ever travel to your district at the expense of a private group, perhaps one inviting you to speak?

Should travel allowances be raised? If so, how much?

5. Have you a standard honorarium for speaking to private groups?
6. Has a testimonial dinner ever been given for you?

(Senators) What was the gravamen of Senator Dodd's offense? Is he unique?

7. Several Members have established office expense funds. Do you have one?

(What effect will the recent Senate approval of office funds have on the practice?)

8. Do you think it is proper to prohibit Members from employing relatives?

(House) What did Mr. Powell do that justified his exclusion?

Campaign Financing

1. Including your estimate of money spent by independent committees, how much did your last campaign cost?

Do you have any idea how much your opponent spent?

2. What use did you make of radio and TV in your last campaign?

What proportion of your total expenditures would you estimate was spent on radio and TV?

(If more than one campaign) Do you have any idea how much your TV costs have increased since you first began using it?

What proportion of your total expenditures would you estimate was spent on newspaper ads?

3. How do you raise funds for your campaigns?
4. What interest groups are your principal supporters?
5. To what extent did you personally participate in fund-raising?
6. Did you know who made contributions and in what amounts?
7. Do you personally acknowledge gifts either during or after a campaign?
8. Do you favor:

—limits on individual political contributions? What amounts?

—limits on spending? (apply to primaries as well?)

—prohibition of contributions from labor and industry (as the law now provides)?

—limits on total TV and radio time?

—free (broadcaster-subsidized) television and radio time, together with limits on purchasing additional time? What about Government-subsidized "free" television?

—tax credits or deductions for political contributions?

—a form of public financing?

9. Have you ever had a campaign surplus? If so, how was it used?

Have you ever had a campaign deficit? If so, how was it paid?

10. Have you ever spent personal funds on a campaign? If so, to what extent?

Conflicts of Interest

1. Do you view conflicts of interest as a problem for a number of Members?

2. Have you ever experienced a conflict of interest?

3. Did you sell any interests when you entered Congress (or joined the X committee) to avoid any potential conflict?

4. Are you in a better (or not so good) financial position than when you entered Congress? Or about the same?

If richer, to what do you attribute the change? If poorer, to what do you attribute the change?

5. Do you have outside income? What are your major sources? (Do you have one major source?)

6. How much time do you spend on your outside interests?

7. Do you believe a Member's outside income-producing activities should be curtailed in any way?

Would it be feasible to raise salaries and ban outside employment?

8. Have you ever made a disclosure statement? (When and where?)

How would full public disclosure affect you if it went into effect today?

(If against disclosure) Would the limited disclosure adopted by the House (list interests over $5,000, legal fees over $1,000) be objectionable also?

(If for disclosure) Why do many Members oppose disclosure?

9. Would you add to the adopted code?

(How do you account for the House code being stronger than the Senate's?)

10. Would you limit a Member's right to practice law?

Practice of Law (lawyers only)

1. Which interest came first—politics or law? How has your political career affected your law practice?

2. Under what circumstances does your firm or any member of it take a case involving the Federal government?

How is your share of partnership income determined?
3. How much time do you devote to law practice?
   What sort of services do you perform?
   How much income do you derive?
4. Would you favor disclosure of clients' names? Or categories of interest, e.g., oil, banking?
5. Do you favor any general limit on law practice?

HOUSE AND SENATE ETHICS CODES AND APPLICABLE PROCEDURAL RESOLUTIONS

SENATE ETHICS CODE: SUBSTANTIVE PROVISIONS

Rules XLI–XLIV of the Standing Rules of the Senate
(adopted, March 22, 1968)

RULE XLI

*Outside Business or Professional Activity or Employment
by Officers or Employees*

1. No officer or employee whose salary is paid by the Senate may engage in any business or professional activity or employment for compensation unless—

(a) the activity or employment is not inconsistent nor in conflict with the conscientious performance of his official duties; and

(b) he has reported in writing when this rule takes effect or when his office or employment starts and on the 15th day of May in each year thereafter the nature of any personal service activity or employment to his supervisor. The supervisor shall then, in the discharge of his duties, take such action as he considers necessary for the avoidance of conflict of interest or interference with duties to the Senate.

2. For the purpose of this rule—

(a) a Senator or the Vice President is the supervisor of his administrative, clerical, or other assistants;

(b) a Senator who is the chairman of a committee is the supervisor of the professional, clerical, or other assistants to the committee except that minority staff members shall be under the supervision of the ranking minority Senator on the committee;

(c) a Senator who is a chairman of a subcommittee which has its own staff and financial authorization is the supervisor of the professional, clerical, or other assistants to the subcommittee except that minority staff members shall be under the supervision of the ranking minority Senator on the subcommittee;

(d) the President pro tempore is the supervisor of the Secretary of the Senate, Sergeant at Arms and Doorkeeper, the Chaplain, and the employees of the Office of the Legislative Counsel;

(e) the Secretary of the Senate is the supervisor of the employees of his office;

(f) the Sergeant at Arms and Doorkeeper is the supervisor of the employees of his office;

(g) the Majority and Minority Leaders and the Majority and Minority Whips are the supervisors of the research, clerical, or other assistants assigned to their respective offices;

(h) the Majority Leader is the supervisor of the Secretary for the Majority. The Secretary for the Majority is the supervisor of the employees of his office; and

(i) the Minority Leader is the supervisor of the Secretary for the Minority. The Secretary for the Minority is the supervisor of the employees of his office.

3. This rule shall take effect ninety days after adoption.

RULE XLII

Contributions

1. A Senator or person who has declared or otherwise made known his intention to seek nomination or election, or who has filed papers or petitions for nomination or election, or on whose behalf a declaration or nominating paper or petition has been made or filed, or who has otherwise, directly or indirectly, manifested his intention to seek nomination or election, pursuant to State law, to the office of United States Senator, may accept a contribution from—

(a) a fundraising event organized and held primarily in his behalf, provided—

(1) he has expressly given his approval of the fundraising event to the sponsors before any funds were raised; and

(2) he receives a complete and accurate accounting of the source, amounts, and disposition of the funds raised; or

(b) an individual or an organization, provided the Senator makes a complete and accurate accounting of the source, amount, and disposition of the funds received; or

(c) his political party when such contributions were from a fundraising event sponsored by his party, without giving his express approval for such fundraising event when such fundraising event is for the purpose of providing contributions for candidates of his party and such contributions are reported by the Senator or candidate for Senator as provided in paragraph (b).

2. The Senator may use the contribution only to influence his nomination for election, or his election, and shall not use, directly or indirectly, any part of any contribution for any other purpose, except as otherwise provided herein.

3. Nothing in this rule shall preclude the use of contributions to defray expenses for travel to and from each Senator's home State; for printing and other expenses in connection with the mailing of speeches, newsletters, and reports to a Senator's constituents; for expenses of radio, television, and news media methods of reporting to a Senator's constituents; for telephone, telegraph, postage, and stationery expenses in excess of allowance; and for newspaper subscriptions from his home State.

4. All gifts in the aggregate amount or value of $50 or more received by a Senator from any single source during a year, except a gift from his spouse, child, or parent, and except a contribution under sections 1 and 2, shall be reported under rule XLIV.

5. This rule shall take effect ninety days after adoption.

RULE XLIII

Political Fund Activity by Officers and Employees

1. No officer or employee whose salary is paid by the Senate may receive, solicit, be the custodian of, or distribute any funds in connection with any campaign for the nomination for election, or the election of any individual to be a Member of the Senate or to any other Federal office. This prohibition does not apply to any assistant to a Senator who has been designated by that Senator to perform any of the functions described in the first sentence of this paragraph and who is compensated at a rate in excess of $10,000 per annum if such designation has been made in writing and filed with the Secretary of the Senate. The Secretary of the Senate shall make the designation available for public inspection.

2. This rule shall take effect sixty days after adoption.

RULE XLIV

Disclosure of Financial Interests

1. Each Senator or person who has declared or otherwise made known his intention to seek nomination or election, or who has filed papers or petition for nomination or election, or on whose behalf a declaration or nominating paper or petition has been made or filed, or who has otherwise, directly or indirectly, manifested his intention to seek nomination or election, pursuant to State law, to the office of United States Senator, and each officer or employee of the Senate who is compensated at a rate

in excess of $15,000 a year, shall file with the Comptroller General of the United States, in a sealed envelope marked "Confidential Personal Financial Disclosure of _____",

(Name)

before the 15th day of May in each year, the following reports of his personal financial interests:

(a) a copy of the returns of taxes, declarations, statements, or other documents which he, or he and his spouse jointly, made for the preceding year in compliance with the income tax provisions of the Internal Revenue Code;

(b) the amount or value and source of each fee or compensation of $1,000 or more received by him during the preceding year from a client;

(c) the name and address of each business or professional corporation, firm, or enterprise in which he was an officer, director, partner, proprietor, or employee who received compensation during the preceding year and the amount of such compensation;

(d) the identity of each interest in real or personal property having a value of $10,000 or more which he owned at any time during the preceding year;

(e) the identity of each trust or other fiduciary relation in which he held a beneficial interest having a value of $10,000 or more, and the identity if known of each interest of the trust or other fiduciary relation in real or personal property in which the Senator, officer, or employee held a beneficial interest having a value of $10,000 or more, at any time during the preceding year. If he cannot obtain the identity of the fiduciary interests, the Senator, officer, or employee shall request the fiduciary to report that information to the Comptroller General in the same manner that reports are filed under this rule;

(f) the identity of each liability of $5,000 or more owned by him, or by him and his spouse jointly, at any time during the preceding year; and

(g) the source and value of all gifts in the aggregate amount or value of $50 or more from any single source received by him during the preceding year.

2. Except as otherwise provided by this section, all papers filed under section 1 of this rule shall be kept by the Comptroller General for not less than seven years, and while so kept shall remain sealed. Upon receipt of a resolution of the Select Committee on Standards and Conduct, adopted by a recorded majority vote of the full committee, requesting the transmission to the committee of any of the reports filed by any individual under section 1 of this rule, the Comptroller General shall transmit to the committee the envelopes containing such reports. Within a reasonable time after such recorded vote has been taken, the individual concerned shall be informed of the vote to examine and audit, and shall be

advised of the nature and scope of such examination. When any sealed envelope containing any such report is received by the committee, such envelope may be opened and the contents thereof may be examined only by members of the committee in executive session. If, upon such examination, the committee determines that further consideration by the committee is warranted and is within the jurisdiction of the committee, it may make the contents of any such envelope available for any use by any member of the committee, or any member of the staff of the committee, which is required for the discharge of his official duties. The committee may receive the papers as evidence, after giving to the individual concerned due notice and opportunity for hearing in a closed session. The Comptroller General shall report to the Select Committee on Standards and Conduct not later than the 1st day of June in each year the names of Senators, officers, and employees who have filed a report. Any paper which has been filed with the Comptroller General for longer than seven years, in accordance with the provisions of this section, shall be returned to the individual concerned or his legal representative. In the event of the death or termination of service of a Member of the Senate, an officer or employee, such papers shall be returned unopened to such individual, or to the surviving spouse or legal representative of such individual within one year of such death or termination of service.

3. Each Senator or person who has declared or otherwise made known his intention to seek nomination or election, or who has filed papers or petitions for nomination or election, or on whose behalf a declaration or nominating paper or petition has been made or filed, or who has otherwise, directly or indirectly, manifested his intention to seek nomination or election, pursuant to State law, to the office of United States Senator, and each officer or employee of the Senate who is compensated at a rate in excess of $15,000 a year, shall file with the Secretary of the Senate, before the 15th day of May in each year, the following reports of his personal financial interests:

  (a) the accounting required by rule XLII for all contributions received by him during the preceding year, except that contributions in the aggregate amount or value of less than $50 received from any single source during the reporting period may be totaled without further itemization; and

  (b) the amount or value and source of each honorarium of $300 or more received by him during the preceding year.

4. All papers filed under section 3 of this rule shall be kept by the Secretary of the Senate for not less than three years and shall be made available promptly for public inspection and copying.

5. This rule shall take effect on July 1, 1968. No reports shall be filed for any period before office or employment was held with the Senate, or during a period of office or employment with the Senate of less than ninety days in a year; except that the Senator, or officer or employee of

the Senate, may file a copy of the return of taxes for the year 1968, or a report of substantially equivalent information for only the effective part of the year 1968.

SENATE PROCEDURAL PROVISIONS

S. Res. 338, 88th Cong., 2d Sess. (July 24, 1964)

RESOLUTION

Resolved, That (a) there is hereby established a permanent select committee of the Senate to be known as the Select Committee on Standards and Conduct (referred to hereinafter as the "Select Committee") consisting of six Members of the Senate, of whom three shall be selected from members of the majority party and three shall be selected from members of the minority party. Members thereof shall be appointed by the President of the Senate. The Select Committee shall select a chairman and a vice chairman from among its members.

(b) Vacancies in the membership of the Select Committee shall not affect the authority of the remaining members to execute the functions of the committee, and shall be filled in the same manner as original appointments thereto are made.

(c) A majority of the members of the Select Committee shall constitute a quorum for the transaction of business, except that the Select Committee may fix a lesser number as a quorum for the purpose of taking sworn testimony. The Select Committee shall adopt rules of procedure not inconsistent with the rules of the Senate governing standing committees of the Senate.

SEC. 2. (a) It shall be the duty of the Select Committee to—

(1) receive complaints and investigate allegations of improper conduct which may reflect upon the Senate, violations of law, and violations of rules and regulations of the Senate, relating to the conduct of individuals in the performance of their duties as Members of the Senate, and to make appropriate findings of fact and conclusions with respect thereto;

(2) recommend to the Senate by report or resolution by a majority vote of the full committee disciplinary action to be taken with respect to such violations which the Select Committee shall determine, after according to the individuals concerned due notice and opportunity for hearing, to have occurred;

(3) recommend to the Senate, by report or resolution, such additional rules or regulations as the Select Committee shall determine to be necessary or desirable to insure proper standards of conduct by Members of the Senate, and by officers or employees of the Senate, in the performance of their duties and the discharge of their responsibilities; and

(4) report violations by a majority vote of the full committee of any law to the proper Federal and State authorities.

(b) The Select Committee from time to time shall transmit to the Senate its recommendation as to any legislative measures which it may consider to be necessary for the effective discharge of its duties.

SEC. 3. (a) The Select Committee is authorized to (1) make such expenditures; (2) hold such hearings; (3) sit and act at such times and places during the sessions, recesses, and adjournment periods of the Senate; (4) require by subpoena or otherwise the attendance of such witnesses and the production of such correspondence, books, papers, and documents; (5) administer such oaths; (6) take such testimony orally or by deposition; and (7) employ and fix the compensation of such technical, clerical and other assistants and consultants as it deems advisable.

(b) Upon request made by the members of the Select Committee selected from the minority party, the committee shall appoint one assistant or consultant designated by such members. No assistant or consultant appointed by the Select Committee may receive compensation at an annual gross rate which exceeds by more than $1,600 the annual gross rate of compensation of any individual so designated by the members of the committee who are members of the minority party.

(c) With the prior consent of the department or agency concerned, the Select Committee may (1) utilize the services, information, and facilities of the General Accounting Office or any department or agency in the executive branch of the Government, and (2) employ on a reimbursable basis or otherwise the services of such personnel of any such department or agency as it deems advisable. With the consent of any other committee of the Senate, or any subcommittee thereof, the Select Committee may utilize the facilities and the services of the staff of such other committee or subcommittee whenever the chairman of the Select Committee determines that such action is necessary and appropriate.

(d) Subpoenas may be issued by the Select Committee over the signature of the chairman or any other member designated by him, and may be served by any person designated by such chairman or member. The chairman of the Select Committee or any member thereof may administer oaths to witnesses.

SEC. 4. The expenses of the Select Committee under this resolution shall be paid from the contingent fund of the Senate upon vouchers approved by the chairman of the Select Committee.

SEC. 5. As used in this resolution, the term "officer or employee of the Senate" means—

(1) an elected officer of the Senate who is not a member of the Senate;

(2) an employee of the Senate, any committee or subcommittee of the Senate, or any Member of the Senate;

(3) the Legislative Counsel of the Senate or any employee of his office;

(4) an Official Reporter of Debates of the Senate and any person

employed by the Official Reporters of Debates of the Senate in connection with the performance of their official duties;

(5) a member of the Capitol Police force whose compensation is disbursed by the Secretary of the Senate;

(6) an employee of the Vice President if such employee's compensation is disbursed by the Secretary of the Senate; and

(7) an employee of a joint committee of the Congress whose compensation is disbursed by the Secretary of the Senate.

HOUSE ETHICS CODE: SUBSTANTIVE PROVISIONS

Rules XLIII–XLIV of the Rules of the House of Representatives
(April 3, 1968)

RULE XLIII
Code of Official Conduct

There is hereby established by and for the House of Representatives the following code of conduct, to be known as the "Code of Official Conduct":

1. A Member, officer, or employee of the House of Representatives shall conduct himself at all times in a manner which shall reflect creditably on the House of Representatives.

2. A Member, officer, or employee of the House of Representatives shall adhere to the spirit and the letter of the Rules of the House of Representatives and to the rules of duly constituted committees thereof.

3. A Member, officer, or employee of the House of Representatives shall receive no compensation nor shall he permit any compensation to accrue to his beneficial interest from any source, the receipt of which would occur by virtue of influence improperly exerted from his position in the Congress.

4. A Member, officer, or employee of the House of Representatives shall accept no gift of substantial value, directly or indirectly, from any person, organization, or corporation having a direct interest in legislation before the Congress.

5. A Member, officer, or employee of the House of Representatives shall accept no honorarium for a speech, writing for publication, or other similar activity, from any person, organization, or corporation in excess of the usual and customary value for such services.

6. A Member of the House of Representatives shall keep his campaign funds separate from his personal funds. He shall convert no campaign funds to personal use in excess of reimbursement for legitimate and verifiable prior campaign expenditures. He shall expend no funds from his campaign account not attributable to bona fide campaign purposes.

7. A Member of the House of Representatives shall treat as campaign contributions all proceeds from testimonial dinners or other fund raising

events if the sponsors of such affairs do not give clear notice in advance to the donors or participants that the proceeds are intended for other purposes.

8. A Member of the House of Representatives shall retain no one from his clerk hire allowance who does not perform duties commensurate with the compensation he receives.

As used in this Code of Official Conduct of the House of Representatives—

(a) the terms "Member" and "Member of the House of Representatives" include the Resident Commissioner from Puerto Rico; and

(b) the term "officer or employee of the House of Representatives" means any individual whose compensation is disbursed by the Clerk of the House of Representatives.

RULE XLIV
Financial Disclosure

Members, officers, principal assistants to Members and officers, and professional staff members of committees shall, not later than April 30, 1969, and by April 30 of each year thereafter, file with the Committee on Standards of Official Conduct a report disclosing certain financial interests as provided in this rule. The interest of a spouse or any other party, if constructively controlled by the person reporting, shall be considered to be the same as the interest of the person reporting. The report shall be in two parts as follows:

PART A

1. List the name, instrument of ownership, and any position of management held in any business entity doing a substantial business with the Federal Government or subject to Federal regulatory agencies, in which the ownership is in excess of $5,000 fair market value as of the date of filing or from which income of $1,000 or more was derived during the preceding calendar year. Do not list any time or demand deposit in a financial institution, or any debt instrument having a fixed yield unless it is convertible to an equity instrument.

2. List the name, address, and type of practice of any professional organization in which the person reporting, or his spouse, is an officer, director, or partner, or serves in any advisory capacity, from which income of $1,000 or more was derived during the preceding calendar year.

3. List the source of each of the following items received during the preceding calendar year:

(a) Any income for services rendered (other than from the United States Government) exceeding $5,000.

(b) Any capital gain from a single source exceeding $5,000, other than from the sale of a residence occupied by the person reporting.

(c) Reimbursement for expenditures (other than from the United States Government) exceeding $1,000 in each instance.

Campaign receipts shall not be included in this report.

Information filed under part A shall be maintained by the Committee on Standards of Official Conduct and made available at reasonable hours to responsible public inquiry, subject to such regulations as the committee may prescribe including, but not limited to, regulations requiring identification by name, occupation, address, and telephone number of each person examining information filed under part A, and the reason for each such inquiry.

The committee shall promptly notify each person required to file a report under this rule of each instance of an examination of his report. The committee shall also promptly notify a Member of each examination of the reports filed by his principal assistants and of each examination of the reports of professional staff members of committees who are responsible to such Member.

PART B

1. List the fair market value (as of the date of filing) of each item listed under paragraph 1 of part A and the income derived therefrom during the preceding calendar year.

2. List the amount of income derived from each item listed under paragraphs 2 and 3 of part A.

The information filed under this part B shall be sealed by the person filing and shall remain sealed unless the Committee on Standards of Official Conduct, pursuant to its investigative authority, determines by a vote of not less than seven members of the committee that the examination of such information is essential in an official investigation by the committee and promptly notifies the Member concerned of any such determination. The committee may, by a vote of not less than seven members of the committee, make public any portion of the information unsealed by the committee under the preceding sentence and which the committee deems to be in the public interest.

Any person required to file a report under this rule who has no interests covered by any of the provisions of this rule shall file a report so stating.

In any case in which a person required to file a sealed report under part B of this rule is no longer required to file such a report, the committee shall return to such person, or his legal representative, all sealed reports filed by such person under part B and remaining in the possession of the committee.

As used in this rule—

(1) the term "Members" includes the Resident Commissioner from Puerto Rico; and

(2) the term "committees" includes any committee or subcommittee of the House of Representatives and any joint committee of Con-

gress, the expenses of which are paid from the contingent fund of the House of Representatives.

HOUSE PROCEDURAL PROVISIONS
Rule XI (19) (April 3, 1968)

All proposed legislation, messages, petitions, memorials, and other matters relating to the subject listed under the standing committees named below shall be referred to such committees, respectively:

* * *

19. COMMITTEE ON STANDARDS OF OFFICIAL CONDUCT
(a) Measures relating to the Code of Official Conduct
(b) Measures relating to financial disclosure by Members, officers, and employees of the House of Representatives
(c) The committee is authorized (1) to recommend to the House of Representatives, from time to time, such legislative or administrative actions as the committee may deem appropriate to establish or enforce standards of official conduct for Members, officers, and employees of the House of Representatives; (2) to investigate, subject to paragraph (d) of this clause, any alleged violation, by a Member, officer, or employee of the House of Representatives, of the Code of Official Conduct or of any law, rule, regulation, or other standard of conduct applicable to the conduct of such Member, officer, or employee in the performance of his duties or the discharge of his responsibilities and, after notice and a hearing, shall recommend to the House of Representatives, by resolution or otherwise, such action as the committee may deem appropriate in the circumstances; (3) to report to the appropriate Federal or State authorities, with approval of the House of Representatives, any substantial evidence of a violation, by a Member, officer, or employee of the House of Representatives, of any law applicable to the performance of his duties or the discharge of his responsibilities, which may have been disclosed in a committee investigation; and (4) to give consideration to the request of a Member, officer, or employee of the House of Representatives, for an advisory opinion with respect to the general propriety of any current or proposed conduct of such Member, officer, or employee and, with appropriate deletions to assure the privacy of the individual concerned, to publish such opinion for the guidance of other Members, officers, and employees of the House of Representatives.
(d) (1) No resolution, report, recommendation, or advisory opinion relating to the official conduct of a Member, officer, or employee of the House of Representatives shall be made, and no investigation of such conduct shall be undertaken, unless approved by the affirmative vote of not less than seven members of the committee. (2) Except in the case of an investigation undertaken by the committee on its own initiative, the committee may undertake an investigation relating to the official

conduct of an individual Member, officer, or employee of the House of Representatives only (A) upon receipt of a complaint, in writing and under oath, made by or submitted to a Member of the House of Representatives and transmitted to the committee by such Member, or (B) upon receipt of a complaint, in writing and under oath, directly from an individual not a Member of the House of Representatives if the committee finds that such complaint has been submitted by such individual to not less than three Members of the House of Representatives who have refused, in writing, to transmit such complaint to the committee. (3) No investigation shall be undertaken of any alleged violation of a law, rule, regulation, or standard of conduct not in effect at the time of the alleged violation. (4) A member of the committee shall be ineligible to participate, as a member of the committee, in any committee proceeding relating to his official conduct. In any case in which a member of the committee is ineligible to act as a member of the committee under the preceding sentence, the Speaker of the House of Representatives shall designate a Member of the House of Representatives from the same political party as the ineligible member of the committee to act as a member of the committee in any committee proceeding relating to the official conduct of such ineligible member.

(e) For the purpose of carrying out the foregoing provisions of this clause, the committee, or any subcommittee thereof, is authorized to sit and act at such times and places within the United States, whether the House is in session, has recessed, or has adjourned, to hold such hearings, and to require, by subpena or otherwise, the attendance and testimony of such witnesses and the production of such books, records, correspondence, memorandums, papers, and documents, as it deems necessary. Subpenas may be issued under the signature of the chairman of the committee or any member of the committee designated by him, and may be served by any person designated by such chairman or member.

MODEL ELECTION REFORM ACT[*]

A BILL TO REVISE THE FEDERAL ELECTION LAWS, AND
FOR OTHER PURPOSES.

*Be it enacted by the Senate and House of Representatives of the
United States of America in Congress assembled,
That this Act may be cited as the "Election Reform Act of ——"*

TITLE I—AMENDMENTS TO CRIMINAL CODE

SEC. 101. Section 591 of title 18 of the United States Code is
amended to read as follows:

"§591. Definitions

"When used in sections 597, 599, 602, 608, and 610 of this title—

"(a) The term 'election' means (1) a general, special, or primary
election, (2) a convention or caucus of a political party held to nominate
a candidate, (3) a primary election held for the selection of delegates to
a national nominating convention of a political party, or (4) a primary
election held for the expression of a preference for the nomination of
persons for election to the office of President.

"(b) The term 'candidate' means an individual who seeks nomination
for election, or election, to Federal office, whether or not such individual
is elected. For purposes of this paragraph, an individual shall be deemed
to seek nomination for election, or election, if he (1) has taken the action
necessary under the law of a State to qualify himself for nomination for
election, or election, to Federal office, or (2) has received contributions
or made expenditures, or has given his consent for any other person to
receive contributions or make expenditures, with a view to bringing about
his nomination for election, or election, to such office;

"(c) The term 'Federal office' means the office of President or Vice
President of the United States, or of Senator or Representative in, or
Resident Commissioner to, the Congress of the United States;

---

[*] This bill essentially combines Title I of S. 1880, 90th Cong. with Title II of
H.R. 11233, 90th Cong. See discussion in Chapter 4, *infra*.

"(d) The term 'political committee' means any individual, committee, association, or organization which accepts contributions or makes expenditures during a calendar year in an aggregate amount exceeding $1,000;

"(e) The term 'contribution' means a gift, subscription, loan, advance, or deposit of money or any thing of value, made for the purpose of influencing the nomination for election, or election, of any person to Federal office, or for the purpose of influencing the result of a primary held for the selection of delegates to a national nominating convention of a political party or for the expression of a preference for the nomination of persons for election to the office of President, and includes a contract, promise, or agreement, express or implied, whether or not legally enforceable, to make a contribution, and also includes a transfer of funds between political committees;

"(f) The term 'expenditure' includes a purchase, payment, distribution, loan, advance, deposit, or gift of money or any thing of value, made for the purpose of influencing the nomination for election, or election, of any person to Federal office, or for the purpose of influencing the result of a primary held for the selection of delegates to a national nominating convention of a political party or for the expression of a preference for the nomination of persons for election to the office of President, and includes a contract, promise, or agreement, express or implied, whether or not legally enforceable, to make an expenditure, and also includes a transfer of funds between political committees;

"(g) The term 'person' or the term 'whoever' means an individual, partnership, committee, association, corporation, or any other organization or group of persons."

SEC. 102. Section 600 of title 18 of the United States Code is amended to read as follows:

"§600. Promise of employment or other benefit for political activity.

"Whoever, directly or indirectly, promises any employment, position, compensation, contract, appointment, or other benefit, provided for or made possible in whole or in part by any Act of Congress, or any special consideration in obtaining any such benefit, to any person as consideration, favor, or reward for any political activity or for the support of or opposition to any candidate or any political party in connection with any general or special election to any political office, or in connection with any primary election or political convention or caucus held to select candidates for any political office, shall be fined not more than $1,000 or imprisoned not more than one year, or both."

SEC. 103. Section 602 of title 18 of the United States Code is amended—

(a) by inserting "(a)" before "Whoever," and
(b) by adding at the end thereof the following new subsection:

"(b) Whoever, acting on behalf of any political committee (including any State or local committee of a political party), directly or indirectly, intentionally or willfully solicits, or is in any manner concerned in soliciting, any assessment, subscription, or contribution for the use of such political committee or for any political purpose whatever from any officer or employee of the United States (other than an elected officer) shall be fined not more than $5,000 or imprisoned not more than three years, or both."

SEC. 104. Section 608 of title 18 of the United States Code is amended to read as follows:

"§608. Limitations on political contributions and purchases

"(a) It shall be unlawful for any person, directly or indirectly, to make a contribution or contributions in an aggregate amount in excess of $5,000 during any calendar year in connection with any campaign for nomination for election, or election, to any political committee or candidate, to two or more political committees substantially supporting the same candidate, or to a candidate and one or more political committees substantially supporting the candidate: *Provided, however,* That nothing contained in this subsection shall prohibit the transfer of contributions received by a political committee.

"(b) (1) It shall be unlawful for any political committee or candidate to sell goods, commodities, advertising, or other articles, or any services (except as provided in the Election Reform Act of ———) to anyone other than a political committee or candidate.

"(2) It shall be unlawful for any person, other than a political committee or candidate, to purchase goods, commodities, advertising, or other articles, or any services (except as provided in the Election Reform Act of ———) from a political committee or candidate.

"(c) Whoever violates subsection (a) or (b) of this section shall be fined not more than $5,000 or imprisoned not more than five years, or both.

"(d) Subsection (b) of this section shall not apply to a sale or purchase (1) of any political campaign pin, button, badge, flag, emblem, hat, banner, or similar campaign souvenir or any political campaign literature or publications (but shall apply to sales of advertising including the sale of space in any publication), for prices not exceeding $25 each, (2) of tickets to political events or gatherings, (3) of food or drink for a charge not substantially in excess of the normal charge therefor, or (4) made in the course of the usual and known business, trade, or profession of any person or in a normal arm's-length transaction: *Provided, however,* That a sale or purchase described in paragraph (1), (2), or (3) shall be deemed a contribution under subsection (a) of this section.

"(e) For the purposes of this section, a contribution made by the spouse or a minor child of a person shall be deemed a contribution made by such person.

"(f) In all cases of violations of this section by a partnership, committee, association, corporation, or other organization or group of persons, the officers, directors, or managing heads thereof who knowingly and willfully participate in such violation shall be punished as herein provided."

SEC. 105. Section 609 of title 18 of the United States Code is repealed.

SEC. 106. Section 611 of title 18 of the United States Code is amended to read as follows:

"§611. Contributions by Government contractors

"Whoever, including a corporation, entering into any contract with the United States or any department or agency thereof either for the rendition of personal services or furnishing any material, supplies, or equipment to the United States or any department or agency thereof or for selling any land or building to the United States or any department or agency thereof, if payment for the performance of such contract or payment for such material, supplies, equipment, land, or building is to be made in whole or in part from funds appropriated by the Congress, at any time between the commencement of negotiations for and the later of (a) the completion of performance under, or (b) the termination of negotiations for, such contract or furnishing of material, supplies, equipment, land or buildings, directly or indirectly makes any contribution of money or other thing of value, or promises expressly or impliedly to make any such contribution, to any political party, committee, or candidate for public office or to any person for any political purpose or use; or

"Whoever knowingly solicits any such contribution from any such person for any such purpose during any such period—

"Shall be fined not more than $5,000 or imprisoned not more than five years, or both."

SEC. 107. So much of the sectional analysis at the beginning of chapter 29 of title 18 of the United States Code as relates to sections 609 and 611 is amended to read:

"§609. Repealed.

"§611. Contributions by Government contractors."

TITLE II—DISCLOSURE OF FEDERAL CAMPAIGN FUNDS
Definitions

SEC. 201. When used in this title—

(a) The term "election" means (1) a general, special, or primary election, (2) a convention or caucus of a political party held to nominate a candidate, and (3) a primary held for the selection of delegates to a national nominating convention of a political party, or for the expression of a preference for the nomination of persons for election to the office of President or Vice President.

(b) The term "candidate" means an individual who seeks nomination for election, or election, to Federal office whether or not such individual is elected. For purposes of this paragraph, an individual shall be deemed to seek nomination for election, or election, if he (1) has taken the action necessary under the law of a State to qualify him for nomination for election, or election, to Federal office, or (2) has received contributions or made expenditures, or has given his consent for any other person to receive contributions or make expenditures, with a view to bringing about his nomination for election, or election, to such an office.

(c) The term "Federal office" means the office of President or Vice President of the United States; or of Senator or Representative in, or Resident Commissioner to, the Congress of the United States.

(d) The term "political committee" means any committee, association, or organization which accepts contributions or makes expenditures during a calendar year in an aggregate amount exceeding $1,000, other than a committee which primarily supports persons seeking State or local office, which does not substantially support Federal candidates, and which does not operate in more than one State.

(e) The term "contribution" means a gift, donation, payment of money, or any thing of value, or loan of money, except to a candidate by a licensed lending institution, or loan of any thing of value, made for the purpose of influencing the nomination for election, or election, of any person to Federal office or as presidential and vice-presidential electors, or for the purpose of influencing the result of a primary held for the selection of delegates to a national nominating convention of a political party, or for the expression of a preference for the nomination of persons for election to the office of President and Vice President, and includes a transfer of funds between political committees.

(f) The term "expenditure" includes a purchase, payment, distribution, loan, advance, deposit, or gift of money or any thing of value, made for the purpose of influencing the nomination for election, or election, of any person to Federal office, or as presidential and vice-presidential electors, and includes a contract, promise, or agreement, whether or not legally enforceable, to make an expenditure, or for the purpose of influencing the result of a primary held for the selection of delegates to a national nominating convention of a political party, or for the expression of a preference for the nomination of persons for election to the office of President and Vice President, and also includes a transfer of funds between political committees.

(g) The term "person" includes an individual, partnership, committee, association, corporation, labor organization, and any other organization or group of persons.

(h) The term "State" includes the District of Columbia, Puerto Rico, Guam, American Samoa, and the Virgin Islands.

Federal Elections Commission

SEC. 202. (a) (1) There is hereby created a commission to be known as the Federal Elections Commission (referred to hereafter in this Act as

"Commission"), which shall be composed of five members, who shall be appointed by the President, by and with the advice and consent of the Senate.

(2) A person may not be appointed to the Commission—

(A) if at the time of his appointment he was not a member of a major political party, or

(B) if his appointment results in more than three persons from his party being members of the Commission.

For purposes of this paragraph, the term "major political party" means a national political party whose candidate for President received either the largest or the next largest popular vote in the preceding presidential election.

(3) One of the original members shall be appointed for a term of two years, one for a term of four years, one for a term of six years, one for a term of eight years, and one for a term of ten years, beginning from the effective date of this title but their successors shall be appointed for terms of ten years each, except that any individual chosen to fill a vacancy shall be appointed only for the unexpired term of the member whom he shall succeed. The President shall designate one member to serve as Chairman of the Commission, and one member to serve as Vice Chairman. The Vice Chairman shall act as Chairman in the absence or disability of the Chairman or in the event of a vacancy in that office.

(b) If there is a vacancy in the Commission which has existed for more than ninety days, the remaining members of the Commission may not exercise any of the powers of the Commission until such vacancy is filled, but in such case the Executive Director of the Commission may exercise any duties previously vested in him by the Commission. Except as provided in the preceding sentence, three members of the Commission shall constitute a quorum.

(c) The Commission shall have an official seal which shall be judicially noticed.

(d) The Commission shall at the close of each fiscal year report to the Congress and to the President concerning the action it has taken; the names, salaries, and duties of all individuals in its employ and the moneys it has disbursed; and shall make such further reports on the matters within its jurisdiction and such recommendations for further legislation as may appear desirable.

(e)(1) Members of the Commission shall, while serving on the business of the Commission, be entitled to receive compensation at a rate fixed by the Director of the Bureau of the Budget, but not exceeding $100 per day, including traveltime; and, while so serving away from their homes or regular places of business, they may be allowed travel expenses, including per diem in lieu of subsistence, as authorized by section 3109 of title 5, United States Code.

(2) The Commission shall, in accordance with chapter 51 of title 5, United States Code, and subchapter III of chapter 53 of title 5, United

States Code, appoint and fix the compensation of an Executive Director and such other officers, agents, attorneys, and employees as it deems necessary to assist it in the performance of its functions.

(3) The Executive Director shall be the chief administrative officer of the Commission. He shall perform his duties under the direction and supervision of the Commission, and the Commission may delegate any of its functions, other than the making of regulations, to him.

(f) The principal office of the Commission shall be in or near the District of Columbia, but it may meet or exercise any or all of its powers at any other place.

(g) All officers, agents, attorneys, and employees of the Commission shall be subject to the provisions of sections 7324 and 7325 of title 5, United States Code, notwithstanding any exemption contained therein.

Organization of Political Committees

SEC. 203. (a) Every political committee shall have a chairman and a treasurer. No contribution and no expenditure shall be accepted or made by or on behalf of a political committee at a time when there is a vacancy in the office of chairman or treasurer thereof. No expenditure shall be made for or on behalf of a political committee without the authorization of its chairman or treasurer, or their designated agents.

(b) Every person who receives a contribution for a political committee shall, on demand of the treasurer, and in any event within five days after the receipt of such contribution, render to the treasurer a detailed account thereof, including the amount, the name and address of the person making such contribution, and the date on which received. All funds of a political committee shall be kept separate from other funds.

(c) It shall be the duty of the treasurer of a political committee to keep a detailed and exact account of—

(1) all contributions made to or for such committee;

(2) the full name and mailing address of every person making any contribution, and the date and amount thereof;

(3) all expenditures made by or on behalf of such committee; and

(4) the full name and mailing address of every person to whom any expenditure is made, and the date and amount thereof.

(d) It shall be the duty of the treasurer to obtain and keep a receipted bill, stating the particulars, for every expenditure made by or on behalf of a political committee in excess of $100. The treasurer shall preserve all receipted bills and accounts required to be kept by this section for periods of time to be determined by the Commission in accordance with published regulations.

Registration of Political Committees; Statements

SEC. 204. (a) Each committee, organization, or association (other than an exempt State or local committee) which anticipates receiving contributions or making expenditures in an aggregate amount exceeding

$1,000 in any calendar year (hereafter in this section referred to as "committee") shall, within ten days after its organization, or, if later, ten days after the date on which it has information which causes it to anticipate it will receive or make contributions or expenditures in such amount, file with the Commission a statement of organization. Each such political committee in existence at the effective date of this Act shall file a statement of organization with the Commission at such time as it prescribes.

(b) The statement of organization shall include—

(1) the name and address of the committee;

(2) the name, address, and relationship of any organization which (under regulations of the Commission) constitutes an affiliated or connected organization;

(3) the area, scope, or jurisdiction of the committee;

(4) the name, address, and position of the custodian of books and accounts;

(5) the name, address, and position of other principal officers, including officers and members of the finance committee, if any;

(6) the name, office sought, and party affiliation of (A) each candidate whom the committee is supporting and (B) any other individuals whom the organization is supporting for nomination or election to public office; or, if the committee is supporting the entire ticket of any party, the name of the party;

(7) a statement whether the committee is a continuing one;

(8) what disposition of residual funds will be made in the event of dissolution;

(9) a listing of all banks, safety deposit boxes, or other repositories used; and

(10) a statement whether the committee is required by law to file reports with State or local officers and, if so, the names, addresses, and positions of such State or local officers.

(c) Any change in information previously submitted in a statement of organization shall be reported to the Commission within a ten-day period following the change.

(d) Any political committee which, after having filed one or more statements of organization, disbands or determines it will no longer receive contributions or make expenditures exceeding $1,000 in the aggregate in any calendar year shall so notify the Commission and file with the Commission a complete report with respect to its funds, including any disposition thereof to date.

Reports by Political Committees and Candidates

SEC. 205. (a) If an individual is a candidate during a reporting period, or if a political committee is in existence during a reporting period, then such individual or the treasurer of such committee (as the case may be) shall file a financial report under subsection (c) with respect to such reporting period. Such report shall be filed on the first reporting date following the close of such reporting period.

(b) For purposes of this section:

(1) Reporting periods shall be established by the Commission by regulation. A reporting period shall begin at least five days before each reporting date and shall end at least five days before the next succeeding reporting date.

(2) Each of the following days shall be a reporting date:

(A) the 31st day of January.

(B) the 10th day of March.

(C) the 10th day of June.

(D) the 10th day of September

In addition to the foregoing reporting dates, (i) in the case of a candidate, or a political committee supporting only such candidate, the 15th day and the fifth day preceding any election in which he is a candidate shall be reporting dates, and (ii) in the case of a political committee supporting more than one candidate, or a person required to make a report under section 206, the Commission shall by regulation prescribe reporting dates with respect to any election in which such committee or person supports a candidate.

(3) A political committee shall be deemed to be in existence during a reporting period if it has filed a statement of organization under section 204(a) before the close of such reporting period (and has not filed a final report under section 204(d) before the beginning of such period).

(c) Each report under this section shall disclose—

(1) the amount of cash on hand at the beginning of the reporting period;

(2) the full name and mailing address of each person who has made one or more contributions to or for such committee or candidate (including the purchase of tickets for events such as dinners, luncheons, rallies, and similar fundraising events), in the aggregate amount or value, within the calendar year, in excess of $100, together with the amount and date of such contributions;

(3) the total sum of individual contributions made to or for such committee or candidate during the reporting period and not reported under paragraph (2);

(4) the name and address of each political committee from which the reporting committee or the candidate received, or to which that committee or candidate made, any transfer of funds, together with the amounts and dates of all such transfers;

(5) each loan to or from any person, except a loan to a candidate by a licensed lending institution, together with the full names and mailing addresses of the lender and endorsers, if any, and the date and amount of such loan;

(6) the total amount of proceeds from (A) the sale of tickets to

each dinner, luncheon, rally, and other fundraising event; (B) mass collections made at such events; and (C) sales of items such as political campaign pins, buttons, badges, flags, emblems, hats, banners, literature, and similar materials;

(7) each rebate, refund, or other receipt not otherwise listed under paragraphs (2) through (6);

(8) the total sum of all receipts by or for such committee or candidate during the reporting period;

(9) the full name and mailing address of each person to whom an expenditure or expenditures have been made by such committee or candidate within the calendar year in the aggregate amount or value in excess of $100 and the amount, date, and purpose of each such expenditure;

(10) the full name and mailing address of each person to whom an expenditure for personal services, salaries, and reimbursed expenses in excess of $100 has been made, and which is not otherwise reported, including the amount, date, and purpose of such expenditure;

(11) the total sum of expenditures made by such committee or candidate during the reporting period; and

(12) the amount and nature of debts and obligations owed by or to the committee, in such form as the Commission may prescribe.

(d) The reports required to be filed by subsection (a) shall be cumulative during the calendar year to which they relate, but where there has been no change in an item reported in a previous report only the amount need be carried forward.

Reports Other Than by Political Committees and Candidates

SEC. 206. Any person (other than a political committee, candidate, or exempt State or local committee) whose expenditures exceed $100 in the aggregate during a calendar year shall file with the Commission on the first reporting date (as defined by section 205 (b) (3)) which occurs five or more days after the first day in such year on which his expenditures exceed $100 a statement containing the information required by section 205(c). If he makes any additional expenditure during such calendar year, he shall file such a statement on the first reporting date which occurs more than five days after such expenditure. Statements under this section need not be cumulative.

Formal Requirements Respecting Reports and Statements

SEC. 207. (a) A report or statement required by this title to be filed by a treasurer of a political committee, a candidate, or by any other person, shall be verified by the oath or affirmation of the person filing such report or statement, taken before any officer authorized to administer oaths.

(b) A copy of a report or statement shall be preserved by the person filing it for a period of time to be designated by the Commission in a published regulation.

(c) The Commission shall have authority to modify, suspend, or waive by published regulation of general applicability such of the requirements of sections 204, 205, and 206 as it finds to be unnecessarily burdensome to the persons required to report thereunder or not to be necessary to effectuate the purposes of this title.

(d) The Commission shall, by published regulations of general applicability, prescribe the manner in which contributions and expenditures in the nature of debts and other contracts, agreements, and promises to make contributions or expenditures shall be reported. Such regulations shall provide that they be reported in separate schedules. In determining aggregate amounts of contributions and expenditures, amounts reported as provided in such regulations shall not be considered until actual payment is made.

Reports on Convention Financing

SEC. 208. Each committee or other organization which—

(1) represents a State, or a political subdivision thereof, or any group of persons in such State, in dealing with officials of a national political party (or with an organization described in paragraph (2)) with respect to matters involving a national convention held in such State or political subdivision to nominate a candidate for the office of President or Vice President, or

(2) represents a national political party in making arrangements for a national convention of such party held to nominate a candidate for the office of President or Vice President.

shall, within sixty days following the end of the convention (but not later than twenty days prior to the date on which presidential and vice-presidential electors are chosen), file with the Commission a full and complete financial statement, in such form and detail as it may prescribe, the sources from which it derived its funds and the purposes for which such funds were expended.

Duties of the Commission

SEC. 209. (a) It shall be the duty of the Commission—

(1) to develop prescribed forms for the making of reports and statements required by this Act;

(2) to prepare and publish a manual setting forth recommended uniform methods of bookkeeping and reporting for use by persons required to make reports and statements required by this Act;

(3) to develop a filing, coding, and cross-indexing system consonant with the purposes of this Act;

(4) to make the reports and statements filed with it available for public inspection and copying during regular office hours, commencing as soon as practicable but not later than the end of the second day following the day during which it was received, and to permit copying of any such report or statement by hand or by duplicating machine, as requested by any person, at the expense of such person;

(5) to preserve such reports and statements for a period of at least ten years from date of receipt, except that reports and statements relating solely to candidates for the House of Representatives shall be preserved for at least five years from the date of receipt;

(6) to compile and maintain a current list of all statements or parts of statements pertaining to each candidate;

(7) to prepare and publish an annual report including compilations of (A) total reported receipts and expenditures for all candidates, political committees, and other persons during the year; (B) total amounts expended according to such categories as the Commission shall determine and broken down into candidate, party, and nonparty expenditures on the National, State, and local levels; (C) total amounts expended for influencing nominations and elections stated separately; (D) total amounts contributed according to such categories of amounts as the Commission shall determine and broken down into contributions on the National, State, and local levels for candidates and political committees; and (E) aggregate amounts contributed by any contributor shown to have contributed a sum in excess of $100;

(8) to prepare and publish from time to time special reports comparing the various totals and categories of contributions and expenditures made in preceding years;

(9) to prepare and publish such other reports as it may deem appropriate;

(10) to assure wide dissemination of summaries and reports;

(11) to make, from time to time, audits and field investigations with respect to reports and statements filed under the provisions of this Act, and with respect to alleged failures to file any report or statement required under the provisions of this title or title III of this Act; and

(12) to report apparent violations of law to the appropriate law enforcement authorities;

(13) to prescribe suitable procedural regulations to carry out the provisions of this Act; and

(14) for the purpose of any audit or investigation provided for in paragraph (11) of subsection (a) or in subsection (b) of this section, the provisions of sections 9 and 10 of the Federal Trade Commission Act (15 U.S.C. 49, 50) are hereby made applicable to the jurisdiction, powers, and duties of the Commission, or any officer designated by it, except that the attendance of a witness may not be required outside of the State where he is found, resides, or transacts business, and the production of evidence may not be required outside the State where such evidence is kept.

(b) Any candidate who believes a violation of this Act has occurred may file a complaint with the Commission. If the Commission determines there is substantial reason to believe such a violation has occurred, it shall expeditiously make an investigation which shall include an investigation of reports and statements filed by the complainant, as well as of the matter complained of. If, on the basis of such investigation and after affording due notice and opportunity for a hearing on the record, it determines such a violation has occurred, the Commission shall issue an order directing the violator to take such action as the Commission determines may be necessary in the public interest to correct the injury occasioned by the violation. Such action may include requiring the violator to make public the fact that a violation has occurred, and the nature thereof, and may also include requiring the violator to make public complete statements, in corrected form, containing information required by this Act. The Commission may also take action to correct such an injury by making public the fact that a violation has occurred, and the nature thereof, and may also make public complete statements (prepared by the Commission itself and its officers and employees) containing the information required by this Act. Any party in interest who is aggrieved by a determination of the Commission under this subsection may, within sixty days after such order is issued, file with the United States court of appeals for the circuit in which he resides or in the United States Court of Appeals for the District of Columbia circuit a petition for review of the action of the Commission in issuing the order. A copy of the petition shall be forthwith transmitted by the clerk of the court to the Commission. The Commission thereupon shall file in the court the record of the proceedings on which it based its action, as provided in section 2112 of title 28, United States Code. The findings of fact by the Commission, if supported by substantial evidence, shall be conclusive; but the court, for good cause shown, may remand the case to the Commission to take further evidence, and the Commission may thereupon make new or modified findings of fact and may modify its previous action, and shall certify to the court the record of the further proceedings. Such new or modified findings of fact shall likewise be conclusive if supported by substantial evidence. The court shall have jurisdiction to affirm the action of the Commission or to set it aside, in whole or in part. The judgment of the court shall be subject to review by the Supreme Court of the United States upon certiorari or certification as provided in section 1254 of title 28, United States Code. Any action brought under this section shall be advanced on the docket of the court in which filed, and put ahead of all other actions (other than other actions brought under this section).

(c) Section 5 (1) of the Federal Trade Commission Act (15 U.S.C. 45 (1)) shall apply to violations of orders of the Commission in the same manner as it applies to violations of orders of the Federal Trade Commission.

Statements Filed with Clerk of United States Courts

SEC. 210. (a) Each person who is required by this title to file a report or statement with the Commission, shall file a copy of such report or statement with the clerk of the United States district court for the judicial district in which is located the principal office of the political committee or, in the case of a statement filed by a candidate or other person, in which is located such person's residence; except that this section shall apply to political committees supporting candidates in more than one State. The Commission may require the filing of copies of reports and statements required by this title with the clerks of United States district courts other than courts where copies are filed under the preceding sentence where it determines the public interest will be served thereby.

(b) It shall be the duty of the clerks under subsection (a)—

(1) to receive and maintain in an orderly manner all reports and statements required by this title to be filed with such clerks;

(2) to preserve such reports and statements for a period of at least ten years from date of receipt, except that reports and statements relating solely to candidates for the House of Representatives shall be preserved for at least five years from the date of receipt;

(3) to make the reports and statements filed with it available for public inspection and copying during regular office hours, commencing as soon as practicable after filing but not later than the end of the second day following the day during which it was received, and to permit copying of any such report or statement by hand or by duplicating machine, as requested by any person, at the expense of such person; and

(4) to compile and maintain a current list of all statements, or part of statements, pertaining to each candidate.

(c) Copies of all reports and statements required to be filed with clerks of court pursuant to subsection (a) by incumbent Members of Congress shall also be maintained in such Member's principal office in his state or Congressional district and shall be made reasonably available to the public for copying.

Prohibition on Contributions in Name of Another

SEC. 211. No person shall make a contribution in the name of another person, and no person shall knowingly accept a contribution made by one person in the name of another person.

Penalty for Violations

SEC. 212. Any person who violates any of the provisions of this title shall be fined not more than $1,000 or imprisoned not more than one year, or both.

Repealing Clause

SEC. 213. The Federal Corrupt Practices Act, 1925, and all other Acts or parts of Acts inconsistent herewith are repealed.

POWELL v. McCORMACK:
AN EXCERPT

395 U.S. 486, 89 S.Ct. 1944, 23 L. Ed. 2d 491
June 16, 1969

(Portions of the opinion of the Court delivered by Chief Justice Warren dealing with the constitutional power of the House of Representatives to judge the qualifications of a Member-elect)

* * *

In order to determine the scope of any "textual commitment" under Art. I, §5, we necessarily must determine the meaning of the phrase to "judge the qualifications of its members." Petitioners argue that the records of the debates during the Constitutional Convention, available commentary from the post-Convention, pre-ratification period, and early congressional applications of Art. I, §5, support their construction of the section. Respondents insist, however, that a careful examination of the pre-Convention practices of the English Parliament and American colonial assemblies demonstrates that by 1787, a legislature's power to judge the qualifications of its members was generally understood to encompass exclusion or expulsion on the ground that an individual's character or past conduct rendered him unfit to serve. When the Constitution and the debates over its adoption are thus viewed in historical perspective, argue respondents, it becomes clear that the "qualifications" expressly set forth in the Constitution were not meant to limit the long recognized legislative power to exclude or expel at will, but merely to establish "standing incapacities," which could be altered only by a constitutional amendment. Our examination of the relevant historical materials leads us to the conclusion that petitioners are correct and that the Constitution leaves the House[44] without authority to exclude any person, duly elected by his con-

[44] Since Art. I, §5, cl. 1, applies to both Houses of Congress, the scope of the Senate's power to judge the qualifications of its members necessarily is identical to the scope of the House's power, with the exception, of course, that Art. I, §3, cl. 3, establishes different age and citizenship requirements for membership in the Senate.

stituents, who meets all the requirements for membership expressly prescribed in the Constitution.

a. The Pre-Convention Precedents.

Since our rejection of respondents' interpretation of §5 results in significant measure from a disagreement with their historical analysis, we must consider the relevant historical antecedents in considerable detail. As do respondents, we begin with the English and colonial precedents.

The earliest English exclusion precedent appears to be a declaration by the House of Commons in 1553 " 'that Alex. Nowell, being Prebendary [*i.e.*, a clergyman] in Westminster, and thereby having voice in the Convocation House, cannot be a member of this House * * *.' " J. Tanner, Tudor Constitutional Documents: 1485–1603, at 596 (2d ed. 1930). This decision, however, was consistent with a long-established tradition that clergy who participated in their own representative assemblies or convocations were ineligible for membership in the House of Commons.[45] See 1 E. Porritt, The Unreformed House of Commons 125 (1963); Taswell-Langmead's English Constitutional History 142–143 (11th ed. T. Plucknett 1960). The traditional ineligibility of clergymen was recognized as a standing incapacity.[46] See 1 Blackstone's Commentaries *175. Nowell's exclusion, therefore, is irrelevant to the present case, for petitioners concede—and we agree—that if Powell had not met one of the standing qualifications set forth in the Constitution, he could have been excluded under Art. I, §5. The earliest colonial exclusions also fail to support respondents' theory.[47]

---

[45] Since the reign of Henry IV (1399–1413), no clergyman had sat in the House of Commons. 1 E. Porritt, the Unreformed House of Commons 125 (1903).

[46] Because the British do not have a written constitution, standing incapacities or disqualifications for membership in Parliament are derived from "the custom and law of parliament." 1 Blackstone's Commentaries *162; see *id.*, at *175. The groups thus disqualified as of 1770 included aliens; minors; judges who sat in the House of Lords; clergy who were represented in their own convocation; persons "attainted of treason or felony"; sheriffs, mayors, and bailiffs as representatives for their own jurisdictions; and certain taxing officials and officers of the Crown. *Id.*, at *175–176. Not until the exclusion of John Wilkes, discussed *infra*, did Blackstone subscribe to the theory that, in addition, the Commons could declare ineligible an individual "in particular [unspecified] circumstances * * * for that parliament" if it deemed him unfit to serve on grounds not encompassed by the recognized standing incapacities. As we explain, *infra*, this position was subsequently repudiated by the House in 1782. A Clerk of the House of Commons later referred to cases in which this theory was relied upon "as examples of an excess of * * * jurisdiction by the Commons: for one house of Parliament cannot create a disability unknown to the law." May's Parliamentary Practice 67 (13th ed. T. Webster 1924).

[47] In 1619, the Virginia House of Burgesses challenged the eligibility of certain delegates on the ground that they did not hold their plantations under proper patents from the Virginia Company in England. See generally, 7 The

Respondents' remaining 16th and 17th century English precedents all are cases of expulsion, although some were for misdeeds not encompassed within recognized standing incapacities existing either at the time of the expulsions or at the time the Constitution was drafted in 1787.[48] Although these early expulsion orders occasionally contained statements suggesting that the individual expelled was thereafter ineligible for re-election, at least for the duration of the Parliament from which he was expelled,[49] there is no indication that any were re-elected and thereafter excluded. Respondents' colonial precedents during this period follow a similar pattern.[50]

Apparently the re-election of an expelled member first occurred in 1712. The House of Commons had expelled Robert Walpole for receiving kickbacks for contracts relating to "foraging the Troops," 17 H.C. Jr. 28, and

---

Federal and State Constitutions, Colonial Charters, and Other Organic Laws 3783–3810 (F. Thorpe ed. 1909) (hereinafter cited as Thorpe). One of them, a Captain Warde, was admitted on condition that he obtain the necessary patent. The others, representatives from Martin's Brandon plantation, were excluded on the ground that the owner of the plantation had claimed that his patent exempted him from the colony's laws. See Journals of the House of Burgesses of Virginia: 1619–1658/59, at 4–5 (1915); M. Clarke, Parliamentary Privilege in the American Colonies 133–134 (1943). The questions presented by these two cases, therefore, seem to be jurisdictional in nature; that is, an attempt was made to gain representation for plantations over which the assembly may have had no power to act. Thus viewed these cases are analogous to the exclusions for failure to comply with standing qualifications. They certainly are not precedents which support the view that a legislative body could exclude members for mere character defects or prior misconduct disapproved by the assembly. See generally, M. Clarke, *supra*, at 132–204; J. Greene, The Quest for Power: The Lower Houses of Assembly in the Southern Royal Colonies: 1689–1776, at 171–204 (1963).

[48] For example, in 1585 the Commons expelled a Doctor Parry for unspecified misbehavior. A Compleat Journal of the Votes, Speeches and Debates of the House of Lords and House of Commons Throughout the Whole Reign of Queen Elizabeth, of Glorious Memory 352 (D'Ewes ed. 1708); and in 1628 Sir Edmund Sawyer was expelled because he had sought to induce a witness to suppress evidence against Sir Edmund in testimony before the House. 1 H.C. Jour. 917.

[49] In expelling Sir Edmund Sawyer in 1628, the Commons declared "him to be unworthy ever to serve as a Member of this House." *Ibid.* Almost identical language was used in the expulsion of H. Benson in 1641. 2 *Id.*, at 301. But by 1642, the formula had been changed to "disabled to sit any longer *in this Parliament as a Member of this House.* * * *" *Id.*, at 703. (Emphasis added.) By the 18th century it was apparently well established that an expulsion by the House of Commons could last no longer than the duration of the Parliament from which the member was expelled. See 1 Blackstone's Commentaries *176.

[50] For example, in 1652, the Virginia House of Burgesses expelled two members for prior conduct disapproved by the assembly, Journals of the House of Burgesses, *supra*, at 85; and in 1683, Rhode Island expelled a member "from acting in this present Assembly" for refusing to answer a court summons. 1 S. Arnold, History of the State of Rhode Island and Providence Plantations 289 (1859). See generally, M. Clarke, *supra*, at 173–204.

committed him to the Tower. Nevertheless, two months later he was re-elected. The House thereupon resolved "[t]hat Robert Walpole, Esquire, having been, this Session of Parliament, committed a Prisoner to the *Tower of London,* and expelled [from] this House, * * * is incapable of being elected a Member to serve *in this present Parliament* * *." *Id.,* at 128. (Emphasis added in part.) A new election was ordered, and Walpole was not re-elected. At least two similar exclusions after an initial expulsion were effected in the American colonies during the first half of the 18th century.[51]

Respondents urge that the Walpole case provides strong support for their conclusion that the pre-Convention English and colonial practice was that members-elect could be excluded for their prior misdeeds at the sole discretion of the legislative body to which they had been elected. However, this conclusion overlooks an important limiting characteristic of the Walpole case and of both the colonial exclusion cases on which respondents rely: the excluded members had been previously expelled. Moreover, Walpole was excluded only for the remainder of the Parliament from which he had been expelled. "The theory seems to have been that expulsion lasted as long as the parliament * * *." Taswell-Langmead's *supra,* at 584, n. 99. Accord, 1 Blackstone's Commentaries *170. Thus, Walpole's exclusion justifies only the proposition that an expulsion lasted for the remainder of the particular Parliament, and the expelled member was therefore subject to subsequent exclusion if re-elected prior to the next general election. The two colonial cases arguably support a some-what broader principle, i.e., that the assembly could permanently expel. Apparently the colonies did not consistently adhere to the theory that an expulsion lasted only until the election of a new assembly. M. Clarke, Parliamentary Privilege in the American Colonies 196–202 (1943).[52] Clearly, however, none of these cases supports respondents' contention that by the 18th century the English Parliament and colonial assemblies had assumed absolute discretion to exclude any member-elect they deemed unfit to serve. Rather, they seem to demonstrate that a member could be excluded only if he had first been expelled.

---

[51] In 1726, the Massachusetts House of Representatives excluded Gershom Woodle, who had been expelled on three previous occasions as "unworthy to be a Member." 7 Journals of the House of Representatives of Massachusetts 1726–1727, at 4–5, 15, 68–69 (1926). In 1758, North Carolina expelled Francis Brown for perjury. He was re-elected twice in 1760 and excluded on both occasions; however, when he was elected at the 1761 general elections, he was allowed to take his seat. 5 Colonial Records of North Carolina 1057–1058 (1887); 6 *Id.* at 375, 474, 662–663, 672–673 (1888). There may have been similar exclusions of two men elected in 1710 to the New Jersey Assembly. See M. Clarke, *supra,* at 197–198.

[52] Significantly, the occasional assumption of this broader expulsion power did not go unchallenged, M. Clarke, *supra,* at 196–202; and it was not supported by the only parliamentary precedent, the Walpole case.

Even if these cases could be construed to support respondents' contention, their precedential value was nullified prior to the Constitutional Convention. By 1782, after a long struggle, the arbitrary exercise of the power to exclude was unequivocally repudiated by a House of Commons resolution which ended the most notorious English election dispute of the 18th century—the John Wilkes case. While serving as a member of Parliament in 1763, Wilkes published an attack on a recent peace treaty with France, calling it a product of bribery and condemning the Crown's ministers as " 'the tools of despotism and corruption.' " R. Postgate, That Devil Wilkes 53 (1929). Wilkes and others who were involved with the publication in which the attack appeared were arrested.[53] Prior to Wilkes' trial, the House of Commons expelled him for publishing "a false, scandalous, and seditious libel." 15 Parl. Hist. Eng. 1393 (1764). Wilkes then fled to France and was subsequently sentenced to exile. 9 L. Gipson, the British Empire Before the American Revolution 37 (1956).

Wilkes returned to England in 1768, the same year in which the Parliament from which he had been expelled was dissolved. He was elected to the next Parliament, and he then surrendered himself to the Court of King's Bench. Wilkes was convicted of seditious libel and sentenced to 22 months' imprisonment. The new Parliament declared him ineligible for membership and ordered that he be "expelled this House." 16 Parl. Hist. Eng. 545 (1769). Although Wilkes was re-elected to fill the vacant seat three times, each time the same Parliament declared him ineligible and refused to seat him. See 11 L. Gipson, *supra*, at 207–215.[54]

Wilkes was released from prison in 1770 and was again elected to Parliament in 1774. For the next several years, he unsuccessfully campaigned to have the resolutions expelling him and declaring him incapable of re-election expunged from the record. Finally, in 1782, the House of Commons voted to expunge them, resolving that the prior House actions were "subversive of the Rights of the Whole Body of Electors of this Kingdom." 22 Parl. Hist. Eng. 1411 (1782).

With the successful resolution of Wilkes' long and bitter struggle for the right of the British electorate to be represented by men of their own choice, it is evident that, on the eve of the Constitutional Convention, English precedent stood for the proposition that "the law of the land had regulated the qualifications of members to serve in parliament" and those qualifications were "not occasional but fixed." 16 Parl. Hist. Eng. 589, 590

[53] Pursuant to a general warrant, Wilkes was arrested, his home ransacked, and his private papers seized. In his later election campaigns, Wilkes denounced the use of general warrants, asserting that he was fighting for liberty itself. See 11 L. Gipson, the British Empire Before the American Revolution 213–214 (1965).

[54] The issue before the Commons was clear: could the Commons "put in any disqualification, that is not put in by the law of the land." 1 Cavendish's Debates 384 (ed. J. Wright 1841). The affirmative answer was somewhat less than resounding. After Wilkes' third re-election, the motion to seat his opponent carried 197 to 143.

(1769). Certainly English practice did not support, nor had it ever supported, respondents' assertion that the power to judge qualifications was generally understood to encompass the right to exclude members-elect for general misconduct not within standing qualifications. With the repudiation in 1782 of the only two precedents for excluding a member-elect who had been previously expelled,[55] it appears that the House of Commons also repudiated any "control over the eligibility of candidates, except in the administration of the laws which define their [standing] qualifications." May's Parliamentary Practice 66 (13th ed. Webster 1924). See Taswell-Langmead's, *supra*, at 585.[56]

The resolution of the Wilkes case similarly undermined the precedential value of the earlier colonial exclusions, for the principles upon which they had been based were repudiated by the very body the colonial assemblies sought to imitate and whose precedents they generally followed. See M. Clarke, *supra*, at 54, 59–60, 196. Thus, in 1784 the Council of Censors of the Pennsylvania Assembly[57] denounced the prior expulsion of an unnamed assemblyman, ruling that his expulsion had not been effected in conformity with the recently enacted Pennsylvania Constitution.[58] In

---

[55] The validity of the House's action against Wilkes rested to a large extent on the validity of the Walpole precedent. Taswell-Langmead's, *supra*, at 585. Thus, the House of Commons resolution expunging, as subversive to the rights of the whole electorate, the action taken against Wilkes was also a tacit repudiation of the similar action taken against Walpole in 1712.

[56] English law is apparently the same today. See May's Parliamentary Practice 105–108 (17th ed. B. Cocks 1964).

[57] The Council of Censors was established by the 1776 Pennsylvania Constitution. It was an elected body that was specifically charged with the duty "to enquire whether the constitution has been preserved inviolate in every part; and whether the legislative and executive branches of government have performed their duty as guardians of the people, or assumed to themselves, or exercised other or greater powers than they are entitled to by the constitution." Pa. Const. of 1776, §47, 5 Thorpe 3091. See Introduction to Pennsylvania Convention Proceedings: 1776–1790 at iv (1825).

[58] In discussing the case, respondents characterize the earlier action as an *exclusion*. The Council of Censors, however, stated that the general assembly had resolved that the member "is expelled from his seat." Pennsylvania Convention Proceedings, *supra*, at 89. The account of the dissenting committee members suggests that the term expulsion was properly used. They note that in February 1783 the assembly received a letter from the Comptroller General charging the asemblyman with fraud. Not until September 9, 1783, did the assembly vote to expel him. Presumably, he held his seat until that time. But, even if he had been excluded, arguably he was excluded for not meeting a standing incapacity, since the Pennsylvania Constitution of 1776 required assemblymen to be "most noted for wisdom and *virtue*." Pa. Const. of 1776, §7, 5 Thorpe 3084. (Emphasis added.) In fact, the dissenting members of the Committee argued that the expelled member was ineligible under this very provision. Pennsylvania Convention Proceedings, *supra*, at 89.

Respondents cite one other exclusion during the period between the Declaration of Independence and the Constitutional Convention 11 years later. In 1780 the Virginia Assembly excluded John Breckenridge because he was a minor. Minority, of course, was a traditional standing incapacity, and Professor Warren

the course of its report, the Council denounced by name the Parliamentary exclusions of both Walpole and Wilkes, stating that they "reflected dishonor on none but the authors of these violences." Pennsylvania Convention Proceedings: 1776–1790, at 89 (1825).

Wilkes' struggle and his ultimate victory had a significant impact in the American colonies. His advocacy of libertarian causes[59] and his pursuit of the right to be seated in Parliament became a *cause célèbre* for the colonists. "[T]he cry of 'Wilkes and Liberty' echoed loudly across the Atlantic Ocean as wide publicity was given to every step of Wilkes's public career in the colonial press. * * *. They named towns, counties, and even children in his honour." 11 L. Gipson, *supra*, at 222.[60] It is within this historical context that we must examine the Convention debates in 1787, just five years after Wilkes' final victory.

b. Convention Debates.

Relying heavily on Professor Charles Warren's analysis[61] of the Convention debates, petitioners argue that the proceedings manifest the Framers' unequivocal intention to deny either branch of Congress the authority to add to or otherwise vary the membership qualifications ex-

---

therefore appears to have been correct in concluding that this exclusion was probably based upon an interpretation of the state constitutional requirement that members must be duly qualified according to law. Va. Const., 7 Thorpe 3816. See C. Warren, The Making of the Constitution 423, n. 1 (1928). Respondents, based upon their misinterpretation of the Pennsylvania case just discussed, criticize Professor Warren for concluding that there had been only one exclusion during this period. Our research, however, has disclosed no other cases.

[59] Wilkes had established a reputation both in England and the Colonies as a champion of free elections, freedom from arbitrary arrest and seizure, and freedom of the press. See 11 L. Gipson, *supra*, at 191–222.

[60] See R. Postgate, That Devil Wilkes 171–172, 173–174 (1929). During the House of Commons debates in 1781, a member remarked that expelling Wilkes had been "one of the great causes which had separated * * * [England] from America." 22 Parl. Hist. Eng. 100–101 (1781).

The writings of the pamphleteer "Junius" were widely reprinted in colonial newspapers and lent considerable support to the revolutionary cause. See 3 Dictionary of American History 190 (1940). Letter XVIII of the "Letters of Junius" bitterly attacked the exclusion of Wilkes. This letter, addressed to Blackstone, asserted: "You cannot but know, sir, that what was Mr. Wilkes's case yesterday may be yours or mine to-morrow, and that, consequently the common right of every subject of the realm is invaded by it * * *. If the expulsion of a member, not under any legal disability, of itself creates in him an incapacity to be elected, I see a ready way marked out, by which the majority may, at any time, remove the honestest and ablest men who happen to be in opposition to them. To say that they will not make extravagant use of their power would be language unfit for a man so learned in the laws as you are. By your doctrine, sir, they have the power: and laws, you know, are intended to guard against what men may do, not to trust what they will do." 2 Letters of Junius, Letter XVIII, at 118 (1821).

[61] See C. Warren, *supra*, at 399–426.

pressly set forth in the Constitution. We do not completely agree, for the debates viewed in the context of the bitter struggle for the right to freely choose representatives which had recently concluded in England and in light of the distinction the Framers made between the power to expel and the power to exclude, indicate that petitioners' ultimate conclusion is correct.

The Convention opened in late May 1787. By the end of July, the delegates adopted, with a minimum of debate, age requirements for membership in both the Senate and the House. The Convention then appointed a Committee of Detail to draft a constitution incorporating these and other resolutions adopted during the preceding months. Two days after the Committee was appointed, George Mason, of Virginia, moved that the Committee consider a clause " 'requiring certain qualifications of landed property & citizenship' " and disqualifying from membership in Congress persons who had unsettled accounts or who were indebted to the United States. 2 The Records of the Federal Convention of 1787, at 121 (M. Farrand rev. ed. 1966) (hereinafter cited as Farrand). A vigorous debate ensued. Charles Pinckney and General Charles C. Pinckney, both of South Carolina, moved to extend these incapacities to both the judicial and executive branches of the new government. But John Dickinson, of Delaware, opposed the inclusion of any statement of qualifications in the Constitution. He argued that it would be "impossible to make a compleat one, and a partial one would by implication tie up the hands of the Legislature from supplying the omissions." *Id.*, at 123.[62] Dickinson's argument was rejected; and, after eliminating the disqualification of debtors and the limitation to "landed" property, the Convention adopted Mason's proposal to instruct the Committee of Detail to draft a property qualification. *Id.*, at 116–117.

The Committee reported in early August, proposing no change in the age requirement; however, it did recommend adding citizenship and residency requirements for membership. After first debating what the precise requirements should be, on August 8, 1787, the delegates unanimously adopted the three qualifications embodied in Art. I, §2. *Id.*, at 213.[63]

On August 10, the Convention considered the Committee of Detail's proposal that the "Legislature of the United States shall have the authority to establish such uniform qualifications of the members of each House, with regard to property, as to the said Legislature shall seem expedient."

[62] Dickinson also said that a built-in veneration for wealth would be inconsistent with the republican ideal that merit alone should determine who holds the public trust. 2 The Records of the Federal Constitution of 1787, at 123 (M. Farrand rev. ed. 1966) (hereinafter cited as Farrand).

[63] On August 10, a delegate moved to reconsider the citizenship qualification. The delegate proposed to substitute a three-year requirement for the seven-year requirement already agreed upon. The motion passed. *Id.*, at 251. However, when this proposal was considered on August 13, it was rejected. *Id.*, at 265–266.

Id., at 179. The debate on this proposal discloses much about the views of the Framers on the issue of qualifications. For example, James Madison urged its rejection, stating that the proposal would vest

> "an improper & dangerous power in the Legislature. The qualifications of electors and elected were fundamental articles in a Republican Govt. and ought to be fixed by the Constitution. If the Legislature could regulate those of either, it can by degrees subvert the Constitution. A Republic may be converted into an aristocracy or oligarchy as well by limiting the number capable of being elected, as the number authorized to elect. * * * It was a power also, which might be made subservient to the views of one faction agst. another. Qualifications founded on artificial distinctions may be devised, by the stronger in order to keep out partisans of a [weaker] faction." *Id.*, at 249–250.[64]

Significantly, Madison's argument was not aimed at the imposition of a property qualification as such, but rather at the delegation to the Congress of the discretionary power to establish any qualifications. The parallel between Madison's arguments and those made in Wilkes' behalf is striking.[65]

In view of what followed Madison's speech, it appears that on this critical day the Framers were facing and then rejecting the possibility that the legislature would have power to usurp the "indisputable right of the people to return whom they thought proper" [66] to the legislature. Oliver Ellsworth, of Connecticut, noted that a legislative power to establish property qualifications was exceptional and "dangerous because it would be much more liable to abuse." *Id.*, at 250. Gouverneur Morris then moved to strike "with regard to property" from the Committee's proposal. His intention was "to leave the Legislature entirely at large." *Ibid.* Hugh Williamson, of North Carolina, expressed concern that if a majority of the legislature should happen to be "composed of any particu-

---

[64] Charles Pinckney proposed that the President, judges, and legislators of the United States be required to swear that they possessed a specified amount of unencumbered property. Benjamin Franklin expressed his strong opposition, observing that "[s]ome of the greatest rogues he was ever acquainted with, were the richest rogues." *Id.*, at 249. He voiced the fear that a property requirement would "discourage the common people from removing to this Country." *Ibid.* Thereafter, "the Motion of Mr. Pinkney [*sic*] was rejected by so general a *no*, that the States were not called." *Ibid.* (Emphasis in original.)

[65] "That the right of electors to be represented by men of their own choice, was so essential for the preservation of all of their other rights, that it ought to be considered as one of the most sacred parts of our constituion * * *. That the law of the land had regulated the qualification of members to serve in parliament and that the free holders * * * had an indisputable right to return whom they thought proper, provided he was not disqualified by any of those known laws * * *. They are not occasional but fixed: to rule and govern the question as it shall arise; not to start up on a sudden, and shift from side to side, as the caprice of the day or the fluctuation of party shall direct." 16 Parl. Hist. Eng. 589–590 (1769).

[66] *Id.*, at 589.

lar description of men, of lawyers for example, * * * the future elections might be secured to their own body." *Ibid.*[67] Mr. Madison then referred to the British Parliament's assumption of the power to regulate the qualifications of both electors and the elected and noted that "the abuse they had made of it was a lesson worthy of our attention. They had made the changes in both cases subservient to their own views, or to the views of political or Religious parties." *Ibid.*[68] Shortly thereafter, the Convention rejected both Gouverneur Morris' motion and the Committee's proposal. Later the same day, the Convention adopted without debate the provision authorizing each House "to be the judge of the * * * qualifications of its own members." *Id.*, at 254.

One other decision made the same day is very important to determining the meaning of Art. I, §5. When the delegates reached the committee of detail's proposal to empower each house to expel its members, Madison "observed that the right of expulsion . . . was too important to be exercised by a bare majority of a quorum: and in emergencies [one] faction might be dangerously abused." *Id.*, at 254. He therefore moved that "with the concurrence of two-thirds" be inserted. With the exception of one State, whose delegation was divided, the motion was unanimously approved without debate, although Gouverneur Morris noted his opposition. The importance of this decision cannot be over-emphasized. None of the parties to this suit disputes that prior to 1787 the legislative powers to judge qualifications and to expel were exercised by a majority vote. Indeed, without exception, the English and colonial antecedents to Art. I, §5, cl. 1 and 2, support this conclusion. Thus, the Convention's decision to increase the vote required to expel, because that power was "too important to be exercised by a bare majority," while at the same time not similarly restricting the power to judge qualifications, is compelling evidence that they considered the latter already limited by the standing qualifications previously adopted.[69]

[67] Wilkes had made essentially the same argument in one of his early attempts to have the resolutions denying him a seat expunged: "This usurpation, if acquiesced under, would be attended with the most alarming consequences. If you can reject those disagreeable to a majority, and expel whom you please, the House of Commons will be self-created and self-existing. You may expel til you approve, and thus in effect you nominate. The original idea of this House being the representative of the Commons of the realm will be lost." 18 Parl. Hist. Eng. 367 (1775).

[68] Professor Warren concluded that "Madison's reference was undoubtedly to the famous election case of John Wilkes * * *." C. Warren, *supra*, at 420, n. 1. It is also possible, however, that he was referring to the Parliamentary Test Act, 30 Car. II st. 2, c. 1 (1678), which had exluded Catholics as a group from serving in Parliament.

[69] Professor Charles Warren, upon whose interpretation of these events petitioners rely, concluded that the Convention's decision to reject Gouverneur Morris' proposal and the more limited proposal of the Committee of Detail was an implicit adoption of Madison's position that the qualifications of the elected "were fundamental articles in a Republican Govt. and ought to be fixed by the Constitution." 2 Farrand 249–250. See C. Warren, *supra*, at 420–421. Certainly,

Respondents urge, however, that these events must be considered in light of what they regard as a very significant change made in Art. I, §2, cl. 2, by the Committee of Style. When the Committee of Detail reported the provision to the Convention, it read:

"every member of the House of Representatives shall be of the age of twenty-five years; shall have been a citizen of [in] the United States for at least three years before his election; and shall be, at the time of his election, a resident of the State in which he shall be chosen." *Id.*, at 178.

However, as finally drafted by the Committee of Style, these qualifications were stated in their present negative form. Respondents note that there are no records of the "deliberations" of the Committee of Style. Nevertheless, they speculate that this particular change was designed to make the provision correspond to the form used by Blackstone in listing the "standing incapacities" for membership in the House of Commons. See 1 Blackstone's Commentaries *175–176. Blackstone, who was an apologist for the anti-Wilkes forces in Parliament,[70] had added to his Commentaries after Wilkes' exclusion the assertion that individuals who were not ineligible for the Commons under the standing incapacities could still be denied their seat if the Commons deemed them unfit for other reasons.[71] Since Blackstone's Commentaries were widely circulated in the Colonies, respondents further speculate that the Committee of Style rephrased the qualifications provision in the negative to clarify the delegates' intention "only to prescribe the standing incapacities without imposing any other limit on the historic power of each house to judge qualifications on a case by case basis." [72]

Respondents' argument is inherently weak, however, because it assumes

Warren argued, "[s]uch action would seem to make it clear that the Convention did not intend to grant to a single branch of Congress * * * the right to establish any qualifications for its members other than those qualifications established by the Constitution itself * * *. For certainly it did not intend that a single branch of Congress should possess a power which the Convention had expressly refused to vest in the whole Congress." *Id.* at 421. See 1 J. Story, Commentaries on the Constitution of the United States §625, at 445 (1873). Although Professor Chafee argued that congressional precedents do not support this construction, he nevertheless stated that forbidding any additions to the qualications expressed in the Constitution was "the soundest policy." Z. Chafee, Free Speech in the United States 256 (1941).

[70] See 10 W. Holdworth, A History of English Law 540–542 (1938).

[71] Holdworth notes that in the first edition of Blackstone's Commentaries Blackstone enumerated various incapacities and then concluded that "subject to these standing restrictions and disqualifications, every subject of the realm is eligible [for membership in the House of Commons] of common right." 1 Blackstone's Commentaries *176. Blackstone was called upon in Commons to defend Wilkes' exclusion and the passage was quoted against him. Blackstone retaliated by writing a pamphlet and making two additions to later editions of his *Commentaries* in an effort to justify the decision of Parliament. W. Holdworth, *supra*, at 540–541.

[72] Appendix D to Brief for Respondents, at 52.

that legislative bodies historically possessed the power to judge qualifications on a case-by-case basis. As noted above, the basis for that conclusion was the Walpole and Wilkes cases, which, by the time of the Convention, had been denounced by the House of Commons and repudiated by at least one State government. Moreover, respondents' argument misrepresents the function of the Committee of Style. It was appointed only "to revise the style of and arrange the articles which had been agreed to * * *." 2 Farrand 553. "The Committee * * * had no authority from the Convention to make alterations of substance in the Constitutions voted by the Convention, nor did it purport to do so; and certainly the Convention had no belief * * * that any important change was, in fact, made in the provisions as to qualifications adopted by it on August 10." [73]

Petitioners also argue that the post-Convention debates over the Constitution's ratification support their interpretation of §5. For example, they emphasize Hamilton's reply to the antifederalist charge that the new Constitution favored the wealthy and well-born:

"The truth is that there is no method of securing to the rich the preference apprehended but by prescribing qualifications of property either for those who may elect or be elected. But this forms no part of the power to be conferred upon the national government. Its authority would be expressly restricted to the regulation of the *times*, the *places*, the *manner* of elections. *The qualifications of the persons who may choose or be chosen, as has been remarked upon other occasions, are defined and fixed in the constitution, and are unalterable by the legislature.*"

The Federalist 371 (Mentor ed.). (Emphasis added in part.)

Madison had expressed similar views in an earlier essay,[74] and his arguments at the Convention leave no doubt about his agreement with Hamilton on this issue.

Respondents counter that Hamilton was actually addressing himself to

---

[73] C. Warren, *supra*, at 422, n. 1. Professor Warren buttressed his conclusion by noting that the Massachusetts Constitution of 1780 "contained affirmative qualifications for Representatives and exactly similar negative qualifications for Senators." *Ibid.* Apparently, these provisions were not considered substantively different, for each house was empowered in identical language to "judge of the elections, returns, and qualifications of their own members, as pointed out in the *constitution.*" Mass. Const. Ptc. 2, c. I, §2, Art. IV, 3 Thorpe 1897, and §3, Art. X, 3 Thorpe 1899. (Emphasis added.) See C. Warren, *supra*, at 422–423, n. 1.

[74] In No. 52 of The Federalist, Madison stated: "The qualifications of the elected, being less carefully and properly defined by the State constitutions, and being at the same time more susceptible of uniformity, have been very properly considered and regulated by the Convention. [He then enumerated the qualifications for both representatives and Senators.] * * * Under these reasonable limitations, the door of this part of the federal government is open to merit of every description, whether native or adoptive, whether young or old, and without regard to poverty or wealth, or to any particular profession or religious faith." The Federalist 326 (Mentor ed. 1961).

criticism of Art, I, §4, which authorizes Congress to regulate the times, places, and manner of electing members of Congress. They note that prominent anti-federalists had argued that this power could be used to "confer on the rich and *well-born* all honours," Brutus No. IV, N.Y. Journal, Nov. 29, 1787, p. 7. (Emphasis in original.) Respondents' contention, however, ignores Hamilton's express reliance on the immutability of the qualifications set forth in the Constitution.[75]

The debates at the state conventions also demonstrate the Framers' understanding that the qualifications for members of Congress had been fixed in the Constitution. Before the New York convention, for example, Hamilton emphasized: "[T]he true principle of a republic is, that the people should choose whom they please to govern them. Representation is imperfect in proportion as the current of popular favor is checked. This great source of free government, popular election, should be perfectly pure, and the most unbounded liberty allowed." 2 Debates on the Federal Constitution 257 (J. Elliot ed. 1876) (hereinafter cited as Elliot's Debates).[76] In Virginia, where the Federalists faced powerful opposition by advocates of popular democracy, Wilson Carey Nicholas, a future member of both the House and Senate and later Governor of the State, met the arguments that the new Constitution violated democratic principles with the following interpretation of Art. I, §2, cl. 2: "[A]s it respects the qualifications of the elected. It has ever been considered a great security to liberty, that very few should be excluded from the right of being chosen to the legislature. This Constitution has amply attended this idea. We find no qualifications required except those of age and residence which create a certainty of their judgment being matured, and of being attached to their state." 3 Elliot's Debates 8.

c.   Post-Ratification.

As clear as these statements appear, respondents dismiss them as "general statements * * * directed to other issues."[77] They suggest that far more relevant is Congress' own understanding of its power to judge qualifications as manifested in post-ratification exclusion cases. Unquestionably,

---

[75] Respondents dismiss Madison's assertion that the "qualifications of the elected, * * * being at the same time more susceptible of uniformity, have been very properly considered and regulated by the convention," as nothing more than a refutation of the charge that the new national legislature would be free to establish additional "standing incapacities." However, this conclusion cannot be reconciled with the pre-Convention history of this question, the Convention debates themselves, and, in particular, the delegates' decision to require a two-thirds vote for expulsion.

[76] At the same convention, Robert Livingston, one of the new Constitution's most ardent supporters and one of the State's most substantial landowners, endorsed this same fundamental principle: "The people are the best judges who ought to represent them. To dictate and control them, to tell them whom they shall not elect, is to abridge their natural rights." 2 Elliot's Debates 292–293.

[77] Appendix D to Brief for Respondents, at 62.

both the House and the Senate have excluded members-elect for reasons other than their failure to meet the Constitution's standing qualifications. For almost the first 100 years of its existence, however, Congress strictly limited its power to judge the qualifications of its members to those enumerated in the Constitution.

Congress was first confronted with the issue in 1807,[78] when the eligibility of William McCreery was challenged because he did not meet additional residency requirements imposed by the State of Maryland. In recommending that he be seated, the House Election Committee reasoned:

"The Committee proceeded to examine the Constitution with relation to the case submitted to them, and find that qualifications of members are therein determined, without reserving any authority to the State Legislatures to change, add to, or diminish those qualifications; and that, by that instrument, Congress is constituted the sole judge of the qualifications prescribed by it, and are obliged to decide agreeably to the Constitutional rules * * *." 17 Annals of Cong. 871 (1807).

Lest there be any misunderstanding of the basis for the committee's recommendation, during the ensuing debate the chairman explained the principles by which the committee was governed:

"The Committee of Elections considered the qualifications of members to have been unalterably determined by the Federal Convention, unless changed by an authority equal to that which framed the Constitution at first; that neither the State nor the Federal Legislatures are vested with authority to add to those qualifications, so as to change them * * *. Congress, by the Federal Constitution, are not authorized to prescribe the qualifications of their own members, but they are authorized to judge of their qualifications; in doing so, however, they must be governed by the rules prescribed by the Federal Constitution, and by them only. These are the principles on which the Election Committee have made up their report and upon which their resolution is founded." *Id.*, at 872.

The chairman emphasized that the committee's narrow construction of the power of the House to judge qualifications was compelled by the "fundamental principle in a free government," *Id.*, at 873, that restrictions upon the people to choose their own representatives must be limited to

[78] In 1799, during the 5th Congress, 1st Session, the House considered expelling Matthew Lyon, a Republican, for sedition. The vote to expel, however, was 49 to 45, and broke down largely along partisan lines. Although Lyon's opponents, the Federalists, retained a majority in the 6th Congress, to which Lyon was re-elected, and although there were political advantages to be gained from again trying to prevent him from taking his seat, there was no effort made to exclude him. See P. Dionisopoulos, A Commentary on the Constitutional Issue in the Powell and Related Cases, 17 J. Pub. L. 107, 123–127 (1968).

those "absolutely necessary for the safety of the society." *Id.*, at 874. At the conclusion of a lengthy debate, which tended to center on the more narrow issue of the power of the States to add to the standing qualifications set forth in the Constitution, the House agreed by a vote of 89 to 18 to seat Congressman McCreery. *Id.*, at 1237. See 1 A. Hinds, Precedents of the House of Representatives §414 (1907) (hereinafter cited as Hinds).

There was no significant challenge to these principles for the next several decades.[79] They came under heavy attack, however, "during the stress of civil war [but initially] the House of Representatives declined to exercise the power [to exclude], even under circumstances of great provocation." [80] Rules of the House of Representatives, H.R. Doc. No. 529, 89th Cong., 2d Sess. §12, at 7 (1967). The abandonment of such restraint, however, was among the casualties of the general upheaval produced in war's wake. In 1868, the House voted for the first time in its history to exclude a member-elect. It refused to seat two duly elected representatives for giving aid and comfort to the Confederacy. See 1 Hinds §§449–451.[81] "This change was produced by the North's bitter enmity toward those who failed to support the Union cause during the war, and was effected by the Radical Republican domination of Congress. It was a shift brought by the naked urgency of power and was given little doctrinal support." Comment, Legislative Exclusion: Julian Bond and Adam Clayton Powell, 35 U. Chi. L. Rev. 151, 157 (1967).[82] From that time until the present,

[79] Another Maryland representative was unsuccessfully challenged in 1808 on grounds almost identical to those asserted in the challenge of McCreery. See 18 Annals of Cong. 1848–1849 (1808). In 1844, the Senate declined to exclude John M. Niles, who was accused of being mentally incompetent, after a special committee reported him competent. Cong. Globe, 28th Cong., 1st Sess., 564–565, 602 (1844). In 1856, the House rejected an attempt to exclude Samuel Marshall for violating an Illinois law prohibiting state judges from running for other offices. 1 A. Hinds, Precedents of the House of Representatives §415 (1907) (hereinafter cited as Hinds). That same year, the Senate refused to exclude Lyman Trumball for violating the same Illinois law. *Ibid.*

[80] Between 1862 and 1867, both the House and Senate resisted several attempts to exclude members-elect who were accused of being disloyal to the Union during the Civil War. See, *Id.*, §§448, 455, 458; Senate Subcommittee on Privileges and Elections, Senate Committee on Rules and Administration, Senate Election, Expulsion and Censure Cases, S. Doc. No. 71, 87th Cong., 2d Sess., 21 (1962) (hereinafter cited as Senate Cases).

[81] That same year the Senate also excluded a supporter of the Confederacy. Senate Cases 40. The House excluded two others shortly thereafter, one for the same offense, and another for selling appointments to the Military and Naval Academies. See 1 Hinds §§459, 464; 2 Hinds §1273.

[82] This departure from previous House construction of its power to exclude was emphasized by Congressman William P. Feddenden: "[T]he power which we have under the Constitution to judge the qualifications of members of the body is not a mere arbitrary power, to be exerted according to the will of the individuals who may vote upon the subject. It ought to be a power subject to certain rules and founded upon certain principles. So it was up to a very later period, until the rebellion. The rule simply was, if a man came here and pre-

congressional practice has been erratic;[83] and on the few occasions when a member-elect was excluded although he met all the qualifications set forth in the Constitution, there were frequently vigorous dissents.[84] Even the annotations to the official manual of procedure for the 90th Congress manifest doubt as to the House's power to exclude a member-elect who has met the constitutionally prescribed qualifications. See Rules of the

---

sented proper credentials from his State, to allow him to take the ordinary oath, which we all took, to support the Constitution, and be admitted, and if there was any objection to him to try that question afterward." Cong. Globe, 40th Cong., 2d Sess., 685 (1868).

[83] For example, in 1870, the House refused to exclude a Texas Congressman accused of a variety of criminal acts, 1 Hinds §465; but in 1882 and again in 1900 the House excluded a member-elect for practicing polygamy. 1 Hinds §§473, 477–480. Thereafter, it apparently did not consider excluding anyone until shortly after World War I, when it twice excluded Victor L. Berger, an avowed Socialist, for giving aid and comfort to the enemy. Significantly, the House committee investigating Berger concluded that he was ineligible under the express provision of §3 of the Fourteenth Amendment. 6 C. Cannon, Precedents of the House of Representatives §§56–59 (1935) (hereinafter cited as Cannon). Berger, the last person to be excluded from the House prior to Powell, was later re-elected and finally admitted after his criminal conviction was reversed. 65 Cong. Rec. 7 (1923).

The House next considered the problem in 1925 when it contemplated excluding John W. Langley for his alleged misconduct. Langley resigned after losing a criminal appeal, and the House therefore never voted upon the question. 6 Cannon §238. The most recent exclusion attempt prior to Powell's occurred in 1933, when the House refused to exclude a Representative from Minnesota who had been convicted of sending defamatory matter through the mail. See 77 Cong. Rec. 73–74, 131–139 (1933).

The Senate has not excluded anyone since 1929; in that year it refused to seat a member-elect because of improper campaign expenditures. 6 Cannon §180. In 1947, a concerted effort was made to exclude Senator Theodore C. Bilbo of Mississippi for allegedly accepting gifts from war contractors and illegally intimidating Negroes in Democratic primaries. See 93 Cong. Rec. 3–28 (1947). He died, however, before a decision was reached.

[84] During the debates over H.R. Res. No. 278, Congressman Celler, chairman of both the Select Committee and the Judiciary Committee, forcefully insisted that the Constitution "unalterably fixed and defined" the qualifications for membership in the House and that any other construction of Art. I, §5, would be "improper and dangerous." 113 Cong. Rec. 1920 (daily ed. March 1, 1967). See H.R. Rep. No. 484, 43d Cong., 1st Sess., 11–15 (1874) (views of minority); H.R. Rep. No. 85, 56th Cong., 1st Sess., 53–77 (1900) (views of minority). In the latter report, the dissenters argued: "A small partisan majority might render the desire to arbitrarily exclude, by a majority vote, in order to more securely intrench itself in power, irresistible. Hence its exercise is controlled by legal rules. In case of expulsion, when the requisite two-thirds can be had, the motive for the exercise of arbitrary power no longer exists, as a two-thirds partisan majority is sufficient for every purpose * * *. The power of exclusion is a matter of law, to be exercised by a majority vote, in accordance with legal principles, and exists only where a member-elect lacks some of the qualifications required by the Constitution." *Id.,* at 76–77.

302

House of Representatives, H.R. Doc. No. 529, 89th Cong., 2d Sess., §12, at 7–8 (1967).

Had these congressional exclusion precedents been more consistent, their precedential value still would be quite limited. See Note, the Power of a House of Congress to Judge the Qualifications of its Members, 81 Harv. L. Rev. 673, 679 (1968).[85] That an unconstitutional action has been taken before surely does not render that same action any less unconstitutional at a later date. Particularly in view of the Congress' own doubts in those few cases where it did exclude members-elect, we are not inclined to give its precedents controlling weight. The relevancy of prior exclusion cases is limited largely to the insight they afford in correctly ascertaining the draftsmen's intent. Obviously, therefore, the precedential value of these cases tends to increase in proportion to their proximity to the Convention in 1787. See Myers v. United States, 272 U.S. 52, 175, 47 S. Ct. 21, 45 71 L. Ed. 160 (1926). And, what evidence we have of Congress' early understanding confirms our conclusion that the House is without power to exclude any member-elect who meets the Constitution's requirements for membership.

d. Conclusion.

Had the intent of the Framers emerged from these materials with less clarity, we would nevertheless have been compelled to resolve any ambiguity in favor of a narrow construction of the scope of Congress' power to exclude members-elect. A fundamental principle of our representative democracy is, in Hamilton's words, "that the people should choose whom they please to govern them." 2 Elliot's Debates 257. As Madison pointed out at the Convention, this principle is undermined as much by limiting whom the people can select as by limiting the franchise itself. In apparent agreement with this basic philosophy, the Convention adopted his suggestion limiting the power to expel. To allow essentially that same power to be exercised under the guise of judging qualifications, would be to ignore Madison's warning, borne out in the Wilkes case and some of Congress' own post-Civil War exclusion cases, against "vesting an improper & dangerous power in the Legislature." 2 Farrand 249. Moreover, it would effectively nullify the Convention's decision to require a two-third vote for expulsion. Unquestionably, Congress has an interest in preserving its institutional integrity, but in most cases that interest can be sufficiently

[85] "Determining the basis for congressional action is itself difficult; since a congressional action, unlike a reported judicial decision, contains no statement of the reasons for the disposition, one must fall back on the debates and the committee reports. If more than one issue is raised in the debates, one can never be sure on what basis the action was predicated. Unlike a court, which is presumed to be disinterested, in an exclusion case the concerned house is in effect a party to the controversy that it must adjudicate. Consequently, some members may be inclined to vote for exclusion though they strongly doubt its constitutionality." 81 Harv. L. Rev., at 679.

safeguarded by the exercise of its power to punish its members for disorderly behavior and, in extreme cases, to expel a member with the concurrence of two-thirds. In short, both the intention of the Framers, to the extent it can be determined, and an examination of the basic principles of our democratic system persuade us that the Constitution does not vest in the Congress a discretionary power to deny membership by a majority vote.

For these reasons, we have concluded that Art. I, §5, is at most a "textually demonstrable commitment" to Congress to judge only the qualifications expressly set forth in the Constitution. Therefore, the "textual commitment" formulation of the political question doctrine does not bar federal courts from adjudicating petitioners' claims.

BIBLIOGRAPHY

Alexander, Herbert E. "Financing Presidential Elections," *Jahrbuch des Offentlichen Rechts der Gegenwart*, XVII (1968), 596–614.
———. *Regulation of Political Finance*. Princeton, N.J.: Citizens' Research Foundation, 1966.
Allen, George E. *Presidents Who Have Known Me*. New York: Simon & Schuster, 1950.
Alsop, Stewart. *The Center: People and Power in Political Washington*. New York: Harper & Row, 1968.
American Society of Corporate Secretaries, Inc. *Corporate Directorship Practices*. National Industrial Conference Board, Inc., Studies in Business Policy, No. 125, 1967.
The Association of the Bar of the City of New York. *Conflict of Interest and Federal Service*. Cambridge: Harvard University Press, 1960.
Bagdikian, Ben H., & Don Oberdorfer. "Conflict of Interest: Can Congress Crack Down on Its Own Members?," *The Saturday Evening Post*, CCXXXV (Nov. 17, 1962), 21–29.
Bailey, Stephen K., & Howard D. Samuel. *Congress at Work*. New York: Henry Holt & Co., 1952.
Baker, Leonard. *The Guaranteed Society*. New York: Macmillan Co., 1968.
Barrow, Roscoe L. "The Equal Opportunities and Fairness Doctrines in Broadcasting: Pillars in the Forum of Democracy," *University of Cincinnati Law Review*, XXXVII (1968), 447–557.
Bates, Ernest Sutherland. *The Story of Congress 1789 to 1935*. New York: Harper & Bros., 1936.
Berman, Daniel M. *In Congress Assembled*. New York: Macmillan Co., 1964.
Bibby, John, & Roger Davidson. *On Capitol Hill: Studies in the Legislative Process*. New York: Holt, Rinehart & Winston, 1967.
Blaustein, Albert P., & Charles O. Porter. *The American Lawyer*. Chicago: University of Chicago Press, 1954.
Borah, William E. "The Lawyer and the Public," *American Bar Association Journal*, II (1916), 776–88.
Boyd, James. *Above the Law*. New York: New American Library, 1968.
———. "Legislate? Who, Me? What Happens to a Senator's Day," *The Washington Monthly*, I (Feb. 1969), 44–53.

Bratter, Herbert (ed.). *A Bank Director's Job* (12th rev. ed.). New York: American Bankers Association, 1968.

Burke, Edmund. "Speech to the Electors of Bristol," *Legislative Politics U.S.A.*, ed. Theodore J. Lowi. Boston: Little, Brown & Co., 1962.

Burns, James MacGregor. *Congress on Trial*. New York: Harper, 1949.

Carlin, Jerome E. *Lawyers' Ethics: A Survey of the New York City Bar.* New York: Russell Sage Foundation, 1966.

Clapp, Charles L. *The Congressman: His Work as He Sees It*. Garden City, N.Y.: Doubleday & Co. (Anchor Edition), 1963.

Clark, Joseph S. *Congress: The Sapless Branch*. New York: Harper & Row (Colophon, rev. ed.), 1964.

Clarke, James P. "Waste of Time or Important Control?," *Public Management*, XLIX (Aug. 1967), 222–26.

Committee on House Administration. *Allowances and Emoluments Authorized for Members of the U.S. House of Representatives* (90th Cong., 2d Sess.). Washington, D.C.: Government Printing Office, 1968.

Committee on House Administration. *Detailed Statement of Disbursements, July 1 to December 31, 1968* (90th Cong., 2d Sess.). Washington, D.C.: Government Printing Office (Committee Print), 1969.

"Conflicts of Interest of State Legislators," *Harvard Law Review*, LXXVI (1963), 1209–32.

Congress and the Nation 1945–1964, ed. Thomas N. Schroth. Washington, D.C.: Congressional Quarterly Service, 1965.

Davidson, Roger H., David M. Kovenock, & Michael K. O'Leary. *Congress in Crisis: Politics and Congressional Reform*. Belmont, Calif.: Wadsworth Publishing Co., 1966.

Deakin, James. *The Lobbyists*. Washington, D.C.: Public Affairs Press, 1966.

Dexter, Lewis Anthony. "The Representative and His District," *New Perspectives on the House of Representatives* (2d ed.), eds. Robert L. Peabody & Nelson W. Polsby. Chicago: Rand McNally & Co., 1969.

Donham, Philip, & Robert J. Fahey. *Congress Needs Help*. With a Foreword by David Brinkley. New York: Random House, 1966.

Donner, Frank J. "Is There an Ethic in the House?," *The Nation*, CCVII (Sept. 23, 1968), 278–80, 282.

Drinker, Henry S. *Legal Ethics*. New York: Columbia University Press, 1953.

——. "Legal Ethics," *The Annals of the American Academy of Political and Social Science*, CCXCVII (Jan. 1955), 37–45.

Eisenhower, Dwight D. "The Ticklish Problem of Political Fund-Raising —and Spending," *Reader's Digest*, LXLII (Jan. 1968), 64–69.

Eulau, Heinz, & John D. Sprague. *Lawyers in Politics: A Study in Professional Convergence*. Indianapolis: Bobbs-Merrill Co., 1964.

Evans, Rowland, & Robert Novak. *Lyndon B. Johnson: The Exercise of Power*. New York: New American Library, 1966.

Evins, Joe Landon. *Understanding Congress.* New York: C. N. Potter, 1963.

Federal Communications Commission. *1968 Survey of Political Broadcasting.* Washington, D.C.: Government Printing Office, 1969.

"The Federal Conflicts of Interests Statutes and the Fiduciary Principle," *Vanderbilt Law Review,* XIV (1961), 1485–1509.

The Federalist. Edited, and with an Introduction and Notes, by Jacob E. Cooke. Middletown, Conn.: Wesleyan University Press, 1961.

Felknor, Bruce L. *Dirty Politics.* New York: W. W. Norton & Co., 1966.

Fenno, Richard F., Jr. "The Appropriations Committee as a Political System," *New Perspectives on the House of Representatives* (2d ed.), eds. Robert L. Peabody & Nelson W. Polsby. Chicago: Rand McNally & Co., 1969.

———. "The Internal Distribution of Influence: The House," *The Congress and America's Future,* ed. David B. Truman. Englewood Cliffs, N.J.: Prentice-Hall, 1965.

———. *The Power of the Purse.* Boston: Little, Brown & Co., 1966.

Ficklen, Mary. "The Day Congress Read the D–ty Words," *Washingtonian Magazine,* IV (Oct. 1968), 69, 91, 93–94.

Financing a Better Election System. New York: Committee for Economic Development, 1968.

Galloway, George B. *Congress at the Crossroads.* New York: Thomas Y. Crowell Co., 1946.

———. *History of the House of Representatives.* New York: Thomas Y. Crowell Co., 1961.

Gellhorn, Walter. *When Americans Complain.* Cambridge: Harvard University Press, 1966.

Getz, Robert S. *Congressional Ethics.* Princeton, N.J.: D. Van Nostrand Co., 1966.

Heard, Alexander. *The Costs of Democracy.* Chapel Hill: University of North Carolina Press, 1960.

Hearings Before a Subcommittee of the House Judiciary Committee on Conflict of Interest Legislation (86th Cong., 2d Sess.). Washington, D.C.: Government Printing Office, 1960.

Hearings Before a Subcommittee of the House Judiciary Committee on Conflict of Interest Legislation (87th Cong., 1st Sess.). Washington, D.C.: Government Printing Office, 1961.

Hearings Before a Subcommittee of the Senate Committee on the Judiciary on Possible Anti-Competitive Effects of Sale of Network TV Advertising (89th Cong., 2d Sess.). Washington, D.C.: Government Printing Office (Committee Print), 1966.

Hearings Before the Senate Select Committee on Standards and Conduct on the Order to Investigate Certain Charges Relating to Senator Thomas J. Dodd (90th Cong., 1st Sess.). Washington, D.C.: Government Printing Office (Committee Print), 1967.

Hearings on Proposals for Standards of Official Conduct Before the House

307

Committee on Standards of Official Conduct (90th Cong., 1st Sess.). Washington, D.C.: Government Printing Office, 1967.

Hearings on S. Con. Res. 21 Before a Subcommittee of the Senate Committee on Labor and Public Welfare (82d Cong., 1st Sess.), Washington, D.C.: Government Printing Office, 1951.

Hearings on Various Proposals for Financing Political Campaigns Before the Senate Committee on Finance (90th Cong., 1st Sess.). Washington, D.C.: Government Printing Office, 1967.

House Committee on Standards of Official Conduct. *Report Under the Authority of H. Res. 418, H.R. Rep. No. 1176* (90th Cong., 2d Sess.). Washington, D.C.: Government Printing Office, 1968.

House Select Committee Pursuant to H. Res. 1. *In Re Adam Clayton Powell, H.R. Rep. No. 27* (90th Cong., 1st Sess.). Washington, D.C.: Government Printing Office, 1967.

House Special Subcommittee on Investigations of the Committee on Interstate and Foreign Commerce. *The Fairness Doctrine and Related Issues, H.R. Rep. No. 257* (91st Cong., 1st Sess.). Washington, D.C.: Government Printing Office, 1969.

Huitt, Ralph K. "The Internal Distribution of Influence: The Senate," *The Congress and America's Future*, ed. David B. Truman. Englewood Cliffs, N.J.: Prentice-Hall, 1965.

Joint Committee on the Organization of the Congress. *Organization of Congress, H.R. Rep. No. 1781, S. Rep. No. 1414* (89th Cong., 2d Sess.). Washington, D.C.: Government Printing Office, 1966.

Jones, Charles O. *Every Second Year*. Washington, D.C.: The Brookings Institution, 1967.

———. "Inter-Party Competition for Congressional Seats," *Western Political Quarterly*, XVII (Sept. 1964), 471–76.

Josephson, Matthew. *The Politicos 1865–1896*. New York: Harcourt, Brace & Co., 1938.

Kaufman, Richard F. "As Eisenhower Was Saying . . . 'We Must Guard Against Unwarranted Influence by the Military-Industrial Complex,'" *The New York Times Magazine*, June 22, 1968, pp. 10–11, 68–72.

Kefauver, Estes, & Jack Levin. *A Twentieth-Century Congress*. New York: Duell, Sloan and Pearce, 1947.

Kelley, Stanley, Jr. *Political Campaigning*. Washington, D.C.: The Brookings Institution, 1960.

Kennedy, John F. *Profiles in Courage*. New York: Harper & Bros., 1955.

Kirwan, Michael J. *How to Succeed in Politics*. New York: Macfadden-Bartell Corp., 1964.

Knebel, Fletcher. "The Economics of Politics," *1968 World Book Year Book*. Chicago: Field Enterprises Educational Corp., 1968.

Krasnow, Erwin G., & Richard E. Lankford. "Congressional Conflicts of Interest: Who Watches the Watchers?," *The Federal Bar Journal*, XXIV (1964), 264–85.

Luce, Robert. *Legislative Assemblies.* Boston: Houghton Mifflin Co., 1924.

Maclay, William. *Journal of William Maclay, United States Senator from Pennsylvania* (1789 to 1791), ed. Edgar S. Maclay. New York: D. Appleton & Co., 1890.

MacNeil, Neil. *Forge of Democracy: The House of Representatives.* New York: David MacKay Co., 1963.

MacNeil, Robert. *The People Machine.* New York: Harper & Row, 1968.

Malone, Ross L. "The Lawyer and His Professional Responsibilities," *Washington and Lee Law Review,* XVII (1960), 191–212.

Manning, Bayless. *Federal Conflict of Interest Law.* Cambridge: Harvard University Press, 1964.

——. "The Purity Potlatch: An Essay on Conflicts of Interest, American Government, and Moral Escalation," *The Federal Bar Journal,* XXIV (1964), 239–56.

Masterson, Thomas, and Carlton Nunan (eds.). *Ethics in Business.* New York: Pitman, 1969.

Matthews, Donald R. *U.S. Senators and Their World,* New York: Vintage Books, 1960.

Mayer, Martin. *The Lawyers.* New York: Harper & Row, 1967.

McCrane, Reginald Charles (ed.). *The Correspondence of Nicholas Biddle.* Boston: Houghton Mifflin Co., 1919.

Miller, Warren E., & Donald E. Stokes. "Constituency Influence in Congress," *New Perspectives on the House of Representatives* (2d ed.), eds. Robert L. Peabody & Nelson W. Polsby. Chicago: Rand McNally & Co., 1969.

Monypenny, Phillip. "The Control of Ethical Standards in the Public Service," *The Annals of the American Academy of Political and Social Science,* CCXCVII (Jan. 1955), 98–104.

Munn, Glenn G. *Encyclopedia of Banking and Finance* (6th rev. ed.), ed. F. L. Garcia. Boston: The Bankers Publishing Co., 1962.

Olson, Kenneth G. "The Service Function of the United States Congress," *Congress: The First Branch of Government.* Washington, D.C.: American Enterprise Institute, 1966.

Osborne, John. "Why Not Ban Paid Political Broadcasting?," *The New Republic,* CLVIII (June 15, 1968), 13–15.

Paul, Randolph E. "The Responsibilities of the Tax Advisor," *Harvard Law Review,* LXIII (1950), 377–88.

Pearson, Drew, & Jack Anderson. *The Case Against Congress.* New York: Simon and Schuster, 1968.

Perkins, Roswell B. "The New Federal Conflict-of-Interest Law," *Harvard Law Review,* LXXVI (1963), 1113–69.

Phillips, A. Cabell. "The High Cost of Our Low-Paid Congress," *The New York Times Magazine,* Feb. 24, 1952, pp. 7, 41–42, 44.

Phillips, David Graham. *The Treason of the Senate.* Edited and with an

Introduction by George E. Mowry & Judson A. Grenier. Chicago: Quadrangle Books, 1964.

Political Broadcast Catechism and the Fairness Doctrine (6th ed.). New York: National Association of Broadcasters, 1968.

Polsby, Nelson W. *Congress and the Presidency.* Englewood Cliffs, N.J.: Prentice-Hall, 1964.

——. "Two Strategies of Influence: Choosing a Majority Leader, 1962," *New Perspectives on the House of Representatives* (2d ed.), eds. Robert L. Peabody & Nelson W. Polsby. Chicago: Rand McNally & Co., 1969.

President's Commission on Campaign Costs. *Financing Presidential Campaigns.* Washington, D.C.: Government Printing Office, 1962.

Price, H. Douglas. "The Electoral Arena," *The Congress and America's Future,* ed. David B. Truman. Englewood Cliffs, N.J.: Prentice-Hall, 1965.

Report of the Commission on Executive, Legislative and Judicial Salaries. Washington, D.C.: Government Printing Office, 1968.

Reuss, Henry S. "An 'Ombudsman' for America," *Congressional Reform: Problems and Prospects,* ed. Joseph S. Clark. New York: Thomas Y. Crowell Co., 1965.

Rienow, Robert, & Leona Rienow. *Of Snuff, Sin and the Senate.* Chicago: Follett Publishing Co., 1965.

Roche, John P., & Leonard W. Levy. *The Congress.* New York: Harcourt, Brace & World, 1964.

Rogow, Arnold A., & Harold D. Lasswell. *Power, Corruption and Rectitude.* Englewood Cliffs, N.J.: Prentice-Hall, 1963.

Secretary of the Senate. *Report from July 1, 1968 to December 31, 1968,* S. Doc. No. 91–6 (91st Cong., 1st Sess.). Washington, D.C.: Government Printing Office, 1969.

Senate Committee on the Judiciary. *Selected Report of the Administrative Conference of the United States,* S. Doc. No. 24 (88th Cong., 1st Sess.). Washington, D.C.: Government Printing Office, 1963.

Senate Committee on Rules and Administration. *Financial or Business Interests of Officers or Employees of the Senate,* S. Rep. No. 1175 (88th Cong., 2d Sess.). Washington, D.C.: Government Printing Office, 1964.

Senate Committee on Rules and Administration. *Financial, Business, or Other Interests or Activities of Present or Former Members, Officers, or Employees of the Senate, with Particular Emphasis on the Allegations Raised in Connection with the Construction of the District of Columbia Stadium, and Matters Related Thereto,* S. Rep. No. 388 (89th Cong., 1st Sess.). Washington, D.C.: Government Printing Office, 1965.

Senate Committee on Rules and Administration. *Senate Election, Expulsion and Censure Cases from 1789 to 1960,* S. Doc. No. 71 (87th Cong., 2d Sess.). Washington, D.C.: Government Printing Office, 1962.

Senate Select Committee on Standards and Conduct. *Report on the Investigation of Senator Thomas J. Dodd of Connecticut, S. Rep. No. 193* (90th Cong., 1st Sess.). Washington, D.C.: Government Printing Office, 1967).

Senate Select Committee on Standards and Conduct. *Standards of Conduct for Members of the Senate and Officers and Employees of the Senate, S. Rep. No. 1015* (90th Cong., 2d Sess.). Washington, D.C.: Government Printing Office, 1968.

Smith, Frank E. *Congressman from Mississippi.* New York: Pantheon Books, 1964.

Smith, William Henry. *Speakers of the House of Representatives of the United States.* Baltimore: S. J. Gaeng, 1928.

Sorauf, Frank J. "The Public Interest Reconsidered," *Introduction to Politics: Essays and Readings,* eds. Nelson P. Guild & Kenneth T. Palmer. New York: John Wiley & Sons, 1968.

Special Subcommittee on Contracts of the House Administration Committee. *Report of Special Investigation into Expenditures During the 89th Congress by the House Committee on Education and Labor and the Clerk-Hire Status of Y. Marjorie Flores (Mrs. Adam C. Powell), H.R. Rep. No. 2349* (89th Cong., 2d Sess.). Washington, D.C.: Government Printing Office, 1967.

Staff of Subcommittee No. 5, House Judiciary Committee. *Federal Conflict of Interest Legislation* (85th Cong., 2d Sess.). Washington, D.C.: Government Printing Office (Committee Print), 1958.

"Statutory Regulation of Political Campaign Funds," *Harvard Law Review,* LXVI (1953), 1259–73.

Subcommittee of the Senate Committee on Labor and Public Welfare. *Report on Ethical Standards in Government* (82d Cong., 1st Sess.). Washington, D.C.: Government Printing Office (Committee Print), 1951.

Suggested Code of Ethics for Municipal Officials and Employees. Chicago: The International City Managers' Association, 1962.

Tacheron, Donald G., & Morris K. Udall. *The Job of the Congressman.* Indianapolis: Bobbs-Merrill Co., 1966.

Udall, Morris K. "The High Cost of Being a Congressman," *Playboy,* Nov. 1967, 232.

Voorhis, Horace Jeremiah. *Confessions of a Congressman.* Garden City, N.Y.: Doubleday & Co., 1947.

Wahlke, John C., Heinz Eulau, William Buchanan, & Leroy C. Ferguson. *The Legislative System.* New York: John Wiley & Sons, 1962.

Weber, Max. "Politics as a Vocation," *From Max Weber: Essays in Sociology.* Translated, edited and with an Introduction by H. H. Gerth & C. Wright Mills. New York: Oxford University Press, 1946.

Wells, Henry, & Robert W. Anderson. *Government Financing of Political Parties in Puerto Rico: A Supplement to Study Number Four.* Princeton, N.J.: Citizens' Research Foundation, 1966.

White, William Allen. *Masks in a Pageant.* New York: Macmillan Co., 1928.

White, William S. *Citadel: The Story of the U.S. Senate.* New York: Harper & Bros., 1956.

Wilson, H. H. *Congress: Corruption and Compromise.* New York: Rinehart and Co., 1951.

Wilson, Woodrow. *Congressional Government.* Boston: Houghton, Mifflin & Co., 1885.

Witmer, Richard T. "The Aging of the House," *Political Science Quarterly*, LXXIX (Dec. 1964), 526–41.

Woodward, C. Vann. *Reunion and Reaction.* Boston: Little, Brown & Co., 1951.

Wright, Jim. "Clean Money for Congress," *Harper's Magazine*, CCXXXIV (April, 1967), 98–102, 105–06.

—— *You and Your Congressman.* New York: Coward-McCann, 1965.

1963 Annual Report of the Director of the Administrative Office of the United States Courts. Washington, D.C.: Government Printing Office, 1963.

NOTES

Notes to the Introduction

1. The Federalist No. 55, at 278 (Cooke ed. 1961).
2. A Subcomm. of the Senate Comm. on Labor and Public Welfare, 82d Cong., 1st Sess., Report on Ethical Standards in Government (Comm. Print 1951).
3. Staff of Subcomm. No. 5, House Judiciary Comm., 85th Cong., 2d Sess., Federal Conflict of Interest Legislation (Comm. Print 1958).
4. Hearings Before a Subcomm. of the House Judiciary Comm. on Conflict of Interest Legislation, 86th Cong., 2d Sess. (1960).
5. Hearings Before a Subcomm. of the House Judiciary Comm. on Conflict of Interest Legislation, 87th Cong., 1st Sess. (1961).
6. The Association of the Bar of the City of New York, Conflict of Interest and Federal Service 15–16 (1960).
7. 18 U.S.C. §§ 201–218 (1969).
8. The relevant order, which is still in effect, is Exec. Order No. 11,222, 3 C.F.R. at 591 (1968), which was issued May 8, 1965. It superseded and revoked several orders and White House memoranda issued between May 1961 and May 1964. President Kennedy's Exec. Order No. 10,939 of May 5, 1961, 3 C.F.R. 469 (1959–63 Comp.), entitled "To Provide a Guide on Ethical Standards to Government Officials," significantly regulated the conduct of Presidential appointees. On Feb. 9, 1962, prior to enactment of the new conflict-of-interest laws, the President sent to all heads of agencies a memorandum entitled "Preventing Conflicts of Interest on the Part of Advisers and Consultants to the Government," 3 C.F.R. 818 (1959–63 Comp.). Subsequent to the enactment of the new conflict-of-interest statutes, under date of Oct. 23, 1962, and effective Jan. 21, 1963, the Department of Justice, with the approval of the President, issued a memorandum on the new conflict-of-interest statutes as a whole, 28 Fed. Reg. 9851; see also Exec. Order No. 11,125 of Oct. 29, 1963, 3 C.F.R. 798 (1959–63 Comp.). On May 2, 1963, President Kennedy issued a memorandum entitled "Preventing Conflicts of Interests on the Part of Special Government Employees," 3 C.F.R. 834 (1959–63 Comp.).
9. Joint Comm. on the Organization of the Congress, Organization of Congress, H.R. Rep. No. 1781, S. Rep. No. 1414, 89th Cong., 2d Sess. 52–55 (1966).
10. Senate Comm. on the Judiciary, Selected Reports of the Administrative Conference of the United States, S. Doc. No. 24, 88th Cong., 1st Sess. 46–49, 165–205 (1963). For an analysis that such contacts create conflicts of interest for administrative officials, see Krasnow & Lankford, Congressional Conflicts of Interest: Who Watches the Watchers? 24 Fed. B.J. 264, 280 (1964).
11. G. Allen, Presidents Who Have Known Me 218 (1950).
12. H. Wilson, Congress: Corruption and Compromise 223–26 (1951).
13. Manning, The Purity Potlatch: An Essay on Conflicts of Interest, American Government, and Moral Escalation, 24 Fed. B.J. 239, 243 (1964).

NOTES TO CHAPTER 1

1. Quoted in W. H. Smith, SPEAKERS OF THE HOUSE OF REPRESENTATIVES OF THE UNITED STATES 261 (1928).
2. G. Galloway, CONGRESS AT THE CROSSROADS 289 (1946).
3. See Weber, *Politics as a Vocation*, in FROM MAX WEBER 85 (H. Gerth & C. Mills eds. & transls. 1946).
4. Quoted in J. Wright, YOU AND YOUR CONGRESSMAN 164–65 (1965).
5. Quoted in D. Tacheron & M. Udall, THE JOB OF THE CONGRESSMAN 30–31 (1966).
6. G. Galloway, HISTORY OF THE HOUSE OF REPRESENTATIVES 125 (1961).
7. Witmer, *The Aging of the House*, 79 POLITICAL SCIENCE QUARTERLY 526, 538 (Dec. 1964).
8. Virtually every book dealing with Congress, and virtually every Congressman writing of his experiences, includes "a day in" his life. See, *e.g.*, S. Bailey & H. Samuel, CONGRESS AT WORK, ch. 4 (1952) (Senator H. Lehman, Rep. W. Ayres, Rep. F. Smith); J. Bibby & R. Davidson, ON CAPITOL HILL, ch. 3 (1967) (Rep. Albert Quie and Senator Mike Monroney); J. Clark, CONGRESS: THE SAPLESS BRANCH, ch. 4 (1964); J. Evins, UNDERSTANDING CONGRESS 24–32 (1963); Galloway, *supra* note 2 at 58–60; E. Kefauver & J. Levin, A TWENTIETH-CENTURY CONGRESS 189–94 (1947); D. Matthews, U.S. SENATORS AND THEIR WORLD 80–82 (1960) (Senator Neuberger); and J. Voorhis, CONFESSIONS OF A CONGRESSMAN 291–301 (1947).
9. J. Roche & L. Levy, THE CONGRESS 204–05 (1964).
10. See Boyd, *Legislate? Who, Me? What Happens to a Senator's Day*, THE WASHINGTON MONTHLY, Feb. 1969, at 44, for a not wholly sympathetic but fairly realistic analysis of a busy Senator's actual legislative time during a day.
11. Matthews reports that "[w]ithin the memory of senate old-timers, a typical Senator's office staff consisted of an executive secretary and a typist or two." Matthews, *supra* note 8 at 82.
12. A study by J. Saloma on the Congressional office work load in Tacheron & Udall, *supra* note 5 at 280, 281, found that during the 88th Congress, 89 Congressional offices received a total of 134,404 visitors, averaging 1,511 visitors per office.
13. D. Berman, IN CONGRESS ASSEMBLED 54 (1964). During 1968 the Senate received an estimated 9.5 million letters; mail to the House totaled 18.7 million. Congressional Quarterly, WEEKLY REPORT, Nov. 14, 1969, at 2282.
14. Clark, *supra* note 8 at 56.
15. W. Gellhorn, WHEN AMERICANS COMPLAIN 58 n. 4 (1966). Former Senator Paul H. Douglas had his staff keep tabs on incoming mail to that office in a typical week. He found that there were 2,953 pieces of legislative mail, 284 pieces of mail involving case work, 16 pieces of mail requiring Executive agency business with no action required, and 380 pieces of miscellaneous mail, for a grand total of 3,633 pieces. Olson, *The Service Function of the United States Congress*, in CONGRESS: THE FIRST BRANCH OF GOVERNMENT 350 (American Enterprise Institute 1966).
16. See Olson, *supra* note 15 at 345. A weekly average of 521 pieces of mail per office is reported by Saloma, *supra* note 12 at 282.
17. This is also true of some Senators, but it would be physically impossible for some to handle personally all the mail which goes out over their names.
18. Reuss, *An "Ombudsman" for America*, in CONGRESSIONAL REFORM: PROBLEMS AND PROSPECTS 295 (J. Clark ed. 1965).
19. Gellhorn, *supra* note 15 at 59–60. Gellhorn continues: "Health, Education

and Welfare received 2,000 calls monthly in its liaison office alone, and these were but a fraction of the congressional contacts with various of the Department's segments. A 1965 analysis of Navy Department operations showed that close to 60,000 letters had been written to congressmen in response to their 20,000 inquiries during 1964; the 'production cost' was three dollars per letter. The Post Office Department's widely dispersed units are said to receive 80,000 matters from congressmen in the course of a year; those that came to the Customers Relations Division in Washington during 1965 typically necessitated five letters in response. Every month the Veterans Administration's liaison office, located in one of the House office buildings, has more than 6,000 contacts—mail, telephone, personal interviews—with congressional staff members." *Id.* at 60 (footnotes omitted).

20. Olson, *supra* note 15 at 338.

21. *Id.* at 340–42. Olson includes in the service function not only requests for help in dealing with the Federal bureaucracy but also requests for information on legislation, for publications, for help in district projects, for assistance in scheduling visits to Washington, and for jobs within the Member's partonage. *Id.* at 347–49.

22. Quoted in C. Clapp, The Congressman: His Work as He Sees It 61 (1963).

23. *Id.* at 60. See generally 56–62.

24. Matthews, *supra* note 8 at 82.

25. P. Underdown, quoted in Galloway, *supra* note 6 at 209.

26. Burke, *Speech to the Electors of Bristol*, in Legislative Politics U.S.A. 151 (T. Lowi ed. 1962).

27. J. Wahlke, H. Eulau, W. Buchanan & L. Ferguson, The Legislative System 267–86 (1962).

28. Galloway, *supra* note 2 at 320–21.

29. N. MacNeil, as quoted in Price, *The Electoral Arena*, in The Congress and America's Future 33 (D. Truman ed. 1965).

30. Dexter, *The Representative and His District*, in New Perspectives on the House of Representatives 9 (2d ed. R. Peabody & N. Polsby eds. 1969).

31. Price, *supra* note 29 at 50.

32. J. M. Burns, Congress on Trial 10 (1949) observes "If [a Member's] position happens to coincide with that of the organized groups in his district, it is not simply because he is controlled by them. It is because he is one of them."

33. Miller & Stokes, *Constituency Influence in Congress*, in New Perspectives on the House of Representatives, *supra* note 30 at 48.

34. See R. Fenno, Jr., *The Appropriations Committee as a Political System*, in New Perspectives on the House of Representatives, *supra* note 30 at 125.

35. R. Davidson, D. Kovenock & M. O'Leary, Congress in Crisis: Politics and Congressional Reform 77 (1966).

36. Quoted in Matthews, *supra* note 8 at 82.

37. See the Report of the Joint Comm. on the Organization of Congress, H.R. Rep. No. 1781, S. Rep. No. 1414, 89th Cong., 2d Sess. (1966). The bill passed the Senate on March 7, 1967, but was bottlenecked in the House Rules Committee throughout the 90th Congress. A full discussion of the objections voiced in the House is found at 1969 CQ Almanac 515–18. Most blueprints for reform of Congress also mention the need for a year-round schedule. Some go so far as to suggest that Congress should provide for regular campaign and election recesses, periodic trips home, set vacations, scheduled trips abroad, and devote the remainder of time to Congressional work. See the conclusions of P. Donham & R. Fahey, Congress Needs Help 194–203 (1966). These authors

suggest that computer and linear programming techniques be used to lay out and adjust Congressional schedules to minimize time conflicts among Members.

38. This account of the entire sequence is in N.Y. TIMES, Feb. 6, 1968, at 25, col. 3.

39. See, *e.g.*, W. White, CITADEL, ch. 7 (1956); Clark, *supra* note 8, especially ch. 6.

40. Matthews, *supra* note 8 at 92–102.

41. The norm of courtesy, very strong in the Senate, probably explains Senator Stennis' unfailing courtesy to Senator Dodd during the Senate Ethics Committee's hearings on the Dodd case and in conveying to Dodd the committee's report prior to its publication. See J. Boyd, ABOVE THE LAW 237–38 (1968).

42. Roche & Levy, *supra* note 9 at 104.

43. R. Evans & R. Novak, LYNDON B. JOHNSON: THE EXERCISE OF POWER, ch. 6 (1966).

44. Fenno, *The Internal Distribution of Influence: The House*, in THE CONGRESS AND AMERICA'S FUTURE, *supra* note 29 at 70.

45. *Id.* at 71–73.

46. *Id.* at 73–76.

47. N.Y. TIMES, May 31, 1969, at 21, cols. 6, 8.

48. See, *e.g.*, Polsby, *Two Strategies of Influence: Choosing a Majority Leader, 1962*, in NEW PERSPECTIVES ON THE HOUSE OF REPRESENTATIVES, *supra* note 30 at 325, 355–58. Polsby contrasts the styles of Lyndon Johnson as Majority Leader and of his successor Mike Mansfield in N. Polsby, CONGRESS AND THE PRESIDENCY 39 (1964). Johnson believed in strong, centralized power, whereas Mansfield believes (as he said in a staff interview) that he is "one of 100 equals."

49. *Cf.* Huitt, *The Internal Distribution of Influence: The Senate*, in THE CONGRESS AND AMERICA'S FUTURE, *supra* note 29 at 89. Huitt talks of the "little governments of the standing committees." This seems to echo Woodrow Wilson's thesis that power in Congress is diffused among committee chairmen who are subject to no central party control. See W. Wilson, CONGRESSIONAL GOVERNMENT, ch. 2 (1885).

50. R. Fenno, Jr., THE POWER OF THE PURSE 692 (1966).

51. Examples of party discipline are set forth in Clark, *supra* note 8 at 147–70.

52. *Id.* at 168.

53. Rarick and Watson lost little seniority, but Williams would have succeeded to the chairmanship of the Interstate and Foreign Commerce Committee but for the caucus action.

54. White, *supra* note 39 at 122.

55. *Id.* at 133.

56. R. Getz, CONGRESSIONAL ETHICS 134–35 (1966).

57. H.R. REP. No. 1176, 90th Cong., 2d Sess. 37–41 (1968).

58. 18 U.S.C. §201(c) (1969).

59. 2 U.S.C. §39 (Supp. 1969).

60. *Cf.* Senator Robert Byrd's speech, "Lobbyist Activities by Bar Associations and by Individual Lawyers and Their Role in the Legislative Process," 113 CONG. REC. 5690 (1967).

61. E.g., The Public Utility Holding Company Act of 1935 requires the registration of anyone who would "present, advocate or oppose any matter affecting any registered holding company . . . before Congress . . . or before the Commission or Federal Power Commission. . . ." 15 U.S.C. §79l(i) (1963). A similar provision which requires filing of shipowners or builders who appear before the Federal Maritime Board, the Secretary of Commerce, or the Congress was included in the Merchant Marine Act of 1936. 46 U.S.C. §1225 (1958).

62. 2 U.S.C. §§261–70 (Supp. 1969). The Act requires that quarterly reports be filed with the Clerk of the House and Secretary of the Senate by any individual or organization soliciting or receiving money "to be used principally to

aid, or the principal purpose of which person is to aid" in influencing legislative action. 2 U.S.C. §266 (Supp. 1969). It should be noted that the Regulation of Lobbying Act does not cover lawyers who appear before Congressional committees. Neither does it empower any person or committee to investigate any reports to ascertain their truthfulness. The Justice Department has conducted only three prosecutions under this Act, and all of them were connected with the 1956 attempt to bribe Senator Francis Case. Light fines were imposed in each case.

63. 34 Stat. 864–65 (1907).

64. 43 Stat. 1070 (1925), as amended, 2 U.S.C. §§241–48 (Supp. 1969), 18 U.S.C. §§591, 597, 599, 602, 610 (1966).

65. Congressional Quarterly, CONGRESS AND THE NATION 1945–1964, at 1420.

66. U.S. CONST., art. I, §6.

67. *United States v. Johnson,* 383 U.S. 169 (1966).

68. Burns, *supra* note 32 at 8.

69. F. E. Smith, CONGRESSMAN FROM MISSISSIPPI 127 (1964) (emphasis added).

70. R. Neuberger, quoted in Matthews, *supra* note 8 at 72–73.

71. Matthews, *supra* note 8 at 68–69.

72. For an incisive discussion of the campaigns of Senator Abraham Ribicoff and Representative Clark MacGregor, see Bibby & Davidson, *supra* note 8, ch. 2.

73. For a discussion of incumbency advantage, see C. O. Jones, EVERY SECOND YEAR 62–71 (1967) and Clapp, *supra* note 22 at 374–76.

74. M. Kirwan, HOW TO SUCCEED IN POLITICS 20 (1964). A recent feature story reports the experience of a new Member who finds that his franking privilege gives him "an almost intimidating advantage" over prospective opponents. WALL STREET JOURNAL, Aug. 4, 1969, at 1, col. 1.

75. Clapp, *supra* note 22 at 375.

76. Quoted in Price, *supra* note 29 at 47.

77. *Id.* at 42.

78. *Id.* at 33. See also Jones, *Inter-party Competition for Congressional Seats,* WESTERN POLITICAL QUARTERLY 461–76 (Sept. 1964).

79. Jones, *supra* note 73 at 50–51.

80. Matthews, *supra* note 8 at 87–88.

81. In the Senate debate on the 1969 Congressional pay increase, Senator Dirksen (R-Ill.) remarked that he did not know "how many lunches I have bought for the Illinois delegation, because nobody ever broke his arm reaching for a check." 115 CONG. REC. S1343 (daily ed. Feb. 4, 1969).

82. One of the Members we interviewed said that his constituents believe residence in Washington taints a person and that they need visible reassurance that their representative has not become "pink."

83. Galloway, *supra* note 2 at 288.

84. W. Maclay, JOURNAL OF WILLIAM MACLAY, UNITED STATES SENATOR FROM PENNSYLVANIA (1789 to 1791), at 175–78, 330–32 (E. Maclay ed. 1890).

85. R. Luce, LEGISLATIVE ASSEMBLIES 412 (1924). It was charged that the bank loaned $1,605,781 to Congressmen over a five-year period, more than the total of all their salaries for the period.

86. CONG. GLOBE, 32d Cong., 2d Sess. 289 (1853). The first conflict-of-interest statute, passed in 1853 (predecessor to present 18 U.S.C. §205), did not cover Congressmen, but it contained a separate section forbidding Members of Congress to prosecute claims against the government for a fee. B. Manning, FEDERAL CONFLICT OF INTEREST LAW 78 (1964).

87. This material is taken from The Association of the Bar of the City of New York, CONFLICT OF INTEREST AND FEDERAL SERVICE 29–44 (1960), discussing the origin of the first conflict-of-interest statute.

88. *Id.* at 32, citing CONG. GLOBE, 38th Cong., 1st Sess. 559 (1864).

89. J. Deakin, The Lobbyists 67 (1966), including quote by K. Crawford.

90. Quoted in Luce, *supra* note 85 at 413.

91. H.R. Exec. Doc. No. 151, 37th Cong., 2d Sess. 6 (1862). Later that year, in July 1862, a criminal act was passed entitled "An Act to Prevent Members of Congress and Officers of the Government of the United States from Taking Consideration for Procuring Contracts, Office or Place from the United States."

92. Senate Comm. on Rules and Administration, Senate Election, Expulsion and Censure Cases from 1789 to 1960, S. Doc. No. 71, 87th Cong., 2d Sess. 32 (1962).

93. Although the 1864 Act did not add much to an earlier (1853) conflict-of-interest statute, our predecessor committee speculated that since "abuses had continued and grown worse with the war, [and since] scandal was in the air, [and] public opinion was aroused, . . . action was the order of the day." The Association of the Bar of the City of New York, *supra* note 87 at 40.

94. C. Woodward, Reunion and Reaction 99–101 (1956); M. Josephson, The Politicos 1865–1896, at 103–08 (1938); W. White, Masks in a Pageant 79 (1928).

95. Deakin, *supra* note 89 at 68–69, including quote by D. Loth. See also E. Bates, The Story of Congress 1789 to 1935, at 262–64 (1936).

96. See also R. & L. Rienow, Of Snuff, Sin and the Senate (1965), which deals with the same period but is somewhat more temperate. The principal villains are Roscoe Conkling, Mark Hanna, Chauncey Depew, and Thomas C. Platt.

Notes to Chapter 2

1. 113 Cong. Rec. 2976 (1967).

2. Senate Comm. on Rules and Administration, Financial or Business Interests of Officers or Employees of the Senate, S. Rep. No. 1175, 88th Cong., 2d Sess. 57–58 (1964).

3. The Rules Committee summarized Baker's financial dealings:

"Robert G. Baker, while serving as secretary to the Senate majority between January 1, 1959, and November 1, 1963, borrowed money or received the benefits from borrowings from 18 banks located in 8 States and 14 cities, including the District of Columbia. The beginning date, January 1, 1959, was chosen because it is the earliest date for which many records were available. In the same period, he participated in borrowing additional money from five organizations or lending institutions in four cities, and, in addition, borrowed as much as $5,000 or more from each of five different individuals. He borrowed money jointly with 11 different individuals or organizations; he purchased stock which was registered in names, other than his own, with 9 individuals involving 8 transactions. In four instances, he bought stock registered in his own name in which five other persons had undisclosed interests.

"In the same period, Baker listed ownership of stock in 27 corporations, including 6 banks located in 6 States. He handled the purchase of stock of the Mortgage Guaranty Insurance Co. for eight separate individuals." *Id.* at 17–18.

4. The statutes cited are 18 U.S.C. §§201–218 (1969).

5. S. Res. 266, 90th Cong., 2d Sess., 114 Cong. Rec. S3245 (daily ed. Mar. 22, 1968).

6. *Steele v. Louisville & N. R.R.*, 323 U.S. 192, 202 (1944).

7. 5 A. Scott, Trusts §504 (3d ed. 1967).

8. 2 A. Scott, Trusts §170 (3d ed. 1967).

9. *Loft Inc. v. Guth*, 23 Del. Ch. 138, 169; 2 A.2d 225, 239 (1938).

10. *Reading v. King*, [1948] 2 K.B. 268, aff'd, [1949] 2 K.B. 232, 1951 A.C.

507. Senator Clifford Case (R-N.J.) cited this in a relevant speech, 114 Cong. Rec. S752–53 (daily ed. Feb. 1, 1968).

11. 217 U.S. 286 (1910).

12. These and other cases are discussed in *The Federal Conflicts of Interests Statutes and the Fiduciary Principle*, 14 Vand. L. Rev. 1485 (1961).

13. Congressional Quarterly, Weekly Report, July 18, 1969, at 1268–69.

14. The Association of the Bar of the City of New York, Conflict of Interest and Federal Service 198 (1960).

15. The statute involved was 18 U.S.C. §434, which has been superseded by 18 U.S.C. §208 (1969), the basic disqualification provision of present law.

16. *United States v. Mississippi Valley Generating Co.*, 364 U.S. 520, 549 (1961).

17. 18 U.S.C. §208 (1969).

18. 49 U.S.C. §11 (1959).

19. 1 Stat. 67 (1789), as amended, 5 U.S.C. §243 (1964).

20. 18 U.S.C. §207(a) (1969).

21. 18 U.S.C. §207(b) (1969).

22. U.S. Const., art. I, §6.

23. 113 Cong. Rec. 2976 (1967).

24. The Association of the Bar of the City of New York, *supra* note 14 at 17.

25. The various concepts and definitions of "the public interest" are discussed in Sorauf, *The Public Interest Reconsidered*, 19 The Journal of Politics 616 (1957), reprinted at Introduction to Politics: Essays and Readings 321 (N. Guild & K. Palmer eds., 1968).

26. Plato, The Republic 543 C.

27. R. Luce, Legislative Assemblies 228 (1924).

28. *Id.* at 232–35.

29. 18 U.S.C. §431 (1966). The corporate exception speaks of contracts "for the general benefit" of a corporation. This has been interpreted to permit a government contract with a corporation 30 percent of whose stock was owned by a Member. 39 Op. Att'y Gen. 165 (1938). We find little evidence of such contracts. One Representative withdrew from a laundry business after adverse publicity occasioned by contracts with a military base. A few may have benefited from leases of buildings to the government by family corporations.

30. 18 U.S.C. §433 (1966) specifically exempts from the provisions of 18 U.S.C. §431 (1966) contracts entered into under the Reconstruction Finance Corporation Act, the Agricultural Adjustment Act, the Federal Farm Loan Act, the Emergency Farm Mortgage Act of 1933, the Farm Credit Act of 1933, the Home Owners Loan Act of 1933, the Farmers' Home Administration Act of 1946, and the Bankhead-Jones Farm Tenant Act. Other laws individually exempt certain agreements from the requirement of 41 U.S.C. §22 (1965), which implements §431 by requiring a compliance provision in contracts. The Federal Crop Insurance Act, 7 U.S.C. §1514(f) (1964), exempts certain crop-insurance agreements made pursuant to chapter 36 of title 7. The Commodity Credit Corporation is exempted by 15 U.S.C. §714*l* (1963) as to certain contracts. Contracts of the United States Information and Educational Exchange Programs are exempted by 22 U.S.C. §1472(2) (1964).

31. 33 U.S.C. §702*m* (1957).

32. 46 U.S.C. §1223(e) (1958).

33. Data on the House disclosures are taken from Congressional Quarterly, Weekly Report, May 23, 1969, at 755–94, as supplemented by Weekly Report, July 4, 1969, at 1172.

34. Congressional Quarterly, Congress and the Nation 1945–1964, at 956–61 (1965).

35. *E.g.*, Kaufman, *As Eisenhower Was Saying . . . "We Must Guard Against*

Unwarranted Influence by the Military-Industrial Complex," N.Y. TIMES, June 22, 1969, §6 (Magazine) at 10.

36. For a brief period it appeared that the FCC favored Congressional applicants as automatically having demonstrated public-service capabilities. Senator William Proxmire introduced legislation in 1960 and 1963 to prevent the FCC from considering this factor. See 109 CONG. REC. 1870 (1963).

37. BROADCASTING, April 17, 1961, at 62; May 6, 1963, at 58; May 17, 1965, at 74.

38. BROADCASTING, Jan. 15, 1968, at 62–63.

39. R. MacNeil, THE PEOPLE MACHINE 243–58 (1968).

40. *Id.* at 246.

41. 114 CONG. REC. H2540 (daily ed. April 3, 1968), in an answer by Ethics Committee Chairman Price (D-Ill.).

42. Quoted in Luce, *supra* note 27 at 410.

43. Luce, *supra* note 27 at 412.

44. 110 CONG. REC. 17,842 (1964).

45. 110 CONG. REC. 17,844 (1964).

46. WALL STREET JOURNAL, July 29, 1969, at 1, col. 1.

47. *Supra* note 2 at 30.

48. Senate Comm. on Rules and Administration, FINANCIAL, BUSINESS, OR OTHER INTERESTS OR ACTIVITIES OF PRESENT OR FORMER MEMBERS, OFFICERS, OR EMPLOYEES OF THE SENATE, WITH PARTICULAR EMPHASIS ON THE ALLEGATIONS RAISED IN CONNECTION WITH THE CONSTRUCTION OF THE DISTRICT OF COLUMBIA STADIUM, AND MATTERS RELATED THERETO, S. REP. No. 388, 89th Cong., 1st Sess. 17 (1965).

49. 18 U.S.C. §201 (1969).

50. 202 U.S. 344 (1906).

51. *United States v. Johnson*, 383 U.S. 169 (1966).

52. 114 CONG. REC. H2540 (daily ed. April 3, 1968).

53. The discussion and the report of the Senate Select Committee on Standards and Conduct are found at 113 CONG. REC. 30,096–98 (1967). A summary appears at 1967 CQ ALMANAC 579–80. Shortly thereafter another investigation was begun. 1967 CQ ALMANAC 583–84.

54. DOD Standards of Conduct, 32 C.F.R. §40.735–15(a)(3) (1969).

55. The Association of the Bar of the City of New York, *supra* note 14 at 249–50.

56. Quoted in D. Phillips, THE TREASON OF THE SENATE 62 (G. Mowry & J. Grenier eds., 1964).

57. National Industrial Conference Board, Inc., American Society of Corporate Secretaries, Inc., CORPORATE DIRECTORSHIP PRACTICES 15, 22 (Studies in Business Policy, No. 125, 1967).

58. The American Bankers Association, A BANK DIRECTOR'S JOB 1 (12th ed. 1968).

59. *Supra* note 57 at 127.

60. *Supra* note 58 at 34–36.

61. 1963 ANNUAL REPORT OF THE DIRECTOR OF THE ADMINISTRATIVE OFFICE OF THE UNITED STATES COURTS 62.

62. See G. Munn, ENCYCLOPEDIA OF BANKING AND FINANCE 663–64 (6th ed. 1962).

63. Congressional Quarterly, WEEKLY REPORT, May 23, 1969, at 756.

64. Exec. Order No. 11,222, 3 C.F.R. at 591 (1968).

65. CIVIL SERVICE COMM. Employee Responsibilities and Conduct, 5 C.F.R. §735 (1968).

66. 47 U.S.C. §154(b) (1962).

67. H.R. Doc. No. 529, 89th Cong., 2d Sess. 171–72 (1967).

68. Bagdikian & Oberdorfer, *Conflict of Interest, Can Congress Crack Down on Its Own Members?*, THE SATURDAY EVENING POST, Nov. 17, 1962, at 26.

69. The Illinois code of legislative ethics contains a commendable effort to codify the factors to be weighed by a legislator considering self-disqualification for personal interest. They are

(a) whether a substantial threat to his independence of judgment has been created by the conflict situation;

(b) the effect of his participation on public confidence in the integrity of the legislature;

(c) whether his participation is likely to have any significant effect on the disposition of the matter;

(d) the need for his particular contribution, such as special knowledge of the subject matter, to the effective functioning of the legislature.

[Ill. S.H.A. ch. 127, §603–202 (1967)].

70. The old provision was ABA Canons of Professional Ethics No. 6. The new Code of Professional Responsibility carries forward the disclosure requirement and strengthens it by requiring that multiple clients be told "the possible effect of such representation on the exercise of his independent professional judgment on behalf of each." ABA Code of Professional Responsibility, DR 5–105(C).

71. In *Commonwealth Coatings Corp. v. Continental Cas. Co.*, 393 U.S. 145 (1968), an arbitration award was denied enforcement because the supposedly neutral member of a three-man arbitration panel had failed to disclose financial relations that had existed between him and one of the parties. The Court assumed that a judge would have had a duty of disclosure or disqualification under similar circumstances.

72. As reported in N.Y. TIMES, June 11, 1969, at 17, col. 1.

73. Congressional Quarterly, WEEKLY REPORT, May 23, 1969, at 755–56.

NOTES TO CHAPTER 3

1. See, *e.g.*, The Association of the Bar of the City of New York, CONFLICT OF INTEREST AND FEDERAL SERVICE 30 (1960).

2. Letters from Daniel Webster to Nicholas Biddle, Oct. 29, 1833, Dec. 21, 1833, in McGrane, THE CORRESPONDENCE OF NICHOLAS BIDDLE 216–17, 218 (1919).

3. M. Mayer, THE LAWYERS 12 (1966).

4. XII Memoirs of J. Q. Adams 225, quoted in R. Luce, LEGISLATIVE ASSEMBLIES 455 (1924).

5. The present statute on uncompensated assistance to claimants, 18 U.S.C. §205 (1969), originated as 10 Stat. 170 (1853). See The Association of the Bar of the City of New York, *supra* note 1 at 32–39 for the history of this provision.

6. Quoted in The Association of the Bar of the City of New York, *supra* note 1 at 35–36.

7. 17 CONG. REC. 5999 (1886).

8. D. Phillips, THE TREASON OF THE SENATE 120 (G. Mowry & J. Grenier eds. 1964).

9. 40 CONG. REC. 9375–76 (1906).

10. In their introduction the editors of the 1964 edition give Phillips such credit, although noting that the work was a failure in several respects. *Supra* note 8 at 41–44.

11. Borah, *The Lawyer and the Public*, 2 A.B.A.J. 776, 780 (1916).

12. D. Pearson & J. Anderson, THE CASE AGAINST CONGRESS 101–27 (1968).

13. *United States v. Johnson*, 215 F. Supp. 300 (D. Md. 1963), *partially rev'd and new trial ordered*, 337 F.2d 180 (4th Cir. 1965), *aff'd*, 383 U.S. 169

321

(1966). Johnson was again convicted, and appellate proceedings are incomplete at this writing.

14. *United States v. Johnson,* 337 F.2d 180, 200. The Court discusses evidence establishing that penciled notations allegedly made by Johnson on legal documents were made after the FBI began investigating the case.

15. 1965 CQ ALMANAC 1513.

16. Senate Comm. on Rules and Administration, FINANCIAL OR BUSINESS INTERESTS OF OFFICERS OR EMPLOYEES OF THE SENATE, S. REP. No. 1175, 88th Cong., 2d Sess. 15 (1964).

17. 1965 CQ ALMANAC 1513. Also Congressional Quarterly, CONGRESS AND THE NATION 1945–1964, at 1777–78 (1965).

18. Quoted in Bonafede, *Ethics: Legislator-Lawyer "Back-Scratching" Pact,* N.Y. HERALD TRIBUNE, June 13, 1965, at 14, col. 1. Also Pearson & Anderson, *supra* note 12 at 119.

19. The events involving Senator Long are summarized at 1967 CQ ALMANAC 583–84.

20. These were among the items listed by four former members of Dodd's staff in a public letter to the Senate Ethics Committee. J. Boyd, ABOVE THE LAW 271–74 (1968).

21. Three issues of LIFE, Aug. 9, 1968, at 20; Aug. 30, 1968, at 13; and Oct. 20, 1968, at 70, contained the derogatory material. The incident is briefly summarized at 1968 CQ ALMANAC 815–16.

22. Knebel, *The Economics of Politics,* 1968 WORLD BOOK YEARBOOK 62, 68–69.

23. Ottenad, *Congressmen and Private Law Practice,* ST. LOUIS POST-DISPATCH, Nov. 12, 1967, at 3B.

24. Of the lawyer-Representatives whom we interviewed, 44 percent disclosed some law practice. The House disclosures, which should reveal all practice income above $1,000, indicate that approximately 80, or 33 percent, had such income in 1968 from unterminated practices. This discrepancy is due in part to the fact that our interviews included some who were not required to file by the House rule because they were not affiliated with a firm of lawyers. These received income as salaried corporate counsel or for independent "solo" services.

25. S. REP. No. 1414, 89th Cong., 2d Sess. 55 (1966).

26. Legislative Reorganization Act of 1946, 2 U.S.C. §198 (Supp. 1969).

27. Congressional Quarterly, WEEKLY REPORT, Dec. 29, 1967, at 2667.

28. The figures for these three delegations are based partly on our research and partly on the financial disclosures made by House Members in April 1969.

29. 18 U.S.C. §204 (1969), originally enacted as 12 Stat. 766 (1863).

30. 25 U.S.C. §700 (1963).

31. 46 U.S.C. §1223(e) (1958).

32. 40 OP. ATT'Y GEN. 289 (1943).

33. COLUMBUS CITIZEN, Sept. 28, 1952, at 1.

34. *Hearings Before the Senate Select Comm. on Standards and Conduct on the Order to Investigate Certain Charges Relating to Senator Thomas J. Dodd,* 90th Cong., 1st Sess. at 1046, 1055 (1967).

35. A. Blaustein & C. Porter, THE AMERICAN LAWYER 98 (1954).

36. Borah, *supra* note 11 at 782.

37. 114 CONG. REC. S8918 (daily ed. July 18, 1968).

38. A Subcomm. of the Senate Comm. on Labor and Public Welfare, 82d Cong., 1st Sess., REPORT ON ETHICAL STANDARDS IN GOVERNMENT 25 (Comm. Print 1951).

39. Ottenad, *Most Lawyers in Congress Receive Fixed Amounts a Year from Partnerships,* ST. LOUIS POST-DISPATCH, Nov. 19, 1967, at 3C.

40. Wendell Wyatt (R-Ore.). Congressional Quarterly, WEEKLY REPORT, May 23, 1969, at 787.

41. ABA Comm. on Professional Ethics, OPINIONS, No. 266 (1945), quoting The Association of the Bar of the City of New York, Comm. on Professional Ethics, OPINIONS, No. 633 (1943). The ABA Opinion incorrectly cites Opinion 109 of the N.Y. County Lawyers' Association.

42. ABA Code of Professional Responsibility DR 2–102(B).

43. Malone, *The Lawyer and His Professional Responsibilities*, 17 WASH. & LEE L. REV. 191, 206 (1960).

44. Borah, *supra* note 11 at 780–81.

45. Paul, *The Responsibilities of the Tax Advisor*, 63 HARV. L. REV. 377, 387 (1950).

46. J. Carlin, LAWYERS' ETHICS: A SURVEY OF THE NEW YORK CITY BAR 48, 50, 53, 144 (1966).

47. H. Drinker, LEGAL ETHICS 107 (1953) (footnotes omitted).

48. N.Y. County Lawyers' Assn., Comm. on Professional Ethics, OPINIONS, No. 350 (1939).

49. ABA Code of Professional Responsibility, *Definitions*.

50. *In Re Bond & Mortgage Guarantee Company*, 303 N.Y. 423, 431–32, 103 N.E.2d 721, 725–26 (1952).

51. ABA Code of Professional Responsibility, *Preliminary Statement*.

52. *Id.*

53. The language of this footnote to the Code is taken from an ABA ethics opinion which summarized a number of opinions issued under old Canon 6. ABA Comm. on Professional Ethics, OPINIONS, No. 192 (1939).

54. *E.g.*, Pearson & Anderson, *supra* note 12 at 119, Bonafede, *supra* note 18, Bagdikian & Oberdorfer, *Conflict of Interest, Can Congress Crack Down on its Own Members?*, THE SATURDAY EVENING POST, Nov. 17, 1962, at 26. The Bonafede article goes so far as to include pictures of the two firms' plaques at the entrances to the Celler law offices.

55. This is indicated by 40 OP. ATT'Y GEN. 289 (1943) and B. Manning, FEDERAL CONFLICT OF INTEREST LAW 37–38, 256–58 (1964). In the absence of such arrangements, a New York Representative and his partners were prosecuted, although unsuccessfully, on the basis of the partners' Federal tax practice. *United States v. Quinn*, 111 F. Supp. 870 (E.D.N.Y. 1953), *reargued*, 116 F. Supp. 802 (E.D.N.Y. 1953), 141 F. Supp. 622 (S.D.N.Y. 1956).

56. ABA Comm. on Professional Ethics, OPINIONS, No. 16 (1929).

57. *Id.*, OPINIONS, No. 72 (1932).

58. *Id.*, OPINIONS, No. 49 (1931).

59. *Id.*, OPINIONS, No. 33 (1931).

60. The Association of the Bar of the City of New York, Comm. on Professional Ethics, OPINIONS, No. 431 (1938).

61. *Id.*, OPINIONS, No. 863, in The Association of the Bar of the City of New York, 19 THE RECORD 424 (1964).

62. For the purpose and legislative history, see The Association of the Bar of the City of New York, *supra* note 1 at 30–38, and *United States v. Johnson*, 337 F.2d 180, 195–96 (4th Cir. 1964), and *Burton v. United States*, 202 U.S. 344, 365–68 (1906). In both 1863–64, when the Act was first debated, and in 1908 when amendments were made, Congress explicitly chose to exclude courts from its coverage. See Manning, *supra* note 55 at 56.

63. The present 18 U.S.C. §204 (1969), originally enacted as 12 Stat. 766 (1863).

64. *Chudoff v. McGranery*, 179 F.2d 869 (3d Cir. 1950).

65. Bonafede, *supra* note 18.

66. *Darlington Mfg. Co. v. NLRB*, 380 U.S. 263 (1965).

67. Ervin was sharply criticized for the sequence of the court appearance and the subcommittee hearings by Donner, Book Review, *Is There an Ethic in the House?*, THE NATION, Sept. 23, 1968, at 278.

68. This was considered in 1962 but prevented by Congressional reluctance to reconsider the right of its Members to handle court cases against the government. Perkins, *The New Federal Conflict-of-Interest Law,* 76 HARV. L. REV. 1113, 1143 (1963). Other inadequacies of the present statutory language are discussed by Manning, *supra* note 55 at 58–65. In *United States v. Johnson,* 383 U.S. 169 (1966), the Supreme Court clarified some of the questions raised by Manning.

NOTES TO CHAPTER 4

1. Letter from James C. Wright to Louis M. Loeb, Mar. 13, 1968.
2. C. O. Jones, EVERY SECOND YEAR 53 (1967).
3. See discussion *supra* pp. 23–27.
4. Senate Comm. on Rules and Administration, SENATE ELECTION, EXPULSION AND CENSURE CASES FROM 1789 TO 1960, S. DOC. No. 71, 87th Cong., 2d Sess. 57 (1962).
5. *Id.*
6. The Court held that Congress lacked jurisdiction over primaries. *Newberry v. United States,* 256 U.S. 232 (1921). Newberry has been effectively overruled by *United States v. Classic,* 313 U.S. 299 (1941).
7. Senate Comm. on Rules and Administration, *supra* note 4 at 119.
8. *Id.* at 123.
9. 2 U.S.C. §248(b)(2) (1927).
10. L. Johnson, Presidential Message, "The Political Process in America," May 25, 1967, quoted in *Hearings on Various Proposals for Financing Political Campaigns Before the Senate Comm. on Finance,* 90th Cong., 1st Sess. 3 (1967) [hereinafter cited as *1967 Hearings*].
11. See A. Heard, The Costs of Democracy 351–55 (1960). The President's Commission on Campaign Costs, chaired by Heard, believed that limits on contributions were also unenforceable. See President's Commission on Campaign Costs, FINANCING PRESIDENTIAL CAMPAIGNS 17 (1962).
12. Not all campaign techniques contribute to the cost spiral. The 1968 campaign of Senator Eugene McCarthy for President suggests that some new techniques are being invented which produce a high "yield" at very low cost. McCarthy showed through his army of canvassers that a vigorous political organization at the grass roots can be highly effective at minimum cost. Former President Eisenhower heartily endorsed this type of campaign. See Eisenhower, *The Ticklish Problem of Political Fund-Raising—and Spending,* READER'S DIGEST, Jan. 1968, at 64–69.
13. Quoted from THE REPORTER in R. MacNeil, THE PEOPLE MACHINE 229 (1968).
14. *Id.* at 232.
15. *Id.* at 327.
16. *Id.* at 228.
17. Wright, *Clean Money for Congress,* HARPER'S MAGAZINE, Apr. 1967, at 100.
18. WALL STREET JOURNAL, July 19, 1968, at 1.
19. See L. Baker, THE GUARANTEED SOCIETY 78–79 (1968).
20. According to a N.Y. TIMES editorial, Federal tax revenues are used to "underwrite inefficient American shipyards, whose average worker is about half as productive as his better foreign counterparts." N.Y. TIMES, July 24, 1969, at 36, col. 1.
21. See LIFE, July 26, 1968, at 42A.
22. WALL STREET JOURNAL, June 28, 1967, at 14, col. 5, where it is reported that executives of a tobacco company raised over $10,000 for Congressmen who had been helpful in passing a mild cigarette-labeling law.

23. Congressional Quarterly, CONGRESS AND THE NATION 1945–1964, at 1742–1743 (1965).
24. N.Y. TIMES, Nov. 3, 1968, at 62, col. 1.
25. Johnson, *1967 Hearings, supra* note 10 at 5.
26. It is assumed that Congress' powers to spend for the general welfare (U.S. CONST., art I, §8) and to regulate Congressional elections (art. I, §4) are sufficiently broad to encompass the election-finance proposals discussed herein.
27. This figure assumes that all qualified candidates would choose public financing. Under the bill, they are given the option of "going public" and foregoing private contributions for the 90 days during the election campaign when public funds would be available. If a candidate does not choose to accept public financing, he is, of course, under no such restrictions.
28. Senate Special Comm. to Investigate Campaign Expenditures in 1936, S. REP. No. 151, 75th Cong., 1st Sess. (1937).
29. Heard, *supra* note 11 at 431.
30. *Id.* at 431–32. See also Tanner, *In France, the Campaign Means Free Time on Air*, N.Y. TIMES, May 22, 1969, at 16, col. 1.
31. S. 3242, 84th Cong., 2d Sess. (1956). The bill was co-sponsored by Senators Wayne Morse, James Murray, Paul Douglas, John Sparkman, Mike Mansfield, William Langer, and Hubert Humphrey. See the discussion in S. Kelley, Jr., POLITICAL CAMPAIGNING 44–48 (1960). Major parties were defined as those which received 10 percent of the total popular vote for a Presidential candidate in the preceding election or which polled the same proportion of the total popular vote in the Senatorial and Congressional races. Individual contributions to candidates were also limited.
32. R. Neuberger, cited in Kelley, *supra* note 31 at 46. Kelley points out that transferring control of campaign funds from local party groups to national committees, the Neuberger proposal, "would have a powerful centralizing effect on the direction of all other party activities." *Id.* at 47. See also the Senate debate on adoption and suspension of the Presidential Election Campaign Fund Act beginning at 112 CONG. REC. 26,383 (1966) and 113 CONG. REC. 8051 (1967).
33. Wright, *supra* note 17 at 98.
34. Udall, *The High Cost of Being a Congressman*, PLAYBOY, Nov. 1967, at 232.
35. 1963 CQ ALMANAC 987.
36. See S. 734, 91st Cong., 1st Sess. (1969).
37. Interviews in Washington, D.C. with Stanley Surrey, Assistant Secretary of the Treasury, May 22, 1968; Stuart Siegal, Assistant Tax Legislative Counsel, Dep't of the Treasury, Mar. 4, 1968; and Lawrence Stone, former Tax Legislative Counsel, Dep't of the Treasury, Feb. 22, 1968.
38. 113 CONG. REC. 12,938–39 (1967). The government would foot approximately half of this bill through tax credits and deductions.
39. Statement of Carlos Moore, Legislative Director, International Brotherhood of Teamsters, Chauffeurs, Warehousemen & Helpers of America, *1967 Hearings, supra* note 10 at 474.
40. Statement of former Senator Paul Douglas, *1967 Hearings, supra* note 10 at 383.
41. H. Alexander, REGULATION OF POLITICAL FINANCE 24 (Citizens' Research Foundation & Institute of Governmental Studies 1966).
42. See S. 411, 91st Cong., 1st Sess. (1969).
43. The legislative history of this measure is discussed in Alexander, *Financing Presidential Elections*, JAHRBUCH DES OFFENTLICHEN RECHTS DER GEGENWART 596–614 (1968), a publication of a paper delivered by the author at the Political Finance Panel of the 7th World Congress of the International Political Science Association, held in Brussels, Belgium, on Sept. 23, 1967.

44. Quotations are taken from the Senate debate on repeal of the Act beginning at 113 CONG. REC. 8051 (1967).

45. Johnson, *supra* note 10. See earlier discussion at p. 122.

46. Although favorably reported by the Senate Finance Committee in September, 1967, the measure never came to the floor.

47. Senator Gore pointed out, "[I]t seems to me the most vulnerable of all [to improper influence] are candidates for the U.S. Senate." *1967 Hearings, supra* note 10 at 105.

48. *1967 Hearings, supra* note 10 at 55–58.

49. The subsidy formula would allow about $14 million for each of the major-party Presidential candidates and between $100,000 and $1.5 million for Senatorial candidates choosing to accept the subsidy.

50. An effort to eliminate all spending *on behalf of* a candidate might be unconstitutional as well as impractical.

51. The cost of the frank for Members "to keep their constituents informed" has been estimated at $9.5 million a year. Comm. for Economic Development, FINANCING A BETTER ELECTION SYSTEM 20 (1968).

52. 12 and 13 Geo. VI C. 68, §79.

53. To reduce the inequities of access to voters, certain states have sponsored and subsidized the publication of voters' pamphlets. In Oregon, for example, the Secretary of State prepares a pamphlet presenting arguments supporting and opposing candidacies and bills. Arguments are submitted by party committees, candidates, or any other persons or organizations opposing candidacies or ballot measures. At a specified time before each primary and general election, the pamphlet is mailed to all registered voters. The state of Washington now follows the Oregon example, and California distributes a pamphlet on ballot measures. See Alexander, *supra* note 41 at 21–22 and Kelley, *supra* note 31 at 37.

The Committee on Economic Development suggests that all election services be "Federalized," including publication and distribution of campaign literature, all registration activities for Federal elections, and payment of Election Day officials. See Comm. for Economic Development, *supra* note 51. TIME MAGAZINE recommended editorially that candidates for Federal office be given office space in Federal buildings during campaigns. TIME, Jan. 5, 1968, at 45.

54. Alexander Heard's observation is typical: "Federal regulation of the air waves provides a fortuitous and feasible way of guaranteeing a degree of equitable access to the electorate to candidates for important offices. The access, moreover, can be assured at no cost, or at reduced cost, to the political contestants. Such a step . . . would assure candidates an opportunity to reach a large segment of voters, and at the same time would reduce campaign costs." Heard, *supra* note 11 at 440.

55. Recent cases carry striking language concerning the public responsibilities of broadcasters and their duty to make air waves available for public dialogue on public issues in partial return for the substantial benefits of their license. See, *e.g., Red Lion Broadcasting Co. v. FCC*, 395 U.S. 367 (1969).

56. 47 U.S.C. §303 (1962).

57. 47 U.S.C. §315(a), (b) (1962).

58. 47 U.S.C. §315(b) (1962).

59. *Red Lion Broadcasting Co. v. FCC*, 395 U.S. 367, 377 (1969).

60. FCC, SURVEY OF POLITICAL BROADCASTING, Table XII (1967).

61. FCC, "Use of Broadcast Facilities by Candidates for Public Office," 31 FED. REG. 6660–74 (1966).

62. MacNeil, *supra* note 13 at 260.

63. National Association of Broadcasters, POLITICAL BROADCAST CATECHISM AND THE FAIRNESS DOCTRINE 12 (6th ed., Apr. 1968).

64. See remarks of Elizabeth Drew and Newton Minow in MacNeil, *supra* note 13 at 243.

65. MacNeil, *supra* note 13 at 245–46.

66. One Member was particularly incensed about "discriminatory" newspaper advertising rates. He has heard publishers justify their rates on the theory that politicians are bad credit risks. Be that as it may, this Member has never seen any politician avoid payment. "They keep your grandmother in the closet until you pay," he said. Our information indicates that newspapers and broadcasting stations normally demand cash payment in advance for any political advertising.

67. During hearings before the Senate Antitrust and Monopoly Subcommittee in 1966, one of the witnesses, Gerald T. Arthur, President of Mercury Media, explained that rate cards are simply a beginning point for bargaining. Sometimes with weaker bargaining factors, such as small, low-budget advertisers, they are adhered to, and at other times they are brushed aside. Occasionally, stations and networks deliberately inflate their rate cards. If they do, almost every sale is made only after prolonged negotiation. *Hearings Before a Subcomm. of the Senate Comm. on the Judiciary on Possible Anticompetitive Effects of Sale of Network TV Advertising,* 89th Cong., 2d Sess. 117 (1966). Further on, Mr. Arthur explains that the general unit of charge in the industry is based on "cost per thousand," which is not reflected on the face of the rate cards. *Id.* at 125.

68. This was done in the 1968 campaign by the CBS network. In our interviews one Senator complained that his spots were frequently pre-empted by his opponent, who could afford the non-preemptible rate.

69. The Commission's guidelines could be quite specific, and, for example, could require stations to assign a given number of minutes for daytime, fringe-time and prime-time spot announcements. Candidates who did not use the time made available in a given week would forfeit such time rather than concentrate it in the week or two before the election.

70. One professional time-buyer indicated that if a well-financed candidate spends only 50 percent more than his opponent, he may still get 75 percent or 100 percent more return because additional advertising below saturation levels has a cumulative effect.

71. See *Why Not Ban Paid Political Broadcasting?*, The New Republic, June 15, 1968, at 13–15.

72. In his meeting with our Committee, Feb. 14, 1968.

73. Eisenhower, *supra* note 12.

74. Time editors estimate that 60 percent of all political broadcasting is wasted in this way. Time, Jan. 5, 1968, at 44.

75. Although numerous Members of Congress claim to be in favor of free television time, it is not unlikely that when they came around to voting on it, many would ask themselves, as Senator Russell Long did, why they should give their opponents free exposure. *1967 Hearings, supra* note 10 at 481.

76. One optimistic observer envisions a possible solution to the problem of making free television time available in large metropolitan areas. He would have stations agree to televise free political programs simultaneously, with the region divided into as many parts as there are stations. In New York City, for example, Channel 2 would televise Brooklyn candidates; Channel 4, Manhattan; Channel 5, New Jersey; and so forth. See B. Felknor, Dirty Politics 246 (1966). This plan presumably would require a suspension or a very broad construction of the antitrust laws.

77. According to some of our consultants, many station owners interpret §315 very literally indeed; if Candidate A purchases one spot and Candidate B purchases 15 spots, these station owners interpret §315 as requiring them to charge Candidate B exactly 15 times what they charged Candidate A, thus depriving B of the advantage a commercial advertiser would get for a similar multiple order.

78. See, *e.g.*, the testimony of Vincent T. Wasilewski, President, National Association of Broadcasters, *1967 Hearings, supra* note 10 at 481.

79. Quoted in MacNeil, *supra* note 13 at 286.
80. FCC, SURVEY OF POLITICAL BROADCASTING (1969).
81. It should be noted that §315 does not prevent broadcasters from presenting campaign *issues* through debates or documentaries. Networks and stations seldom do this.
82. Comm. for Economic Development, *supra* note 51 at 23.
83. *Red Lion Broadcasting Co. v. FCC*, 395 U.S. 367, 385 (1969).
84. The *Red Lion* case, *id.*, leaves little doubt that Congress would not be acting unconstitutionally in establishing a structure of reduced political-broadcasting rates. Any lost revenue resulting from these plans would surely be too modest to be deemed confiscatory.
85. *Office of Communication of United Church of Christ v. FCC*, 38 U.S.L.W. 2002 (D.C. Cir., June 20, 1969).
86. Congress' Constitutional power to regulate Federal-campaign spending has not been seriously questioned since *Newberry v. United States*, 256 U.S. 232 (1921). *United States v. Classic*, 313 U.S. 299 (1941), affirms the broad power in Congress over Federal elections both in art. I, §4 and in art. I, §8, the necessary-and-proper clause. See also *United States v. CIO*, 77 F. Supp. 355 (D.D.C. 1948), affirming the prohibition of union and corporate political contributions in §304 of the Labor-Management Relations Act of 1948. The Supreme Court upheld the lower-court decision, 335 U.S. 106 (1948), but did not reach the Constitutional question.
87. 18 U.S.C. §608(a) (1966).
88. 18 U.S.C. §610 (1966).
89. The problem is compounded by the fact that few states have effective reporting and disclosure rules for campaign contributions and expenditures. See generally Alexander, *supra* note 41. A WALL STREET JOURNAL correspondent indicates that a group was organized in Texas for the support of a particular candidate. Contributions came from outside of Texas, but the committee was exempt from the Federal Corrupt Practices Act disclosure rule because it operated in only one state, and it was exempt from Texas law because it was seeking solely to influence a national (Vice-Presidential) election. WALL STREET JOURNAL, June 28, 1967, at 14, col. 6.
90. The registration and reporting requirements in the Senate version are somewhat stricter than those in the House. The House version exempts intrastate committees which primarily support candidates for non-Federal offices and do not substantially support Federal candidates.
91. In a variant version of S. 1880 proposed by Senator Clark (D-Pa.) and others, the Comptroller General was made responsible for receipt, analysis, and publication of campaign-spending reports. This feature was rejected by the Senate Rules Committee, and the Clerk/Secretary custodianship was retained. When the bill came to the Senate floor, Senator Clark tried unsuccessfully to substitute the Comptroller General for the two internal officers.
92. The present Clerk of the House, W. Pat Jennings, took unprecedented action in November 1968, when he referred to the Justice Department for possible prosecution late and incomplete reports of 21 Presidential campaign committees. Congressional Quarterly, WEEKLY REPORT, Nov. 22, 1968, at 3178. For a review of the enforcement record prior to 1953, see Note, *Statutory Regulation of Political Campaign Funds*, 66 HARV. L. REV. 1259, 1260 (1953).
93. No political committee may receive contributions or make expenditures of more than $3 million in any calendar year. Candidates for Senator are limited to expenditures of $25,000;; candidates for Representative, to $5,000.
94. See Note, *supra* note 92 at 1265, n. 56. Senator Gore believes that spending limitations are desirable and says that the law can hold a candidate accountable for what his committees spend. While this may be theoretically possible,

given a determination by the Justice Department and U.S. Attorneys to vigorously enforce the law, there would still be the difficulty of holding a candidate responsible for what is done gratuitously in his behalf. It seems likely that if the limitation were strictly enforced, it would be circumvented by claiming that moneys above the limit were spent without the candidate's authority and against his will.

95. President's Commission on Campaign Costs, *supra* note 11 at 17.

96. Eisenhower, *supra* note 12.

97. A predecessor version of the House bill removed ceilings on individual contributions as well as on total spending, in line with the recommendation of the Heard Commission. This was amended in committee, and the $5,000 limit on contributions was reinstated and tightened.

98. N.Y. TIMES, Oct. 25, 1968, at 29, col. 1.

99. This would eliminate the present procedure of going to the Clerk's office in the Capitol and painstakingly copying out the data in longhand.

100. Note, *supra* note 92 at 1262.

101. Quoted in Congressional Quarterly, WEEKLY REPORT, Sept. 15, 1967, at 1803.

102. N.Y. TIMES, Jan. 13, 1969, at 46, col. 1.

NOTES TO CHAPTER 5

1. This amount, of course, was based on part-time Congressional service when sessions lasted only several weeks a year. As shown in Chapter 1, the full-time Congress is generally regarded as a post-World War II phenomenon.

2. See R. Luce, LEGISLATIVE ASSEMBLIES 541 (1924).

3. *Id.*

4. *Id.* at 542.

5. N. MacNeil, FORGE OF DEMOCRACY: THE HOUSE OF REPRESENTATIVES 144–45 (1963).

6. Luce, *supra* note 2 at 543.

7. REPORT OF THE COMMISSION ON EXECUTIVE, LEGISLATIVE, AND JUDICIAL SALARIES 3 (December 1968), hereinafter referred to as the *Salaries Commission.*

8. Raises were subsequently provided for the Vice President and Speaker (from $43,000 to $62,500) and for the Majority and Minority Leaders of both the House and the Senate, and the President Pro Tempore of the Senate (from $42,500 to $49,500). H.R. 7206, 91st Cong., 1st Sess., 15 CONG. REC. S9376 (daily ed. Aug. 7, 1969), amending 2 U.S.C. §31 and 3 U.S.C. §104.

9. *Salaries Commission, supra* note 7 at 13.

10. *Id.* at 37.

11. 115 CONG. REC. S1312–51 (daily ed. Feb. 4, 1969).

12. Rep. William L. Hungate (D-Mo.). See 115 CONG. REC. E5040–41 (daily ed. June 18, 1969).

13. Latest figures of the Bureau of the Census, U.S. Commerce Department, Current Population Report on Consumer Income, Series P–60, No. 53, Table 18.

14. A check of available sources for Members' addresses indicates that about one third of the Members from districts or states within a 200-mile radius of the Capitol do not maintain a second residence in Washington. But any money thus saved is undoubtedly absorbed by these Members' increased travel home.

15. Other allowances and emoluments which have no ascertainable pecuniary benefit to the Member are discussed in the succeeding sections on Congressional allowances.

16. All Members' lives are insured for $20,000 upon payment of a monthly premium of $10.83. Health-insurance premiums vary according to coverage.

17. One Senator whom we interviewed commented ruefully that many people believe that Members of Congress get free hospital care. The rate may be reduced, he said, but it certainly is not free.

18. See 5 U.S.C. §§2251–68 (Supp. 1969).

19. There were no pensions for Congressmen until they were provided by the Legislative Reorganization Act of 1946.

20. S. Alsop, THE CENTER 289 (1968).

21. In the 90th Congress, Rep. Wayne Hays (D-Ohio) proposed a bill to require Members to pay into the Members' retirement fund 10 percent of their salaries in place of 7.5 percent at present required. They would receive 3.33 percent credit for each year of service, as opposed to 2.5 percent under the present system and would thereby be entitled to receive the maximum 80 percent of their final salary after 24, rather than 32, years of Congressional service. The surviving female spouse of a Member would receive survivor's benefits of 65 percent of the decedent's annuity, as opposed to 55 percent under present law. H.R. 77, 90th Cong., 1st Sess. (1967). Former Congresswoman Edna Kelly (D-N.Y.) pointed out that surviving *male* spouses get nothing under the present plan.

22. The information contained in this section was obtained from conversations with IRS officials.

23. Until 1953, fifteen agents were assigned from the national office of the IRS to help with Members' returns. In 1953 the function was transferred to the D.C. field office of the Baltimore District, and the staff was reduced to its present size.

24. 26 U.S.C. §162(a) (1967).

25. 115 CONG. REC. S1341 (daily ed. Feb. 4, 1969).

26. The original House bill [H.R. 7977, 90th Cong., 1st Sess. (1968)] creating the Federal Salaries Commission empowered it to inquire into amounts and kinds of expenses and allowances, as well as rates of pay. The Senate opposed the quadrennial Commission altogether. While Senate conferees agreed to the establishment of the Commission, they refused to permit the Commission to determine allowances and expenses. Accordingly, the Salaries Commission had no power to recommend increases in the cost-of-living deduction. See 1967 CQ ALMANAC 608–09.

27. See Comm. on House Administration, ALLOWANCES AND EMOLUMENTS AUTHORIZED FOR MEMBERS OF THE U.S. HOUSE OF REPRESENTATIVES, 90th Cong., 2d Sess. (1968).

28. The present Subcommittee on Legislative Appropriations is chaired by Senator Montoya (D-N.Mex.), and its members include Senators Proxmire (D-Wis.), Yarborough (D-Tex.), Pearson (R-Kans.), and Cotton (R-N.H.). Of these five, only Yarborough comes from a large state. Small-state Senators appear to be reluctant to give large-state Senators expanded staff and office space. It has been argued in their behalf that they do as much research on legislative issues as large-state Senators, and thus there is no reason for large-state Senators to get larger staffs except to handle their extra mail.

29. 2 U.S.C. §§60g-l, 92 as amended by H.R. Res. 357, 91st Cong., 1st Sess., 115 CONG. REC. H5208 (daily ed. June 25, 1969). $37,000 in "base" and 13 staff members are allowed if a Member's constituency exceeds 500,000. When Congressional districts are reapportioned following the 1970 census, the population discrepancies in sections 60g-l and 90 of Title 2 should be eliminated in accordance with recent Supreme Court decisions.

30. D. Tacheron & M. Udall, THE JOB OF THE CONGRESSMAN 45 (1966).

31. See 115 CONG. REC. S6572 (daily ed. June 17, 1969).

32. Baker's criminal conviction for tax evasion, fraud, and larceny was based in part on evidence that he received funds purportedly intended as campaign

contributions for named Senators but never passed them on to the intended recipients. 1967 CQ ALMANAC 1166.

33. 114 CONG. REC. S3179 (daily ed. Mar. 21, 1968).
34. 39 U.S.C. §4161 (1962).
35. Luce, *supra* note 2 at 574.
36. *Id.*
37. *Id.* at 575.
38. 2 U.S.C. §42a (Supp. 1969).
39. 2 U.S.C. §46a (Supp. 1969).
40. 2 U.S.C. §46b–1 (Supp. 1969). See discussion *supra* at pp. 162–63.
41. See 2 U.S.C. §§46d-4, f, g (Supp. 1969).
42. See *e.g.*, Secretary of the Senate, REPORT FROM JULY 1, 1968 TO DECEMBER 31, 1968, S. DOC. No. 91–6, 91st Cong., 1st Sess. 391–93 (1969).
43. See *id.* at 77–82.
44. 2 U.S.C. §§52, 122 (Supp. 1969).
45. 2 U.S.C. §53 (Supp. 1966). See also Secretary of the Senate, *supra* note 42 at 374–90; Comm. on House Administration, 90th Cong., 2nd Sess., DETAILED STATEMENT OF DISBURSEMENTS, JULY 1 TO DECEMBER 31, 1968, 13–37 (Comm. Print 1969).
46. Tacheron & Udall, *supra* note 30 at 51–52.
47. U.S.C. §§53, 122(a) (Supp. 1969).
48. See 2 U.S.C. §112a (Supp. 1969).
49. Luce, *supra* note 2 at 563.
50. *Id.* See also 2 U.S.C. §43 (1927).
51. 2 U.S.C. §43b (Supp. 1969).
52. One Congressman shuns air travel and always uses his car to go to his Massachusetts district; he claims that this way he is able to make money from his travel allowance.
53. 2 U.S.C. §§127, 127(a) (Supp. 1969).
54. The Joint Committee on the Organization of the Congress, reporting before the House voted itself one trip for every month Congress is in session, recommended that Senators' round trips to their home states be increased from six to seven and Representatives' round trips be increased from four to seven. Joint Comm. on the Organization of Congress, ORGANIZATION OF CONGRESS, H.R. REP. No. 1781, S. REP. No. 1414, 89th Cong., 2d Sess. 38 (1966).
55. Senate Select Comm. on Standards and Conduct, STANDARDS OF CONDUCT FOR MEMBERS OF THE SENATE AND OFFICERS AND EMPLOYEES OF THE SENATE, S. REP. No. 1015, 90th Cong., 2d Sess. 15–16 (1968).
56. C. Clapp, THE CONGRESSMAN: HIS WORK AS HE SEES IT 55 (1963).

NOTES TO CHAPTER 6

1. J. Deakin, THE LOBBYISTS 68 (1966).
2. B. Montesquieu, SPIRIT OF THE LAWS, bk. V, ch. XVII, at 79 (1748).
3. H. Wilson, CONGRESS: CORRUPTION AND COMPROMISE 146–54 (1951).
4. A Subcomm. of the Senate Comm. on Labor and Public Welfare, 82d Cong., 1st Sess., REPORT ON ETHICAL STANDARDS IN GOVERNMENT 23 (Comm. Print 1951).
5. 113 CONG. REC. 15,695 (1967).
6. As quoted by Senator Long at 113 CONG. REC. 16,029 (1967).
7. As quoted by Senator Stennis at 113 CONG. REC. 16,277 (1967).
8. 113 CONG. REC. 16,272 (1967).
9. S. Alsop, THE CENTER 283 (1968).
10. The House Rule accords with the IRS regulation which presumes, in the

absence of evidence to the contrary, that contributions to a political candidate are not intended for his unrestricted personal use. See Rev. Proc. 68–19, 1968–1 Cum. Bull. 810.

11. WALL STREET JOURNAL, Aug. 9, 1967, at 1.

12. U.S. CONST., art. I, §9.

13. Congressional Quarterly, CONGRESS AND THE NATION 1945–1964, at 1748.

14. See *Defense Firms Are Eager to Provide Courtesy Flights for U.S. Officials,* WASHINGTON POST, Mar. 5, 1966, at A16.

15. Senate Select Comm. on Standards and Conduct, STANDARDS OF CONDUCT FOR MEMBERS OF THE SENATE AND OFFICERS AND EMPLOYEES OF THE SENATE, S. REP. No. 1015, 90th Cong., 2d Sess. 16 (1968).

16. DoD Standards of Conduct, 32 C.F.R. §40.735–5(a) (1969).

17. Telephone conversation with a member of committee staff, June 25, 1969.

18. All three of the Senators and six of the nine Representatives were among those randomly selected, which may indicate that the practice is less rare among the entire membership than it is among the leadership or those "ethically conscious." Moreover, the leaders and committee chairmen have special or committee staffs and allowances at their disposal.

19. N.Y. TIMES, Sept. 19, 1952, at 1.

20. N.Y. TIMES, Oct. 13, 1968, at 78.

21. Congressional Quarterly, CONGRESS AND THE NATION 1945–1964, at 1761 reports that Billie Sol Estes, Texas financial manipulator, contributed $1,700 to Senator Yarborough's radio fund as part of more than $7,000 in campaign contributions to Senator Yarborough.

22. Senate Select Comm. on Standards and Conduct, *supra* note 15 at 15–16.

23. *Id.* at 14.

24. *Id.* at 16. The Ethics Committee's discussion skirts a dilemma. They justify office funds on the theory that office allowances are not adequate, but also indicate that most, if not all, of the expenses covered by such funds are *political* expenses which would not be appropriate for coverage by Senatorial allowances.

25. *Id.*

26. Because of 18 U.S.C. §209 (1969), one of the conflict-of-interest statutes.

27. 114 CONG. REC. S3159 (daily ed. Mar. 21, 1968).

28. *Id.* at S3163.

29. *Id.* at S3159.

30. 114 CONG. REC. S3240 (daily ed. Mar. 22, 1968). The Senate Ethics Committee construes this provision to include a Senator's travel within his state.

31. Id. at S3227–30.

32. N.Y. TIMES, May 16, 1969, at 22.

33. WASHINGTON POST, June 3, 1969, at A18.

34. Senate Select Comm. on Standards and Conduct, *supra* note 15 at 29.

35. Quoted in Phillips, *The High Cost of Our Low-Paid Congress,* N.Y. TIMES, Feb. 24, 1952, §6 (Magazine) at 7.

36. Congressional Quarterly, WEEKLY REPORT, May 23, 1969, at 748.

37. R. Getz, CONGRESSIONAL ETHICS 99 (1966).

38. *Id.* at 115 n.30.

39. WASHINGTON EVENING STAR, May 16, 1969, at A–3, col. 1.

40. Congressional Quarterly, *supra* note 36 at 748–49.

41. *Id.* at 749–54.

42. WALL STREET JOURNAL, July 11, 1969, at 1.

43. Three Senators reportedly apply all honoraria to charitable or educational uses. Congressional Quarterly, *supra* note 36 at 748.

44. House Comm. on Standards of Official Conduct, REPORT UNDER THE AUTHORITY OF H. RES. 418, H.R. REP. No. 1176, 90th Cong., 2d Sess. 19 (1968).

NOTES TO CHAPTER 7

1. U.S. CONST., art. I, §6. Members are also privileged from arrest while attending, going to, or returning from a session, except in cases of "Treason, Felony and Breach of the Peace."

2. *U.S. v. Johnson*, 383 U.S. 169 (1966), discussed in Chapter 3, *supra*.

3. Getz lists seven nineteeth-century cases of Congressional discipline for accepting bribes and three for sale of appointments to military academies. R. Getz., CONGRESSIONAL ETHICS 85–89 (1966).

4. *In Re Chapman*, 166 U.S. 661, 669–70 (1897).

5. 395 U.S. 486 (1969).

6. 109 CONG. REC. 1769–71 (1963).

7. N.Y. TIMES, Feb. 21, 1963, at 10, cols. 6–8.

8. 109 CONG. REC. 3525–31 (1963).

9. 1966 CQ ALMANAC 521–22.

10. N.Y. TIMES, Sept. 23, 1966, at 1, col. 4.

11. Special Subcomm. on Contracts of the House Administration Comm., REPORT OF SPECIAL INVESTIGATION INTO EXPENDITURES DURING THE 89TH CONGRESS BY THE HOUSE COMMITTEE ON EDUCATION AND LABOR AND THE CLERK-HIRE STATUS OF Y. MARJORIE FLORES (MRS. ADAM C. POWELL), H.R. REP. NO. 2349, 89th Cong., 2d Sess. 7 (1967).

12. *Id.* at 82–83.

13. 113 CONG. REC. 27 (1967).

14. N.Y. TIMES, Jan. 10, 1967, at 1, col. 8.

15. House Select Comm. Pursuant to H. Res. 1, IN RE ADAM CLAYTON POWELL, H.R. REP. NO. 27, 90th Cong., 1st Sess. 33 (1967).

16. 113 CONG. REC. 23 (1967).

17. *Id.* at 5037–38.

18. *Kilbourn v. Thompson*, 103 U.S. 168, 204–05 (1880).

19. H.R. RES. 2, 91st Cong., 1st Sess., 115 CONG. REC. H21–22 (daily ed. Jan. 3, 1969).

20. *Kilbourn v. Thompson*, 103 U.S. 168, 189–90 (1880).

21. Until recently few persons knew the exact nature of the obscene material because it was expunged from the Record. It is partially revealed in Ficklen, *The Day Congress Read the D--ty Words*, WASHINGTONIAN MAGAZINE, Oct. 1968, at 69, where it is noted that the 1921 Record's expunged portions are on file in the Library of Congress.

22. See Getz, *supra* note 3 at 85–98.

23. *Id.* at 86, 88.

24. A. Rogow & H. Lasswell, POWER, CORRUPTION AND RECTITUDE 60–62 (1963) (footnotes omitted).

25. H. Wilson, CONGRESS: CORRUPTION AND COMPROMISE 222 (1951).

26. Getz, *supra* note 3 at 84.

27. *Id.* at 100.

28. See *Id.* at 121, where Getz tabulates the partisan voting patterns.

29. Wilson, *supra* note 25 at 221.

30. *Id.* at 323.

31. *Hearings on S. Con. Res. 21 Before a Subcomm. of the Senate Comm. on Labor and Public Welfare*, 82d Cong., 1st Sess. 259 (1951).

32. 109 CONG. REC. 1929 (1963). Full discussion and text at 109 CONG. REC. 1927–33, 1934–37 (1963).

33. S. RES. 212, 88th Cong., 1st Sess., 109 CONG. REC. 19181–82 (1963).

34. Senate Comm. on Rules and Administration, FINANCIAL OR BUSINESS IN-

TERESTS OF OFFICERS OR EMPLOYEES OF THE SENATE, S. REP. No. 1175, 88th
Cong., 2d Sess. 107 (1964).
35. Getz, *supra* note 3 at 130–31 (footnotes omitted).
36. Senate Select Comm. on Standards and Conduct, STANDARDS OF CONDUCT
FOR MEMBERS OF THE SENATE AND OFFICERS AND EMPLOYEES OF THE SENATE,
S. REP. No. 1015, 90th Cong., 2d Sess. 2 (1968).
37. 114 CONG. REC. S3120 (daily ed. Mar. 20, 1968).
38. Joint Comm. on the Organization of the Congress, ORGANIZATION OF
CONGRESS, H.R. REP. No. 1781, S. REP. No. 1414, 89th Cong., 2d Sess. (1966).
39. 112 CONG. REC. 27,729 (1966). Complete debate at 27,713–30.
40. 113 CONG. REC. 9448 (1967).
41. *Id.* at 5032.
42. H.R. RES. 1099, 90th Cong., 2d Sess., 114 CONG. REC. H2544–45 (daily
ed. Apr. 3, 1968).
43. Address by former Chief Justice Earl Warren, Jewish Theological Semi-
nary's Louis Marshall Award Dinner, New York, New York, Nov. 11, 1962.
44. The so-called Pagan Oath of Hippocrates:
I swear by Apollo Physician, by Asclepius, by Health, by Heal-all, and by
all the gods and goddesses, making them witnesses, that I will carry out,
according to my ability and judgment, this oath and this indenture:
To regard my teacher in this art as equal to my parents; to make him
partner in my livelihood, and when he is in need of money to share mine with
him; to consider his offspring equal to my brothers; to teach them this art, if
they require to learn it, without fee or indenture; and to impart precept, oral
instructure, and all the other learning, to my sons, to the sons of my teacher,
and to pupils who have signed the indenture and sworn obedience to the
physicians' law, but to none other.
I will use treatment to help the sick according to my ability and judgment,
but I will never use it to injure or wrong them.
I will not give poison to anyone though asked to do so, nor will I suggest
such a plan. Similarly I will not give a pessary to a woman to cause abortion.
But in purity and holiness I will guard my life and my art.
I will not use the knife either on sufferers from stone, but I will give place
to such as are craftsmen therein.
Into whatsoever house I enter, I will do so to help the sick, keeping myself
free from all intentional wrongdoing and harm, especially from fornication
with woman or man, bond or free.
Whatsoever in the course of practice I see or hear (or even outside my
practice in social intercourse) that ought never to be published abroad, I will
not divulge, but consider such things to be holy secrets.
Now if I keep this oath and break it not, may I enjoy honor, in my life and
art, among all men for all time; but if I transgress and forswear myself, may
the opposite befall me.
Quoted in The American Academy of Political and Social Science, 297 THE
ANNALS 29 (1955).
45. Drinker, *Legal Ethics*, The American Academy of Political and Social Science, *supra* note 44 at 37, 38.
46. These groups are subjects of individual articles: The American Academy of
Political and Social Science, 297 THE ANNALS (1955). Recent developments in
the business field are the subject of ETHICS IN BUSINESS (T. Masterson & J. Nunen
eds. 1969).
47. CODE OF ETHICS FOR GOVERNMENT SERVICE:
Any person in Government service should:
1. Put loyalty to the highest moral principles and to country above loyalty
to persons, party, or Government department.

2. Uphold the Constitution, laws and legal regulations of the United States and of all governments therein, and never be a party to their evasion.

3. Give a full day's labor for a full day's pay; giving to the performance of his duties his earnest effort and best thought.

4. Seek to find and employ more efficient and economical ways of getting tasks accomplished.

5. Never discriminate unfairly by the dispensing of special favors or privileges to anyone, whether for remuneration or not; and never accept, for himself or his family, favors or benefits under circumstances which might be construed by reasonable persons as influencing the performance of his governmental duties.

6. Make no private promises of any kind binding upon the duties of office, since a Government employee has no private word which can be binding on public duty.

7. Engage in no business with the Government, either directly or indirectly, which is inconsistent with the conscientious performance of his governmental duties.

8. Never use any information coming to him confidentially in the performance of his governmental duties as a means for making private profit.

9. Expose corruption wherever discovered.

10. Uphold these principles, ever conscious that public office is a public trust.

H.R. Con. Res. 175, 85th Cong., 2d Sess., 72 Stat. 312 (1958).

48. The Canons of Judicial Ethics of the American Bar Association were adopted in 1924.

49. Exec. Order No. 11,222, 3 C.F.R. at 591 (1968).

50. Civil Service Comm., Employee Responsibilities and Conduct, 5 C.F.R. §735 (1968).

51. Each Executive department and independent administrative agency issues its code of conduct as a separate publication and will supply copies upon request. They are also published in the Code of Federal Regulations.

52. The International City Managers' Association, 1313 East 60th Street, Chicago, Illinois 60637, promulgated a model municipal code in a pamphlet entitled A Suggested Code of Ethics for Municipal Officials and Employees (1962). It was reported in 1967 that 60 cities and towns in 27 states and the District of Columbia have adopted codes since New York City adopted its code in 1959. See Clarke, *Waste of Time or Important Control,* reprinted from the August 1967 issue of Public Management in the *Hearings on Proposals for Standards of Official Conduct Before the House Comm. on Standards of Official Conduct,* 90th Cong., 1st Sess. 272 (1967).

53. See *Note, Conflicts of Interest of State Legislators,* 76 Harv. L. Rev. 1209, 1230 (1963). Comprehensive state legislative codes enacted through 1968 are: Ariz. Rev. Stat. §§41–1281–1297 (Supp. 1969); Cal. Gov't Code §§8920–55 (West Supp. 1969); Fla. Stat. Ann. §§112.311–319 (Supp. 1969); Haw. Rev. Stat. 84-1-3, 11–18, 21, 31–36 (1968); Ill. S.H.A. ch. 127, §§601-101–607-101 (1967); Ia. Code Ann. 68B:1–10 (Supp. 1969); Kan. Stat. Ann. §§75-4301–4307 (Supp. 1968); La. Rev. Stat. §§42:1141–48 (1965); Mass. Ann. Laws c. 268A, §§1–12, 23 (Supp. 1966); Mich. Stat. Ann. §§4.1700(1)–(12) (1969); Minn. Stat. Ann. §§3.87–92 (1967); N.Y. Pub. Officers Law, §§73–74 (McKinney Supp. 1969); 74 Okl. St. Ann. §§1401–14 (Supp. 1969); 46 Pa. Stat. §§143.1–143.8 (Supp. 1969); Tex. Civ. Stat. Ann., art 6252–9 (1962); Wash. Rev. Code Ann., §§42.21.010–08C (Supp. 1968). Statutes of the states of Kentucky, Michigan, Missouri, New Jersey, and West Virginia contain special provisions on legislators' conflicts of interest.

54. H. Eulau & J. Sprague, LAWYERS IN POLITICS, A STUDY IN PROFESSIONAL CONVERGENCE 139–41 (1964) (footnotes omitted).

55. A Subcomm. of the Sen. Comm. on Labor and Public Welfare, 82d Cong., 1st Sess., REPORT ON ETHICAL STANDARDS IN GOVERNMENT 35–36 (Comm. Print 1951).

56. For the statements by Senator Stennis, see 114 CONG. REC. E9547 (daily ed. Nov. 1, 1968) and, generally, 114 CONG. REC. S2906 (daily ed. Mar. 15, 1968).

57. S. RES. 266, 90th Cong., 2d Sess., 114 CONG. REC. S3245 (daily ed. Mar. 22, 1968).

58. H.R. REP. No. 1176, 90th Cong., 2d Sess. 5 (1968).

59. Monypenny, *The Control of Ethical Standards in the Public Service*, The American Academy of Political and Social Science, *supra* note 44 at 98, 100–01.

60. S. RES. 112, 90th Cong., 2d Sess., 113 CONG. REC. 17,011 (1967).

61. U.S. CONST., art. III, §1.

62. 113 CONG. REC. 16,270 (1967).

63. Senate Select Comm. on Standards and Conduct, REPORT ON THE INVESTIGATION OF SENATOR THOMAS J. DODD OF CONNECTICUT, S. REP. No. 193, 90th Cong., 1st Sess. 26, 31–32 (1967).

64. Hays reported this fact to the House during the debates on Powell's punishment by the House in the 91st Congress. 115 CONG. REC. H9 (daily ed. Jan. 3, 1969). The subcommittee's report had merely recommended that the full House Committee on Administration take such action. *Supra* note 11 at 7–8. The procedural rules governing the House Ethics Committee require it to obtain House approval before referring evidence of law violations to enforcement agencies.

65. 115 CONG. REC. H5023 (daily ed. June 19, 1969).

INDEX

349